The Principle of

The Principle of Sufficient Reason (PSR) says that all contingent facts must have explanations. In this volume, the first on the topic in the English language in nearly half a century, Alexander Pruss examines the substantive philosophical issues raised by the PSR, which currently is considered primarily within the context of various cosmological arguments for the existence of God. Discussing several forms of the PSR and selected historical episodes from Parmenides, Aquinas, Leibniz, Hume, and Kant, Pruss defends the claim that every true contingent proposition must have an explanation against major objections, including Hume's imaginability argument and Peter van Inwagen's argument that the PSR entails modal fatalism. Pruss also provides a number of positive arguments for the PSR, based on considerations as different as the metaphysics of existence, counterfactuals and modality, negative explanations, and the everyday applicability of the PSR. Moreover, Pruss shows how the PSR would advance the discussion in a number of disparate fields, such as metaethics and the philosophy of mathematics.

Alexander R. Pruss is Assistant Professor of Philosophy at Georgetown University. He has published many papers on metaphysics, philosophy of religion, applied ethics, probability theory, and geometric symmetrization theory. With Richard M. Gale he is coeditor of *The Existence of God*.

The Principle of Sufficient Reason

A Reassessment

ALEXANDER R. PRUSS

Georgetown University

CAMBRIDGE UNIVERSITY PRESS
Cambridge, New York, Melbourne, Madrid, Cape Town, Singapore,
São Paulo, Delhi, Dubai, Tokyo, Mexico City

Cambridge University Press
32 Avenue of the Americas, New York, NY 10013-2473, USA

www.cambridge.org
Information on this title: www.cambridge.org/9780521184397

First published 2006
First paperback edition 2010

A catalog record for this publication is available from the British Library

Library of Congress Cataloging in Publication data
Pruss, Alexander R.
The principle of sufficient reason : a reassessment/Alexander R. Pruss.
p.   cm. – (Cambridge studies in philosophy)
Includes bibliographical references and index.
ISBN 0-521-85959-x (hardback)
1. Sufficient reason.   I. Title.   II. Series.
BD591.P78   2006
111–dc22   2005015857

ISBN 978-0-521-85959-2 Hardback
ISBN 978-0-521-18439-7 Paperback

For my father and mother

Contents

Acknowledgments

I am grateful for encouragement, discussions, comments, and/or suggestions to Denis Bradley, Robert Brandom, Robert Clifton, William Lane Craig, Kevin Davey, Wayne Davis, William Dembski, James Dreier, Thomas Flint, Peter Forrest, Richard Gale, Jerome Gellman, Alfonso Gomez-Lobo, Michael Gorman, John Haldane, Jeremy Heis, Christian Jenner, Chauncey Maher, David Manley, Mark Murphy, Thane Naberhaus, J. Brian Pitts, Alvin Plantinga, Nicholas Rescher, Lionel Shapiro, Richard Sisca, Ernest Sosa, Thomas Sullivan, Joanna Tamburino, Peter van Inwagen, Linda Wetzel, and anonymous readers who went beyond the call of duty. I would also like to thank Mark Pitlyk for a thorough proofreading of the manuscript, and the National Endowment for the Humanities and Georgetown University for summer research support.

Portions of Chapter 13 are taken from my article "*Ex Nihilo Nihil Fit*: Arguments New and Old for the Principle of Sufficient Reason," in: J. Campbell, M. O'Rourke, and H. Silverstein (eds.), *Explanation and Causation: Topics in Contemporary Philosophy*, Cambridge, MA: MIT Press (2006), copyright © 2006 MIT Press, with kind permission of the MIT Press. Chapter 19 is largely taken verbatim from my article "The Actual and the Possible," in Richard M. Gale (ed.), *Blackwell Guide to Metaphysics*, Oxford: Blackwell (2002), pp. 317–333, copyright © 2002 Blackwell Publishing, with kind permission of Blackwell Publishing. The extended footnote 6 of Chapter 16 is adapted from footnote 2 in my article "The Cardinality Objection to David Lewis's Modal Realism," *Philosophical Studies* 104 (2001), pp. 167–176, copyright © 2001 Kluwer Academic Publishers, with kind permission of Springer Science and Business Media.

I would also like to thank Susan Thornton and Barry Koffler for patiently correcting many infelicities and unclarities in my original manuscript. Any remaining ones I take full responsibility for, of course.

Part One

The Principle of Sufficient Reason and the Causal Principle

1

Introduction

Nothing happens in vain, but everything for a reason and under necessitation.
                                        – Leucippus (Diels and Kranz, 1985, 67B2)

1.1. THE SIGNIFICANCE OF THE PSR

An airplane crash is investigated thoroughly. No cause for the malfunction is found. The investigative team reports that the plane crashed for no cause. We naturally object: "You mean, it crashed for no *apparent* cause." But the team insists that in fact there was no cause.[1] Of course we might question the epistemic bona fides of this finding. After all, there could always be some cause beyond our ken. But can we do more? Can we insist that there *must* have been a cause?

The Principle of Sufficient Reason (PSR) claims we can. Everything that is the case must have a reason why it is the case. Necessarily, every true or at least every contingent true proposition has an explanation. Every event has a cause. The PSR in various guises is as old as philosophy. Parmenides used it to argue that there was no such thing as change. St. Thomas proved the existence of God with a version of it apparently based on his distinction between being and essence. Spinoza's version implied that there is no contingency. Leibniz attacked Newtonian absolute space for violating it and, together with Spinoza, used the PSR as part of an argument against libertarian free will. Kant grounded a phenomenal version of it in the causal nature of time and, arguably, based his transcendental idealism on a noumenal version (cf. Rescher, 2000b).

---

1 This example is taken from Rescher (1995, p. 2).

3

In late-twentieth-century Anglo-American philosophy the PSR was primarily the preserve of the philosopher who, following St. Thomas, came up with increasingly rigorous cosmological arguments for the existence of God. There must be an explanation of why there exist contingent beings at all, and this explanation, at the pain of vicious circularity, cannot itself essentially involve the existence of a contingent being, so there must be a first cause whose existence is itself necessary. Indeed, despite some notable dissent, it now appears generally established that once one grants an appropriate version of the PSR, it follows that there is a necessary first cause of the cosmos, that is, of the aggregate of all contingent beings. This leaves two issues for the cosmological arguer to settle: whether this first cause can be identified with the God of traditional theism and, more basically, whether the PSR is true. And much of the twentieth-century discussion of the formulation and truth of the PSR took place in this context.

But it would be a philosophical mistake to leave the PSR to purely theological uses. Philosophy starts in wonder, and wonder impels us to find reasons for things. As the opening example shows, scientists and ordinary people do presume events to have causes, though they do not always reflect on whether the PSR is exceptionless and necessary. But even a PSR contingently true and only true most of the time calls for reflection. What kind of a reason do we have to believe in the PSR even to this extent? And is it not then a puzzling fact about the universe that the PSR is in fact true in as many cases as it is? Does this fact itself have an explanation, or is this fact itself one of the exceptions to the PSR?

On some accounts of scientific practice, the scientist makes an inference to the best available potential explanation. Philosophy of science has not given us a fully satisfactory account of how we are justified in assuming that the best available potential explanation is in fact true. Does this problem become any more pressing if one allows for the possibility that not only the best available potential explanation is not true, but in fact there is no true explanation?

Quantum mechanical indeterministic transitions are often taken to be reasons to reject the PSR. But at the very same time, the indeterminism, and hence the apparent violation of the PSR, motivates some, perhaps even some as brilliant as Einstein, to prefer deterministic theories.

One of the most powerful arguments against traditional Humean regularity theories of laws of nature is that mere regularities are not explanatory: that As are always followed by Bs does not explain why a given token of A is followed by a given token of B. If the PSR is accepted, one then has reason to reject regularity theories, since then the things that we normally think have causal explanations do not in fact have causal explanations. But if the PSR is false, then the Humean can simply accept the charge that mere regularity is not explanatory, but continue to talk with the vulgar by using a stipulative notion, *explains**, such that a token of A being followed by a token of B is explained* by A's always being followed by B. A decision on the PSR is, thus, prima facie most relevant to the debate on laws of nature.

In the philosophy of mind, the PSR would allow the objector to property dualism to make the following opening gambit: The property dualist needs to explain why it is that in fact the beings that have such-and-such physical states – for example, the physical states we have in virtue of having human brains – also have such-and-such mental states. If the PSR were not true, the property dualist could simply insist this is a brute contingent fact about our universe, one not having any explanation.

But there are cases in which bringing in the PSR could conclusively clinch an argument. There is a discussion since the time of Molina, motivated by concerns of providence, grace, and free will, about whether there are any nontrivially true conditionals about what a person would freely do in nonactual circumstances. The question is particularly vexed in the case in which the person in question is herself nonactual. Are there any contingently true conditionals of the form, "Were there to exist a person x satisfying C, then x would freely do A," where *freely* is understood in the libertarian sense and where no person identical with a person satisfying C exists? Alvin Plantinga insists that there are. David Manley, in conversation, offered basically the following refutation. By the PSR (perhaps in some limited form), such a conditional would have to have an explanation. But there is nothing in terms of which the conditional could be explained in a world in which the agent does not exist. For instance, there cannot be a nomological explanation, since that would require a law of nature that persons satisfying C do A, which would vitiate the supposed libertarian freedom of the agent. Nor can there be an explanation in terms of the action of any person, since the only possible candidate for such a person would be the nonexistent x, as it is inconceivable how anybody else could bring it about that such a conditional would hold without thereby vitiating the hypothetical freedom of x.

5

This is an instance of a general argument form:

(1) The proposition F is such that if it were contingent and true, then its obtaining could not be explained.
(2) But all contingent true propositions have explanations.
(3) Therefore, F is necessary or false.

For another case, consider the following argument against Hartry Field's view that mathematical objects do not exist but *could* have existed. If the PSR is true, then there must be an explanation of *why* mathematical objects do not in fact exist, and if the PSR is *necessarily* true, then in the possible world at which mathematical objects exist, there must be an explanation of why they exist. On the plausible assumptions that the explanations of the existence or nonexistence of contingent objects are necessarily causal and that mathematical objects cannot stand in causal relations,[2] we see that Field's philosophy of mathematics is incompatible with the PSR. Similarly, we may argue on the basis of the necessity of the PSR that mathematical truths, including unprovable ones such as the ones Gödel showed to exist, are all necessary. For what could explain, were it a contingent truth, why a mathematical proposition, especially an unprovable one, in fact holds? Descartes did think mathematical truths could be given a causal explanation in terms of divine causality. But the notion of causing a mathematical truth to be the case is most dubious.

Another example would be the following argument for the necessity of moral truths. Specifically, the thesis to be argued for is that there is no world just like ours in its non-moral features but in which there are different deontic truths – say, torturing the innocent is a duty. Therefore, if C is a complete description of the non-moral properties of our cosmos, and p is any true deontic proposition, the proposition $C \supset p$ is a necessary truth. Moreover, this is true in every possible world. Thus, necessarily, any deontic proposition p is a necessary truth when the circumstances of application are sufficiently elaborated. Alternately, this can be put by

---

2 Field himself holds that mathematical objects cannot be *causes* and therefore would not impinge on our consciousness if they existed. This is in fact a part of his reason for thinking that they do not in fact exist. But it is hard to see what reason there is for thinking that they could not be causes that is not based in general considerations according to which they are the sort of being that simply cannot stand in causal relations at all. Moreover, if in fact mathematical objects could be *caused*, then there would be a possibility that somehow our minds might be capable of causing them to exist, and thus that we could know their existence through our intentional knowledge – our knowledge of that which we intentionally bring about. If this were so, then Field's argument for the nonexistence of mathematical objects would be weakened.

saying that the deontic features of our world supervene on the non-moral ones.[3]

How to argue for a claim like this? The idea of a possible world just like this one non-morally but where torturing the innocent is a duty seems absurd. One might try to argue by simply saying: "Don't you see the evil of torture? Once you see it, you will see that torture *couldn't* be right." But there is a more metaphysical argument. If the PSR is a necessary truth, we can explain what is absurd about worlds differing in deontic features but not in other features: We simply cannot see what could *explain* such a difference. If contingent truths are ultimately to be explained causally, then this is particularly clear. What could *cause* it to be the case that torturing the innocent is a duty? The very idea of causing a deontic proposition to be the case, other than by causing the non-moral circumstances of its application, seems to be absurd. If we were utilitarians, we might say that if evolution caused it to be the case that somehow torturing the innocent were to cause them extremely intense pleasure ten years later, then torturing the innocent might increase utility. But this difference in deontic features would be achieved precisely through a difference in non-moral features.

We might, of course, admit some cases of noncausal explanation of contingent propositions. Thus, if p and q are contingent propositions with p true and q false and with the disjunction p *or* q itself contingent, we might want to say that the disjunction is explained by p's being true. But ultimately we still will want a causal explanation: for instance, we may want to get to a causal explanation of p's being true, unless p is itself disjunctive. Likewise, if p is reductively explained by q, say the metal's being hot by its molecules moving rapidly, we will still want a causal explanation for q or for something that q is in turn reductively explained by, and it appears that an endless chain of reductive explanations, with nothing ultimate that things are reduced to, is explanatorily unsatisfactory.

The idea of something's directly *causing* a moral truth, without causing some set of non-moral circumstances to be actualized, seems absurd. Moral truths, properly qualified in the form $C \supset p$ where C is a sufficiently precise description of the non-moral circumstances, just do not seem to be the sort of thing one can cause. The one example on the books of such causal interaction is a divine voluntarism: God directly brings it

3   This claim is quite close to that which occurs at the *locus classicus* of the notion of supervenience, which is the claim that goodness supervenes on non-moral properties (Hare, 1964, p. 80ff).

about that some actions are duties, some are impermissible, and some are neither, even though he could have brought it about differently. He does not do this by engaging in some speech act such as engraving "Thou shalt not murder" on a clay tablet, but by directly bringing about some moral propositions. One is likely to be puzzled by this kind of a view precisely because deontic properties just do not seem to be the sorts of properties that can be caused except by causing the non-moral circumstances of application of a moral truth. Once we admit that the deontic properties of this world if not supervenient on the non-moral properties could not be explained, then, given the PSR, we have good reason to hold to the thesis that deontic truths, when properly qualified in terms of non-moral circumstances, are necessary truths. This is not a knock-down argument. But it shows where the discussion should be focused: What would deontic facts have to be like if they were contingent and capable of being brought about not through bringing about non-moral facts? It at least seems likely that something like divine voluntarism would have to be true were moral facts to be contingent.[4]

Neither does it really help here to note that causal explanations need not have the state of affairs reported in the explanans causing the state of affairs in the explanandum: the relationship can be more complicated. For instance, that E caused F is a paradigmatic explanation of why F occurred. But E's causing F does not cause F. This is a case of a causal explanation, but for categorial reasons we do not want to say that the state of affairs reported by the explanans causes that reported by the explanandum. Similarly, an agent- or substance-causation account can provide an explanation, but there is no state of affairs causing anything at all there. When we say that some event happened because Fred, a substance, caused it, there is no causal relation, except perhaps as a *façon de parler*, between any state of affairs or event and an event: the whole point of the theory is that the relation is between a substance and an event. There may be more complicated relations. For instance, I will argue in Chapter 7 for the prima facie strange claim that it makes sense to say that in

---

4   Observe that social constructivism would not be a counterexample here. Either social constructivism is an error theory about morality that says that there are no moral truths but only moral "truths," or else social constructivism thinks that there are moral facts but they are produced by society. The first view does not provide a counterexample. But on the second view, the social constructivist does not hold that society *directly* brings about certain moral truths. Rather, society brings about moral truths, given social constructivism, through engaging in certain speech acts. The occurrence or nonoccurrence of such speech acts can be thought of as part of the circumstances.

some cases it could be self-explanatory that an agent freely chose something. This is a causal explanation in the sense that causation is invoked – the agent freely chose something. But since nothing can be causa sui, this is another case in which what is reported in the explanans does not cause what is reported in the explanandum. Nonetheless, none of these other kinds of causal explanations seems to help us explain an allegedly contingent moral claim.

Similar things could be said in favor of other supervenience claims, such as that of the aesthetic on the nonaesthetic or of epistemic statuses on things other than epistemic statuses. Consider the latter case. If the PSR were false, we could give a very simple epistemology, which the attentive reader will notice is a straw-man version of Plantinga's Reformed epistemology. Some belief-forming processes just happen to be "properly functioning" and "truth directed." There is no explanation as to which processes have one or both of these properties – this is just a brute, unexplained contingent fact. Any true proposition delivered by properly functioning truth-directed belief-forming processes is knowledge. No counterexample can be given to this theory. Suppose you give me some case where it seems that knowledge arose not from a truth-directed belief-forming properly functioning process. Then I can just say that the process in these particular circumstances *happens* to be truth directed and properly functioning. Or if you give me a Gettier-type case where a truth-directed properly functioning process delivers a true belief that is not a case of knowledge, I can say that appearances notwithstanding, in these circumstances the process *happened* not to be truth directed and properly functioning.

You might criticize my naive epistemology on the grounds that the contingency involved is contrary to our modal intuitions. We have the modal intuition that there is no world like ours in terms of features other than epistemic statuses but in which peering into a crystal ball on some particular occasion, and only on that occasion, delivers knowledge of the distant future. But I can explain your intuition as simply based on our firm knowledge – that is, the deliverance of a truth-directed properly functioning process – that *in our world* crystal-ball peering is not a properly functioning truth-directed process. And if you do not accept this, then I can just make a modal move. Yes, indeed, crystal ball peering is *necessarily* not a properly functioning truth-directed process in a world with laws of nature like those of our world. But I refuse to give you a criterion for which processes are necessarily like this – there just is no explanation for the fact that some processes are necessarily properly functioning and truth directed and others are not. Given a sufficiently strong PSR, one can reject this whole line of reasoning. If there is no explanation as to why some processes have this epistemic status (contingently or necessarily) and others do not, then it cannot be a fact that some have it and others do not. However, the version of the PSR invoked here is stronger than the one defended in this book – a PSR for necessary truths would be required to make this argument go through, while I will defend one only for contingent truths. Nonetheless, this should motivate us to investigate the PSR in general.

Finally, observe that while the PSR does not solve the problem of skepticism, it may let one at least infer that if one's perceptions are contingent, then they have causes, and this at least takes us to some extent beyond our perceptions. If the PSR is true, and if our perceptions are contingent, then they cannot be all there is. There must be an explanation of why we have these perceptions and not others. Thus, were the PSR self-evident, it could be the start of a climb out of skepticism.

1.2. A RESTRICTION TO CONTINGENT TRUTHS

The PSR that I will defend will not be general enough for *all* of the preceding applications. I will only defend the claim that, necessarily, every contingently true proposition has an explanation. The restriction to contingent propositions is natural and forced by the current state of the art. We simply do not have a good handle on the nature of explanations of necessary propositions.

Aristotle's account of science supposes there are such. In Aristotelian scientific explanations we start with propositions that are "in themselves" more understandable and proceed to propositions that are less understandable in themselves, though of course in the order of knowledge we first know these less understandable propositions, say, that there are rainbows, and proceed from them to the more understandable ones, say, the laws of optics, to give a contemporary example. Thus, if we could identify which *necessary* propositions are "more understandable" or "objectively more basic," for instance which mathematical propositions are more properly considered as axiomatic, then we might have hope of an Aristotelian account of mathematical explanation.

Unfortunately, given the plethora of different logically equivalent axiomatizations for a single mathematical theory, it is not clear which axiomatization counts as objectively more basic, and the PSR is, after all, concerned with *objective* explanations. We could include among the other axioms of Euclidean geometry the parallel postulate that given a line and a point not on the line there is a unique parallel line through the point and derive the Pythagorean theorem. Or we could instead make the Pythagorean theorem among the other axioms and derive the parallel postulate. Which is the genuine explanation? Traditional geometry used the former approach, but a mathematician accustomed to thinking in Cartesian ways might start with the Pythagorean theorem, which lays down a Euclidean metric on the plane, and proceed from there.

While the mathematician Paul Erdős talked of some "proofs from the Book," where the Book was the imaginary heavenly book of the optimal proofs for each theorem, no one knows exactly what it means for a proof to be "from the book." At the same time, we know that some proofs are more explanatory than others. A proof of a geometrical fact that is done in a Cartesian algebraic fashion will sometimes quite "obscure" the geometrical issues, while a different such proof will, the mathematician may say, "clarify" the issues where a "geometrical" proof would obscure them beneath the complexities of a diagram covered with myriad lines. The Four Color Theorem, that every map can be colored by using only four colors without countries that share a border ever having the same color, was proved by a computer checking over a thousand different cases (Appel and Haken, 1989). The proof could in principle be written out, but the proof thus written out would no doubt be quite unenlightening to us. It is not an *explanatory* proof to us. For all we know, the proof might be quite enlightening to a smarter being who could understand all the cases at once. What counts as an explanation in the sphere of mathematical necessary propositions, thus, may paradoxically be quite contingent and mind dependent, in a way in which the explanation of contingent propositions is not. On the other hand, Thomas Sullivan (conversation, 2002) might be right in thinking that when we subsume a number of mathematical theorems under a single more general theorem, we *do* explain things, by showing how such-and-such results follow from such-and-such general properties of mathematicals.

Perhaps more worrying is that given Gödelian unprovable mathematical truths, it is not clear what could explain *those* truths,[5] whereas it seems unlikely that they are self-explanatory. Thus, the PSR extended to them might be false, unless of course mathematical truths are grounded in something deeper yet, say, the nature of modality itself (i.e., whatever

---

5   This argument is due to the father of Joanna Tamburino, an undergraduate student of Richard M. Gale.

it is that in virtue of which it is impossible for there to exist a concrete counterexample to a mathematical truth) or the nature of God's mind.

All this suggests that there may be a significant difference between the cases of contingent and necessary propositions with respect to explanation, and hence the restriction of the PSR to contingent propositions is not ad hoc, in the way that a restriction to single events would be.

Nonetheless, there is some reason to think that we have a commitment to a PSR for necessary truths. Defense of such an argument is beyond the scope of this book, but we may sketch a possibility. Consider a certain species of the phenomenon of refusal to philosophize. The species in question refuses to move to general principles behind judgments. Yes, our interlocutor claims, it is necessarily wrong to kill brown-eyed people but it is never wrong to kill blue-eyed people. Our request for the principle behind this is rebuffed. "That's just the way it is! Brown eyes – good, blue-eyes – bad." What about people with one brown eye and one blue eye? "That depends on which eye is brown and which is blue. If it is the left one that is blue, killing is good but supererogatory. If the right one is blue, killing is prohibited." What if someone had four eyes, two brown and two blue? "I have no view about this case."

There is obviously something irrational about this attitude. One sort of irrationality here has to do with *warrant*. How could our interlocutor justify her moral beliefs? But she might well justify then on the basis of testimony. She might claim that she witnessed great miracles of prediction of the future that made it likely that an infallible supernatural being was speaking to her, and this being told her these things. Or she might claim that she had a very clear moral intuition, of the same sort that we may have with regard to the wrongness of torturing babies. We could dispute an epistemology that allows for such clear moral intuitions, but one feels there is something more deeply wrong here than just lack of warrant.

A version of the PSR is just what we need to solve the problem. There must be an explanation of the moral truths. The proposition, p, that it is right to kill the blue-eyed and wrong to kill the brown-eyed certainly would not be self-explanatory, the way Bentham would claim the proposition that pain is bad to be self-explanatory, even if, *per impossibile*, p were necessarily true. Nor can we possibly see how the proposition could be derived from self-explanatory moral truths, because we would not likely accept a moral truth as self-explanatory if it treated brown-eyedness (or some other property entailed by it but not by blue-eyedness, say) as significantly morally different from blue-eyedness, as a moral truth that entails

12

p would have to. Thus, by a PSR applied to necessary propositions, *p* cannot be true.

One might think that there is a different way of arguing against *p*. One might argue that it is a basic moral truth which we know through some sort of moral intuition that there is no morally significant difference between blue-eyedness and brown-eyedness. But is not our use of the concept of a "morally insignificant difference" itself dependent on the PSR? Is not a "morally insignificant difference" just the sort of difference that cannot *explain* a difference in appropriateness of treatment, so that absent the PSR, we are still no further ahead?

Or perhaps we might argue against the irrational view on the grounds that we have a clear moral intuition that killing innocent people is always wrong. However, the example can be modified. Take some difficult case in which we do not have a clear moral intuition, and imagine someone claiming that the answer depends entirely on the eye colors of the persons involved but again refusing to philosophize or adduce any principles.

We have here a refusal to philosophize, a refusal we all see in less extreme forms in various cases. A different example would be the naive epistemology discussed in Section 1.1, where it is a brute fact about which processes are warrant conferring and which are not. Much of philosophy rests on a rejection of these kinds of views, and we see the Socratic dialogues, in which Socrates seeks definitions of concepts and refuses to accept lists of items falling under the concepts, as cases of this rejection. We call views that refuse to philosophize as in the naive epistemology or in the moral case "ad hoc." Admittedly, in some cases we can criticize the views on the grounds that our interlocutors happen not to be warranted in believing them. But that surely is not the whole story.

There might, thus, be a PSR for necessary propositions. However, investigating such a PSR will have to await an advance in our understanding of the concepts of mathematical and philosophical explanation.

1.3. WHY ACCEPT THE PSR?

These observations, together with the distinguished history of the PSR, suggest that, indeed, whether the PSR is true is highly relevant to a number of disparate fields of philosophy. But while a significant amount of work in the twentieth century was put into discussions of attempts to disprove the PSR, whether by counterexample or by reduction to absurdity, with some notable exceptions there has been surprisingly little done to motivate the PSR. One explanation of this is that those philosophers who accept the PSR typically do so because they take it to be *self-evident* and hence in need only of refinement and defense from attempts at disproof, but not in need of proof. Moreover, some take the PSR to be a first principle in the Aristotelian sense, and if it is such, then any valid noncircular argument for the PSR will have to make use of premises less evident than the PSR itself.

The claim that a principle is self-evident tends to be a dialectical dead end inviting the response "But it's not evident to me!" or, worse, "But its falsity is evident to me!" And this is an unnecessary dead end, since the philosopher who accepts the PSR as self-evident can take the Aristotelian line that even if the PSR is in and of itself self-evident, it need not be self-evident to everyone, and one might still construct dialectical arguments based on principles that are, in themselves, less self-evident than the PSR but which the PSR's opponent accepts. Or, alternately, a principle can be justified in terms of its theoretical utility, much as David Lewis (1986, Section 1.1) justified his theory that every possible world exists as a concrete physical universe by citing the many apparent philosophical benefits of this account.

A different explanation of the paucity of arguments for the PSR can be found in the view widely held by contemporary philosophers that we have good reasons to think the PSR to be false. Specifically, there are two reasons that appear to be quite common. First, with greater intellectual respectability, it is claimed that quantum mechanics on its leading interpretations is incompatible with the PSR, and hence the PSR is empirically seen to be false. Second, there is a fear that acceptance of the PSR will force one to accept various theological conclusions. This sort of a fear is only a good reason for denying the PSR if in fact (a) the existence of a first cause can be shown to follow from an appropriate version of the PSR, and (b) there is evidence that that kind of first cause does not exist. Note for instance that the argument from evil against the existence of God is only relevant as an argument against the PSR if one can show that a first cause would have to be omnipotent, omniscient, and perfectly good. But while there is a long philosophical tradition of thinking that this can be shown, one suspects that the philosophical atheist is unlikely to give credence to the arguments of this tradition – even if, as I think, the arguments are defensible – and hence she is unlikely to be able to use the argument from evil justifiedly as an argument against the PSR. Since the history of late-twentieth-century philosophy of religion strongly suggests that it is the argument from evil that is the only truly interesting positive argument against the existence of God, theophobia is no excuse for rejecting the PSR.

I will begin by sketching five episodes in the history of the PSR: Parmenides, Aquinas, Leibniz, Hume, and Kant. The survey will show a variety of forms that the PSR has taken, for instance, as a causal principle in Aquinas or as a principle of the existence of explanations in Leibniz, and will naturally lead us to distinguish several forms of the PSR. I will argue that we should see the best of these as embodying the insight that contingent propositions always have explanations, though some of the forms are arbitrarily restricted, say, to the explanation of those contingent propositions that make certain existential claims. One of the central claims defended there will be that as soon as we accept even a relatively weak version of the principle, such as that *ex nihilo nihil fit* (nothing comes from nothing), we should for the same reason accept the stronger one that every contingent proposition has an explanation. This will allow us to harness the intuitions behind the *ex nihilo nihil fit* principle and arguments specifically tailored to this principle as evidence for the full PSR once we move on to giving arguments for the PSR.

After having discussed the PSR itself, we will need to defend it against attack. The two main objections that will be considered will be the already discussed argument from quantum mechanics and Peter van Inwagen's *modus tollens* version of Spinoza's PSR-based argument for modal fatalism, the view that there are no contingent truths: the PSR entails modal fatalism, modal fatalism is necessarily false, and hence so is the PSR. In doing this, we will need to discuss the interplay between the PSR and libertarian notions of free will.

From responses to criticisms, we will move to a clarification of the notion of self-evidence. We will see that the fact that the PSR is under dispute is not an objection against the thesis of self-evidence: other plausibly self-evident principles such as the Law of Excluded Middle share this feature with the PSR.

But if an interlocutor does not or will not see the PSR as self-evident, self-evidence will be a dialectical dead end for the PSR's defender. Hence, we will need to move on to giving a positive cumulative argument for the PSR. We will examine Thomas Aquinas's being-essence argument from his *De Ente et Essentia*, Kant's arguments based on his theory of time, as well as some contemporary modal arguments for the PSR. Furthermore, a better modal argument will be offered: I will show that, on plausible and non-question-begging assumptions about the logic of counterfactuals, if it is possible that y has a cause, then in fact y has a cause.

15

I will, further, argue that an attractive Aristotelian account of the nature of possibility entails the truth of the PSR. Moreover, we will look at how far scientific practice assumes the PSR. For instance, I will argue that on an Aristotelian conception of the laws of nature, taking the PSR, as we empirically must, to be a merely contingent and only for the most part true proposition is not a feasible option: it is just too unlikely that the PSR should be true as often as it is if it is not in fact necessarily true. Obviously an argument of this form will have to be very carefully defended.

The PSR is a powerful tool in philosophy. PSR-based considerations may well get used in a covert way in much philosophical analysis. Is not all philosophical research itself a quest for explanation? Once we see that the PSR is itself capable of defense, there will be no need to be ashamed of it and to hide our use of it behind other labels. We will not need to say that Hartry Field's theory is "incomprehensible": we will simply be able to say that it posits uncaused contingent beings. We will not have to express our discomfort with epiphenomenalism by saying that it posits an excessive ontology: dislike of the theory may well be caused by a puzzlement as to what could explain the correlation between the realm of the mental and that of the physical.

At the same time, the version of the PSR that I will be defending will be a limited one, and hence one that will not be sufficient for every application in which someone may wish to make use of it. I will end up restricting the PSR to the explanation of contingent true propositions, and not requiring that the explanation have any teleological component. Whether stronger versions of the PSR hold is a fruitful subject for investigation and, as we have seen in the case of the naive epistemology, one that has philosophical application. But we will have our hands full with the more limited version.

1.4. WHAT ARE WE TALKING ABOUT?

Throughout we will be using the notions of explanation and of a cause, but nowhere will the reader find an analysis of these notions. Rather, through the investigation as a whole, we will learn more about what explanation and causation are like. Pace Socrates, we do not need a definition of a commonly used notion in order to make use of it. We know many things about explanation and causation. We know that explaining A by B and then B by A is viciously circular. We know that that the apple was dropped and gravity was operative explains why the apple fell. We know that it is both true that I am the cause of this book and that my writing this book caused this book to come to exist.

At the same time, more needs to be said about the notions to make clear argumentation later and to make explicit some assumptions. Explanation is always a relation between two facts, that is, two true propositions (I will stipulatively use the word *fact* to mean a true proposition, unless stated explicitly otherwise). Thus, necessarily, if *p* explains *q*, then the explanans *p* and the explanandum *q* both hold. As the preceding examples show, the notion of explanation does not, however, require that the explanation be *final* or *ultimate* in the sense that no mystery remains. An ultimate explanation is one in which the explanans itself does not call out for further explanation because it is either self-explanatory or necessary or both.

However, we will usually require explanations to be *full*. This notion requires some explication. An explanation is full provided that it does not allow a puzzling aspect of the explanandum to disappear: anything puzzling in the explanandum is either also found in the explanans or else explained by the explanans. It would not do to explain why John is sad and excited by saying that he was made sad by the death of his dog, Fido. That would miss out on a part of the explanandum, namely, why he is also *excited*. One way to give a full, though not ultimate, explanation is to say that John is made sad by the death of his dog, Fido, and excited by a job offer he has received.

But there are other ways to give a full explanation that do not require that one actually explain *both* conjuncts. For instance, one might simply say that John is excited *and* the death of his dog saddened him. This does not give an explanation of all of the explanandum, but it also does not let a part of the explanandum slip from grasp. In fact the PSR ultimately will require that every contingent conjunct have an explanation. For we can apply the PSR again: Why is it that his dog died and he is excited? Either we will generate an infinite chain of explanations with no ultimate explanation or we will have come to the ultimate explanation. If we have an ultimate explanation, then we must have arrived at something self-explanatory or necessary. Since the claim that John is excited is neither, it follows that along the way we must have explained why John is excited. On the other hand, as we shall see in Chapter 3, the PSR is not compatible with an infinite chain of explanations that has no ultimate explanans. Thus, proceeding chainwise, it does not matter whether we insist that a full explanation explain every conjunct, as long as whatever puzzling aspects remain unexplained in the explanandum are carried over into the explanans.

17

If a full explanation explains every contingent aspect of the explanandum, then I will call the explanation *complete*.

We will not make any scientistic assumption that science is the ultimate arbiter of what is an explanation or of what is a cause. Scientific explanation is one species of explanation, with deductive-nomological explanation, where the initial conditions and laws of nature are cited as an explanation of a later state of affairs that is entailed by these initial conditions and laws, as a distinguished subspecies. But there are other species. There is mathematical explanation, for instance, which we have touched on already. And there is personal explanation, as when we explain an event by saying that a person freely brought it about. It is prima facie possible that some forms of explanation can be reduced to others. Thus, an occasionalist thinks scientific explanation can be reduced to theistic personal explanation. A reductive physicalist thinks personal explanation can be reduced to scientific explanation. Spinoza thinks all explanation can be reduced to something very much like mathematical explanation. But no such reductionist assumptions will be made, and indeed it will be tacitly assumed that Spinoza is wrong because there really is contingency.

A guiding intuition to be kept in mind is that there are a close connections among explanation, wonder, and mystery. One commonsensical way to look at explanation is as a removal or transfer of puzzlement or mystery. If knowing that q does not leave rational room for puzzlement about why p holds, then q explains p. Of course there will be a different puzzlement as to why q holds, unless q is an ultimate explanation.

The opponent of the PSR may argue that this is a problematic notion of explanation, for the concept of a puzzle or mystery entails the existence of a solution. To see this, suppose we have some contingent proposition that lacks an explanation, say, the proposition that this plane crashed. Then once one knows that there is no explanation, one thereby has removed all room for puzzlement about why the plane crashed. Thus that there is no explanation for the crash explains the crash on this view of explanation, which is truly absurd. Note that the proponent of the PSR might accept this as a reductio ad absurdum, though not of this notion of explanation but of the possibility of the denial of the PSR (if there were no explanation, then saying that there is no explanation would remove all puzzlement; but if all puzzlement were removed, an explanation would thereby be given; hence if there is no explanation, there is an explanation). But both the opponent and the proponent would be wrong, for were one to learn that the airplane crashed for no reason, the mystery would not thereby be removed – it would deepen, if anything.

Likewise, no analysis of causation is offered. However, it is assumed that causation is non-Humean. That *A*s are always followed by *B*s is neither sufficient nor necessary for *A*'s causing *B*. There can be single-instance causal relations and it is quite possible that *A*s should be followed by *B*s merely coincidentally. There is a possible world with the same laws of nature as ours but in which, completely by chance, no shaman has ever clapped his hands except immediately before a rainstorm. All clappings by shamans are followed by rainstorms in that world, then, but it does not follow that the clappings cause the rainstorms.

No prior assumptions are made about entailment relations between explanans and explanandum or between the fact of the occurrence of the cause and the fact of the occurrence of the effect. Hume thought that the connection in the latter case was always contingent, but that is not obvious. That Jones's intentionally brought it about that *E* happens causes *E*, even though it also logically entails that *E* happens. Many think that the explanans should entail the explanandum, but we will see in Section 6.3 that this condition is dispensable, even if we are talking of full explanations.

One might object that one cannot investigate the PSR and claims such as that all events have causes without a prior investigation of the notions of explanation and causation. But this is mistaken, I take it. At the same time, the various arguments I will end up making concerning explanation and causation will in the end be constraints on which accounts of explanation and causation are plausible. But to draw out such conclusions would be the task of another work. Aquinas thought that we could know *that* God exists, though our knowledge of exactly *what* God is like is quite shaky. Likewise, one might know *that* all contingent events have causes, while not knowing *what* exactly causes are. After all, do we not *all* know at least that some events have causes, while few if any of us know what causes are?

2

Reflections on Some Historical Episodes

Let us begin with some instructive historical episodes. Of these, Parmenides and the truthmaker principle will be crucial at important points in the book. Aquinas is important historically and we will eventually extend his metaphysical ideas to provide Thomistic arguments for the PSR. Leibniz is probably the most famous proponent of the PSR, but we shall, alas, see that he does not seem to give us a sufficient argument for it. Hume's argument against the PSR is still one of the most powerful. And, finally, Kant's arguments for the Causal Principle will give us an example of an original and interesting argument that simply fails.

2.1. PARMENIDES

2.1.1. Truthmakers and the First Argument for the ex Nihilo Nihil *Principle*

The PSR first shows itself clearly in Parmenides' second argument against becoming. If something comes to be, it does so from something or from nothing. It is against this second possibility that the PSR is ranged. Parmenides asks: "[W]hat need would have driven it later rather than earlier, beginning from the nothing [*tou mêdenos arxamenon*], to grow?" (Fr. 8, 9–10).[1] If we have a state where nothing exists, and then something comes to exist – think of a universe as a whole to make the argument particularly forceful – why did it come to exist when it did, rather than, say,

---

1 Throughout, the translation of Parmenides will be based on that in Kirk, Raven, and Schofield (1990), with occasional modifications, perhaps at times inspired by the commentary of Sider and Johnstone (1986).

five minutes earlier? An empty universe is temporally homogeneous: "the nothing" was no different five minutes earlier than it is now. The question calls for an answer, but the supposition that nothing existed makes an answer impossible. The unstated assumption here is that why-questions of this sort do have answers, that is, that every proposition has an explanation.

Thus, Parmenides employs the PSR to argue for the *ex nihilo nihil* principle. This may seem a little strange to us, because the *ex nihilo nihil* principle is likely to seem less controversial than the PSR. The PSR says that every true proposition, or maybe every contingently true proposition, has an explanation. The *ex nihilo nihil* principle states that no entity comes into existence out of nothing. If we grant that an entity that once did not exist is a contingent entity, then the claim that starting with nothing we will not get anything follows from the PSR restricted to the case of contingently true propositions reporting the existence of an entity that came to be in time. Thus, the *ex nihilo nihil* principle seems to be simply a special case of the PSR, and so a rational person who was unsure about the *ex nihilo nihil* principle would for the same reason be skeptical about the PSR. We would not convince someone who was not sure whether all *material* beings are in flux by baldly telling her that in fact *all* beings are in flux.

However, in fact, the *ex nihilo nihil* principle is not in the first instance a principle about explanation or causation. In one of its cosmological forms, it says that a universe with an empty past will not have a nonempty present or future. Parmenides has the insight that if we had an empty past and then something coming into existence, then this thing's coming into existence when it does would itself be unexplained. It would be unexplained because there would be nothing in existence for it to be explained by, and it makes no sense to explain something in terms of nothing. Behind this lies Parmenides' most basic insight: "that [it] is not and that it is needful that [it] not be, that I declare to you is an altogether indiscernible track: for you could not know what is not – that cannot be done – nor declare it, since what is there to be thought [of] and what there is are the same thing" (Fr. 2–3). This insight is essential to seeing the connection between the *ex nihilo nihil* principle and the PSR. If one thought that explanation could invoke a nonthing, something that is not, then one might deny the *ex nihilo nihil* principle and accept the PSR. We will see later in Chapter 4 that Nicholas Rescher thinks that explanations can be given not only in terms of what is, but also in terms of principles. If so, then we might well have nothing in existence, but nonetheless some principle might obtain that says that the universe is to come to exist at t_0.

This might contradict the homogeneity of time but is not so absurd once one admits that one can explain beings in terms of nonbeings.

Henceforth we will take the *ex nihilo nihil* principle to be implied by the PSR. But this is a substantial claim about explanation: it is an acceptance, correct I believe, that it makes no sense to invoke a shadowy realm of "principles" poised between being and nonbeing in terms of which beings are to be explained. Once we look at the PSR as implying the *ex nihilo nihil* principle, we can modify the principle from merely being a principle about what time slices of the universe can *follow* what time slices of the universe, namely, that nonempty times cannot follow empty times, to being a principle that says that things that come to be in time always have *causes*. Once we see that causality and hence explanation is what the essential insight in the *ex nihilo nihil* principle is about, we might, while retaining the words *ex nihilo nihil fit*, abandon the requirement that the cause should precede the effect in time. The cause might, in fact, not be in time. Indeed, if the Big Bang singularity shows, as Grünbaum (1998) argues, that the past is finite and yet there is no first moment in time – the set of moments in time is a set of t such that $t > t_0$ and t_0 does not mark an actual moment in time – then any application of the *ex nihilo nihil* principle to the universe will have to posit an extratemporal reality.

It is worth noting that while Parmenides' basic insight that coming into existence out of nothing would violate the PSR is correct, since why the thing exists at all would be unexplained, his precise argument is one we should perhaps not embrace. In its cosmological form, the argument posits two ways things could be: the way they actually are and the way they would be if all events in fact happened earlier than they did. The claim made is that no reason can be given for why the former rather than the latter is in fact the case. This argument, if sound, shows a lot more than Parmenides uses it for. In fact, it shows that there cannot be change. For if there were change, then shifting over all events in time would produce a different state of affairs. Parmenides did not seem to see this further application, though of course he accepted the conclusion that there is no change.

Crucial to this argument against change and becoming are two assumptions that can be challenged. The first is that the ways things could be, the actual way and the shifted way, are in fact distinct, pace those who accept a relational theory of time. The second is that no explanation could be given for one rather than another, pace Samuel Clarke's response to Leibniz, where Leibniz argued on the basis of the PSR against a uniform absolute Newtonian space and Clarke responded that there might be a libertarian free will explanation in terms of the will of a creator.

In these days of doxastic timidity, rather than concluding from Parmenides' argument that there is in fact no change, one is more likely to conclude that the PSR to which he appeals is false – assuming that the controversial auxiliary hypothesis about the nonrelational nature of time holds. This, of course, is not the only way to get out of the argument: we could instead adopt a relational theory of time. We will, however, consider a very similar argument in greater detail in Chapter 9.

2.1.2. The Second Argument

But back to the historical Parmenides, where we get two more arguments for the *ex nihilo nihil* principle in its acausal form. The first of these is simply that it makes no sense to talk of something's coming to be from *nothing*, that is, from nonbeing, because then we are talking of nonbeing and "it is not to be said nor thought that it is not" (Fr. 8, 7–8). This is a restatement of Parmenides' proscription of talking about what is not. This proscription can be read as a statement of the controversial *truthmaker* principle. To be true, a proposition needs to be true *of* something, indeed of something that exists. Truth requires a responsiveness to reality; there must be an aspect of reality *of* which a true proposition is true. Something that is not about something is not the sort of thing that can be true or false, and hence is not a proposition.

The truthmaker theory in the form that will interest us here states that for every true proposition there is an aspect of reality in virtue of which the proposition is true, a truthmaker for the proposition. That Socrates is sitting is true in virtue of the sitting Socrates or the sitting of Socrates or Socrates' being seated. In fact, we can always express the truthmaker of a proposition in terms of the participial nominalization of the sentence that expresses the proposition. That Socrates was a war hero who taught Plato is made true by Socrates' having been a war hero and having taught Plato. Depending on what one's underlying ontology is, what this item, *Socrates' having been a war hero and having taught Plato*, is will differ. It might be an accident of Socrates. It might be some sort of relational entity. It might be a *state of affairs*, considered not just as a true proposition but as a concrete entity that exists when and only when the state of affairs occurs. The point is made by Parmenides in saying that we can only think of what *is*, that is, any proposition we think is a proposition *about* something, namely, about its truthmaker.

23

The defender of the truthmaker theory will hold that it simply spells out what is implicit in realism: realism claims that true propositions correspond to realities. Well, these realities are the truthmakers of the proposition. But the truthmaker theory is more controversial than realism! For instance, one might worry what existent reality can make true a negative claim such as that there are no seven-legged dogs. One could posit a negative state of affairs, such as *there not being any seven-legged dogs*, but that might be thought to trivialize the truthmaker theory (unless one supposed that the negative state of affairs was a bona fide positively existing being, say in a Tractarian ontology) as well as undercut Parmenides' argument. Alternately, one could follow Gale (1976) and say that what makes it true that there are no seven-legged dogs would be something like *everything's being either A_1, or $A_2, \ldots$, or A_n, and A_1's having some positive property incompatible with being a seven-legged dog, A_2's having some positive property incompatible with being a seven-legged dog, \ldots, and A_n's having some positive property incompatible with being a seven-legged dog.*

Some, however, reject the truthmaker theory in favor of a more general theory espoused by David Lewis and possibly even Aristotle in his famous claim that to speak truly is either to say "of what is that it is or of what is not that it is not [*to on einai kai to mê on mê einai*]" (*Metaphysics* Γ, 1011b27). The more general theory says that while true positive propositions have truthmakers, false negative propositions have *falsemakers*. I, or perhaps I considered insofar as I am human, am a falsemaker for the proposition that there are no humans. We can then say that at least for some set of relatively logically simple propositions, a true proposition is true either in virtue of being a positive proposition having a truthmaker or of being a negative proposition lacking a falsemaker. This allows purely negative realities, the absences of falsemakers, to have a role in making true propositions be true. For many purposes it does not matter whether we take the simple truthmaker theory or the more complicated truth-maker/falsemaker theory, and so I will confine myself to the truthmaker case. For instance, suppose an ethicist seeks truthmakers of moral propositions. It is of little help to be told that perhaps the search should be for falsemakers: it is as hard to find a falsemaker for the negation of the claim that it is wrong to torture little babies as to find a truthmaker for it, and if we find a *plausible* candidate for a truthmaker, then in the absence of a simpler falsemaker account of the proposition, we will opt for this candidate truthmaker.

However, for Parmenides' argument against things' coming into existence to work, it seems we *need* a pure truthmaker theory. A truthmaker/

falsemaker theory appears insufficient. Yet, one may object, a truthmaker/ falsemaker theory is superior to a pure truthmaker theory.

Moreover, one might object to the argument that we are talking of "nothing" when we are talking of something come to be *ex nihilo* as this confuses:

(4) $\sim\exists x(y$ comes from $x)$

and

(5) $\exists x(y$ comes from x and x is nothing).

Clearly, (5) is absurd, but should not be confused with (4), which is only absurd if one accepts a sufficiently strong version of the truthmaker principle. One might accept a limited truthmaker principle only for positive states of affairs and then claim that (4) is a negative state of affairs and hence the truthmaker principle does not apply to it.

2.1.3. The Third Argument

Finally, Parmenides has a third argument against coming into existence out of nothing. This is a general argument against coming into existence. Suppose x comes into existence. Imagine ourselves at a time prior to x's coming into existence. At that time, x did not exist. What are we talking about, then, when we say, truly, "x will exist"? If it *will* exist but does not now, then it does not exist, and hence we are talking of an x that does not exist: "For if it came into being, it is not: nor is it if it is ever going to be in the future. Thus coming to be is extinguished and perishing unheard of" (Fr. 8, 20–21).

The ways out of the argument should be familiar, of course. One might deny the existence of facts about the future that cannot be sufficiently grounded in present states of affairs. One might hold that future things exist *simpliciter*, for instance by becoming a B-theorist. Or one might go for determinism, claiming that it makes sense to talk about the future because we are really then talking about the present states of affairs that determine the future ones. Note that this last solution does not work in the special case of coming into existence *ex nihilo*, for then there are not going to be enough present facts, presumably, to determine the future states of affairs. So if one does not wish to go for the B-theory or to deny future states of affairs, one may find this a sound argument for the *ex nihilo nihil* thesis.

25

Observe that this argument, specialized to a case of coming into existence out of nothing, is stronger than just the Parmenidean argument that it makes no sense to talk of coming into existence *out of nothing*. For while the simpler argument needed an unrestricted truthmaker thesis, the new argument can observe that future states of affairs are obviously not *negative* states of affairs, and hence there should be some positive present state of affairs in which they are to be grounded. But of course the B-theoretic approach is still available as an attractive way to avoid the argument.

2.2. THOMAS AQUINAS

The PSR shows up in the guise of causal principles in Aquinas's Five Ways, at least four of which demand explanations. Why is there movement? Why are there causal connections? Why do contingent things exist? Why is there order in the universe? While no one of the Ways invokes the PSR in its full generality, it is in the background: it is assumed that, indeed, these things have explanations, and given the wide categorial range that "these things" takes, this would be most implausible unless in fact just about everything had an explanation.

Each Way makes an explanatory demand and then claims that the only thing that can fill that demand is something godlike. The succeeding articles in the *Summa Theologica* then try to argue that this thing is indeed God. The explicit way the PSR enters into the Five Ways is through causal principles (CPs): nothing moves without being moved, contingent beings have causes, and so on. However, there is an implicit way that the PSR also enters in. A causal principle, as such, is compatible with an infinite regress. The cause of A can be B, and that of B can be C, and so on. Thomas Aquinas rejects infinite regresses on many grounds. They may involve an actual simultaneous infinity of movers, for instance, whereas an actual infinity is impossible. This argument does not impress us as much since Cantor showed us how to talk coherently of actual infinities. Or a regress may violate some aspect of Aristotelian physics, but once again we are no longer Aristotelians in physics.

But there is a deep way in which the PSR can be seen as entering in. The best objection to an infinite regress with no initial element is that it just does not constitute an ultimate explanation: one could still ask why the whole infinite chain took place. By the PSR, we need something over and beyond the infinite chains with no initial elements. Observe here one of the differences between a PSR and a CP: the CP is prima facie compatible with infinite chains with no initial elements.

Note that this argument does not rule out the possibility of an infinite chain *with* an initial element. Consider, for instance, the infinite number of states that a cannonball goes through from firing to landing, given the continuity of time.[2] This is an infinite chain with an initial element, namely, the firing of the cannon, and this initial element explains the whole infinite chain. An Aristotelian theory of time on which there is only a finite number of actual moments of time in any interval, with the other moments being merely potential, would rule out this example, but Thomas accepted a different kind of example: he was willing to entertain the logical possibility of the cosmos's having in fact always existed, as long as God had, from outside time, created it – that would be an infinite chain *with* an initial element.

In the *Summa Theologica*, St. Thomas does not give us an argument for the PSR or the CP. But we do get hints of an argument in the earlier *De Ente et Essentia* based on the distinction between existence or the act of existing (*esse*) and essence or quiddity (*essentia, quidditas*). In Thomistic ontology, the existence of a thing is that by which the thing *exists* at all. The essence of a thing is that by which it is what it is. "I can know what a man or a phoenix is and still be ignorant whether it exists in reality. From this it is clear that the act of existing (*esse*) is other than the essence or quiddity, unless, perhaps, there is a being whose quiddity is its very act of existing" (Aquinas, 1949, chap. 4). The latter exceptional being would be a necessary being, one that exists simply in virtue of the kind of being it is, that is, in virtue of its essence, though Thomas has not yet argued that there is any such being.

The distinction between *esse* and *essentia* is more basic than the hylomorphic distinction between form and matter. For instance, it would apply to contingent beings that have no matter: for them, too, there would be a difference between their act of existing and that which defines their identity. The distinction is parallel to a distinction one can draw in a somewhat Fregean context between a property *P* and the metaproperty of *P's being instantiated*.

The important point is that unless a being is a necessary one, it must have two different principles in it, the *esse* and the *essentia*. Both of these are thought of as real principles found in a given thing. Socrates is a human being by virtue of his essence, which is not something extrinsic to him that he merely participates in as the Platonists claimed.

---

2   A similar example was given by Cain (1995). See also Hill (1982).

Socrates exists by virtue of his act of existence, which is something real in him.[3]

Thomas concludes from this that there is a CP for contingent beings, that is, for all beings in which existence differs from essence:

> Now, whatever belongs to a being is either caused by the principles of its nature, as the capability of laughter in man, or it comes to it from some extrinsic principle, as light in the air from the sun's influence. But it is impossible that the act of existing be caused by a thing's form or its quiddity, (I say *caused* as by an efficient cause); for then something would be the cause of itself and would bring itself into existence – which is impossible. Everything, then, which is such that its act of existing is other than its nature must needs have its act of existing from something else. (Aquinas, 1949, chap. 4)

Thus, we have a CP for contingent beings. St. Thomas goes on to argue that there must be a *first* cause, but our interest right now is just in the CP.

At first sight, Thomas's argument simply begs the question. The *esse* of a thing must arise from its essence or from outside. But in saying this, Thomas leaves out precisely the option an opponent who denies the CP will choose: the *esse* of a thing not being caused by anything and not following from the thing's essence. A simple explanation why Thomas does not feel obliged to discuss this option, crucial as it appears to philosophers these days, might be that it is intuitively obvious to him that if you have a composition of two factors, in this case the existence and the essence, there has to be an explanation of why there is such a composition.

Obviously, this will not do if we are trying to find an *argument* for the CP in Aquinas. What we need to do is ask whether a Thomistic *esse-essentia* ontology does not in fact commit one to the impossibility of the indicated third option, a commitment that might have been obvious to Thomas. I will argue in Chapter 12 that indeed this is so: Thomistic ontology does commit one to the CP.

2.3. LEIBNIZ

If there is one philosopher who is most famously associated with the Principle of Sufficient Reason, it is Leibniz.

> Our reasonings are founded on *two great principles, that of Contradiction* ... [a]nd *that of Sufficient Reason*, in virtue of which we consider that no fact can be real

---

3 See Miller (1983) for a philosophy of language–based justification of the *esse-essentia* distinction.

or actual [*existent*], and no proposition [*Enonciation*] true, without there being a sufficient reason for its being so and not otherwise, although most often these reasons cannot at all be known by us.[4]

Leibniz uses the PSR most famously in his arguments against Newtonian absolute space and time. If space and time are absolute, then the world would have been different had things been shifted over in space or time. But the homogeneity of space and time means that no reason can be assigned why the universe occupies one position in space and time rather than another, contrary to the PSR. Hence, space and time cannot be absolute. We already saw the ingredients of this argument in Parmenides. Samuel Clarke responded that a reason can be given, namely, God's free choice to create the universe in such and such a place and time rather than another. Leibniz, in turn, queried what grounds God had for such a choice. Clarke as a libertarian grounded this in a reasonless free choice. Leibniz found such a choice incomprehensible.

Nowadays, the Leibnizian argument is not likely to be used for showing space and time to be relative. In fact, the argument is more likely to act as an attempt at a reductio ad absurdum of the PSR. We will consider it under that head in Chapter 9.

Can Leibniz give an argument for the PSR? In the *Theodicy* (section 44, quoted in Rescher, 1990, p. 116), he writes of the PSR: "Were it not for this great principle we could never prove the existence of God, and we should lose an infinitude of very just and very profitable arguments whereof it is the foundation." In a more skeptical age this argument sounds less impressive. On the other hand, the argumentative pattern here is perhaps not one we should dismiss immediately. We saw in the Introduction that the PSR does give us a number of useful arguments for the plausibility of theses such as the falsity of a completely ad hoc epistemology. Is it only wishful thinking to think that this counts a little in favor of it? Or is it that the plausibility of those theses in fact derives from the intuitive plausibility of the PSR? And consider, after all, what may be one of the main reasons driving the acceptance of the Axiom of Choice by mathematicians. Accepting the Axiom of Choice lets mathematicians prove many handy theorems, such as the Hahn-Banach theorem. Admittedly this kind of pragmatic argumentation is a little strange from a rationalist such as Leibniz, but perhaps the pragmatic aspects of his thought need more examination.

4 *Monadology*, 31–32 (Rescher, 1991, translation modified slightly).

Leibniz also offered an argument for the PSR based on something like the truthmaker principle and his inherence account of the properties of a monad as found within the complete individual concept of a monad (cf. Rescher, 1991, pp. 124–125; Gerhardt, 1960–1961, vol. 7, p. 300). When we say that Napoleon was short, that is because the complete individual concept of Napoleon is (with the ellipses indicating infinitely many omissions) *the concept of someone born on August 15, 1769, in Corsica, . . . who was short, . . . who lost at Waterloo, . . .* Thus, an explanation can be given of why Napoleon is short: he is short because his complete individual concept, which itself is an eternal and necessarily existing idea in the mind of God, contains shortness. At the same time, this very reason is what makes it possible to predicate shortness of Napoleon.

Thus, the ground of predication is the same as the explanation of the proposition on this way of looking at Leibniz (cf. Heidegger, 1974). It is true that this way of looking at the matter will only give a PSR for propositions of the form *x is F*, where *x* is a monad. But because monads and their properties are all there is, it seems that the Leibnizian account explains everything. All truths supervene on truths about monads, and all truths about monads are of the form *x is F*. The PSR follows from Leibniz's take on what the grounds for predication are, that is, on Leibniz's take on what the truthmaker principle implies in the case of *x-is-F* propositions.

However, Leibniz's account neglected *existence*. The explanation of why Napoleon is short, namely, because his complete individual concept includes shortness, is exactly parallel to an analysis of why Sherlock Holmes is tall: the complete individual concept of Sherlock Holmes includes tallness. But all this fails to explain why Napoleon Bonaparte, and not Sherlock Holmes, exists.

It is here, of course, that Leibniz will bring in the principle of optimality: Napoleon Bonaparte and not Sherlock Holmes exists because there is a possible world that is better than every other world, and this best possible world includes Napoleon but not Holmes. But here the PSR and the truthmaker principle seem to part ways: it is not because of any truthmaker-based consideration that Napoleon exists. Instead of admitting this apparent parting of the ways as real, one might distinguish between two PSRs in Leibniz, the weaker holding in all possible worlds and simply consisting in the inherence principle, and the stronger being the principle of optimality that holds only in the best possible world. On this account, we can say that the weaker PSR is grounded in the truthmaker principle, while the stronger is an independent principle.[5] But if so, then it is the stronger principle that I am interested in. For instance, only the stronger one is sufficiently strong to support the claim that *ex nihilo nihil fit*.

This does not mean that there is no argument showing that the PSR cannot be reduced to the truthmaker principle. We will see in Chapter 12 that there is a way of looking at Aquinas's being-essence argument for a version of the causal principle as based on something like truthmakers. But be that as it may, the two principles are prima facie different. They both talk of ground, but there are many kinds of ground. The PSR talks of explanatory ground. The truthmaker principle talks of the ontological ground of truth. And the epistemologist talks of epistemic grounds. There may be times when all three grounds coincide. For instance, perhaps Leibniz's account of predicative truths holds at least for statements such as that *bachelors are unmarried*. What makes this statement true is that the concept *bachelor* includes *being unmarried*. What explains its truth is just this, too. And what gives us knowledge of this fact is this very fact. But this is a very special case. There may be a deep unity among these three kinds of ground, but it is not clear what it might be.

2.4. HUME

2.4.1. The Basic Argument

The PSR understood as a necessary truth entails a CP that claims both that a contingent event cannot occur without a cause and that a contingent being cannot come to exist without a cause. But Hume insists that there is no absurdity in imagining a brick's coming into existence without a cause. Hence, the CP is at most contingent, and hence the PSR cannot be a necessary truth. This argument may be thought to parallel the argument from the self-evidence of the PSR that we will consider later, since the claim that a brick's coming into existence without a cause is nonabsurdly imaginable appears to be taken to be self-evident. This argument does not lead to the conclusion that the PSR is false, but only that it is not necessarily true. But this itself would seriously damage the credibility of

---

5 See also Rutherford (1992), which shows how one can read texts that appear to suggest a distinction between a contingent and a necessary PSR as showing a distinction not between two PSRs but between the PSR and a Principle of Intelligibility.

31

the PSR. For instance, it would make it untenable that the PSR is self-evident in the sense of being such that to understand it is to see that it is true.[6]

2.4.2. The Annihilation Principle

There can be more to the argument than the bald assertion that a brick can come to exist without a cause. The argument might further be based on Hume's principle (Hume, 1779, part IX), that anything thought to exist can likewise be thought not to exist, supplemented with the additional qualification that everything other than the denied item can be thought to continue existing. We can imagine the brick's coming to exist from the clay under the hand of a craftsman. Just hold that in the imagination, but remove the clay and the craftsman from the picture, and you will have imagined a brick's coming to exist *ex nihilo*. Or, alternately, the argument can simply take a more logically minded form. There are perfectly coherent mathematical models describing possible worlds in which the only thing that exists is a brick (or a bricklike entity, if bricks conceptually require brickmakers and a society that has certain purposes for them) and its parts. One way to construct such a model is just to take a list L of the states of the particles of some *actual* brick, take the time series to start at some time t_0 at which the actual brick exists, and posit that the states in L are in fact instantiated at t_0. Then, a brick exists at t_0, without a cause. But bricks are not necessary beings, and so an uncaused contingent being exists in this model, and since the model is coherent, the PSR cannot be necessarily true.

Now a quick caution is needed. Actually, the world described in the model contains no bricks. To be a brick is to play a certain role in our society, to be made for certain constructive purposes, say. But no

---

6 I do not say it would *entail* that the PSR is not self-evident, because there might be contingently true propositions, such as that I exist, that could be argued to be self-evident in this sense. For it might be that for *me* to understand the proposition *that I exist* is for me to understand it to be true. Whether this implies self-evidence depends on controverted questions about *de se* propositions. If there are *de se* propositions, then *that I exist* might be a *de se* proposition that is self-evident, because anyone who grasps it sees that it is true (of herself, for that is the nature of a *de se* proposition). If there are not *de se* propositions, and *I* in "I exist" is a rigid designator, then *that I exist* will be self-evident only if it cannot be communicated – only if no one other than I can grasp that proposition (e.g., your attempt to grasp it can at best get to "He exists" or "Pruss exists," which are different propositions). How one should answer these questions is unclear. But it is deeply implausible that the PSR is a contingently true self-evident proposition analogous to *that I exist*: the issues with the latter seem to be specific to indexical propositions.

32

matter: whether we have modeled a *brick* or some other bricklike aggregate of particles, we have modeled something contingent and uncaused. However, this should caution one in general about Humean intuitions that we can always coherently excise parts of worlds while keeping everything else fixed: cutting humans out of the picture, for instance, brings it about that none of the things that would otherwise have been made by us are artifacts. We must be careful in our imaginative world-constructions: there can be unintended logical effects.

2.4.3. Modal Imagination

But is it indeed intuitively clear that a brick can come to exist *ex nihilo*? Note, first, that the *can* here is a *can* far removed from ordinary usage. In daily life, most of our uses of modal language indicate either epistemic possibilities or causal possibilities. An epistemic possibility is something that might be true for all we know. It is certainly not self-evident that a brick comes to exist *ex nihilo* for all we know: on the contrary, we know (inductively, if in no other way) that such events do not *in fact* happen. On the other hand, there is no *causal possibility* of a brick's coming into existence *ex nihilo*, because *p* is causally possible if and only if there in fact exists or existed a causal agent *x* such that *x* could have initiated a causal chain capable of leading to its being the case that *p*. But, by definition, nothing can initiate a causal chain capable of leading to the existence of an *uncaused* brick.

Of course it will immediately be objected that this is quite unfair as an objection. Surely, it will be pressed, I know perfectly well the sense of *can* involved in the claim that there can be an uncaused brick, and it is neither causal nor epistemic but logical. While that may be correct, the important point here is that purely logical possibility is not an item in everyday conversation. It is not something about which the ordinary person has much in the way of intuition: the ordinary person thinks primarily about causal and epistemic possibilities. It will even be argued in Chapter 19 that the right account of modality has causal possibility at its heart. Now, a proposition containing a term that has a meaning far removed from ordinary life is not a proposition in whose self-evidence we can be very confident, unless of course the proposition is self-evident in the sense of being a tautology, which the Humean claim is not. This is not to say that a self-evident proposition cannot reach beyond the concerns of everyday life. *Modus ponens* while applicable to propositions about groceries and dogs is also applicable to the most abstruse parts

33

of mathematical physics. However, the statement of *modus ponens* does not take us beyond the ordinary uses of language. We use conditionals every day, and the concept of a conditional is certainly one we all have mastered.

Thus an argument from the alleged self-evidence of the claim that an uncaused brick could exist would not be particularly strong. And while Hume's own argument is from the self-evidence of the *imaginability* of an uncaused brick's coming into existence, we know that the inference from imaginability to possibility is fallible.

Now, of course if one restricts the *logical possibility* sufficiently narrowly in the Humean claim to be merely a claim that within some specified system of logic no contradiction can be proved from the proposition that there is an uncaused brick, the claim may become true, but it will also become irrelevant to metaphysics. For if mathematical truths are all logically necessary truths in the metaphysically relevant sense, then by showing the existence of unprovable (within appropriate first-order systems) mathematical truths, Gödel has shown us that there are mathematical falsehoods that are in a sufficiently narrow sense "logically possible." Since these falsehoods are metaphysically impossible, and since the PSR is meant to be a *metaphysically* necessary thesis, showing that the PSR is not narrowly logically necessary will not challenge the claim that the PSR is metaphysically necessary.

Or a weaker point can be made. We can imagine an evolutionary process by which a one-horned horselike animal – call any such an animal a "unicorn" – could have come to exist. We cannot sketch the process in detail, any more than we can sketch the evolutionary history of any animal, but we have a rough idea that the DNA could mutate in such a way that a unicorn comes to be born. The story does not have to be probable, but we are confident that a story can be given. In fact, it is plausible that the only way to have full confidence of a claim of metaphysical possibility is to have a story about how the supposed possibility had come about. But this is precisely what we cannot do in the case of a contingent proposition that violates the PSR: if something violates the PSR, then obviously there is no story to be told about how it came to be true.

But besides all this, the alleged Humean possibility, as has been noted, is an outlandish one. Let me imagine the brick's coming to exist *ex nihilo*. Do we not feel an impulse to ask, "How did this happen?" Do we not feel a pull toward saying that there must have been some physical process that brought it about? And while the Humean will reject these intuitions, is not their presence, especially when added to the preceding considerations, at least evidence for the Humean possibility's *not* being self-evident? It may be that the intuition here can be captured by the weaker notion that such events are very unlikely, but as we shall see much later, it is difficult to account for this "unlikelihood" (see Section 17.4.2).

The second argument was from the idea that any part of reality can be denied while holding everything else fixed. This is the basic Humean intuition. But this intuition is questionable. It implies that it was possible for nothing to have existed. But that possibility is a dubious one. For instance, such a possibility would violate the unrestricted truthmaker principle that every true proposition is true in virtue of some positive reality – ex hypothesi in a world in which nothing existed, it would be *true* that nothing exists. Furthermore, it certainly is at least not obvious that it might have been that nothing existed.

Moreover, the Humean intuition implies that various sorts of holism are false. For instance, if material reality consists of global fields, then the possibility of making local changes while keeping everything else fixed is questionable. Nor is the intuition supported by ordinary thought. When faced with a claim like "The David could have existed without Michelangelo" or "Kennedy could have died of a bullet wound even if Oswald had never lived," we do not generally try to imagine a world where everything else is fixed but Michelangelo or Oswald did not exist. Rather, we try to imagine a world where someone or something *other than* Michelangelo created the David and where someone else shot Kennedy. If we have a Kripkean view of the matter, we will think we cannot even imagine the David's being made by someone else, but this stronger claim is irrelevant here. All I need is that ordinarily when we imagine possible modifications of reality, we do not imagine the effect's staying in the total absence of *any* cause, but simply in the absence of the *particular* cause that caused the effect. And when asked to imagine a world where the cause did not occur, we imagine a world where the effect does not occur as well, because such imagining is ordinarily associated with counterfactuals and the counterfactual *were no cause of E to occur, E would not occur* is generally true for a caused event *E*.

Thus, the exercise in modal imagination in this Humean principle is again removed from ordinary use. This does not mean that the exercise is hopelessly flawed. But what it does do is force us to be careful here. If there were good conceptual reason to think that the matter *cannot* be imagined coherently, if there were good conceptual reason to accept the PSR, the weak intuitive evidence for Hume's principle would be defeated.

2.4.4. A Possible Diagnosis

It is worth noting that Hume's own intuitions about the falsity of the CP or PSR might have been colored by his view of causation. If causation is nothing but constant conjunction, then the denial of the necessity of the CP is just the claim that a contingent event can happen that is not the second term in any constant conjunction. But just about everyone's modal intuitions will support *this*. For instance, consider the rotation of a star's causing the formation of a planet, indeed the universe's first planet. It surely might have been the case that after the first planet was formed, the universe was annihilated. But then the formation of a planet would not have been the second term of any constant conjunction, since it would have been a one-time event and hence uncaused: while the star's rotation would have preceded it, it would not have caused it. On Hume's view of causation, then, the nonnecessity of the CP is not a controversial matter. Now Hume's view of causation is highly implausible. For instance, it makes the question of whether x causes y sometimes depend on future events as in the preceding example, in which it depends on whether the universe is annihilated right afterward. But whether x causes y certainly should not logically depend on anything in the future of x and y. Once x and y occur, apart from exercises of exotic backward causation if such is at all possible, nothing can bring it about that x did or did not cause y. But on the Humean view, one could bring it about that x did not cause y without any exotic exercises of backward causation, but simply by preventing future tokenings of A, where A is the type that x falls under.

Given the implausibility of Humean views of causation and the possible contamination of a Humean's intuitions about the PSR by these views of causation, the Humean's intuitions about the PSR are indeed a little suspect.

Moreover, on a Humean view, one might well argue that there is nothing more mysterious about a brick's coming into existence after a brickmaker has been laboring than there is about a brick's coming into existence *ex nihilo*. This is because both are equally unexplained: if causation is just constant conjunction, then causal statements do not explain, just as "Everybody does it!" is not only not a justification but also not an explanation of why one did it, unless supplemented with additional claims about a common human nature. Thus, in fact, Hume is committed to the necessary falsity of the PSR in just about all cases, simply because he is committed, though he will deny this, to there being no causal *explanations*. All this is reason to reject the Humean view of causation, but it

36

also shows that a Humean's intuitions about the PSR may be biased by the necessity of her rejection of the PSR.

A new and scientifically informed version of Hume's argument, inspired by some remarks by J. Brian Pitts, will, however, still need to be discussed in Chapter 4.

2.5. KANT

In his Second Analogy, Kant tackles the problem of the direction of time. We perceive time as having a direction. Of two nonsimultaneous events, one precedes the other. Not only do we perceive the events successively, that is, first perceive one and then the other, but we also perceive them *as* successive, which is of course quite different. Indeed, we might note that it is only a coincidence that we usually perceive the earlier event first. If I see a puff of smoke from a distant cannon and hear the explosion later, then I have aurally perceived the explosion after I have visually perceived its effect, the smoke. Moreover, perception of events as successive is essential to beings like us having experiences at all. Furthermore, when we actually successively perceive two events, we at least sometimes perceive our phenomena to be successive. Thus, we simply cannot get away from the fact that somehow we must be capable of perceiving successiveness.

What makes one event be later than the other is, according to Kant,

The *relation of cause and effect*; of these two, the cause is what determines the effect in time, and determines it as the consequence.... Therefore experience itself – i.e., empirical cognition of experiences – is possible only inasmuch as we subject the succession of appearances, and hence all change, to the law of causality. (Kant, 1996, p. B234)

Thus, what makes *B* later than *A* is nothing but that *A* causes *B*.

Next, Kant argues that there cannot be something empirical without something empirical preceding it as a cause. "For an actuality succeeding an empty time, i.e., an arising not preceded by any state of things, cannot be apprehended any more than empty time itself" (Kant, 1996, p. A192/B237). Kant has already argued in the First Analogy that time can only be perceived through the perception of substances persisting in time, thereby ruling out the possibility of an empty perceptible time, that is, an empty time in the phenomenal realm. But if succession arises from causation, then it is nonsense to say that some phenomenal event occurred after no cause, since the after is to be analyzed in terms of causation, and hence one would be saying that the phenomenal event was caused by the absence of causes, which is nonsense.

The argument here resembles Aristotle's argument for the eternity of time, which we will discuss in Section 3.2. It may seem to share a flaw with it, due to an ambiguity in the claim that no cause preceded x. This claim can be disambiguated in two ways:

(6) Before x it was the case that (there is no cause of x).
(7) It is not the case that (before x, there is a cause of x).

Of these, (6) makes no sense if temporal succession depends on causation in the way Kant suggests. But (7) seems to make perfect sense.

However, in fact, even (7) will not be acceptable on Kantian grounds. We are dealing here with the phenomenal order. Truths within the realm of the phenomenal must be empirical. But how could (7) be empirical? To verify it, we would need to search thoroughly the region of space-time that is before x, and make sure that it lacks a cause for x. But we can only designate that region of space-time in reference to the cause of x, which ex hypothesi does not exist. Of course, it is plain that we cannot search *all* of space-time for the cause of x – however far we searched, we could not have perceived empirically that we had searched it all, even if in fact we had.

It is thus crucial to the Kantian argument that it should refer to the phenomenal realm. However, the argument seems to have a serious shortcoming. To derive an order for time, it might be thought that we do not need *all* pairs of successive events to be causally connected. This is certainly going to be true if we are allowed to help ourselves to a nondirected betweenness relation that lets us say when an event B is between events A and C, without the relation's saying which events occur first and which do not. It is simply a mathematical fact that *if* we have a timeline with a betweenness relation isomorphic to that had by the real numbers, where we say that y is between x and z providing $x < y < z$ or $z < y < x$, and if we have an ordering between *just one* pair of distinct instants on that timeline, say, A and B with A earlier than B, then we can derive an ordering between all pairs of distinct instants. For instance, if x and y are such that A lies between x and B and y lies between x and A, then we can stipulate that $x < y$, and we can easily formulate a number of other such rules, which will yield a linear ordering.

Thus, while the order of time may require some instances of causation, just one instance of causation between nonsimultaneous events is enough given a timeline with a betweenness relation. And we could get a timeline with a betweenness relation on it simply by attending to our empirically most successful physical theories without reference to an asymmetric notion of causation (cf. Grünbaum, 1974, chap. 7). Admittedly, the physical theories may not yield an order of time by themselves unless we choose stipulatively simply to define this order in terms of something like entropy,[7] but as long as we can perceive one instance of nonsimultaneous causation we will be fine. And we *can* perceive one instance of nonsimultaneous causation. When I drop a rock, my act of will causes the rock to hit the ground.

However, this neglects just how far Kant's critique cuts. Kant is not simply trying to solve the problem of the "arrow of time," the problem of distinguishing past from future, while taking for granted a timeline with a betweenness relation. The timeline is itself a problem. If we are to build a timeline out of causal relations, we cannot take for granted any particular betweenness topology. Similarly, if we could take for granted simultaneity relations, then we could define how an uncaused event A stands with respect to the past, by seeing how it stands with respect to the causes of events simultaneous with A. But it is also puzzling how simultaneity is to be perceived. The simultaneous perception of objects is not the same as the perception of the objects as simultaneous.

However, there is available a different solution here. Kant does not need the strong principle that every event has a full cause. All he needs is that every event is affected by past events. For instance, we now know that every object in the universe is affected, at every moment of its existence, by gravitational forces exerted by other objects in its past. The Newtonians thought gravity was instantaneous, but they were wrong: gravity only propagates at the speed of light. If some item came into existence causelessly, from the first moment of its existence it would have been affected causally by the influences of various past events. And these influences might be sufficient to define a timeline in the absence of a full CP.

---

7 It is not at all clear how one should relate the asymmetry in entropy with what is arguably the crucial intuition about an asymmetry of time, namely, that the future is open in a way in which the past is not. See the discussion in Sklar (1993, pp. 397–404). Unfortunately the one view surveyed by Sklar that had much plausibility as a way of grounding intuitive asymmetries with the entropic asymmetry was the work of David Lewis (1979) on counterfactuals and the arrow of time, which has been refuted now (Elga, 2001; Pruss, 2004b). For these reasons, one might be skeptical about the philosophical significance of the undeniable entropic asymmetry. The causal intuition that causation goes from past to future, or at least tends to do so, seems much more significant.

But even if these counterarguments work contingently in our universe, one might still seek something stronger, especially if one puts more weight on intuitions than Kant does. As a necessary principle, the principle that every contingent event is *affected* by other events is intuitively inferior to a CP that claims that every contingent event is *effected* or *caused* by other events. Even though the principle of affectedness is formally weaker than the CP, all of its intuitive force is derivative from the CP. We do not have any independent intuitions about the principle of affectedness. The discovery of universal forces such as gravity was a *surprise*. Thus, it can only be plausible that the principle of affectedness is necessary if it is plausible that the CP is necessary. But, of course, one could say that the existence of a past-future distinction, and indeed of a timeline or space-time structure even remotely like that which we have, is only a contingent fact, and so its being grounded in a merely contingent fact is no worry here. The people who would like to ground the past-future distinction in entropic asymmetries are quite willing to accept the contingency of the distinction, after all (but see Elga [2001] and Pruss [2004b] for a critique of the most prominent such account).

3

The Causal Principle and the PSR

3.1. CHAINS OF CAUSES

3.1.1. *The Hume-Edwards-Campbell Principle*

Say that a chain of causes is ungrounded if it does not contain a first cause that causes everything else in the chain and if, further, there is no cause outside the chain that causes the chain as a whole. One major difference between a Causal Principle and a PSR is that a CP, prima facie, is compatible with an ungrounded infinite chain of causes, while a PSR is not, since there is no explanation for the whole chain. The latter incompatibility claim can be objected to, however. Hume writes: "Did I show you the particular causes of each individual in a collection of twenty particles of matter, I should think it very unreasonable, should you afterwards ask me, what was the cause of the whole twenty. This is sufficiently explained in explaining the cause of the parts" (Hume, 1779, Part IX).

The Hume–Edwards principle (see Edwards, 1959) states that if one has explained each conjunct of a proposition or each member of an aggregate, then one has explained the whole. One might then try to explain why some aggregate of all contingent beings exists by saying that being A exists because it is caused by B, being B exists because it is caused by C, ad infinitum.

↻ The Hume–Edwards principle, however, is false. The principle depends crucially on explanation's being agglomerative: if one has explained the conjuncts, one has explained the conjunction. But explanation is not agglomerative, as Gale (1991, pp. 254–255) has argued. For instance, even if one had explained why one Mason was at the corner in terms of his desire to buy bread at the bakery on the corner, and why another Mason was at the corner in terms of his desire to eat at the café on the corner,

41

and why a third Mason was at the corner in terms of its being his usual way to work, and why a fourth Mason was at the corner in terms of his having to get his watch repaired at the jeweler's there, it does not follow that one would thereby have explained why the four Masons were there. For all of the preceding is compatible with the proper explanation of the conjunction's being a *Masonic conspiracy* that took them to that location, and ensured that the fourth went to this jeweler rather than to another, and so on.

But as Campbell (1996) has noted, to refute the incompatibility of the PSR with the existence of an infinite ungrounded chain, it is not necessary to show that conjunctions are *always* explained when the conjuncts are explained, but that for any one conjunction it is epistemically possible that it would be explained were the conjuncts explained. If there were no conspiracy that took all the Masons to the same location, then in fact the full and correct explanation of the conjunctive fact would be given by the explanations of the conjuncts.

3.1.2. The Problem with the Principle

However, the Hume–Edwards–Campbell (HEC) principle that it is epistemically possible that one has explained the conjunction whenever one has explained the conjuncts is only true in the special case in which either at least one of the explanations goes beyond the set of conjuncts or at least one of the conjuncts is a self-explainer. In the case of the four Masons, the explanations offered were indeed in terms of something outside the set of conjuncts. Or, if the presence of one of the Masons was somehow self-explanatory and it explained the presence of the other Masons, then we would have a fine explanation. But if, on the other hand, we explained the presence of each of the Masons in terms of the presence of the other Masons, we would not have thereby explained the conjunction. Our explanation, on the contrary, would have been viciously circular. Even if causal circles were logically possible, they would not be *explanatory*: the question of why the whole circle exists would still have to be answered.

The plausibility of the HEC principle lies in examples in which the agglomerative explanation does not become viciously circular or viciously regressive. Presumably, Hume's twenty particles are to be explained in terms of something outside the set: it is not the case that particle A caused particle B to be present, and so on, for all the particles – that would be viciously circular, since given the finite number of particles our causal chain would eventually have to loop back on itself.

42

3.1.3. Regress of Explanations

It is, admittedly, not immediately obvious that a regress of explanations is as vicious as a circle of explanations. But there is a way of closing the gap between these two. Suppose we admit the HEC principle, and therefore claim that we might have an infinite series $p_1, p_2, \ldots$ of distinct propositions such that p_n is explained by p_{n+1}, and such that the conjunction of them all, $p_1 \& p_2 \& \ldots$, has thereby been explained. There is no conspiracy in this case: there is nothing more to the explanation of the conjunction than the explanation of the conjuncts. Let P indicate the conjunction of all of these propositions. Let E be the conjunction of the even numbered ones. Let O be the conjunction of the odd numbered ones. Every conjunct of E then has an explanation in terms of O, since p_{2n} is explained by p_{2n+1}, with none of the propositions being self-explanatory. Therefore, O has the resources for an explanation of E, if we are dealing with a case in which the conjunction can be explained simply by giving explanations of the conjuncts. But by exactly the same reasoning, every conjunct of O has an explanation in terms of E, since p_{2n+1} is explained by p_{2n+2}. Therefore, E has the resources for an explanation of O. Thus, we explain E in terms of O and O in terms of E, once we admit the sort of reasoning that the HEC principle posits.

But it is highly plausible that two conjunctions of distinct propositions, having no propositions in common, cannot be mutually explanatory: that would be just a vicious circularity. Indeed, the only way two conjunctive propositions could be mutually explanatory, I suspect, is if they have in common a self-explanatory proposition that explains all the other propositions, or perhaps if their mutual explanatory power is derivative from some further explanation. An example of the latter case could be that when looking at two pieces of a jigsaw puzzle that fit together, we can explain the shape of each piece in terms of the shape of the other, and vice versa, but the explanatory power of this shape is completely derivative from a further explanation, namely, that someone designed the jigsaw puzzle so that the pieces should fit. In fact, one might argue that in a case like that, the initial circularity in explanation ends up being only apparent, because the description of the two explanations was elliptical: the further explanation should have been mentioned.

The argument above going from regress to circularity can be put more vividly. Suppose we have an infinite sequence of chickens and eggs, each egg giving rise to a chicken and each chicken giving rise to a subsequent

43

egg. Then, the above argument shows that if we accept infinitely regressive explanations, then we should be willing to say that the existence and activity of the members of the set of eggs are explained by the existence and activity of the members of the set of chickens while the existence and activity of the chickens are explained by that of the eggs. This is circular and clearly fails to answer the question of why there are chickens and eggs at all.[1]

3.1.4. The Cannonball's Causeless Flight

There is also another way to see that the HEC principle fails. Consider a cannon that is fired exactly at t_0, and the cannonball flies until t_1. Let B_t be a proposition reporting the state of the cannonball at time t. Then, B_{t^*} causally explains B_t whenever $t^* < t$. Let P be the infinite conjunction of the B_t where $t_0 < t \leq t_1$. Then, by the HEC principle, P could be self-explaining. For, each conjunct of P, say, B_t, is causally explained by B_{t^*} where t^* is chosen such that $t_0 < t^* < t$, and hence each conjunct of P explained by another conjunct of P. But surely P not only is not but could not be self-explaining: the path of a cannonball could not be self-explanatory. At best, it could perhaps be *unexplained* if the PSR were to fail, whereas of course it is the contention of this book that it does not.[2]

One objection to this example is that B_{t^*} does not explain B_t. A full explanation must make reference to the operative causal laws of nature. But no worry! Just as P could not be explained by itself, neither could P be explained by $P\&L$, where L are the laws of nature. For that would basically mean that L is doing all the explanatory work. But to explain the path of a cannonball one needs more than the laws: one needs *initial* conditions.

1   For a very similar argument see Forrest (1996, p. 92). See also Rowe (1970). In Pruss (1998) we also find an objection to the Hume–Edwards principle based on the related observation that even were circularities in causation possible, say, through consistent time travel, the whole circular cycle would remain unexplained, pace Hume and Edwards.

2   William Vallicella (1997) has offered a variant of Hume's account. On Vallicella's story, we are mistaken if we think that we always explain a proposition with a proposition. Sometimes we explain a proposition with more than one proposition. A conjunctive proposition, then, is explained by its conjuncts: Why is p & q true? It is just because p is true and q is true. Unfortunately, the cannonball example shows this account to be false, too, for on this account we have nothing left unexplained after we have explained every conjunct of P in terms of another conjunct and then explained the conjunction by the conjuncts. But it is plain that something *is* left unexplained by this, and it is natural to say that this is P itself.

But perhaps the opponent will be willing to bite the bullet and allow that P is self-explanatory. We can then give the following argument against P's being self-explanatory. Let x_0 be the position of the cannonball at t_0 and let p_0 be the proposition that this is the position at that time. Let p_0^* be the proposition that the limit of cannonball positions at $t > t_0$ as t tends to t_0 is x_0. Observe that neither p_0 entails p_0^* nor p_0^* entails p_0 — it is, after all, logically possible that a cannonball's movement be discontinuous at t_0, perhaps in which case the limit of positions at t as t tends to t_0 will not match the actual position at t_0. However, assuming we are working within classical mechanics, p_0 and L entails p_0^* since L entails that movements are continuous. Unlike p_0, proposition p_0^* is not about what happens at t_0 but what happens at times t such that $t_0 < t \leq t_1$. Observe, too, that p_0^* is entailed by P, since we calculate the limit in terms of the positions that are reported by P.

Now, if we have an explanation of P, I claim we can make this explanation into an explanation of p_0^* just by appending a necessary truth. Let N be the true proposition that the sequence of cannonball positions mentioned in P has limit x_0 as t tends to t_0. Even though P is contingent, N is a necessary truth, because propositions have their meanings essentially — indeed, propositions could even be thought of as identical with meanings — and hence claims about what follows logically from the meaning of a proposition, even a contingent one, are necessary truths. It is clear that once we have explained why P is true, and tacked on to that explanation the necessary truth N, then we know why p_0^* is true. Thus, if q explains P, then q & N explains p_0^*: there is no further mystery about p_0^*, assuming we have a genuine explanation of P on hand.

Therefore, if P is self-explanatory, P & N explains p_0^*. But this conclusion is absurd. To see this, note first that none of the conjuncts B_t in P individually does *anything*, even in combination with N, to lighten the mystery about why p_0^* holds. For, it is true for every $t > t_0$ that p_0^* tells us about what happens before t, and B_t plainly makes no contribution to explaining what happens before the time t. Now, it might be possible in general to have a conjunction no conjunct of which makes a contribution to explaining some proposition but in which the conjunction explains the proposition. However, the defender of the HEC principle cannot claim this in the case of P, because the HEC principle insists that there might be nothing more to P than its conjuncts, and the conjunction of these conjuncts introduces no new element to be explained. But by parity of reasoning, the conjunction should introduce no new explanatory element either. Surely the correct explanation of this limit is rather that the cannonball was in fact at x_0 at time t_0 and that cannonball movements are continuous by the laws of nature.

In fact, this last consideration connects with an important fact about self-explanation. The original Hume-Edwards principle claims that P is self-explanatory in every case. But if there was a cannon firing, then there is another explanation besides P itself, namely, one in terms of the initial conditions and laws. We thus would have *two* explanations for P: it is both self-explanatory and explained in terms of something else. Admittedly, in general a proposition can have two actual explanations. For instance, in some cases explanation is transitive so from r explaining q and q explaining p we also get r explaining p so that p is explained both by r and by q. Alternately, we might have a case of causal overdetermination, with each overdetermining cause providing an explanation. However, it is highly implausible that a self-explanatory proposition could have a further explanation. After all, if the proposition is by itself self-explanatory, that further explanation seems to have no force and there is no need for it. In the transitivity example of a proposition's having two actual explanations, one of the explanations is more final than the other. But if a proposition is self-explanatory, then it does not call out for any further and more final explanation. Nor can we have a case of causal overdetermination here. That would require us to deal with something that both causes itself and is caused by something else – and the first conjunct here is already absurd enough. Besides, in cases of overdetermination it is true that were one of the overdetermining explanations not to have taken place, the explanandum would still have occurred. Thus, if q explains p and p explains p via overdetermination, then were q not to hold, p would still hold. So far so good. But we would also have the absurd conditional: were p not to have happened, p would still have happened. Thus, it is highly plausible that a self-explanatory proposition cannot have a further explanation. Since P has a further explanation, it is not self-explanatory.

But what of Campbell's variant of the Hume-Edwards principle? Perhaps P is only self-explanatory when it in fact has no further explanation, such as that in terms of the cannon firing. Thus, it is self-explanatory if and only if it lacks a further explanation. But this cannot be right. A self-explanatory proposition is one in which the explanation is based on facts and relations reported by that very proposition. The internal structure of what P reports does not change on the basis of whether P has a further explanation or not. If in the one case P explains itself, it does so in the other.

3.1.5. Chains of Causes

Thus indeed the Hume-Edwards objection to the claim that the PSR rules out ungrounded infinite chains fails. The CP, prima facie, does not rule out such chains. Now, the intuition behind the CP is something like this. If we take some event in the world, say, a plane crash, we can trace back a series of causes for the event. There is some set of events significantly before the crash that causes the crash, whether it be the metal's being fatigued or the plane's being boarded by terrorists. But the CP by itself does not actually give us this conclusion, for the CP by itself is compatible with the following scenario: The airplane's crash, E_0, is caused by a certain event E_1 half a minute before the crash. The event E_1 is caused by some further event E_2 two-thirds of a minute before the crash. E_2 is caused by an event E_3 three-quarters of a minute before the crash. And so on: E_{n-1} is caused by an event E_n that happened $1-1/(n+1)$ minutes before the crash. But there is, in fact, no cause *one* minute before the crash or earlier responsible for the crash. Rather, right after one minute before the crash an ungrounded infinite chain of events eventuated, for no reason at all, that led to the plane's crashing. For another example, recall the flight of the cannonball.

Thus, principles such as the CP that are compatible with ungrounded infinite chains cannot yield any principle of the form: for every event E in time there is an event C an hour (say) before E that causes E. For we can always have an ungrounded infinite chain of duration less than an hour that causes E.

The CP can be applied to events or to the existences of contingent beings. In the latter case, the CP might say that every contingent being existing at a time t has a cause of its existing at t. This can be taken to be a spelling out of intuitions behind the *ex nihilo nihil* principle, but in fact, given the preceding observations, this CP is quite compatible with a brick's popping into existence *ex nihilo*. All that is needed is that there not be an initial moment of time at which the brick exists. If the brick exists at all times t such that $t_0 < t < t_1$, all is well vis-à-vis the CP: the existence of the brick at a time t in this interval is just caused by the existence of the brick at an earlier time t^* also in this interval. But the brick has no cause located at t_0. If one objects that it is incorrect to speak of an earlier time slice of the brick as an object that causes a later time slice of the brick to exist, imagine instead that there pops into existence an infinite sequence of *distinct* bricklike objects, all densely sandwiched into the interval of times t such that $t_0 < t < t_1$, with each object that exists in this interval

47

causing the next and being caused by a previous one. This, too, would plainly violate the *ex nihilo nihil* principle.

A related observation has been used by Łukasiewicz (1961), and quite possibly even Kant in some posthumously published notes (see Shapiro, 2001), to give an argument for the compatibility of determinism and free will.[3] If determinism only means that for every event or physical event there is a prior event or physical event that deterministically causes it, as it is sometimes sloppily defined, then this is just like a CP, except with "causes" strengthened to "deterministically causes" and "event" replaced by "physical event." For instance, Roy C. Weatherford in *The Oxford Companion to Philosophy* (Honderich, 1995, p. 194) in the article "Determinism" discusses "the very general thesis about the world that all events without exception are effects – events necessitated by prior events. Hence any event of any kind is an effect of a prior series of effects, with every link solid." But even the staunchest Cartesian incompatibilist can accept the compatibility of libertarian free will with determinism as defined in this way, as long as it is restricted to physical events. Acts of free will, the Cartesian insists, are not themselves physical events, and so this definition of determinism is compatible with the claim that a free act of will at t_0 initiates an infinite chain of physical events over the interval of time $\{t\colon t_0 < t \leq t_1\}$, up to and including the action's performance at t_1.

And so, from the preceding weak definition of determinism, even when one does not restrict it to physical events, one cannot conclude as Weatherford goes on to that "future events are as fixed and unalterable as the past is fixed and unalterable" (p. 194), at least if one does not assume something like the PSR. For the preceding weak definition of determinism is compatible with the idea that several different possible futures could occur tomorrow, as long as each were actualized by an infinite series of events starting some time later today with no first event and the series as a whole had no explanation. And Weatherford's claim may fail even if one *does* assume the PSR, since it might be that the infinite chain of events is explained by some nonevent, such as a timeless divine willing, or that it is explained in a nondeterministic way by some event that causes but does not necessitate it.

These arguments for the compatibility of libertarian free will and an open future with determinism should not satisfy anyone. For it is just too

---

3 Cf. also an argument that Earman (1986, Section III.9) gives for the claim that Newtonian mechanics does not entail determinism.

weak a formulation of determinism to say that every physical event has a prior physically determining cause. This formulation of determinism is too weak to do justice to the incompatibilist's intuitions. Minimally, the incompatibilist needs to define determinism by saying that for every physical event and *every* earlier time t there was a physically determining cause at t of the given event, and not just that for every physical event *there is* such an earlier time.

Likewise the CP, by itself, is too weak to do justice to the intuitions behind it, intuitions about back-traceability of chains of causes or the intuition that things cannot just pop into existence *ex nihilo*. To do justice to these intuitions, one should go for the full PSR. Note, though, that the analogy with determinism is not perfect. The analogue of the better definition of determinism earlier would be a claim that every event has a prior cause at every moment of time prior to the event. While this kind of a quantified claim is enough for defining determinism, since the determinism of concern to the compatibilist tends to be of a scientific variety, the CP is a metaphysical principle, and because it is such, it is unnatural to restrict it from applying to chains of events such that there is no time prior to the chain as a whole whether because time and the chain start simultaneously or because the chain goes back an infinite amount of time. I will argue further for a claim like this shortly.

The preceding considerations strongly suggest that the CP is an unnaturally restricted version of the PSR, much as the principle that all blue-eyed human beings are mortal is an unnaturally restricted version of the principle that all human beings are mortal. There is no reason to suppose that being blue-eyed has anything to do with mortality, and in the absence of additional evidence suggesting how these may be connected, once one accepts that all blue-eyed human beings are mortal, one should also accept that all human beings are mortal. Likewise, once one accepts that all events have causes or that every contingent being's coming to be in time has a prior cause, one should more generally accept that all contingently true propositions have explanations. The CP is, essentially, the PSR as restricted to propositions reporting single events or the existence of contingent beings that come to be in time. But this is an evidently unnatural restriction, since it fails to do justice to the intuitions grounding the principles in question.

One might question the preceding argument in the case of the CP for events, though. Consider the chain of events $E_1, E_2, \ldots$, with E_n happening $1 - 1/(n + 1)$ minutes before the plane crash. One might say that there is a *further* event: the temporally extended event of the chain as a whole. And *this* chain requires the CP. This is a reasonable response. After all, it may well be that all events are temporally extended. But this response is grist for the PSR defender's mill, for once one accepts that a chain of events is itself an event, the sort of thing that requires a cause, then much of the distance between the PSR and the CP is bridged.

Anyway, what seems at first sight to be a punctual physical event – say, a neuron firing – is likely to be temporally extended, and perhaps even in such a way that it can be broken up into an infinite chain of subevents. For all we know, there might not be a first moment of time in the chain (i.e., the chain might stretch over an open or half-open interval of time of the form $\{t : t_0 < t < t_1\}$ or $\{t : t_0 < t \leq t_1\}$, respectively). The CP would be practically useless if it did not apply to the chain. So the CP should be extended to chains if the CP is accepted.

Of course, there will still be some differences from the PSR even if one extends the CP to chains of events. One might argue, for instance, that the CP is compatible with a scenario on which every chain of events has a cause, but this cause is not always itself an event, and hence sometimes a chain of events is explained by a contingent nonevent, which does not itself have an explanation and is not self-explanatory. This is a scenario compatible with the PSR but incompatible with the CP as extended to chains.

But what reason would there be, then, to restrict the CP only to events and not also to this mysterious contingent and non-self-explanatory nonevent? Failing such a reason, we would want to extend the CP to these kinds of things, too: we would want the CP, in other words, to cover chains of contingent entities of a sort S sufficiently general that any cause of an entity or chain of entities of sort S would also be in S. This would be a very strong CP, for just as the Cosmological Argument, as we shall see in Chapter 4, allows one to conclude from the PSR that there is a necessary being, so too this version of the CP would let one conclude that there is a subset of S-type entities, each member of which is self-explanatory, and such that the members of this subset causally explain all the other S-type entities.

3.1.6. The Putnam-Meyer Cosmological Argument

3.1.6.a The Argument. Let us make this precise. Suppose S is a set of entities, partially ordered under the relation $<$ of causal explanation, where

50

$x < y$ if and only if y causally explains x.[4] Suppose that the sort of causation we are working with is such that this relation is transitive ($x < y$ and $y < z$ implies $x < z$) and asymmetric ($x < y$ and $y < x$ cannot hold simultaneously), and that any self-explanatory members of S do not themselves have causal explanation. (An entity more general than an event can be said to be self-explanatory provided the proposition reporting its existence is self-explanatory.)

Then, a *chain* is a set U of entities such that for any distinct entities x and y in U we have $x < y$ or $y < x$. Suppose we have the following CP: For any chain U of non-self-explanatory entities in S, there is an entity z of S which causally explains all the members of U, of course other than z if z is a member of U, and for any non-self-explanatory entity x in S there is an entity y of S that causally explains x. It follows from this that in fact for *any* chain U of members of S there is a z that causally explains all the members of U, other than z if z is a member of U, even though we have assumed this to be true only for chains of non-self-explanatory entities. To see this, suppose that U is a chain containing a self-explanatory entity, z. Then, for every other x in U we must have $x < z$ or $z < x$. The latter is impossible since a self-explanatory entity has no causal explanations.

As Robert Meyer (1987) following Hilary Putnam has noted, it follows from these assumptions and the set-theoretic Axiom of Choice that there is a member z_0 of S such that z_0 is not causally explained by any member of S. By our CP, this z_0 must be self-explanatory, since otherwise it would be causally explained by some member of S. The proof will be given momentarily in a more general form.

More generally, for any entity x in S, let S_x be the set consisting of x and all members of S that causally explain x. Then, S_x is a nonempty "inductively ordered" set under $<$. An "inductively ordered" set A is one that under a partial ordering $<$ has the property that if U is any chain that is a subset of the set, then there is a member z of A that has the property that $y < z$ for all members y of U, other than z if z is a member of U. That S_x is inductively ordered can easily be shown. Let U be a nonempty chain in S_x (the case of the empty chain is trivial: just let $z = x$). Then by our CP, there is a member z of S such that $y < z$ for all y in U other than z if z is in U. Note that then z in fact must be in S_x by transitivity of $<$. For, let y be any member of S_x other than z. Then

---

4   Note that S might have to be the set not just of events and other eventlike things or of objects, but of aggregates of them, since sometimes the cause of something is not a single thing but an aggregate.

either $y = x$ or $x < y$. Since $y < z$, it follows in either case that $x < z$ and hence z is in S_x. Thus, indeed, S_x is inductively ordered under $<$. Then, Zorn's Lemma (see, e.g., Lang, 1984, p. 697), which follows from the Axiom of Choice, states that S_x has a maximal element z_x, that is, an element such that $y < z_x$ for every y in S_x other than z_x itself. If z_x were not self-explanatory, then there would be a u in S such that $z_x < u$. By exactly the same reasoning as previously, we would then have $x < u$ and hence u would be in S_x, and this would contradict the maximality of z_x.

Then, let Z be the set of all the self-explanatory members of S. For any non-self-explanatory entity x of S there is a member of Z, namely, z_x, which causally explains x. Thus, indeed, the members of Z causally explain all the other members of S. This is a very strong conclusion that is drawn. Hence, if we strengthen the CP very naturally to cover *chains* of causes, it becomes a principle that gives *global* explanations, just as the PSR does when we apply the PSR to something like the conjunction of all contingent propositions, as we shall see later.

One might, of course, question the use of the Axiom of Choice (AC) implicit in Zorn's Lemma in the preceding argument. The AC states that for any set A of disjoint nonempty sets, there exists a set that contains exactly one member from every set that is a member of A. There is intuitive plausibility to this axiom. It functions in mathematics as a kind of principle of plenitude for sets. Mathematicians tend to accept the AC because it is needed for important theorems such as the Hahn-Banach theorem on the extension of linear functionals on infinite-dimensional vector spaces, even though it has been shown that the AC cannot be proved from the other axioms of set theory. Of course, the AC does lead to some paradoxes, such as the Banach-Tarski theorem that a solid sphere can be disassembled into a finite number of pieces that can be reassembled to form two spheres of the same size. However, arguably, such paradoxes are not much stranger than the "usual" paradoxes of infinity such as Hilbert's hotel, and how applicable our intuitions about space are to these cases depends on how well Euclidean $\mathbf{R}^3$ models the "space" that our intuitions are about. Giving up the AC would indeed be a high price to pay for whatever philosophical benefits might result from this. We will discuss the AC further in Chapter 11.

Or, alternately, one might argue that there is a difference between infinite chains of causes that stretch back a finite amount of time, as in the case of the cannonball, and infinite chains of causes that stretch back an infinite amount of time, as one might have if one wanted to apply the CP to the universe's history, if this history is in fact infinite. However, it is not clear what significant difference there is there. Consider the sets $S = \{t: 0 < t < 1\}$ and $T = \{t: -\infty < t < 1\}$. There seems to be no intrinsic difference between the structure of the time orderings on the two sets. In fact, the two sets are isomorphic: there is a one-to-one function f that maps S onto all of T such that $f(t) < f(u)$ if and only if $t < u$. For instance, $f(t) = 2 - 1/t$ is an example of such a function. Because of this lack of intrinsic difference, it follows that an infinite ungrounded chain stretching backward along T is just as unexplanatory as an infinite ungrounded chain stretching backward along S. The reason for extending the rationale behind the CP is that a finite-temporal-length infinite chain with no first member, as in the case of the cannonball's flight, fails to be self-explanatory, and the same rationale applies just as well to an infinite chain with infinite temporal length.

But while there is no intrinsic difference between a chain stretching backward along T and one stretching along S, there is an *extrinsic* difference. In the case of S, there is an instant of time prior to the whole chain, while in the case of T there is not. It is, it can be argued, in fact the existence of this instant of time prior to the chain that makes the case of the cannonball's flight so compelling a counterexample to the HEC. However, consider now a thought experiment, one whose possibility the opponent here cannot deny. Start with the standard case of the cannonball fired at t_0 and flying until t_1. This happens in some possible world, say, w, at which one cannot explain the set of states that the cannonball takes at times strictly between t_0 and t_1 without saying something about the state at t_0. Now, modify w into a world w^* whose whole time sequence is $\{t: t > t_0\}$ – just take w and lop off the instant t_0 from its time sequence as well as everything before t_0. Then the flight of the cannonball strictly between t_0 and t_1 does not in any way become more self-explanatory when we move from w to w^*. Nor does noting that the whole time sequence starts right after t_0 do anything to render the flight any more explainable. Insofar, then, as it was intuitions about causal explanation that grounded the CP and its extension to infinite chains, then the question whether there is an instant of time prior to a chain is irrelevant.

Of course, one might object that w^* is not a possible world. Perhaps time *must* go infinitely far back, despite apparent astronomical evidence to the contrary.[5] But even if so, then the construction of w^* still makes

---

5 This evidence consists in the astronomical evidence for the Big Bang, such as red shifts and background radiation, together with an interpretation on which there could not have been time before the Big Bang (cf. Grünbaum, 1998).

a point about the logic of explanation, a point that remains even if the construction is a *per impossibile* one.

3.1.6.b Duration. One might also object that duration is an intrinsic feature of time, and there is thus an intrinsic difference between order-isomorphic time sequences. Note that if one makes this objection, then, as Peter Forrest has observed, one loses one way to refute arguments for the *actual* universe's having a cause. We have good empirical reason to think that the actual universe has finite age. The Kalām claim that whatever has finite age has been caused to exist is highly plausible. One important objection to it has been that a finite age sequence can be isomorphic to an infinite age one (cf. Grünbaum, 1998). But once this objection falls through, the Kalām Cosmological Argument can be made to run.

That said, we can make two other responses. First, on Kantian views on which the order of time supervenes on the order of causation, it does not appear that there is room for duration to be an intrinsic feature of a time sequence. However we rescale the spacing between events, if the causal interconnections remain, the same objective facts about time obtain. A similar thing may be true on Aristotle's view that time is the measure of motion, at least on one interpretation.

But even if duration is an intrinsic feature of time, there does not seem to be any reason why duration should be relevant to what has a cause and what does not. Why is it that a sequence of events ..., E_{-n}, E_{-n+1}, ..., E that are respectively at times ... $< t_{-n} < t_{-n+1} < ...$ $< t_0$ would need a cause outside the sequence if the spacing between the events decreases as one goes "left" in the sequence in such a way that the t_{-n} converge to some finite value, but would not need a cause if the events are spaced sufficiently sparsely that t_{-n} goes to $-\infty$ as n goes to infinity? At the very least, the onus of proof here would be on the one alleging such a difference, and she would need to explain why duration is relevant in this way to the CP.

3.1.7. Resisting the Extension to Chains

There is, however, a way to resist this argument. One's reasons for accepting the CP might not have anything to do with explainability intuitions. One might instead see the CP as grounded in the very nature of time by holding with Kant that an event at one instant of time succeeds an event at another instant of time only when the latter causes the former. This would mean that one would object to the possibility of a present event

E that lacks a cause at some past *existing* instant of time, given that the pastness of that instant relative to E is constituted precisely by something's at that instant causing E, without objecting to the possibility of a world like w^* since there there are no past instants at t_0 or earlier whose pastness would need to be constituted causally. We have, however, seen in Section 2.5 that the Kantian argument for the CP fails.

Thus, the preceding arguments connecting the original highly restricted CP with less restricted versions that are much more like the PSR only apply if one's grounds for accepting the CP are explanatory-type intuitions. But I submit that it is these intuitions that are what really ground the CP insofar as it seems intuitive to us.

There is another way to argue against restricting the CP, inspired by Thomas Aquinas, who argues:

In an ordered series of movers and things moved, . . . it is necessarily the fact that when the first mover is removed or ceases to move [that which it moves], no other mover will move [that which it moves] or be moved. For the first mover is the cause of motion for all the others. But, if there are movers and things moved following an order to infinity, there will be no first mover, but all would be as intermediate movers. Therefore, none of the others will be able to be moved, and thus nothing in the world will be moved. (Aquinas, 1975, I, 13, 14)

A similar argument is given in the Third Way. Edwards (1959) has alerted us to the danger that Aquinas may commit in his Cosmological Argument the fallacy of confusing removal of the first mover, which would indeed remove the series of movers as a whole, with removal of the *firstness* of the first mover, which would cause no such harm. Such an interpretation is uncharitable, but it does recognize that Thomas sees something special about *firstness*. There is a generic difference between a moved mover and an independent mover. The former only passes the motion along while the latter originates it. One thinks of the difference between an electrical generator and the cables transmitting the electricity from it to the outside world.

Consider the case of the explanation of the Earth's failing to fall down in terms of its being held up by a single tortoise. The tortoise's being where it is may well be accepted as causing the Earth to stay put until we learn that the tortoise itself is suspended in midair. Once we learn this, the explanatory power of the tortoise may be vitiated. We only accepted the tortoise as explanatory because we thought we were moving closer to the ultimate explanation of the Earth's failure to fall. Once we learn that we are no closer to such an explanation, we may no longer see the tortoise as explanatory. And it makes no difference here how many tortoises we have; be it one, two, three, or infinity, the Earth is still just as unsuspended. The perhaps legendary old lady's response "But it's turtles all the way down!" to the objection that on the tortoise theory nothing holds up the tortoise does not help.[6]

To see this more clearly, imagine instead of antiquated cosmology, a rock. This rock is a couple of feet off the ground. Why is it off the ground? Because it is held up by a small tortoise. The tortoise itself, however, is also floating in the air, for no cause at all – this is a brute fact. The tortoise does nothing, in fact, to explain things. In fact, it is more puzzling that a rock and tortoise be suspended in the air than that just a rock be there. The tortoise's presence was presumed to have explanatory power, but the presumption was punctured by learning that it was in midair itself.

To back this intuition up further, imagine a case of overdetermination. When an effect is overdetermined by two different sufficient explanations, the explanatory power of neither is thereby vitiated. But suppose that our rock, in addition to being suspended on a tortoise, is suspended also on a lobster beside the tortoise that is holding the rock. The lobster, however, does not float in midair. It is carefully perched atop a pillar of twenty other lobsters that is firmly anchored on the ground. It would be fine to cite the top lobster in an explanation of why the rock is at that particular height. But it would not do to cite the top tortoise to this purpose. In this situation, it is only the lobster that is genuinely explanatory. The tortoise is useless. Likewise, an infinite series of tortoises that did not touch the ground would be just as useless explanatorily – imagine a series in which each tortoise is thinner than the one above it, so that the total thickness of the tortoises is finite and less than the distance from the rock to the ground.

Tortoises and lobsters are intermediate supporters. The support they lend to that which they support is support that itself has been lent to them, and they have no supportive role on their own. An unsupported tortoise or lobster gives no support. Nor does an unsupported finite or infinite pillar of them give any support. Likewise, a chain, finite or infinite, of moved movers where each receives what it needs for motion from the previous mover is not explanatory, for no source is given thereby to that which the movers pass along the chain. Similarly, a chain of causes of existence, without a necessarily existent anchoring cause, is only a

---

6   The story has, apparently, been told of Russell and Eddington. See, for instance, the beginning of Hawking (1988).

chain of things that pass existence along – without that from which it is passed.

Unfortunately, it is not clear how well all the metaphors work. Is one event causing another relevantly like an object physically supporting the weight of another? Is an event that itself is caused by another event really like a cable passing on electricity, rather than a genuine cause that would be at least *somewhat* explanatory even were it to exist on its own, and that would be more explanatory, even if not completely so, were it to be caused by an infinite chain of causes, itself contingent and causeless?

But once the CP is accepted as a necessary truth for single contingent events or objects, then we might well have to think of the analogies as good. If it is necessary that a contingent event have a cause, then it is plausible that this is necessary because something is lacking without a cause, something needed for its occurrence and thereby for its, in turn, having causal efficacy. Thus, if the CP is true, then it *is* plausible that contingent events exhibit a dependence sufficiently similar to the examples mentioned to ground the intuition that an infinite chain is no more helpful than a finite chain.

Alternately, one might attack the analysis of the tortoise case. One might claim that a single tortoise, even if itself unsupported, *is* explanatory. The puzzle shifts from the rock's being above the ground to the tortoise's being above the ground. But, nonetheless, the tortoise's being there *does* explain the rock's being there. The rock is genuinely pressing down on the tortoise's back. The tortoise genuinely exerts upward pressure on the rock. Admittedly, we have no explanation for why the tortoise is where it is. But perhaps we still have given an explanation for why the rock is in midair, though not an ultimate or final one. The unsupportedness of the tortoise does not, perhaps, entirely vitiate the explanatory prowess of the tortoise. Indeed, if *A* explains *B*, then *A* would still explain *B* even if *A* had no explanation.

However, note what is going on all the time when we think of these cases. We cannot help but talk about them in terms of explanation. The notion of causation is so tightly bound up with the notion of explanation that when we wonder about the tortoise's causal activity in suspending the rock, we are wondering about the explanation for the rock's being there. Thus, even if this criticism were accepted, we would still see the CP as a principle of explanation. And there would still be no reason to limit the demand for explanation to a demand for the explanation of single objects or events. It would still remain true that there really is no significant *explanatory* difference between an infinite chain of contingent events and a finite chain of contingent events; it may be that, pace Aquinas, both do some explaining of the given event, but it is also clear that both leave much unexplained. And the reason why we could not rest with the given event as a brute unexplained fact was our intuition that an explanation of a thing, a cause, is needed for the thing to exist or take place. This reason, however, remains in the more global and general cases.

3.2. THE *EX NIHILO NIHIL* PRINCIPLE, THE PSR, AND THE CP

The *ex nihilo nihil* principle (ENNP) can be given in two forms. There is a local form that says that no object that came to exist in time ultimately arose from nothing – every object (a) is itself eternal, or (b) has a causal history stretching back to something that is eternal or had existed for an infinite amount of time, or (c) has an infinite causal history. And there is a cosmic version that says simply that the preceding is true of one special object: the cosmos as it is now, that is, the aggregate of all the contingent things that exist now.

Observe that "had existed for an infinite amount of time," cannot be replaced by "had always existed," because the latter option would allow for an object to come to exist *ex nihilo* as long as time had come to exist simultaneously with the object. For if an object came to exist simultaneously with time, then that object could be said to have always existed – that is, existed at every past time – and we have seen in the last section that this case is just as mysterious as a case in which the object came to exist a finite amount of time ago but not simultaneously with time itself.

The ENNP in either form could be interpreted either as incompatible with the idea that the universe arises in time as a result of the causal influence of a timeless entity or as compatible with it. The idea here would either be a theistic account on which a timeless God creates the cosmos in time, or an account on which the Big Bang originates from some timeless quantum vacuum kind of state (cf. Hartle and Hawking, 1983), or some other scientific account based on an eternally existing substance or quasi substance, say, whatever entity or entities it is that make the laws of nature be laws (lawmakers in the terminology of Section 16.3.2). If *eternal* in the ENNP includes the possibility of a timeless existence, then it is compatible with an account like this. If *eternal* means "existing in time, but at every time," then it is incompatible. Although the Greeks subscribed to the stronger ENNP that excludes the cosmos's coming to exist a finite amount of time ago because of the causal influence of a timeless entity, there is really little reason to accept such a stronger ENNP. The weaker versions do just as much justice to the intuition that nothing comes from nothing: a timeless cause is not nothing.

The ENNPs as stated previously are clearly causal-type principles. One might instead formulate the ENNPs in a weaker, noncausal way. One might simply say, for the cosmic form, that either there is something eternal or there is an infinite past at every moment of which something existed or both. Formulated this way, the ENNP is essentially a thesis about the nonexistence of empty time slices, and about the infinity of the past if we take eternal entities to exist by courtesy at every time slice. The latter stipulation may seem awkward, but those who like abstracta such as propositions and numbers also like to say that these "always exist," even if strictly speaking one might say that they exist at no time, because they exist timelessly.

However, an acausal ENNP would be too weak. One of the aspects of change that worried the Greeks was that change seemed to be a type of replacement. The sophist Dionysodorus presents the worry in Plato's *Euthydemus*:

But now, said [Dionysodorus], you want [Clinias] to become wise.

[Socrates:] Most certainly.

But now, said he, is Clinias wise or not?

He says, not yet, said I [Socrates]. He's no boaster, you know.

And you people, said Dionysodorus, want him to become wise, and not to be a dunce?

We agreed.

Then you wish him to become one that he is not, and no longer to be one that he is.

I was troubled when I heard this, and he, seeing me troubled, took me up: One further word. Since you want him no longer to be one that he is now, you want him to be destroyed, it seems! Indeed, precious friends and lovers they must be who would give a great deal [of money for education] to have their darlings done away with! (*Euthydemus*, 283c–d, in Plato, 1961)

If change is replacement of one entity by another, then change is a kind of coming to be *ex nihilo*. To see this, consider the following three scenarios. In Scenario A, a billiard ball appears at t_0 with nothing having existed before t_0. This clearly violates the ENNP in any reasonable form. But consider Scenario B. Here, we have a universe that contains a rock. The rock exists up to but not including t_0. Then the rock pops out of existence and a billiard ball appears at t_0, coincidentally in the same place where the rock used to be. Scenario C is the same, except that instead of a preexisting rock, it is a blue billiard ball, and what pops into existence at t_0 is a red billiard ball. Our intuitions are, I take it, such that we do not see any difference in the kind of paradoxicality that Scenario A posits and that Scenario B posits. And there is little difference between Scenario B and Scenario C. Thus, if we reject Scenario A, we should for exactly the same reason reject Scenario C: things do not arise from nothing, but the red billiard ball arose from nothing.

What puzzled the Greeks, as illustrated by the preceding quote from the *Euthydemus*, was how to distinguish Scenario C from Scenario D where the billiard ball changes color from blue to red at t_0. They feared that all change would be replacement, and thus a violation of the *ex nihilo nihil fit* principle. This may be a yet further important reason why Parmenides when arguing against change took the trouble to argue for the ENNP. Finally, of course, Aristotle solved the difficulty by noting that the difference between Scenario C and Scenario D is that in D there is a persisting substance, which at first was actually blue and potentially red and which actualized its potentiality for redness.

If we take the ENNP to be a weaker acausal principle about empty times' not being followed by nonempty times, then this development from Parmenides to Aristotle can no longer be understood as being prompted by the ENNP, for an acausal ENNP is satisfied quite well in Scenarios B and C.

Moreover, what reason could one have for accepting an acausal version of the ENNP? Any intuition we have about things' not popping into existence out of nothing is surely violated by Scenario B, but to rule *that* out we need a causal form of the ENNP. Thus, it seems that the evidence for the ENNP in its acausal form is also evidence for it in its causal form.

Furthermore, if one thought that Scenario B was possible, then it would seem that Scenario A should be possible as well. Just imagine that that rock never existed. Since the rock does not actually causally affect the billiard ball's coming into existence in Scenario B, it follows that it is true at the world of Scenario B that had the rock not existed, then the billiard ball would still have existed. In fact, had the rock not existed, Scenario A would have eventuated. Since it is plainly possible that the rock had not existed, it follows that Scenario A is possible. For if we have the counterfactual were p to hold, then q would hold holding, and if p is possible, then q is also possible. Thus, indeed, one should not restrict the ENNP in such a way that it covers only Scenario B but not Scenario A.

But perhaps there *is* an argument for the ENNP in its acausal form that does not imply an ENNP in its causal form. Suppose that

(8) Necessarily, there is an infinite past.
(9) Necessarily, time can only exist in the presence of concrete objects.

It follows from (8) and (9) that at every moment in an infinite past concrete objects had existed. This yields a cosmic ENNP in an acausal form. With the objects' being further required to be in motion or changing in the context (9), Aristotle used this argument to argue for the eternity of motion in Book Λ of the *Metaphysics*.

However, what reason do we have to believe (8)? In favor of (8), Aristotle says that priority and posteriority depend on time. Thus, without time there is no priority. Aristotle does not say how an absurdity follows from this, but consider this. Suppose t_0 is the first moment of time. Then, plainly

(10) Before t_0, nothing existed.

But priority depends on time. Thus, if there was no time before t_0, then there was no "before": it makes no sense to talk about what happened *before* the first moment of time.

However, the argument here is fallacious. For we can disambiguate (10) into

(11) It is the case before t_0 that $\sim\exists x(x$ exists).
(12) $\sim\exists x(x$ exists before t_0).

Of these, (11) is plainly nonsensical if t_0 is the first moment of time. But there is nothing absurd about (12).

It appears then that whatever good reason one may have for accepting the ENNP in its acausal form is also good reason for accepting it in its causal form. Moreover, any reason to accept the cosmic form of the ENNP will surely be reason to accept the local form. One object's popping into existence is not less innately absurd than the cosmos as a whole's popping into existence. Just imagine a walnut-sized cosmos, perhaps even one where the whole of physical reality just *is* one walnut, and note that surely the actual size of the cosmos should not matter.[7] Thus, as soon as one accepts an ENNP in an appropriate form, one should accept a CP.

---

7   This thought experiment is inspired by Taylor (1974, chap. 10).

However, there are two kinds of CP. The event-form of the CP was the chief concern of the previous section. The ENNP leads instead to an object- rather than event-form of the CP: every contingent object has a cause. The CP in this form, when extended to chains as I have argued it should be extended in the previous section – in part arguing precisely on the basis of the ENNP – and assuming the Axiom of Choice, leads to the conclusion that there exists at least one *necessarily* existent object, for the only way the existence of an *object* can be self-explanatory is if the object is a necessary being, even if there should happen to be contingent self-explanatory propositions, as will be argued in Section 5.1.

We have by now argued for a claim that was announced in the Introduction: What we have seen is that the intuitions behind the CP and the ENNP are really intuitions for a PSR that says that every contingent proposition has an explanation, for the primary difference between the PSR and the CP or ENNP limited to single events or entities is globality. The PSR applies to more global states of affairs, such as the existence of chains of events. But if the CP or ENNP should not, on its own founding intuitions, be limited to local uses, then what we get is basically the PSR. Indeed, if we can apply the CP to every chain of causally connected events, then in fact we get the PSR *simpliciter*, since if we have explained every chain of causally connected events, then, plausibly, we have explained every contingent proposition, for, plausibly, the truth values of contingent propositions supervene on the actual events, as long as we construe *events* widely enough, in such a way that by explaining the events we have explained the propositions.

3.3. RESISTING THE EXTENSION TO NECESSARY TRUTHS

At the outset I have already restricted the PSR to contingent truths. But perhaps this restriction is ad hoc. Only a part of the motivation for the restriction was due to any considerations of the truth of the matter, such as that explanation in the case of necessary truths seems to be a different sort of thing from explanation in the case of contingent truths. Another part of the motivation was the fact that as yet we do not understand explanation in the sphere of the necessary.

In fact, just as we gave arguments moving from the CP to the PSR, we might give an argument of Peter Forrest's going from the PSR for contingent truths to the PSR for all truths. For a reductio, assume the PSR to hold for necessary and fail for contingent propositions. Let p be a necessary truth that has no explanation. Let q be a contingent truth. Then

p & q is a contingent truth and must have an explanation. But if p has no explanation, then neither does p & q.

This argument can, however, be resisted. Why is it that the apple has fallen *and* 7 is a prime? It is because of initial conditions J, the force of gravity, *and the fact that 7 is a prime*. In other words, we can give an explanation of p & q as p & r, where r is an explanation of q. And we can keep on doing this, proceeding along a chain of explanations of explanations of . . . of q, and keeping p as a conjunct. Of course, p never gets explained. But that is fine.

There is, however, a variant of this argument that seems more powerful. In Section 6.3.2, I will defend the notion of a contingent self-explanatory proposition. This is a proposition such that by understanding that it is true, we see that there is no further mystery as to why it is true. Suppose there is such a proposition, s. Let p be our unexplainable necessary proposition. Then, what explains p & s? There is no further proposition r that explains s, it seems, so we cannot say that p & s is explained by p & r. But neither is p & s self-explanatory, for then p would either be self-explanatory, or be explained by s, or be jointly explained by itself and by s. One move one can make here, however, is to stipulate that a self-explanatory proposition is explained by whatever conceptual or necessary truths make it be the case that there is no mystery in the proposition. If, for instance, a truth of the form *God freely chose A for R* is self-explanatory, it is self-explanatory in light of certain necessary facts about libertarian free choice providing ultimate explanations of actions. If so, then we can find a necessary r that explains s, and then say that p & s is explained by p & r. Since p & r is necessary, the PSR for contingent truths no longer applies.

If one does not accept that p & q is explained by p & r when r explains q, then something else will have to be done: I will have to stipulate throughout this book that by *explanation* I mean "explanation modulo necessary truths" and illustrate this notion ostensively, by saying that if p is a necessary truth and q is a contingent truth, then any explanation of q is also an explanation of p & q modulo necessary truths.[8]

---

8 Peter Forrest has suggested an alternative on which the PSR says that for every contingent proposition p, there is a logically equivalent proposition q that has an explanation, where p and q are logically equivalent, providing that, necessarily, each holds if and only if the other does. Unfortunately, this yields a PSR that might be too weak, at least given some Kripkean intuitions. Let p be the proposition that Phaenarete and Sophroniscus conceived Socrates. Let q be the proposition that Socrates existed. Then, if the Kripkeans are right, p and q are logically equivalent. Socrates could not exist without being conceived by Phaenarete and Sophroniscus, and clearly if Socrates is conceived, then he exists. Thus, the modified PSR

One might, however, opt to follow Taylor (1974, Chap. 10) in restricting the PSR to contingent positive states of affairs such as that the lightbulb is glowing or that Bucephalus existed, without requiring explanations of why there are no unicorns. This would have the advantage that it is prima facie compatible with the possibility that the cosmos might have been empty, in which case there would have been nothing to explain.

However, as it turns out, starting from such a restricted PSR (R-PSR) if one thinks this R-PSR to be a necessary truth – and that is what it is surely supposed to be, at least insofar as it is argued for on grounds of a priori self-evidence, say – one can get to a full PSR for contingently true propositions.

To see this, let a "positive proposition" be a proposition reporting a positive state of affairs. Let a "negative proposition" be the denial of a positive proposition. The R-PSR then states that, necessarily, if p is a contingent true positive proposition, then p has an explanation. Now, suppose q is a contingent true negative proposition. Then, q is of the form $\sim s$ for some contingent false positive proposition s. We *can* now explain $\sim s$ as follows. By the R-PSR, it is necessarily true that if s holds, then there is an explanation of why s holds. Let R be the set of all propositions r such that r could explain s, that is, propositions r such that in some possible world r explains s. Explanation has an "existential commitment": necessarily, if r explains s, then r and s are true. Then, let e be the proposition that no member of R explains s. It is now a necessary truth that if e is true, then q is true. For if q were false, then s would be true, and by the R-PSR, s would have an explanation.

We can now say that e together with a number of necessary truths, such as the R-PSR and the claim that all possible explanations of s are in R, explains why s does not hold. It does not hold because none of the possible explainers of it in fact explain it. I am not claiming here that any proposition r that entails q also explains q. But e does, since this case of explanation is very close to an ordinary language pattern of explanation. Why did the yogurt fail to ferment? It failed to ferment because none of the usual explanations of fermentation, namely, the presence

would be perversely satisfied in respect of p without our needing to give *any* explanation of the actions of Socrates' parents, for p is logically equivalent to q, we have assumed, and q does have an explanation – the explanation is p!

of bacteria, were there to explain it, and there was no unusual cause. Why did the dog not bark? It did not bark because no stranger approached it and none of the other possible causes of barking caused it to bark.

Thus, if the R–PSR is necessarily true, it is also necessarily true that all negative contingent true propositions have explanations. If one thinks that given explanations of all contingent true positive and negative propositions, one could construct an explanation of *all* contingent true propositions, then the PSR follows. To argue for the claim in the antecedent, let p be the conjunction of all contingent true positive propositions. This itself is a contingent true positive proposition, and hence has an explanation. Let q be the conjunction of all contingent true negative propositions. This is a contingent true proposition but need not be a negative one (unless one takes a disjunction of positive propositions to be positive). However, q can be explained by citing the R–PSR and noting that there is no explanation for *any* of the negations of the conjuncts of q.

Let e be an explanation of p. Then let f be the preceding explanation for q, namely, the claim that none of the negations of the conjuncts of q has an explanation while the R–PSR holds. Then, although in general explanation is not agglomerative, it is highly plausible, if we think about it, that in *this* case e & f explains p & q. Agglomerativeness can fail if some sort of vicious regress or circularity is induced. But none is induced in this case. It is genuinely true that once we have stated e and added that none of the negations of the conjuncts of q has an explanation whereas by the R–PSR they would have to have one if they held, then we have explained p & q. Now, the truth values of all contingent true propositions can in principle be determined from p & q if the truth values of all propositions supervene on the truth values of the union of the classes of the positive and negative contingent propositions, whereas from the truth of p & q one can derive the truth values of all positive and of all negative contingent propositions. The latter fact follows from the observation that any positive contingent proposition either is true, in which case it is a conjunct of p, or is false, in which case its negation is a conjunct of q. Likewise, any negative contingent proposition either is true, in which case it is a conjunct of q, or is false, in which case it is the negation of a conjunct of p. Thus, knowing p & q and knowing all necessary truths, one can in principle read off the truth values of all contingent true propositions. It is highly plausible that this implies that there is nothing more to the explanation of all contingent truths than a bunch of necessary truths conjoined with e & f.

We have looked at two closely related principles, each of which has several different versions. First, consider the Causal Principle :

(13) Every contingent event has a cause.
(14) Every contingent event has a cause that is itself an event.
(15) Every contingent being that once did not exist has a cause.
(16) Every contingent being that comes into existence has a cause.
(17) Every contingent being has a cause.

Some logical interconnections are obvious: (17) $\Rightarrow$ (16) $\Rightarrow$ (15) and (14) $\Rightarrow$ (13). If events are themselves beings, then (17) $\Rightarrow$ (13).

Since the coming-into-existence of a being is itself an event, (13) $\Rightarrow$ (16). This has been disputed by Adolf Grünbaum, who has argued (1998) that the Big Bang, which is the universe's coming-into-existence, should not be thought of as an event. The argument relies on the claim that there was no initial moment of time at which the Big Bang happened, since such a moment of time would involve a singularity – a time when the universe has infinite density and other absurdities occur – and furthermore there was no time before the Big Bang. However, there is nothing absurd about an event's happening over a finite interval of time instead. Typical events, such as the waving of an arm or the explosion of a bomb, happen over intervals of time. It is not obvious that there is a fact of the matter as to when on the standard interpretation of quantum mechanics indeterministic collapse occurs. It occurs "at the time of measurement," but specifying this more precisely is notoriously difficult, and it might turn out that there is no single moment of measurement, but an interval of time. Thus, the lack of a single moment of time at which to locate the Big Bang is not a problem. We can just think of the event of the universe's expansion over the interval $\{t: t_0 < t < t_0 + \delta\}$, where t_0 is numerically equal to the limit of the times as we approach the beginning of the universe and δ is small and positive.[9] Nor is there any reason why for something to be an event there should have to be moments of time *before* it.

It is not clear whether there are converses to a number of the preceding implications. One can argue that (13) $\Rightarrow$ (14) by arguing that if A causes

---

9   More precisely, t_0 is the *infimum* of the times at which the universe is in existence, where the infimum of a set S is the unique largest number (possibly infinite) x such that $x \leq y$ for all y in S. Note that t_0 is not itself actually a *time* if Grünbaum is right, but only a number, relative to whatever units time is measured in.

an event E, whatever kind of ontological item A might be, then A's exercise of causal power should count as an event. On the other hand, if it is a conceptual truth that if an event is a cause, then it should precede the effect in time, and if time began with the Big Bang, which itself is an event, then (14) is in fact false. However, I will not actually be very much interested in (14), since my main interest is the PSR, which in itself does not further specify what sorts of causes or explanations are allowable, though of course some of the arguments for or against it will rest on such a specification.

One could coherently hold to principle (15) while rejecting principle (16). To do so justifiedly, one would have to have a reason to think there is a relevant difference between comings-into-existence prior to which there was a time and ones, perhaps like the Big Bang, such that it is not the case that prior to them there was any time. Now, it seems that there is no intrinsic difference between such comings-into-existence, and the difference appears precisely extrinsic: it concerns whether time exists before the event. We do not see why the flight of a cannonball that was *not* preceded by a cannon firing should any less require a cause if it is in fact the first event in time. Just imagine such an absurdly causeless flight's occurring yesterday, starting at noon, and then imagine that in fact time started yesterday at noon. The flight would become no less absurd.

One might accept (15) without accepting (16) or (17), however, if one thinks that the very nature of time is constituted by causation in such a way as to make (15) true. The one way on the table for doing this is the Kantian approach; we have seen in Section 2.5 that it fails, however. The most serious failing was that we did not need *every* event to have a cause to make the Kantian account of time work.

I have argued previously that if one accepts any version of the CP for isolated events, one should likewise accept a version for chains of events, since a CP for isolated events is not in fact sufficient to do justice to the intuitions of dependency or explanation behind the CP. If we accept this, then although one can certainly coherently believe (16) without believing (17), it is not obvious that one can do so justifiedly. For the only difference between (17) and (16) is that (17) applies to a contingent entity that has always existed. But there is no reason why, once one has accepted a CP for a chain of entities, each causing the next, one should reject a CP for an entity that simply has perdured for an infinite amount of time. Moreover, in a sense there is no *intrinsic* difference, we saw, between perduring over $\{t: -\infty < t < t_1\}$ and perduring over $\{t: t_0 < t < t_1\}$, since these two time sequences are isomorphic. If one accepts the CP for the latter kinds of entities, one should do so likewise for the former.

If the reasons for accepting the CP are explainability or dependency considerations, then it seems that one cannot justifiedly accept any one of (13), (15), (16), and (17) without likewise accepting all of the others. The same is true if one's reasons are based on Thomistic ontology, since the Thomistic arguments, as we shall see in Chapter 12, are dependency arguments starting with an *esse-essentia* distinction. It is true that one might want to limit this distinction to substances, in which case one might get (15)–(17), without however getting (13). But it is plausible that one will be able to get something at least analogous to an *esse-essentia* distinction for events, or maybe one will be able to get it for the accidents of substances while insisting that all events supervene on the accidents of substances on an Aristotelian ontology.[10] After all, Socrates' being seated seems to be something that corresponds to an essence, although one that the scholastics call "an accidental essence," namely, something like *being a seated Socrates*, an essence one can know without knowing that it is in fact actualized.

And if, as has been argued, there cannot be ungrounded infinite dependency chains, then the Thomistic arguments also imply chainwise versions of the principles. Admittedly, most of the arguments about chains were made in terms of explanatory chains, whereas the Thomistic arguments will not use intuitions about explanation but will be based on dependency considerations. However, the arguments on chains of support did concern precisely dependency chains and a number of the explanatory chain arguments also apply in the dependency case. For instance, if we accept an infinite ungrounded chain of support as solving a dependency problem, then we might be stuck with saying that an infinite chain of chickens is supported by an infinite chain of eggs and vice versa, thereby showing that acceptance of infinite ungrounded chains implies acceptance of vicious circularities in the order of dependency.

If this is right, then one cannot both justifiedly accept any one of (13), (15), (16), and (17) without accepting all the others, and moreover accepting them all as applicable chainwise. Furthermore, if there are any other contingent items in our ontology besides events and substances, say,

---

10   Thomas does not think accidents ordinarily have *esse-essentia* composition (*Summa Theologica* III, 77, 1, objection 4 and reply 4). However, this does not rule out the possibility of something analogous, such as a composition between the substance's act of sustaining the accident and the accidental essence.

accidents, our reasoning is likely to apply to them as well, and we will extend the CP to such items as well. Now, if every individual contingent item of our ontology has a cause and hence an explanation, and if likewise we can come up with causal explanations for chains, then it is hard to resist the conclusion that in fact every contingent true proposition has an explanation.

There is a difficulty here in that it has been argued against Hume and Edwards that explanation is not in fact agglomerative. Explanations of the conjuncts need not in general explain the conjunction, and so it is not obvious that we can agglomerate the explanations of the chains to produce a total explanation.

But there are cases in which agglomerativeness holds and I shall argue that we can make an agglomerative explanation work in this case. If p and q are explained by one and the same proposition r, then r surely also explains the conjunction p & q. The same will be true for infinite conjunctions. Now, we have seen in two special cases that a CP extended to chains of items will lead us to a *first cause*. In order to block a call for a further application of the CP, each first cause will have to be a necessary being. To block fatalism, at least some of the first causes will have to exercise their causal power in an indeterministic way: the essential nature of the first cause cannot determine the effects. I will for now assume that such exercise of causal power by a first cause is indeed explanatory of everything down the road in the chain; a detailed discussion of this issue will be found in Chapters 6 and 7.

Given this, let q be a proposition reporting the conjunction of all the exercises of causal power by the first causes and the necessary existence of these first causes. Then, q explains every contingent item in our ontology, since we could start our chainwise argument for a first cause from any contingent item in our ontology. But if so, then we have, with a single proposition q, explained every primitive contingent proposition such as that some substance exists, or that some substance has some accident, or that some event occurs. This proposition q, together with principles of logic and the limited agglomerativeness thesis that says that if one and the same explanation explains every conjunct then the conjunction is explained, explains every contingent true proposition, or at least explains its contingent aspects. The proposition *that $2 + 2 = 4$ and horses exist* is a contingent proposition, but our proposition q will only explain its contingent conjunct, unless one stipulates that all necessary truths are self-explanatory.

If all this is correct, then once we accept any version of the CP, we should also accept

(18) Every true contingent proposition has an explanation at least of its contingent aspects.

I will henceforth stipulate necessary propositions to be self-explanatory or else to have their explanation in their necessity. The latter solution says that if p is necessary, then that Lp (i.e., necessarily p) explains that p. This leads to a regressive sequence, of course: LLp explains Lp, LLLp explains LLp, and so on. But by our stipulation, we can explain the whole sequence by noting that every proposition in the chain is necessary and hence so is their conjunction: L(p & Lp & LLp & LLLp & ...).[11] If either solution is acceptable, then from (18) it follows that

(19) Every true proposition has an explanation.

If not, then all we have is (18).

I will, stipulatively if necessary, assume henceforth that to explain a contingent proposition all that has to be explained are its contingent aspects. Given this, we see that once one accepts any version of the CP, one should also accept

(20) Every true contingent proposition has an explanation.

I will refer to this as the PSR, and it is this that I shall argue for in Part III. Some of the arguments will proceed by showing our commitment to different versions of the CP, a commitment that, by the preceding arguments, should also lead us to accept the PSR. It would be ad hoc to accept the CP but balk at the PSR. At the same time, a reader not convinced by this might find some of the arguments convincing her only of something weaker than the PSR, say, some version of the CP.

Finally, a note on necessity. It is implausible to suppose the CP is merely contingently true. Our confidence in the CP goes beyond our confidence in something that we learned empirically – I will argue for this claim in Section 16.4. Indeed, we judge empirical claims by means of the CP. And if the CP were contingently true, we could surely only know it empirically. Nor should we think of the CP as having merely nomic

---

11 One might wish to extend this regress up the ordinals, but similar considerations should apply, since one will be forming a class of propositions every member of which is necessary, and then it will be necessary *that* every member of the class is necessary, and this will be sufficient to explain the chain as a whole.

necessity. Again, it would have to be argued for empirically then, and there will be further considerations given in Section 16.4, based on a theory of laws of nature, against the nomic necessity view of the CP. This makes the CP metaphysically necessary. And, by the preceding, once one accepts the CP as metaphysically necessary, one should accept the PSR as such, too. Thus, versions (13), (15), (16), and (17) of the CP; the metaphysical necessity of these versions; the PSR; the metaphysical necessity of the PSR; and some versions of the ENNP should be accepted either all or none.

Part Two

Objections to the PSR

4

A Modern Version of the Hume Objection

4.1. TOY MODELS

An impressive variant of the Humean argument, inspired by ideas of J. Brian Pitts, is as follows. The cosmological literature is full of "toy models," complete coherent physical models of universes. Those toy models that model a universe with a finite past, such as the Robertson–Walker hot Big Bang model, are models of universes that come to exist for no cause, since models in physics generally do not include any universe-creating deity. Insofar as the models are coherent, we see that it is possible for something, namely, the universe, to come to exist out of nothing, pace all the forms of the PSR that entail that the *ex nihilo nihil* principle is a necessary truth. Moreover, in fact, physicists think that the models are compatible with at least a subset of the laws of nature. But if so, then surely they are self-consistent and metaphysically possible.

It will not do to challenge this argument on the basis of the claim that the physical laws the physicists invoke are false, for even if they are false, one might think that similar models could be constructed using the true ones, unless we are completely wrong about what the true laws look like. Moreover, even if the laws are false, they surely describe logically possible situations, and that is all that is needed.

One way to gloss the argument is just to say that any internally coherent mathematical theory describes a possible reality. But this is not sufficient for the conclusion. Consider a first-order mathematical theory that can be given in full by us. This typically consists of a language and a set of rules for forming well-formed formulas (wffs), as well as a finite or recursively generable set of axioms. We can then say that the theory "describes a possible reality" if and only if there is a possible world and an interpretation that assign to every constant term in the theory an object in the world, to every predicate term in the theory a property (perhaps understood as a set of satisfying objects) in the world, and to every relation term in the theory a set-theoretic relation in the world, such that a closed formula in the theory's language translates into a proposition about the world, and a theorem translates into a true proposition. I will say that in that case the theory is modeled by the world under the interpretation. I will restrict the discussion to first-order theories, which after all are the theories with which physicists typically deal.

4.2. A POSSIBILITY PRINCIPLE

The claim that any consistent theory describes a possible reality is tantamount to the following possibility principle:

(PP) For any consistent theory there are a possible world and an interpretation of that theory such that the theory is true at that world under that interpretation.

But we will now see that this is not enough to undercut the metaphysical necessity of the PSR, because of the multiplicity of interpretations. I will make the point by means of an example, but the example shows the problem in general. Suppose our theory has a language with only three constants, X, Y, and Z, and one relation, C, which we intend to mean "causes to exist." We suppose further that there are two predicates, F and G, which we intend to mean "is a particle of type 1" and "is a particle of type 2," say. Our theory then is that X is a particle of type 1, Y and Z are particles of type 2, and X causes Y to exist, and there is nothing else in existence and no other causal relations obtain. The model thus is of a system in which there is at least one uncaused item, namely, Z. Our axioms, then, are

(21) $\forall x(x = X \text{ or } x = Y \text{ or } x = Z)$
(22) $\forall x \forall y(xCy \supset (x = X \mathrel{\&} y = Y))$
(23) $Fx \mathrel{\&} {\sim}Gx \mathrel{\&} Gy \mathrel{\&} {\sim}Fy \mathrel{\&} Gz \mathrel{\&} {\sim}Fz$
(24) $X \neq Y \mathrel{\&} Y \neq Z \mathrel{\&} X \neq Z$
(25) XCY

Then, it is supposed to be the case that any world that acts as a model will contain only three entities, of which only one is caused. Unless we think that in fact there exist two necessary beings, and indeed two necessary *particles*, it seems we will have to conclude that in that world there is at

76

least one contingent uncaused being, the one that corresponds to X or the one that corresponds to Z.

However, this conclusion does not follow. All that our previous principle of possibility gives us is that there are a possible world and *an interpretation* of the theory under which the theory is true. If we are to have a contradiction to the necessity of the PSR, it is incumbent on the Humean to show that if the PSR holds, there is no possible world and interpretation of the theory on which the theory comes out true in that world. But the defender of the PSR might reasonably think there *is* such a world. For instance, the defender of the PSR might be a theist. Consider, then, a world w containing only God, who is supposed to be a necessary being, and two substances, say, Ed and Fred, and suppose that Fred knows nothing about Ed. We can now give an interpretation of the preceding theory in this world. Interpret X, Y, and Z as God, Ed, and Fred, respectively. Interpret F and G as the predicates "is infinite" and "is finite," respectively. Interpret C as the relation " . . . knows . . . to be identical with Ed." Then, God and Ed stand in this relation, but no other pair does. It is easy to see that (21)–(25) come out true on this interpretation, and so the world models the theory under the given interpretation. And yet the PSR can hold, since God may have created Ed and Fred. Thus, (21)–(25) holding in a world under some interpretation does not logically contradict the PSR's holding in that world.

Thus, even though we seemed to have had a nice and consistent mathematical theory about a situation containing a contingent uncaused being, the principle that every consistent mathematical theory is modeled by some possible world under some interpretation is seen to be insufficient to yield the contradiction to the PSR. The reason for this is that the "under some interpretation" condition allows enough leeway to reinterpret the theoretical language's relation-term that was intended to signify causation to signify a relation other than causation.

4.3. A STRONGER POSSIBILITY PRINCIPLE

The preceding response seems disingenuous. The Humean need only strengthen her principle to the strong possibility principle (SPP) and claim that this is what she meant all along:

(SPP) Every consistent mathematical theory is modeled at some possible world under an interpretation that interprets the term C intended by the theory's proponent to signify causation as causation in that world.

While this principle as combined with the theory of (21)–(25) is sufficient to yield a reductio of the necessity of the PSR, this principle is false. Consider the following consistent mathematical theory:

(26) $\forall x(x = X$ or $x = Y)$

(27) XCY & YCX

(28) $X \neq Y$

While this theory is consistent, there is no possible world that models it under an interpretation that interprets C as causation. The reason for this is that there is no possible world at which there are two entities each of which causes the other. A causal circle would yield a circularity in explanation, and it is a conceptual truth that there cannot be any such.

Thus, the original PP appears to be too weak to yield the desired conclusion, while the SPP is too strong to be true.

4.4. THE EMPTY WORLD

But the preceding defenses of the necessity of the PSR do neglect one possible refutation. Consider the following consistent theory:

(29) $\forall x(x \neq x)$.

This theory can only be modeled by an empty world. Therefore, the possibility principle with the interpretation unconstrained, that is, the PP, implies that it is possible for there to be an empty world. But the PSR is not satisfied at an empty world, because were an empty world actual, there would be no explanation of the fact that nothing exists.

One might respond by restricting the PSR to explanations of positive states of affairs: at the empty world there are none such, and hence a PSR restricted thus is true by default. But there is no need to go this far. For, precisely to the extent that the PP implies that it is possible for there to be an empty world, the PP is implausible. We do not have any reason to suppose there to be an empty possible world. The idea leads to truthmaker-based paradoxes, as noted earlier. It implies the existence of a world at which it is true that nothing, not even "the cosmos," exists. This possibility is itself sufficiently suspicious metaphysically that a principle that implies this possibility is thereby made dubious. In light of this, one might be tempted to suppose some weaker principle, such as that every consistent mathematical theory that is consistent with the existence of at least one object is modeled by a possible world or that every consistent mathematical theory is modeled by a subset of a possible world. But these versions do not threaten the necessity of the PSR.

An alternate challenge to the original PP is that by implying that there can be an empty world it implies that there are no necessary beings – not even numbers, sets, or propositions are necessary. To overcome this unwelcome conclusion, one might weaken the principle by saying that every consistent mathematical theory is modeled by the subset of a possible world consisting of all the *contingent* objects of that world, so that quantifiers are interpreted as running over the contingent objects. However, a principle thus weakened is no longer a challenge to the necessity of the PSR, even if we impose the implausibly strong condition that causation is the interpretation of C. For instance, take the first example theory (21)–(25). Consider now a world in which there contingently exist three particles, one of type 1 that causes another one of type 2, and one of type 2, and in which there is a necessarily existent God who freely creates each of the three particles. The claim in the theory threatening the PSR is that the only two objects that stand in relation C are X and Y. But if the quantifiers in the interpretation are restricted to run only over the contingent objects, then this claim does not threaten the possibility of God's creating X, Y and Z, if God is a necessary being .

4.5. PHYSICISTS ARE NOT MERELY LOGICIANS

However, the preceding ways of fleshing out the "scientific" form of the Humean anti-PSR argument neglects one important point. When dealing with toy models of universes, we are not dealing merely with models that *logicians* have created. Rather, we have theories that *physicists* have come up with on the basis of well-confirmed laws of physics. For instance, a physicist would not come up with the theory that says that XCY and YCX, because the physicist knows that causation is not circular.

The argument is empirical and inductive: competent physicists rarely come up with the sorts of theories on which the strongest possibility principle, that a consistent theory is modeled by some possible world under an *intended* interpretation, is violated. But now the argument becomes not only scientific but scientistic. Scientists are very good judges of what reality could be like in its physical aspects. If they say that some theory is physically possible, then probably there is a metaphysically possible world whose physical aspects are modeled, under an intended interpretation, by the given theory: that is, the world is modeled by the theory if we restrict quantifiers to all physical objects. But unless we take a scientistic view that science is the measure of all things, the scientist need not be a good judge as to what reality could be like *simpliciter*, not just in its physical aspects but also in its metaphysical aspects. For instance, the scientist is not, qua scientist, qualified to judge whether there can be a world that contains no universals or no numbers or no deities or no Forms.

Thus, the scientist's intuitions behind a toy model that has a universe coming to exist with no cause only make probable that there is a possible world at which the *physical* universe comes to exist with no *physical* cause. But such a supposition is, of course, fully compatible with the necessity of the PSR, since the PSR does not assert that the causes of physical phenomena are always themselves physical.

In fact, consider two physicists, one a traditional Western monotheist and the other an atheist. They discuss some toy model of the universe. They agree on the model's adhering to the standards of the profession and our best knowledge of the laws of nature. But they have a disagreement. The atheist says that the toy model could describe *all* of reality while the theist believes that, necessarily, there is a God, and hence the toy model could describe not all of reality but rather that part of reality that God created. This is surely not a disagreement about *physics*, but a philosophical disagreement.

We cannot imagine what sorts of *physical* considerations, whether theoretical or observational, could possibly have a bearing on the discussion, unless the atheist can argue that her model *excludes* the existence of God on *physical* grounds. The only way I can see that it might do that (apart from considerations of evil, which are not in the province of physics) would be as follows. The toy model might be of a completely *self-explaining* universe.[1] Now, a self-explaining universe could not coexist with a God, because if God exists, then every contingent being is created by God and hence is not self-explaining but explained by God. But however much this kind of an argument might be a challenge to *theism* (though because of the arguments like those in Section IV of the Introduction to Gale and Pruss [2003] it would not likely be a very serious one), it would be no challenge at all to the necessity of the PSR: the self-explaining universe

---

1 The philosophical interpretation by Quentin Smith (1994a) of the already somewhat philosophically charged work of Hartle and Hawking (1983) is somewhat close to this. See Section IV of the Introduction to Gale and Pruss (2003) for a critical discussion.

certainly satisfies the PSR. It is only the toy models of non-self-explaining universes that can be a concern.

Thus, the special competence of the physicist does not help settle the issue in favor of the toy model's giving theories of possible worlds at which the PSR fails. We have seen, therefore, that none of the Humean arguments give significant reason to reject the PSR.

5

The Anti-theological Argument That There Are No Necessary Beings

5.1. COSMOLOGICAL ARGUMENTS

One objection to the PSR is that it is simply false because it entails the existence of a causally efficacious necessary being. Consider applying the PSR (or, in the third case, a version of the CP) to one of these:

(30) The proposition that there exists at least one contingent being
(31) The conjunction of all contingent true propositions
(32) The contingent existence of the actual aggregate of all contingent beings (i.e., of the universe)

All of these explananda have the property that any explanans must entail the existence of a causally efficacious necessary being. The explanation of why there is a contingent being or why the aggregate of all contingent beings exists cannot itself, at the pain of circularity, proceed by citing the causal efficacy of any contingent being.

The case of the conjunction of all contingent true propositions – call this conjunction the Big Conjunctive Contingent Fact (BCCF) – takes a little bit more thought. Swinburne (1968) has argued that human beings have available only two kinds of explanations (as a friendly amendment we may add, in addition to reductive explanation): scientific explanations in terms of boundary conditions and laws and personal explanation in terms of the free activity of a person. No scientific explanation of the BCCF can be given, assuming for now that the laws are contingent – alternate proposals will be discussed in Sections 5.3.2 and 5.6. Then the laws of nature are themselves conjuncts in the BCCF, and they are also not self-explanatory, so that it would be viciously circular for the laws of nature to enter into an explanation of the BCCF. This argument uses the principle that only a self-explanatory proposition can enter into the explanation of a proposition of which that proposition is a conjunct. Nor are the boundary conditions self-explanatory, but they too are contingent. Thus, there is no scientific explanation of the BCCF. Therefore, by the PSR, there must be a personal explanation, in terms of a person's (or persons') freely bringing it about that p, where p is the BCCF. Now the person by whose free actions the BCCF is to be explained cannot exist contingently, for the contingent existence of this person would then be a part of the BCCF and the person's free action would end up explaining her own existence, and that would be absurd: the person would be *causa sui* in the worst possible way. Thus the person must be necessary.

The preceding argument neglects the possibility of a reductive explanation. Reductive explanations may or may not involve laws of nature. Thus, that a riding elected Fred as a member of Parliament reduces to Fred's getting the greatest share of the votes legally cast in the riding and is also explained by it. That the iron is hot is explained by and reduced to the molecules in it having high kinetic energy. However, allowing reductive explanation really does not help to escape the necessary existence of the person whose free actions explain the BCCF. Reductive explanations are never final. If a contingent proposition r reduces to a contingent proposition q, then the question of explanation resurfaces for q. Why did the greatest number of votes fall to Fred? Why do the molecules have the high kinetic energy? If the explanation here, in turn, is reductive, we are off to a regress. But for exactly the same reasons as ungrounded causal regresses are not explanatory, infinite reductive regresses are not explanatory. Thus something beyond the regress of reductive explanations would be needed. And it is not plausible that ultimately everything, when seen as appropriately reduced, is self-explanatory.

Besides which, in any case, the explanation of the BCCF must be either a necessary proposition or a contingent self-explanatory proposition. There cannot be a reductive explanation of a contingent proposition in terms of a necessary one, since propositions inherit their modal status from that to which they reduce. On the other hand, what would a contingent self-explanatory proposition look like? The *explanatory* part of self-explanatory would not be understandable in reductive terms: obviously every state of affairs can be trivially said to reduce to itself, but this is in no way explanatory. Nor can it involve a scientific explanation, since scientific explanations have non-self-explanatory propositions in the explanans. The only remaining option is a personal explanation. Granted, it is hard to see what the explanans would look like, but it is the only remaining option and hence must be right. And the personal explanation, as argued, would have to involve a necessarily existing person, or it would have no chance for being self-explanatory.

I will argue in Chapter 7 that we can coherently take this explanation to consist in the proposition that a necessary being freely brought it about that p, perhaps with the codicil, "for reason R." In Chapter 6 we will consider a different attempt to refute the PSR, one in effect based on the idea that this proposition, being contingent, cannot be self-explanatory. But we do not need this here. All we need here is that the PSR as applied to the BCCF entails that there is a necessary being that is causally efficacious, since that is the only explanatory possibility.

5.2. NECESSARY BEINGS AND ABSURDITY

But, it is often claimed, the notion of a necessary being is absurd. For it is propositions that are necessary, not beings, and hence talk of a necessary being is a category mistake. However, this is an uncharitable argument, since the claim that A is a necessary being can be translated into the claim that the proposition $\exists x(x = A)$ is necessarily true, or perhaps that there is some *individual essence* E of A that is a property that only A can have and that is such that $\exists x(x$ has $E)$ is necessarily true. Talk of necessary and contingent beings will henceforth usually be understood in this way, though there is also a Thomistic model on which a necessary being is one whose *esse* and *essentia* are identical.

A better argument against the existence of a necessary being is that by a principle of Hume, anything that can coherently be thought to exist can also be thought not to exist. This by itself does not yield a satisfactory argument, however. It is not obvious that the totality of all existing things can be thought not to exist, that it could have been that there is nothing in existence. Moreover, this would imply that propositions, mathematical objects, and properties have merely contingent existence, an implication that may well be thought to be absurd since the proposition that $2 + 2 = 4$ would be true no matter what, and it could not be true unless it existed, as nonexistent things lack properties, even properties such as *truth*. Moreover the proposition that there *is* a solution to the equation $3x^2 + x - 7 = 0$ is also necessarily true.

But the objector to the PSR will not bat an eyelash at this response. Propositions, numbers, and properties are *abstract* objects, whereas the necessary being whose existence the PSR implies when applied to the BCCF is explanatorily efficacious and hence nonabstract.

84

A different response to this argument is to deny that the PSR as applied to any of (30)–(32) implies the existence of a necessary being. The classic way of responding in this way involves the Hume-Edwards principle that if one has explained every item in an aggregate, one has explained the whole aggregate. We might explain the BCCF by having one proposition in the BCCF be explained by another, ad infinitum. And we might explain why there are contingent beings by explaining the existence of one by another, and so on. However, we have seen in Section 3.1 that this response is not successful because the Hume-Edwards principle is false.

5.3.1. Systematic Explanation

Nicholas Rescher has recently offered two other ways to escape the conclusion that the PSR entails the existence of a necessary being. The first distinguishes two sorts of explanation. One can explain a set of propositions *subsumptively*, by subsuming them under causal laws and connecting them without boundary conditions. Or, one can explain a theory *systematically* by its internal unity and coherence, and its fit with the observational data (Rescher, 2000a, chap. 4). Thus, the contingent events of the universe might be explained subsumptively by a theory, whereas the theory itself would be explained systematically in terms of its internal unity and coherence, and the fit it has with the contingent events of the universe.

As the internal unity and coherence of a theory is a necessary truth about that theory, since it is a purely formal fact, what we have, modulo necessary truths, is the circular explanation of the events by the theory and the theory by the events. One might try to reject this simply on the grounds that explanation cannot be circular. However, Rescher can respond that while it cannot be that A explains B and B explains A where the same sort of explanation occurs in both cases, nonetheless you can have A explaining B and B explaining A if the two explanations are of a radically different sort, as the subsumptive and systematic explanations are.

But even if one can buy the idea of a circularity in explanation, there is a serious problem for Rescher's theory. It is just not clear whether "systematic explanation" constitutes explanation. Certainly, belief in a theory is *justified* by its internal unity and coherence, and its fit to the data. But justification and explanation often go in opposite ways. My justification for believing the proposition that Smith died is that I saw him being buried and I trust the funeral home not to bury people who are alive. But this justification in no way provides an explanation of the proposition that Smith died: that would only be provided by identifying the cause of death.

Moreover, one might think that the explanation of contingent phenomena is always to some extent in the end causal. That is why we reject deductive-nomological explanations of the form: Tomorrow, the positions, velocities, and masses of the planets will be such and such; the law of gravitation holds; therefore, today the positions of the planets are such and such. The contingent events reported in the explanans cannot be later than those in the explanandum. The only way we could admit an exception would be if backward causation were possible. Then, indeed, we would allow one to explain a past event by a future one. And this case itself shows that what is at issue is causation: the reason we generally do not accept explanations of present events in terms of future ones is just that we do not think backward causation is very common if it ever occurs. Now, Rescher's systematic explanation is noncausal. Admittedly, it is not the explanation of a contingent event, but it is nonetheless an explanation of a contingent fact, namely, the fact that the theory in question is true. If one thinks that the explanation of contingent facts is always to some extent causal, one will reject Rescher's systematic explanations.

Finally, there is just the argument that on a non-Humean view the laws of nature do not hold in virtue of the events governed by them. The laws of nature already held even before there were enough events for the laws to be explained in terms of the data they fit with, and the laws of nature might well still have held even if the boundary conditions were such that there would never have been enough data for the laws to be explained in terms of the data.

5.3.2. Optimalism

Rescher (2000a, chap. 8) also has a second account of how the argument from the PSR to a necessary being could be blocked. That argument insisted that one always explains the existence of things in terms of the existence of other things. But Rescher thinks the idea that we explain beings by beings is flawed. In addition to explaining beings by beings, we can explain beings by *principles*. Thus, Rescher proposes to explain everything by the principle of optimality: that everything is for the best. This principle is itself self-explanatory. Why is there a principle that everything be for the best? Well, surely because it is better for there to be such a principle than for there not to be! In fact, the principle, on Rescher's view, is metaphysically necessary. Other axiological explanations of the cosmos have been given by Ewing (1973), Rice (2000), and Leslie (2001).

Why should we believe such a radical view? Leibniz argued for his optimalism by first arguing for a God, and then arguing that God would only create the best of all possible worlds. Rescher (cf. Rescher, 2000a, chap. 8) has argued instead for optimalism on the grounds that it is the best explanation of why we have such beautifully simple laws of nature.

But the sheer amount of evil in the world makes it prima facie implausible that this would be the best possible world. Rescher has two solutions here. First, he could say that our ordinary axiological notions are mistaken. Sure, there is a lot of pain and suffering, but the disvalue of pain and suffering is much less than the value of the symmetry of the global laws of nature. We must not be too parochial in our judgments of value. How plausible one finds this will depend on how plausible it is that moral values are not the most important ones.

Second, Rescher can avail himself of some of the responses to the argument from evil against the existence of God. Probably, Rescher cannot avail himself of *all* such responses. The libertarian free-will-based theodicies will not be available to an optimalist, since these responses, transposed to a view in which God is seen as trying to optimize the cosmic condition, would claim that God was justified in creating a world that would be less than optimal if the falling short of optimality were due to the free will of creatures. But an optimalist such as Rescher cannot take *this* response, because it presupposes that indeed conditions are worse than they could have been: conditions would have been better had people made better free choices.

Optimalism in fact has two disadvantages over theism vis-à-vis the problem of evil. The first was already alluded to: the optimalist cannot make the same use of free will considerations. The second is that the theist need not argue that this is the best world God could have created. The theist need only defend the claim that this world is such that God was justified in creating it, and this claim does not require that this be the best of all possible worlds. For instance, Robert M. Adams (1972) has argued that God would not have been less than perfectly kind to anyone had he created a world than which there is a better if it is at least true that (a) none of the creatures of the actual world were such that it would have existed in the best world, (b) no creature's life is such that it would be better for it not to have existed, and (c) no creature is worse off than it is in any other world.

Thus, the first difficulty facing the optimalist is the problem of evil in a particularly virulent form.[1] The second is that optimalism either does or does not imply modal fatalism, the thesis that all true propositions are metaphysically necessary. If optimalism implies modal fatalism, then it implies that there is no metaphysical contingency, and that implication is highly implausible. Modality collapses. The optimalist can still allow for a narrower notion of *logical* necessity such that some metaphysically necessary propositions are not logically necessary, but this does not seem to be sufficient as a response. For instance, even some compatibilists − though not Leibniz − think that the metaphysical possibility of having done otherwise, if not the physical possibility, is necessary for human freedom.

On the other hand, if optimalism does not imply modal fatalism, it follows that there is more than one optimal world. Call a world *maximal* if there is no better world. All pairs of maximal worlds are then either tied or incommensurable in respect of value. If optimalism does not imply modal fatalism, then optimalism fails to explain why this one of the maximal worlds is actual rather than some other, and hence the principle of optimalism does not succeed in saving the PSR from having to imply the existence of a necessary being. Of course, an analogous objection can be made to the PSR given the existence of a necessary being, but given some theses about the free will of the necessary being, this objection can be overcome, as can be seen from the arguments in Chapter 7.

1 One solution worth mentioning in passing is that of Donald Turner (1994, 2003), who holds that there is a God who actualized all possible universes that are above the cutoff line, which are such that it would be better for them to exist than not. The superuniverse consisting of all of these universes is arguably the best of all possible worlds, since it contains all possible goodness. To the argument that matters could still be better, namely, God could create *two* of every type of possible universe, Turner argues that indiscernible universes cannot be individuated from one another, since indiscernibles can only be individuated through spatiotemporal relations, and each universe has its own space-time structure so there are no spatiotemporal relations between them. It is reported that Nicholas Rescher has criticized the view on the grounds that a superuniverse of this sort is too complex and disorderly to count as optimal. But we may not share Rescher's axiology here. Apart from the incredulous stare objection leveled so often against David Lewis, a major problem with Turner's view is that if all possible universes above the cutoff line were made to exist concretely, then there would be a *set* of them, for surely there is a set of any kind of concrete entity. But there is no set of all possible worlds above the cutoff line, for exactly the same reason that there is no set of all cardinalities: that the argument in Pruss (2001) extends to the Turner case is left as an exercise to the reader. Plenitude theodicies have also been given by McHarry (1978) and Forrest (1981) and are discussed in Forrest (1996, Section 8.2).

There may be one way to save optimalism from this dilemma. Suppose that as it happens there is more than one maximal world, and moreover there are some libertarian-free choices that persons in our world could make that are such that were they made, another maximal world would have been actual. In that case, the full explanation of why this world is actual involves the free will of some of the persons in it. This would escape modal fatalism and allow for some libertarian free will. But the libertarian would no doubt find implausible that there is no free choice in the history of the universe that both could metaphysically have been different and was such that conditions would have been either better or worse had that choice been made.

It is also worth noting that Rescher's own optimalism also arguably implies the necessary existence of God, for it is better that there be a God than that there not be a God, and hence by optimalism, there necessarily exists a God. Hence one does not escape positing a necessary being. But, in fact, we do not even need to talk about God: Socrates is a necessary being, too, on this view!

The most serious objection to Rescher's account is in the question of what kind of a thing a principle is. To say that there is a metaphysical principle of optimality is to say more than just that everything is for the best. The principle here is not a mere rule of logical grammar. It would be absurd to think that it is a *logical* principle that everything should be for the best.

Nor is the principle just a law of nature, at least not of the type we are familiar with: laws of nature do not seem to assert the existence of things, but how things that exist relate to one another and occasionally how things that exist cause other things to exist. Substantivalist understandings of relativity theory may seem to be a counterexample, but even if we are substantivalists who think that in a real sense space-time pushes particles around, we have no reason to say that there is a *law* that space-time exists. Rather, it seems better to say that there is a law that *if* space-time has such and such properties, then as a result particles move about in such and such ways. In practice, there seems to be a difference in our nomicity attributions when we infer existential and relational claims. When I find that there is a common and particular cause behind a diverse group of phenomena unified in some way, say, a single mastermind behind a number of criminal operations that share a common feature, I do not infer that there is a law that that particular cause should exist. On the other hand, when instead of inferring an entity I infer a relation between entities, as I might upon finding that massive objects attract, I have prima facie grounds for supposing a law. Furthermore, the crucial distinction between an accidental and a nomic generalization and the complex empirical/theoretical methods we use to distinguish between these do not appear applicable in the case of the existence of a particular entity. This does not rule out the possibility that we might have here a law of nature, but if so, it will be one of a sort that is quite unfamiliar to us.

In any case, if one accepts the truthmaker principle, then the principle of optimality will have to be grounded in some existent reality that is such as to make it be the case that everything must be for the best. But if so, and if, as would be plausible, this existent reality is the same in every metaphysically possible world, then we have returned to a necessary being under a new name. Thus, Rescher must reject the truthmaker principle if he is to hold that his principle explains reality without explaining it in terms of a being. But it is most obscure and mysterious what the principle is. What is it we are saying about reality when we say that there is a principle of optimality, beyond affirming that in fact matters are optimal?

5.4. IS THE NOTION OF A NECESSARY BEING ABSURD?

It seems we cannot escape the conclusion that the PSR implies the existence of a necessary being that does the explanatorily relevant work. Recall now the response to the abstracta as counterexamples to the claim that there are no necessary beings. That response insisted that the necessary being whose existence the PSR implies is causally efficacious, whereas the unproblematic abstracta like propositions and numbers are causally inefficacious.

A radical response to this is to question the dogma that propositions and numbers are causally inefficacious. Why should they be? Plato's Form of the Good looks much like the abstracta, but we see it in the middle dialogues as being explanatorily efficacious, with the *Republic* analogizing its role to that of the Sun in producing life. It might seem to be a category mistake to talk of a proposition or a number as causing anything, but why should it be? Admittedly, propositions and numbers are not spatiotemporal. But whence the notion that to be a cause one must be spatiotemporal? On the contrary, one might even opt for one of the views of time on which the notion of causality is prior in the order of being to the notion of temporality (cf. Section 2.5), and hence temporality depends on causality, and that would leave only spatiality as a problem. But why should one think that only objects in space can be causes? It is by no means obvious that spatiality, as such, has much to do with making causation possible unless we are mechanists. If we agree with Newton against Leibniz that action at a distance is at least a metaphysical possibility, although present physics may not support it as an actuality, the pressure to see spatiality as such as essential to causality is likely to dissipate.

Admittedly, a Humean account of causation on which causation is nothing but constant conjunction only works for things in time, since the Humean distinguishes the cause from the effect by temporal priority. But unless we are dogmatically beholden to this Humean account, to an extent that makes us dogmatically a priori deny the existence of deities and other nonspatiotemporal causally efficacious beings, this should not worry us.

Moreover, there is actually some reason to suppose that propositions and numbers enter into causal relations. The primary problem in the epistemology of mathematics is of how we can get to know something like a number given that a number cannot be a cause of any sensation or belief in us. It is plausible that our belief that some item x exists can only constitute knowledge if either x itself has a causal role in our formation of this belief or some cause of x has such a causal role. The former case occurs when we know from the smoke that there was a fire, and the latter when we know from the sound of a match struck that there will be a fire. But if something does not enter into any causal relations, then it seems that our belief about it is in no way affected by it or by anything connected with it, and hence our belief, if it coincides with the reality, does so only coincidentally, and hence not as knowledge. Of course, there are attempts on the books to solve the conundrum. But at least the puzzle gives us some reason to rethink the dogma that numbers can neither cause nor be caused.

But even if abstracta like numbers, propositions, and properties are causally inefficacious, why should we think that there cannot be a non-abstract necessary being that is causally efficacious? One answer was already alluded to: some will insist that only spatiotemporal entities can be causally efficacious and it is implausible that a necessary being be spatiotemporal. But it was difficult to see why exactly spatiotemporality is required for causal connections.

A different answer might be given in terms of a puzzlement about how there could be a nonabstract necessary being. The traditional way of expressing this puzzlement is Findlay's (1948), though Findlay may have since backpedaled on his claims. A necessary being would be such that it would be analytic that this being exists. But it is never analytic that something exists. If $\exists x(Fx)$ is coherent, so is $\sim\exists x(Fx)$. Basically, the worry is caused by the Humean principle that anything that can be thought to exist can also be thought not to exist, a principle we have already discussed in Section 2.4. But it is by no means obvious why this principle should be restricted, without thereby doing something ad hoc, to nonabstract beings.

Why should abstract beings be allowed as necessary? Why should $L\exists x(x$ is a deity) be more absurd than $L\exists x(x$ is a number)? Presumably the answer is going to be that we can *prove* the existence of a number. In fact, mathematicians prove the existence of numbers all the time. Already in ancient times, it was shown that there exist infinitely many primes.

However, these proofs presuppose axioms. The proof that there are infinitely many primes presupposes a number system, say, with the Peano axioms or set theory. But a statement of the Peano axioms will state that there *is* a number labeled 0 and there *is* a successor function s such that for any number n, sn is also a number. Likewise, an axiomatization of set theory will include an axiom stating the existence of some set, for instance, the empty set. If our mathematical conclusions are existential, at least one of the axioms will be as well. The mathematical theory $\sim\exists x(x = x)$ is consistent as a mathematical theory. If we are realists about numbers, we will be admitting something that exists necessarily and does not do so simply in virtue of a proof from nonexistential axioms.

Of course one might not be a realist about abstracta. One might think that we do not need to believe that there necessarily exist propositions, properties, or numbers to be able to talk about necessarily true propositions or necessarily true relations between numbers or properties. But if the critic of the PSR had to go so far as to make this questionable move, the argument against the PSR would not be very plausible. Note, too, that the main argument against mathematical Platonism is epistemological. But an epistemological argument can only establish that we have no reason to think there are mathematicals. It would require a dubious verificationist principle to conclude from this that the existence of mathematicals is absurd.

Fortunately for the Platonist, not all necessity is provability. We have already seen that the work of Gödel questions the thesis that all necessity is provability or analyticity (see Section 2.4). Kripke (1980), too, has questioned the same thesis on different grounds. That horses are mammals is a proposition we discover empirically and not one we can prove a priori. But it is nonetheless a *necessary* thesis. So is the proposition that every dog at some point in its life contained a carbon atom.

Now, it is admittedly true that the Kripkean necessities are not necessities of the *existence* of a thing. But they provide us with a model as to how a proposition might be necessary even though it is not analytic. Another such model might be truths of a correct metaphysics, such as that it is impossible that a trope exists, or that it is necessary that a trope exists in any world containing at least two material objects that are alike in some way. A different model for a necessary being would be that provided by the ontological argument. The ontological argument attempts to show that from the concept of God one can derive the necessary existence of God. A necessary being would then be one for which there was a successful ontological argument, though perhaps one beyond our logical abilities. While the extant ontological arguments happen to fail, though not so much on account of being invalid as on account of being question begging, thinking about them gives us an idea of what it would be like to have a successful ontological argument for the existence of something. Finally, a different account of necessity here could be that the true general metaphysics, the true ontology, might end up entailing the existence of a necessary being.

5.5. PHILOSOPHY OF MIND OBJECTIONS

A different necessary-being-based argument against the PSR would start with materialism in the theory of mind. The necessary being creating the universe would have to have a mind. There is much more plausibility in Humean arguments against necessary existence in the case of material beings. Given a material being m, it does not appear difficult to conceive of m as absent from any particular point of space-time. And it does not seem much more difficult to imagine it as absent from *all* points of space-time. Moreover, our best empirical theories seem to imply that there are no material beings that have existed at all times, or at least that no material beings capable of explaining the BCCF are like that, and we might think that a necessary being would exist at all times if it existed in time.

But, the argument goes on, necessarily, all minds are material, and all material objects are contingent. However, the evidence for a materialism of a sort that claims that necessarily all minds are material is weak. It is highly plausible that even if our minds were material, nonetheless mind-edness could be realized in some other material way, and if in another material way, why not in an immaterial one, too?

But there are more sophisticated arguments available. For instance, one might think that intentionality is produced by, or at least requires, two-way causal interaction with the world,[2] whereas God (at least as traditionally thought of) is not subject to mutual interaction. If this objection were correct, it would constitute an argument for the nonexistence of God, of course.

In response, first of all one could try to argue that God could be at least in one-way causal interaction with the contingent parts of the cosmos, by being their cause, and moreover has the potential for nonactual causal interactions, and the connection of the divine thinkings with this potential may be sufficient to give them intentionality. But this would be only a promissory note, and it would be unclear whether it could be filled out.

Alternately, one can argue that there is no reason to believe that the correct account of intentionality will have to involve two-way causal interaction. For instance, the failure of the existing accounts that construct intentionality out of mere efficient causal interactions to handle the problem of reinterpretation – namely, the problem that any given functional system can have its "beliefs" interpreted in multiple incompatible ways along the lines of Putnam's paradox (cf. Putnam, 1980) – gives one little confidence for thinking that the correct account of intentionality will involve *solely* such interaction. And as to the intuition that causal interactions are necessarily at least a *part* of any correct account of intentionality, one might counter it with the intuition that intentionality at least sometimes can be had without causal interaction, namely, in mathematical thought.

Finally, one might try to counter the materialist theory of mind objection by using a panoply of the standard arguments for theism, since once it is established that there *is* a God, whether necessarily existing or not, it follows that indeed it is possible to have intentionality without two-way causal interaction.

Note that someone who holds the PSR to be true does not need to presuppose the conceptual possibility of a necessary being. The existence of a necessary being is a consequence of the PSR. But when defending a principle that entails some other proposition, we do not need to start off by defending the possibility of the latter proposition. All we need to do is to refute arguments offered against it. Relativity theory, on a certain metaphysical interpretation, implies the nonexistence of absolute simultaneity. But the theory does not need to presuppose the possibility of simultaneity's being relative. The evidence for the theory, rather, gives

---

2 I am grateful to Robert Brandom for this objection.

evidence for the actuality of simultaneity's being relative, and *thereby* gives evidence for the possibility, though of course the relativity theorist needs to defend herself against objections. Likewise for the PSR, even if it should happen — and we shall see in Part III that it does not — that the only evidence for the PSR is self-evidence.

5.6. LAWMAKERS AND LAWS

But perhaps the necessary being is not a person after all and so the worries about a necessarily existing person are out of place. For instance, one suggestion, due to Peter Forrest, is that the necessary being might be a necessarily existing *lawmaker*, where a lawmaker is the truthmaker for the proposition *that p is a law of nature*, where *p* in fact is a law of nature: the lawmaker is that which makes the law a law (the notion will be further discussed in Section 16.3.2). On Armstrong's account, for instance, the lawmakers are universals, and laws supervene on their relations.

It is not clear, however, what kind of a lawmaker could do the job here. It cannot just be an Armstrongian universal, because on Armstrong's view, universals cannot exist apart from their exemplifiers. Nor can it be a universal of the sort contemporary Platonists believe in, since these are causally inert. Given the plausibility of the claim that all material beings are contingent, it would be an immaterial, nonpersonal being, rather like the Forms of Plato himself.

How plausible one finds this possibility depends on many questions that we cannot settle here. For instance, after the discussion in Chapter 7, the reader might come to think that indeterministic causation can only be explanatory in cases of agency, where in addition to a cause a reason is given.

Likewise, a reader might think that there seems to be too much "arbitrariness" in the actual laws of nature for them to be both necessary and of the sort needed here. One might think that the only plausible account of laws that makes them necessary is that they supervene on metaphysically necessary truths about the essences of existing things, as on Armstrong's view and other Aristotelian views. Such views allow one to make sense of the intuition that nomically necessary things could have been otherwise by saying that although water could not fail to boil at a hundred degrees Celsius, another substance that otherwise behaves just as water could. But metaphysically necessarily true laws of this sort are explanatorily inert in the absence of the beings, such as water molecules, whose behavior they describe. The law that water boils at a hundred degrees Celsius may be true and nomic in the absence of water – even this is not obvious, given difficulties of reference to nonexistent natural kinds – but it has no explanatory power then. For even if the essences on which these laws supervene exist necessarily, pace Armstrong, still it seems likely that their efficacy depends on the exemplifiers of these essences or on persons who think about them. Horseness accomplishes nothing apart from horses or people who think about horses.

Note that this last objection applies not just to the idea of a necessarily existing lawmaker but to the idea of a necessarily true law as lying at the heart of the explanation of the BCCF. While it may well be that some or even all laws of nature are necessary, the most plausible accounts of such necessary laws will not let them do the explanatory work needed here.

It may just be necessary for the PSR's defender to accept a necessarily existing deity. But this conclusion is not an absurd one, and there may even be independent evidence for it.

6

Modal Fatalism

6.1. VAN INWAGEN'S ARGUMENT

Peter van Inwagen (1983, pp. 202–204) has formulated an influential and elegant reductio ad absurdum of the PSR. Let p be the conjunction of all contingent truths. If p has an explanation, say, q, then q will itself be a contingent truth, and hence a conjunct of p. But then q will end up explaining itself, and that would be absurd. We can formulate this precisely as follows:

(33) If the PSR holds, then every true contingent proposition has an explanation. (Premise)

(34) No necessary proposition explains a contingent proposition. (Premise)

(35) No contingent proposition explains itself. (Premise)

(36) If a proposition explains a conjunction, it explains every conjunct. (Premise)

(37) A proposition q only explains a proposition p if q is true. (Premise)

(38) There is a Big Conjunctive Contingent Fact (BCCF) that is the conjunction of all true contingent propositions, perhaps with logical redundancies removed, and the BCCF is contingent. (Premise)

(39) Suppose the PSR holds. (For reductio)

(40) Then, the BCCF has an explanation, q. (By (33), (38) and (39))

(41) The proposition q is not necessary. (By (34), (38), and (40) and as the conjunction of true contingent propositions is contingent)

(42) Therefore, q is a contingent true proposition. (By (37), (40), and (41))

(43) Thus, q is a conjunct in the BCCF. (By (38) and (42))

(44) Thus, q is self-explanatory. (By (36), (40), and (43))

(45) But q is not self-explanatory. (By (35) and (42))

(46) Thus, q is and is not self-explanatory, and that is absurd. Hence, the
   PSR is false.

Versions of this argument have been defended by James Ross (1969,
pp. 295–304), William Rowe (1975, 1984), and more recently Francken
and Geirsson (1999).

The argument is plainly valid. Thus, the only question is whether the
premises are true. Premises (33) and (37) are unimpeachable. Premise (36)
is hard to deny. Admittedly the explanation of the conjunction might have
more information in it than is needed to explain just one of the conjuncts,
but certainly it at least will furnish an explanation of the conjunct, though
perhaps with some irrelevant data thrown in.

This leaves the technical premise (38) about the existence of a BCCF,
and two substantive claims, (34) and (35), about explanation.

Something like this argument is central to Spinoza's argument for
modal fatalism. Thus, a defender of the PSR might embrace this argument as showing there are no contingent propositions. This would be a
denial of (38). However, few contemporary defenders of the PSR other
than possibly Rescher are willing to deny metaphysical contingency.

Christopher Hill (1982) has attempted to salvage the PSR from van
Inwagen's attack by restricting the PSR to propositions smaller than the
BCCF, citing a "Maxim of Minimum Mutilation." Hill appears to accept
all of van Inwagen's premises, then, other than (33). Unfortunately, it is not
plausible that such a restriction would be of any help. To see this, partition
the BCCF into two subconjunctions. The first, p_1, is the conjunction of
all horsey facts, that is, contingent true propositions that entail that there
is a horse. The second, p_2, is the conjunction of all unhorsey facts, that is,
contingent true propositions that do not entail that there is a horse. Then,
by Hill's restricted version of the PSR, p_1 has an explanation q_1 and p_2 has
an explanation q_2 since both propositions are smaller than the BCCF. If
q_1 is itself a horsey fact, then the van Inwagen argument applies to p_1 and
q_1 and leads to absurdity. Likewise, if q_2 is itself an unhorsey fact, then the
van Inwagen argument applies to p_2 and q_2 and leads to absurdity.

Thus, to escape the van Inwagen argument, Hill has to claim that q_1 is
an unhorsey fact and q_2 is a horsey fact. The horseyness of q_2 is plausible,
since a conjunct of p_2 might be that there are tracks as of a horse, whose
explanation is the horsey fact that a horse made these tracks. But the
unhorseyness of q_1 is more problematic, given that the main argument
for (34) is that the explanans has to entail the explanandum, as we will
see, and an unhorsey fact does not entail that there are horses, which the

explanandum p_1 does entail. Moreover, even supposing that an unhorsey fact – say, some evolutionary story that falls short of entailing that horses exist – can explain why there are horses, we have a problem. Since q_1 then is a conjunct of p_2, it follows that q_1 is in turn explained by q_2, since q_2 explains all of p_2. By exactly the same reasoning, q_2 is explained by q_1. Thus, we have a case of viciously circular explanation.

It certainly does appear, then, that some of van Inwagen's premises will have to be questioned if one is to defend the PSR.

6.2. THE EXISTENCE OF THE BIG CONJUNCTIVE CONTINGENT FACT

We have already met the BCCF in Chapter 4. There, the existence of the BCCF was not questioned, because the BCCF was involved in only one of three arguments for the same conclusion. Here the BCCF needs to be subjected to more criticism. The following critique of the existence of the BCCF is based on the argument of Davey and Clifton (2001), who were responding to a Cosmological Argument in which Richard Gale and I used the existence of the BCCF, except that instead of using $T(p)$, they used $E(p)$, the proposition that p has an explanation.

If p is a proposition, then let $T(p)$ be the proposition that p is true. If p is a proposition, so is $T(p)$, since surely it always makes sense to say of a proposition that it is true. Now some formulas, such as the infinite formula

(47) $1 = 1$ and $(1 = 1$ and $(1 = 1$ and $(1 = 1$ and $(1 = 1...))))$,

figure as proper subformulas of themselves: In this example, the second conjunct is itself the same as the whole formula.

Let a be the conjunction of all contingent true propositions. Now let a^* be the subconjunction of all contingent true propositions p such that p is not a proper subformula of itself. Since the conjunction of contingent true propositions is contingently true, a^* is contingently true. Thus, $T(a^*)$. But now we get a contradiction. Either $T(a^*)$ is a proper subformula of itself or it is not. If $T(a^*)$ is a proper subformula of itself, then $T(a^*)$ must in fact be a subformula, proper or not, of a^*, since the only proper subformulas of $T(a^*)$ are the subformulas of a^*. In fact, because $T(a^*)$ is not itself a conjunction, it follows that $T(a^*)$ must be a subformula of one of the conjuncts, say, p, of a^*. But p is a subformula of a^* and hence a proper subformula of $T(a^*)$. Therefore, p is a proper subformula of $T(a^*)$, which in turn is a subformula of p; hence p is a proper subformula of p. But if p is a proper subformula of p, then it is not one of the conjuncts of a^*, and hence we get the absurdity that p is both a conjunct of a^* and not a conjunct of a^*. On the other hand, if $T(a^*)$ is not a proper subformula of itself, it will be one of the conjuncts of a^*, and hence will be a proper subformula of itself, and that is absurd. Thus, whether $T(a^*)$ is a proper subformula of itself or not, a contradiction ensues.

This is not quite a reductio of the existence of the BCCF a. It is only a reductio of the claim that a^* is a proposition. However, if supplemented with the premise that for every conjunctive proposition any subconjunction is also a proposition, the argument becomes a reductio of the existence of the BCCF, since a^* is a subconjunction of the BCCF.

However, the collection of all contingent true propositions is not a set. One way to see this is as follows. Where k is an infinite cardinality, let p_k be the proposition that there exist exactly k objects (if one dislikes talking of objects in general, then just be concrete and say "photons")[1] in the universe. Then, every p_k is a contingent proposition: it could be but need not be that there are k objects in the universe. Furthermore, all but at most one of the $\sim p_k$ is true. If the collection of all contingent true propositions is a set, then the collection of all the true $\sim p_k$ is a set. But then the collection of all the $\sim p_k$ will be a set, too, since this collection contains at most one more member, namely, $\sim p_n$, where n is the actual number of objects in the universe, if this number is infinite. But there is no set of all the $\sim p_k$ because as is well known, there is no set of all cardinalities (see, for instance, Pruss, 2001).

If the collection of all contingent true propositions is not a set, then we cannot blithely talk of arbitrary subcollections, and likewise we cannot blithely talk of arbitrary subconjunctions of the BCCF. On the other hand, once one has admitted that there are some properties P of propositions, for example, *being contingently true and not a subformula of itself*, such that there is no conjunction of all propositions having P, why should one think there is a conjunction of all propositions having the property of *being contingently true*? One possible answer is that a given candidate for a proposition should be innocent until proven guilty. We have seen it proved

---

1 There is a technical reason why we are talking of photons here. It is possible for two or more photons to share the same physical state, a condition that would not be possible for electrons. To have a large cardinality of photons in a space-time such as ours would require that some photons be in the same place, and indeed in the same state.

earlier that the conjunction of all contingent true propositions that are not subformulas of themselves is guilty, that is, is not a proposition. But the BCCF is still innocent.

But even if the BCCF is problematic, one might, as Davey and Clifton (2001) note in their context, make van Inwagen's argument work by restricting the BCCF. How exactly we would do that would depend on ontological issues. For instance, if one's ontology were one that included some workable notion of "basic propositions," then we might let BCCF* be the conjunction of both of the following:

(48) all true contingent basic propositions and
(49) all logically uncompounded true propositions reporting causal relations.

The crucial step in the van Inwagen argument that does not straightforwardly adapt to this case is (43), which now would have to be the claim that the explanation of the BCCF*, if it is contingent, must be a conjunct in the BCCF*. Instead of this, one has to note that the explanation of the BCCF*, if it is contingent, must be constructible out of the ingredients in the BCCF*. After all, the explanation presumably is going to be a causal one of some sort, and hence it will be constructible out of the ingredients in (48) and (49). But one can then strengthen (36) to say that if q explains a proposition p out of whose conjuncts a proposition p^* can be in some appropriate sense formed, then q explains p^*. The argument then continues as before, and it is plausible that some such modification of the van Inwagen argument can be made even if the BCCF is not itself tenable.

We can also find in Ross (1969) a variant of the van Inwagen argument that does not depend on a BCCF. In our propositional setting, this is as follows. Start with any contingent proposition p_0. Then, by the PSR, there is an explanation, p_1. This proposition is likewise contingent by (34) and distinct from p_0 by (35). Applying the PSR to p_1, we generate a proposition p_2 that explains p_1. And so on. We thus generate an infinite regress or a vicious circularity. Then, use the additional premises:

(50) The obtaining of an infinite chain of non-self-explanatory propositions is non-self-explanatory and contingent.
(51) The obtaining of a circular collection of explanations is non-self-explanatory and contingent.

These are eminently plausible, once we explain what exactly we mean by explaining a chain or circle of propositions, for instance, by saying that by this we mean explaining their conjunction.[2]

Thus, the PSR enjoins us to find an explanation of the obtaining of the infinite regress or circularity. And then we need to find an explanation of that. And so on, ad infinitum. We cannot escape from the infinite chains of explanations, which are truly vicious, where "[a] regress is vicious with respect to a certain end E iff with each step of the regress E is unattained, and even if the regress is infinite E is still unattained. The E in question ... is its being the case that every contingent fact is explained" (Ross, 1969, p. 364).

Or, if we do not like to have to distinguish vicious from non-vicious regresses, we might instead use the approach of the Putnam–Meyer Cosmological Argument here (see Section 3.1). That approach has the disadvantage, however, of using heavy-duty set-theoretic constructions, whereas as noted previously there is no set of all contingent propositions, and it is therefore not clear whether these constructions can be made to work in this setting.

Finally, a variant form of the argument can be found in Rowe (1975). Rowe asks us, What explains why there is a positive contingent state of affairs at all? Rowe defines positive states of affairs as states of affairs that entail the existence of a contingent being. A necessary state of affairs cannot explain why there are positive contingent states of affairs, since there might have failed to be positive contingent states of affairs. Let us grant this assumption for the sake of argument. Thus it must be a contingent state of affairs, and it will also have to be a *positive* one. But this seems to be viciously circular.

But van Inwagen's formulation is superior to Rowe's. Rowe's argument assumes the principle that if it is contingent whether a state of affairs of type *F* exists, then no state of affairs of type *F* can explain why there are any states of affairs of type *F*. But this is false. Consider *horsey states of affairs*, namely, the ones that entail that there is at least one horse. It is contingent that there are any horsey states of affairs. But now consider the following proposition (*p*): A mammal of type *A* evolved under circumstances *C* into a horse. This proposition explains why there are horses, and hence it also explains, and does so noncircularly, why there are any horsey states

2 Rowe (1984, p. 363) works in terms of states of affairs rather than propositions and simply talks of the contingent state of affairs that this rather than another infinite or circular chain obtains.

of affairs. The state of affairs that p reports, however, is a horsey state of affairs, since it entails the existence of horses. Sometimes, thus, a type F state of affairs can *noncircularly* explain why there are any type F states of affairs at all, implausible as this might seem a priori.[3]

6.3. THE NATURE OF EXPLANATION

The defender of the PSR has no choice, it seems, but to question (34) or (35). I will argue that there is reason to deny *both* of these premises. The general structure of the response to the van Inwagen argument will be that first I will show how one can avoid the negative conclusion by arguing against (34). Next, I will do this in the case of (35). This will be sufficient to respond to the van Inwagen argument. However, in Chapter 7 I will take up in greater detail the explanation of libertarian free actions and argue that a plausible libertarianism has to hold that libertarian free actions are not counterexamples to the PSR. Because libertarian actions cannot be explained by citing prior conditions that determine the effect, this will provide another argument that at least one of (34) and (35) is false. Finally, in Section 7.8 it will be noted that even if all of these arguments failed, the defender of the Principle of Sufficient Reason could retreat to a Principle of Good Explanation that is still quite nontrivial – for instance, it, too, implies the existence of a first cause.

6.3.1. Could a Necessary Proposition Explain a Contingent One?

6.3.1.a The Entailment Principle. Premise (34) says that a necessary proposition cannot explain a contingent one. There is a natural subsidiary argument for this:

(52) If q explains p, then q entails p.
(53) But if q is necessary and entails p, then p is also necessary.

Since the second of these propositions follows from basic axioms of modal logic, indeed from the system M, which is much weaker than S5, it is on the "entailment principle" (52) that criticism should focus.

In favor of (52), one might cite the very term *Principle of Sufficient Reason*. The sort of explanation that the PSR envisions is an explanans that is *sufficient* for the explanandum. If the explanans fails to entail the

---

3 See also two different attempts at counterexamples in Smith (1995).

explanandum, then it is not sufficient for it: the explanans could hold even though the explanandum does not. However, the word *sufficient* can be read in two different ways: the reason given can be *logically* sufficient for the explanandum, or it can *sufficiently* explain the explanandum. If the reason is to be *logically* sufficient for the explanandum, then one would do better to talk of the Principle of Logically Necessitating Reason (PLNR). Admittedly, when Leibniz and Spinoza used the PSR, they took it to be in some sense equivalent to the PLNR. But we need not follow them in this: we could see them as having an incorrect view of explanation, a view that made them think that a sufficient explanation entails the explanandum.

However, there is some reason to think that a sufficient explanation will entail the explanandum − and in the context of the PSR we mean sufficient explanation by *explanation*. When we explain a proposition, we try to clear up a mystery about the explanandum. We need not clear up the mystery completely, because some of the mystery may transfer to the explanans. Thus, while explaining why Jones died in terms of a bullet's entering his brain is quite legitimate, one's puzzlement about the matter then transfers to the question why a bullet entered his brain. However, if we have a *sufficient* explanation, then everything that calls out for explanation in the explanandum is either completely explained by the explanans or else transferred to a puzzlement about the explanans itself. To formulate this principle more precisely, we need the idealized notion of an ultimate explanation. An ultimate explanation of a proposition leaves nothing unexplained and does not itself call out for further explanation. Then, if q sufficiently explains p, the proposition q is such that were we to have an *ultimate* explanation of q, we would thereby have a complete or ultimate explanation of p. But suppose now that q fails to entail p. Then the possibility is open that we will know exactly why q happened without thereby knowing why p happened as well. For there is a puzzle that is not cleared up by explaining q, namely, the puzzle of why p followed from q.

However, this line of thought, though attractive, may well be confusing explanation with prediction. We shall see soon that there are reasonable forms of explanation that do not satisfy (52), forms of explanation that have an ordinary language claim to be giving "sufficient explanations."

6.3.1.b Leibniz's Response. Leibniz, on the other hand, has a way out of this argument through his moral/metaphysical necessity distinction. For Leibniz, a proposition is *metaphysically necessary* if it has a finite proof and *morally necessary* if it has a proof, finite or infinite. Corresponding to this distinction, we can also distinguish moral entailment and metaphysical entailment: q morally (metaphysically) entails p providing that $q \supset p$ is morally (metaphysically) necessary. Thus, q metaphysically entails p if a finite proof can go from q to p, and if the proof is infinite or finite, then there is a moral entailment. Leibniz could then grant (52) in the case of *moral* entailment. Leibniz would then grant (53) in the case of moral entailment and moral necessity, or metaphysical entailment and metaphysical necessity. Combining the preceding with all the premises of van Inwagen's argument with the modalities being disambiguated as moral ones will yield an argument for the claim that the BCCF is morally necessary. Leibniz accepts this form of fatalism but does not see it as problematic. Our intuitions about contingency should be taken as dealing with *metaphysical* contingency. If we are unwilling to make Leibniz's distinction, of course, then this solution is of no help, however.

6.3.1.c An ad Hominem Response. But now consider a refutation of (52) on the assumption that the PSR is actually false, which will show that the opponent of the PSR should not herself agree with (52), but owes us a special argument for why the defender of the PSR should accept it. Suppose the PSR is false. Then, by the plausibility arguments in Section 3.5 and the sections leading up to it, it is possible for events to occur without causes. But we certainly allow the following form of explanation: E did not occur because nothing capable of causing E occurred. Sometimes the explanans will give several examples of causes of E that did not occur (the dog did not bark because it did not see a stranger, and no other cause of barking took place). But note that in this explanation, the explanans only entails the explanandum if it is impossible that E occur causelessly. Thus, the PSR's opponent should allow this as a case in which the explanans does not entail the explanandum. The only downside of this ad hominem refutation of (52) is that in Chapter 15 it will be argued more thoroughly that acceptance of these sorts of explanations commits one to the *truth* of the PSR and so the PSR's opponent might stop accepting these sorts of explanations once she learns this. This argument, thus, is purely ad hominem.

6.3.1.d Is an Explanans Always a Proposition? A radical way to question (52) would be to claim that the explanans of a proposition need not itself be a proposition. Following Aristotelian agent-causation intuitions, one might say that the cause is always an explanation, but the cause does

105

not entail the existence of the effect, since the cause is not categorically the sort of thing that enters into entailment relations. When I move the stone, there is a causal relation between me and the stone's movement, but it would be nonsense to say that I entail that the stone moves. Strictly speaking, only propositions entail. However, this answer seems to confuse causation and explanation. While causation is explanatory, it is not the *cause* that explains the effect, but a proposition reporting something about the cause that explains a proposition reporting the effect.

Alternately, one might try to formulate the thesis that the explanans is a substance by saying that the explanans explains the explanandum in the sense that understanding of the explanans allows us to understand why the explanandum took place.[4] Since both propositions and worldly entities can be understood, this allows the explanans to be a substance. Or one might try to translate Aristotelian agent-causation into an explanatory relation between propositions. One attempt to do so might be to say that if a substance x causes an effect E, then the proposition that x has certain causal powers explains the proposition that E has occurred. If there being such causal powers is not sufficient to entail that E has occurred, then this will be a counterexample to (52). But it is not completely clear that this is a genuine explanation: surely, a genuine explanation requires more than just mention of causal powers. Perhaps, then, the Aristotelian can say that the proposition *that E has occurred* is explained by the fact that some of x's causal powers have been activated and that x has such and such causal powers. This furnishes a counterexample to (52) only if the causal powers are such that their activation does not entail a particular result, and it is precisely then that one might object that an explanation has not been provided by the Aristotelian claim.

To strengthen the Aristotelian account, one might say that giving the complete cause of an effect *is* paradigmatically giving a sufficient explanation of the effect. It is not required here that the complete cause should logically necessitate the effect, just that it be the complete cause. And in paradigmatic cases of agent causation, which are the most interesting instances of substance causation, the agent and her powers *are* the complete causes of the effect, without there being any entailment relation.

Furthermore, if one takes statistical explanations to be genuine explanations, then one must admit that the explanans need not entail the explanandum. That Jones has syphilis and that most people who have

---

4   This suggestion is inspired by remarks by Peter Forrest.

syphilis are periodically in pain explains why Jones is periodically in pain. That Spot is the offspring of two Dalmatians and that most offspring of two Dalmatians have spots explains why Spot has spots. However, in neither case does the explanans entail the explanandum.

It is also worth noting that while the two preceding cases had the explanans making the explanandum more probable than $1/2$, the defender of the PSR should not insist on this as a necessary condition for a genuine probabilistic explanation. In fact, she should probably not even insist on the explanans's making the explanandum more probable than it otherwise would have been. If there is indeterminism, and the statistical counterexamples to (52) are only going to be satisfactory answers to van Inwagen if in the end there is indeterminism and the probabilities are not merely due to our ignorance, then it is quite probable that sometimes an improbable event will happen. More precisely, given enough indeterministic events, while some of them will have been highly probable given antecedent conditions, others will not be thus probable. Even though it is unlikely in any given spin of the roulette wheel that the number 17 should come up, and hence we can probabilistically explain the number 17's not coming up in terms of its having a low probability given the initial conditions of the spin, occasionally the number *will* come up. The defender of the PSR, if she accepts indeterminism, will then have to say that despite the low probability that the initial conditions conferred on the roll, the roll's outcome is to be explained in terms of a low-probability probabilistic process. We will discuss this issue further when we talk about the quantum mechanical challenge to the PSR in Chapter 8.

6.3.1.e Ceteris Paribus Laws. As a somewhat different counterexample to (52), consider ceteris paribus laws of nature. These are indeed explanatory, and we do not usually make it an explicit part of the explanans that the ceteris were in fact paribus. Ceteris paribus, an apple dropped on Earth, given present laws of nature, falls. The falling of the apple is explained by the law of gravitation and the initial conditions. But the law of gravitation and the initial conditions do not entail that the apple will fall. The apple might have very high positive electric charge, and the ceiling of the room might have very high negative charge, and so the apple might instead fly upward to the ceiling: this is a possibility consistent with the explanans. We do not, however, generally pack, and do not need to pack, into the explanans all the negative facts such as that the apple was not electrically or magnetically attracted to the ceiling, that the apple was not repelled from the ground by a power jet of air gushing out of the floor, that no alien force[5] (a force that does not in fact ever occur but could occur if an object had an alien property, namely, a property not instantiated in the actual world) occurred, and so on.

Note further that if Newton's law of gravitation had turned out to be correct, then Newton would have had a perfectly good explanation of why the apple fell even if Newton had no knowledge of the laws of electromagnetics, which he would have needed to state some of the negative facts that would need to be packed into the explanans to make it entail the explanandum.

One might object that the explanans, besides stating the initial conditions and the law of gravity, is assumed to have implicit within it some clause such as "These factors are the only relevant ones operative," and the explanans then starts to entail the explanandum. But to what are the factors supposed to be relevant? There are many other forces acting on the apple besides the gravitation, and they are highly relevant to various other things. To the apple grower, the influence of decay is relevant. To the person doing aerodynamic experiments, air resistance and the resulting slowdown are relevant. What the clause means is that the initial conditions and law of gravity are the only factors relevant to the *effect* in question, that is, relevant to whether the apple falls or not.

But that, too, is not quite right. For suppose that the apple has high electric charge opposite to that of the floor. Then, even in the absence of gravity, the apple would have fallen. Thus, the apple's electrical attraction to the floor *is* relevant to whether the apple falls or not, precisely to the extent that gravity is relevant. But we do not need to cite this electrical attraction in the explanation. In a case of overdetermination, any one of the overdetermining explanations is a sufficient explanation.

Rather, then, the implicit clause allegedly in our explanans is presumably something like this:

(54) And no factor sufficient to prevent the apple from falling is present.

But an explanation including a clause like this is not very far from the nonexplanation:

(55) The causes needed for the apple to fall were present.

After all, the absence of causes needed for the apple to fall would *itself* be a factor (albeit a negative one – but negative factors, such as the absence

5   I am grateful to Peter Forrest for this case.

of mass in the apple, must also be ruled out) sufficient to prevent the apple from falling.

Note that it will not do to have as the implicit clause

(56) And no factors sufficient to counteract gravity are present.

For we can only talk of counteracting the other factors relative to some effect. There might be a slight movement of the air. This is sufficient to counteract the force of gravity in respect of the apple's falling straight down, but not sufficient to counteract the force of gravity in respect of the apple's falling. In fact, presumably, there will always be factors that are sufficient to counteract the listed factors in respect of *some* effect.

The difficulty then is that if the implicit clause specifies too clearly that there is no factor present that prevents the explanandum from resulting, the implicit clause begins to do all the explanatory work on its own. But if the clause is not relativized to the effect, it becomes false. But perhaps the implicit clause can take the following middle course:

(57) And no factors are present sufficient to counteract the effect of gravity with respect to whether the apple falls or not.

This formulation neither tells us by itself that the apple will fall nor is too general to be true. It simply says that in this case whether the apple falls or not is sufficiently determined by the other factors.

However, (57) is ambiguous between

(58) And no factors are present that jointly in fact suffice to counteract the effect of gravity with respect to whether the apple falls or not

and

(59) And no set of factors is present that is such as to be ceteris paribus sufficient to counteract the effect of gravity with regard to the question of whether the apple falls or not.

Unfortunately, neither option will do, for suppose first the implicit clause is (58). Take a case in which a very strong jet of air shooting up from the floor pushes the apple upward more strongly than gravity pulls it down. However, the force of this jet is completely balanced by the fact that the apple has a strong magnet in it and the floor is iron. Then, (58) together with the citation of the force of gravity is sufficient to imply that the apple will fall. But if the only force we have mentioned is the gravitational one, then we have not in fact *explained* why the apple fell just by citing gravity, the initial conditions, and (58). There was in fact a strong counteracting force, a force sufficient on its own to counteract the force of gravity, and this force ensured that an explanation of why the apple fell would have to cite both gravity *and* magnetism.

Now I submit that when we find ourselves thinking that the explanation only in terms of initial conditions and gravity is incomplete in the original paradigmatic case, this is because we think that the explanation should report *all* relevant factors, including relevant *negative* factors, such as the lack of an air jet pushing the apple upward. In other words, we think that the explanans should be sufficiently strong to entail the absence of any possible counteracting factor. But (58) is *not* strong enough to entail the absence of any possible counteracting factor because (58) is logically compatible with the earlier scenario in which there *are* counteracting factors, albeit counteracting factors that are themselves counteracted.

What if we move to (59) instead? Then, our explanans must cite, if only cursorily or in summary, every factor or combination of factors that would have, ceteris paribus, sufficed to counteract gravity. But that demands much too much. Suppose that the air jet underneath the apple is switched off. Suppose that the switch for it is a big button on the ground. Above the switch a big framed picture is hanging. Then the following quadruple of factors is ceteris paribus sufficient to prevent the apple from falling: the air jet machinery's being under the apple, the button's being under the picture, the picture's being suspended over the button a couple of seconds before the apple was dropping, and gravity's pulling the picture toward the button. If these were all the relevant factors, the picture would have fallen, pressed the button, turned on the air jet, and prevented the apple from falling. Therefore, this scenario fails to satisfy (59). However, to spell out the case further, what prevents all these factors from preventing the apple from falling is the fifth factor: that the picture is *nailed to the wall*. But it is absurd to say that all these five factors enter into an explanation. If the air jet was not in fact functioning, then the force of gravity is enough. Thus, (59) is too strong as a proviso since it rules out some genuine cases in which we have an explanation, namely, the scenario with the air jet, button, and nailed picture.

In frustration, we might simply say that the implicit clause in a ceteris paribus nomic explanation is one that says that we have given a good enough explanation. But this is ambiguous between saying we have given a good enough explanation in stating everything *other* than this clause and saying that *with* this clause we have given a good enough explanation. In the former case, the clause is not essential to giving an explanation, since ex hypothesi the other clauses are sufficiently explanatory, and we do indeed have a counterexample to (52) in the ceteris paribus nomic explanation as desired. Consider then the latter case. On this view, the explanation that the apple fell looks like this:

(60) The apple was suspended in midair.
(61) The force of gravity was pulling the apple down.
(62) (Implicit:) Propositions (60)–(62) explain why the apple fell.

Note that claim (62) is essentially self-referential. Bertrand Russell would say that this itself is reason enough to claim (62) to be meaningless. This is not obvious. The proposition that all propositions are true or false is self-referential in the sense that it also says something about itself but is not logically problematic. However, there are also problematic self-referential statements. The most famous is the liar paradox:

(63) Proposition (63) is false.

Claim (62) does not seem to be problematic in *this* sense – it does not seem to generate such a paradox. But while the liar proposition (63) is problematic, so is the truthteller "proposition":

(64) Proposition (64) is true.

It is not that we can derive a paradox from (64). Whether we take (64) to be true or take it to be false, no contradiction ensues. The problem, rather, is that (64) is not a proposition. There is no fact of the matter about whether it is true or false. We can equally well stipulate it to be true as to be false, and we cannot see what kind of a claim about reality (64) makes such that if we could know whether reality is thus and so we would know whether (64) is true.

The reason (64) is meaningless is that it is a putative proposition that attempts to bootstrap its meaning out of itself. As we read (64), we realize that to see what content it has we must already have a grip on it under the description "content of (64)," before we finish reading (64). It is a putative proposition such that to grasp it we must have *already* grasped it. In brief, much of the content of (64) arises from its very self-referentiality. And (64) is disanalogous in this way to the bona fide proposition that all propositions are true or false, because we do not need to have grasped what the latter proposition means before grasping what it means.

Claim (62) is a slightly less clear case of meaninglessness than (64), but it shares the same bootstrapping feature, for if (62) is anything more than the claim that (60) and (61) explain why the apple fell – and we have supposed it to be more − then this additional content itself must derive from the very self-referentiality of (62). Both (62) and (64) are putative propositions that try to pull themselves up by their bootstraps. If we did not already know what additional content (62) adds to the claim that (60) and (61) explain why the apple fell before reading (62), we will not know it afterward.

One might, of course, try to make (62) be non-self-referential, but' then it will collapse to the claim that (60) and (61) explain why the apple fell, a claim that does not sustain this objection against the ceteris paribus nomic explanation counterexamples to (52). What is ultimately wrong with these attempts to save (52) by introducing an implicit clause is a failure to recognize that the claim that the explanans explains the explanandum need not itself be a part of the explanans − and adding it to the explanans is pointless, because then either we will get vicious self-referentiality or the addition will add nothing.

Alternately, one might claim that ceteris paribus nomic explanations are only *partial* explanations. To give a "full explanation," we would need to include additional conjuncts in the explanans (cf. Rowe, 1984, p. 369 n. 18), perhaps conjuncts that we do not actually know. Thus a full explanation of the apple's falling would invoke all the forces of nature, together with initial conditions that entail that only the force of gravity is relevant, together with a claim that the forces of nature cited are all the forces there are. This is, however, not a natural way of talking. We want to say that upon discovering the force of gravity, one could explain why the apple fell. It is not necessary to know about the electromagnetic force to know all about why the apple fell.

6.3.1.f Theism. Finally, one might object as follows to the idea that the notion of explanation requires (52). A notion of explanation should not presuppose that traditional theism is false. But a part of traditional theism is the doctrine of omnipotence, which is generally taken to imply that God is not bound by the laws of nature. If this is so, then consider the following explanation of why the apple fell. Let L be a conjunction of all true propositions of the form, *It is a law of nature that.* . . . Assume further that the laws are all deterministic. Let I be a conjunction of all the initial conditions when the apple is being dropped. Then, clearly, in the ordinary case, $L \& I$ explains why the apple fell. But $L \& I$ does not entail that the apple fell. That entailment would require a further proposition that God did not work a miracle. But it is not very plausible to suppose that the theist needs to add to every nomic explanation the codicil "And God

112

worked no miracle."[6] Note that there are two ways L & I might fail to entail that the apple fell. The first way might be that the theist's notion of a law of nature might be such that *it is a law of nature that p* need not entail *it is the case that p*. The second way, taken by C. S. Lewis (1960), is that laws of nature have the ceteris paribus clause "in the absence of other causes," and God's express miraculous intervention is just such a clause. Note that this argument does not presuppose the *truth* of traditional theism. Rather, the point is to show on the supposition that theism is true, a suppostion that seems coherent, it is quite natural to say that L & I explains why the apple fell even if L & I fails to entail that the apple fell, and hence (52) does not follow from the notion of explanation.

6.3.1.g "Fred Died Because He Died of Being Shot." The sentence "Fred died because he died of being shot" sounds very strange. Instead we would say, "Fred died because he was shot." In ordinary language, then, the explanans is that he was shot. Suppose we take this seriously, and not as merely a pragmatic matter or an instance of our dislike of reduplication. This means that in general knowing the explanans is not sufficient for knowing why the explanandum holds, for, plainly, a necessary condition for knowing why the explanandum holds is knowing *that* it holds, and knowing the explanans is not sufficient for that, since many people are shot but do not die.

Moreover, it is not even enough to know both the explanans and explanandum to know why the explanandum holds. For I may know that Fred died and that Fred was shot without knowing that Fred died *because* he was shot. Nor is this simply because being shot does not entail dying. For suppose that there is a set of laws L whose conjunction with the proposition, q, that Fred fell from a ten-story building onto concrete entails that, p, Fred died. Plainly, L & q explains p. But nonetheless knowledge of L & q and of p is insufficient to give us knowledge of why p holds, for, as we all know, Fred might have instead been shot to death on his way down, and might have died of being shot, and we may suppose that we do not know that this did not happen. Thus, we can know L & q and p without knowing that L & q explains p, even though we know that L & q entails p and even though L & q does explain p.

It thus appears that to know why p holds, it is not enough to know the explanans, q, or even p together with the explanans. It is necessary to know

6   That some of the pious say, in future-tense statements, "God willing," does not mean that they include "and God *was* willing" in explanations.

that q in fact *is* the explanans for p. This has some useful consequences for the defender of the PSR.

First, even if the entailment principle were correct, the stronger claim that

(65) If q explains p, then q entails that (q explains p)

appears to be false. Now, the entailment principle (52) is actually no more plausible than (65). The intuition that gets us to assent to the entailment principle is that we would not know why the explanandum is true if the proposed explanans could be true without the explanandum's being true. One of the best ways to back up this intuition is to observe that the thesis is a principled way of saying what is wrong with certain insufficient attempts at explanation.

For instance, that Bob drank a liquid is, according to the entailment principle, not enough to explain why he died. Something is missing from the story. A plausible principled way to show that something is missing is to note that one can drink a liquid and not die. And indeed we all want to know what it was that he drank. However, suppose that we have this additional information. Thus, we know that Bob drank concentrated arsenic, and we know that this fact, conjoined with some relevant laws L, entails that Bob would die. We have seen that it is still not the case that knowledge of the explanans is sufficient for knowledge of why the explanandum holds. We do not know why the explanandum holds if we do not know that Bob was not shot to death before the arsenic took effect. To know why the explanandum holds, we need something beyond the explanans: we need the claim that the explanans is the explanans.

Now suppose that instead of adding the laws L and the fact that the liquid was arsenic to our explanans, we look at whether we know why Bob died if we know that Bob drank a liquid and died because of that liquid. I think the answer is actually positive. We *do* know why Bob died: he died because of drinking that liquid. Now, there is much that we do not know. For instance, we do not know why drinking that liquid caused his death. But we do have an explanation of why Bob died. Once we see that to know why something happened we in general need to know not only that the explanans holds but also that the explanans is the explanans, we will, I think, become more liberal than van Inwagen about what counts as an explanation and allow the entailment thesis to be violated, for the entailment thesis is intuitively just a special case of the prima facie plausible claim (65), which is in fact false.

114

6.3.1.h Without the Entailment Principle. But even if the defender of the PSR manages to show that (52) is unwarranted or false, the van Inwagen objection can be pursued in a different way. Suppose we grant all the premises in the van Inwagen argument other than (34). Then, the argument shows that the BCCF p of the actual world is explained by some necessary proposition q.

Because q is necessary and p is contingent, it follows that there are possible worlds in which q is true but p is not. Thus, although q explains p, there are possible worlds where q is just as true but where p is false. If the defense of the PSR up to this point was acceptable, this is not a problem: the ceteris paribus laws of nature and some of the initial conditions can explain the occurrence of some event in the actual world even though there are possible worlds where the laws and conditions hold, and the event does not occur as a result of some other cause. However, the defender of the PSR tends to believe, more strongly, that the PSR is a necessary truth. Write p_w for the BCCF of the world w: this is the conjunction of all contingent propositions true at w, with logical redundancies removed. If we grant as conceptual truths all the premises of the van Inwagen argument other than (34), it follows in exactly the same way that p_w is explained at w by some necessary proposition q_w.

Now, either the proposition q_w is the same proposition for every possible world w or it is not. If it *is* the same proposition, then we have the absurdity that one and the same proposition $q = q_w$ can explain every possible contingent state of affairs. For, given any possible proposition r, there is a possible world w at which r holds, and hence such that r is a conjunct of p_w, which is explained by q, so that r, too, is explained by q by (36). A universally explaining proposition q, which for any contingent proposition r can explain both r and $\sim r$, depending only on which of r and $\sim r$ happens to be true, seems rather absurd, so this alternative does not seem tenable.

Therefore, there will be two possible worlds, w and w^*, such that q_w is not the same as q_{w^*}, and such that q_w explains the BCCF p_w of w and q_{w^*} explains the BCCF p_{w^*} of w^*. But the propositions q_w and q_{w^*} are both *necessarily* true. Thus, we have a pair of worlds w and w^*, and a pair of mutually incompatible propositions a and a^* such that a is true at w and a^* is true at w^*, and a pair of propositions b and b^* true at *both* of the worlds w and w^* such that b explains a at w and b^* explains a^* at w^*. And one may think this absurd even if one did not think it absurd that some proposition b that actually explains a proposition a is true at another world at which a does not hold. Consider the reason for not thinking the latter absurd:

115

b might be a bunch of reports of ceteris paribus laws of nature together with initial conditions, and then b might hold without a holding providing that we are in a world where the ceteris are not paribus. But in the latter world, there is an explanation for why $\sim a$ holds: this explanation involves the citation of some additional causal factor that overrides the presumption in favor of a's following from b. But this additional causal factor does not occur in the actual world where b does explain a. However, in the new absurdity, all the resources for explaining why a happened are available at the world at which a^* happens, and vice versa. This seems quite absurd.

6.3.1.i A First Look at Libertarian Free Will. However, there is a way of looking at libertarian free will that would allow for this kind of a situation. Suppose that Jones has two strong incompatible desires, one for ice cream and the other for a steak. Consider two possible worlds, w and w^*. At w, Jones eats ice cream at t. At w^*, Jones eats steak at t. Consider the following two propositions:

(66) Jones had a strong desire for ice cream and freely chose what to eat.
(67) Jones had a strong desire for steak and freely chose what to eat.

It seems quite compatible with ordinary usage to say that at w proposition (66) explains why Jones ate ice cream and that it is true at w^* that (67) explains why Jones ate steak. In fact, we might even say that at w proposition (66) explains why Jones ate ice cream rather than steak and that it is true at w^* that (67) explains why Jones ate steak rather than ice cream.

This may seem to be a misunderstanding. Surely if we say the preceding things, then at w^* Jones had a stronger desire for steak than for ice cream, and it is *this* that explains why he ate steak, whereas at w Jones had a stronger desire for ice cream. But it is by no means obvious that we have to suppose this. Let the two desires be equal or incommensurable. We still will ordinarily say that the reason Jones opted for the ice cream was because of his desire for ice cream, and there is no reason to take this to have the hidden implication that this desire was stronger. In any case, that this is so is an epistemic possibility at least until we examine free will more carefully, as we shall in the next chapter.

To see how an explanation of a BCCF could be given following this suggestion, suppose that there necessarily exists an essentially good God. A good God might be thought to be moved by good reasons when trying to decide what kind of a cosmos to create. This God then surveys the possible worlds. But the first thing he finds in the survey is that no world is best of all. Some worlds are better because simpler – at the head of this list is the world in which God is the only being – and others are better because more diverse. Some are better because they contain less vice and others are better because although they contain more vice they also contain the virtues that vice makes possible, such as courage in the face of persecution. In the end, for each pair of genuinely possible worlds, let us suppose, there is some consideration because of which the first is better than the second and there is another, equal or incommensurable, consideration because of which the second is better than the first. Worlds whose values are strictly dominated by those of others will on this hypothesis be impossible.

On this picture, for each world w there is a set R_w of reasons in favor of actualizing w. These reasons might be, for instance, simplicity, complexity, balances of simplicity and complexity, and they may even be, for instance, *containing the* de re *lovable Mr. Jones* – indeed, each possible person might count as a reason in favor of creating those worlds in which she exists, if God is motivated by love. For any possible world w, then, were w actualized, the BCCF of w could be explained by some proposition of the form:

(q_w) *God appreciated the reasons in* R_w *and chose what to create.*

Now, the curious fact is that each of the q_w is a necessary truth, since it is a necessary truth that God appreciates all the reasons there in fact are. But while each of the q_w is a necessary truth, it is a contingent truth that one of the q_w in fact has explanatory *oomph*, a contingent fact explained in turn by that very q_w.

There is, however, an objection to be made against this account. One might think it is a conceptual truth that if q explains p, and r is any other true proposition, then likewise q & r explains p. If this is correct, then this approach collapses into biting the bullet and allowing that the very same proposition can explain incompatible propositions. For suppose that q_w explains the BCCF p_w of w for every w. Let w and w^* be any two worlds. Then, let Q be q_w & q_{w^*}. By the conjunctiveness principle earlier, Q explains p_w at w and Q explains p_{w^*} at w^*. Indeed, generalizing to the case of infinite conjunctions, if Q is the conjunction of all the propositions q_w, then necessarily Q explains every contingent true proposition. And this we thought before was absurd. The absurdity can even be seen in the preceding example. Surely that Jones has both a desire for ice cream *and* a desire for steak and that Jones chooses does not explain why Jones eats ice cream.

117

But perhaps the claim that if r is true and q explains p, then q & r explains p is suspect. Although an argument is not made invalid by the addition of an irrelevant true premise, explanation is not the same as proof. Explanation has a pragmatic aspect. Adding irrelevancies to the explanans can obscure matters, and perhaps it can obscure them to the point at which we no longer have an explanation. Comparing explanation to causation is helpful. Even if there were conjunctive events, it would not always be the case that if C causes E and D occurs, then C & D causes E. It is not my sneezing *and* conviction by the Athenian court that caused Socrates' death: it is the conviction alone. One might, however, respond that my having sneezed and the Athenian court's having convicted Socrates does explain why Socrates died: it just does not do so as perspicuously as the explanation in terms of the conviction alone. And, furthermore, if the notion of explanation involved in the PSR is such that that lack of perspicuity vitiates a putative explanation, then we have no reason at all to think the PSR true. For while it might well be plausible that everything has an explanation, it is rather unlikely that matters are so nice that everything has a *perspicuous* explanation.

Yet, the addition of obscuring factors may vitiate some kinds of ordinary language explanations. Suppose John drank some poison and consequently died. That John drank the poison explains why John died. Suppose that there is one more piece of information: Jennifer immediately ran to him to try to induce vomiting. However, she did not get to him before he died. Then, that John drank the poison explains why John died. But, plainly, that John drank the poison *and Jennifer immediately ran to him to try to induce vomiting* does not explain why John died. Once one adds the second conjunction, one also needs a third to have an explanation: *and she did not get there in time.*

It might be objected that Jennifer's running to John to try to induce vomiting vitiates the initial explanation of John's death in terms of his drinking poison. Thus, John's drinking poison does not explain his death. This goes back to the discussion of ceteris paribus nomic explanations. We do not require such an explanation to cite the absence of a factor's preventing the explanandum from following in the usual way from the explanans. Nor is Jennifer's running to save John's life even one of the factors the ceteris paribus clause in the law *those who drink poison die* excludes: if it were one of the factors excluded, then its presence would indeed have to be cited in an explanation, and its defeater would further have to be cited. But what the ceteris paribus clause excludes is the induction of vomiting – not someone's running to induce vomiting.

The disadvantage of the preceding way out of van Inwagen's argument is that it relies on a rather anthropocentric notion of explanation. Perhaps explanation should be understood as a more idealized concept, one on which we take ceteris paribus nomic "explanations" to be mere sketches of a full explanation that the speaker cannot or does not want to supply. The more anthropocentric our notion of explanation, the less probable the PSR becomes. Yet, at the same time, our anthropocentric concepts are all we have: perhaps we should not try to jump out of our skin. Moreover, although an ordinary language argument can be given that the ceteris paribus nomic explanations are in fact taken to be *sufficient* explanations, one might also worry that this is stretching the word *sufficient* too far. If so, then the preceding is a defense of something a little weaker than the PSR, a Principle of Explainability or Reason, rather than a Principle of *Sufficient* Explainability or Reason.

6.3.1.j A Parallel. What all my responses have to defend is the claim that a necessary truth such as *q* can sufficiently explain a contingent truth such as *p*. Once this claim is granted, the defender of the PSR need not be embarrassed by any further question about what explains why *q* explains *p*. The additional explanatory burden of this question can be borne by adding some conceptual truths to the explanans, as we shall see in the next section. But of course we have not yet done much to defend a view of free will on which a necessary truth about a God's reasons could explain a contingent truth about what God chooses.

The parallel to this discussion in the sphere of causation is the claim, famously defended by Elizabeth Anscombe, that while the effects *depend* on the cause, they need not be determined by the cause.

For example, we have found certain diseases to be contagious. If, then, I have had one and only one contact with someone suffering from such a disease, and I get it myself, we suppose I got it from him. But what if, having had the contact, I ask a doctor whether I will get the diseases? He will usually only be able to say, "I don't know – maybe you will, maybe not."

But, it is said, knowledge of causes here is partial; doctors seldom even know any of the conditions under which one invariably gets a disease, let alone all the sets of conditions. This comment betrays the assumption that there is such a thing to know. Suppose there is: still, the question whether there is does not have to be settled before we can know what we mean by speaking of the contact as cause of my getting the disease. (Anscombe, 1993, p. 91)

One might respond, however, that we all intuitively believe in determinism. Thus, we do not need to find out empirically that there is a necessitating set of conditions. Rather, we believe this a priori, and hence we assume that if the contact with the sufferer is a partial cause of the disease, then we *can* add enough conditions to make for necessitation.

It is not obvious, however, that we do all believe in determinism. Is it at all intuitively clear that if we knew the initial conditions of a coin's being flipped we could predict how it will go? Is this not an *empirical* discovery, if it is true at all, one that might well not have turned out to be so? But, yet, we *do* accept that the contact causes the disease prior to having any warrant for thinking that we could give a necessitating set of conditions that includes the contact. Note that we do not even require the contact to make contracting of the disease highly probable to be sure that there is a causal connection.

Consider also any paradigmatic instance of macroscopic causation.[7] One billiard ball strikes another and causes the latter to move. Do we not, pace Hume, perceive the first ball as *pushing* against the second, with the *pushing* being a causal concept? And even if this is not granted, do we not feel *pushed along*[8] or *scraped?*[9] Yet if indeterministic quantum mechanics is to be believed, then there was a tiny but nonzero probability that given the same initial conditions the second ball should rest immobile. Yet this does not deprive us of confidence in saying that in *this* case, the case in which the second ball did in fact move, we have a genuine instance of causation. Likewise when Jones in fact chose to have ice cream, this is explained by his having chosen freely while having a desire for it.

6.3.1.k What Explains Explanatory Claims? Consider finally the following issue already raised by Ross (1969) and more recently by Francken and Geirsson (1999). Suppose we do indeed have a case in which some necessary proposition q explains the BCCF p. What, then, explains why qEp, where E stands for "explains"? This seems to be a further explanatory problem. Since it is contingent that qEp, this proposition is itself a conjunct in p. Thus, q must explain why qEp, since q explains every conjunct in p. But if it is contingent that q explains p, then how can q explain why q explains p? Its being contingent that q explains p while yet q is necessary shows that in fact q is not sufficient to explain why q explains p.

However, it is not obvious why q cannot explain both p and qEp. Consider first an unproblematic case of explanation. Suppose that L is the

---

7 This argument is also inspired by one in Anscombe (1993), but more remotely.
8 This observation is due to David Armstrong.
9 Cf. Anscombe (1993).

conjunction of all true propositions of the form *P is a basic law of nature that holds universally*, that *J* is a report of the initial conditions, and further that *L* & *J* evidently entail *A*, the proposition that the apple fell. Then certainly *L* & *J* explains *A*. Let *N* be a conjunction of all the conceptual truths about the nature of explanation, truths such as that laws conjoined with initial conditions are explanatory, together with the necessary truth that *L* & *J* entails *A*. Then, *L* & *J* & *N* also explains *A* – getting clearer on the nature of explanation does not obscure a particular explanation. But note that the claim (*L* & *J* *N*)*EA* now need not be thought of as a *further* claim to be explained. It is already sufficiently explained by *L* & *J* & *N*. Once we know that *L* & *J* & *N*, we have all we need for explaining *A* and for explaining why (*L* & *J* & *N*)*EA*. Observe, too, that here it is also the case that (*L* & *J* & *N*)*EA* is contingent, since it entails *A*, which is contingent. Thus, there are cases in which the same proposition *q* explains both *p* and *qEp*.

In fact, it is quite plausible that this happens more often. If *q* explains *p*, then *q* and various conceptual truths should also, at least in many cases, make it clear to us why *q* explains *p*. Take the free will case, and suppose we are talking of a free choice by a necessary being, and our explanans is of the form, (*q*) *God appreciated the reasons in R_w and chose what to create.* If we accept *q* as an explanation of why (*p*) God actualized world *w*, we will likewise accept *q* conjoined with some conceptual truths about explanation as explaining why *qEp*, for *q* explains why God actualized *w*. But we understand *why q* explains this: *q* explains this because God necessarily acts on the basis of reasons that incline but do not necessitate and because such reason-based explanations are in fact good ones. To the extent that this seems unsatisfactory, it seems unsatisfactory because we may not be convinced that in fact *q* explains why God actualized *w*, given that *q* could have been true without God's actualizing *w*. But once we accept *q* as giving a bona fide explanation, then presumably we have no further mystery as to *why* it gives such an explanation – the facts about explanation that get us to accept *q* as a genuine explanation explain why it is such.

We can see this more clearly by considering the relation of *putative explanation*. A proposition *q* putatively explains *p* if and only if *q* would explain *p* were both *p* and *q* true. When we claim that *q* explains *p*, we can be seen as claiming that *q* putatively explains *p* and both *q* and *p* hold. Now, in the case in which *q* is necessary, taking all necessary truths (stipulatively if needed) to be self-explanatory, if *q* explains *p*, then *q* explains why both *q* and *p* hold, simply because *q* explains why *p* holds and *q* explains why *q*

121

holds, by self-explanatoriness. So, the only remaining thing to show is how q explains why q putatively explains p. But in the previous case, given that God necessarily acts on reasons, if I am right about its being a conceptual truth that God's appreciating the reasons in R_w and choosing what to create would explain why God actualized w if God in fact actualized w and in fact appreciated the reasons in R_w and chose what to create, it is a *necessary* truth, and hence one that does not require explanation since it is self-explanatory, that q *putatively* explains p.

Observe that this does not apply to all cases of explanation. For instance, in a ceteris paribus nomic explanation, it is not a conceptual truth that the explanans putatively explains the explanandum. There are possible worlds where there is gravity, the apple is dropped, and the apple falls, but gravity does not explain why the apple falls. For instance, gravity might be counteracted by something else while the explanation of why the apple falls might lie elsewhere. However, this argument applies in the case of the free will explanation of God's action if this is a good putative explanation.

6.3.2. Could a Contingent Proposition Explain Itself?

6.3.2.a Paradigmatic Self-Explanatory Propositions. If the response to the van Inwagen argument through questioning the claim that a necessary proposition cannot explain a contingent one fails, then there is only one way out for the defender of the PSR: she must acknowledge that there are self-explanatory contingent propositions. The explanation of the BCCF of the actual world needs to be itself a self-explanatory contingent proposition. The difficulty here is that our most clear paradigmatic examples of self-explanatory propositions are propositions that are also self-evident and necessarily true: that $1 = 1$, that material objects take up space, that nothing is both true and false at the same time and in the same respect, and so on. The explanation of the BCCF will not be necessarily true, we have assumed; it is also most unlikely to be self-evidently true.[10]

6.3.2.b What Is a Self-Explanatory Proposition? We could say that a self-explanatory proposition p is a proposition p such that p explains p. But that would not tell us anything. What could it mean for p to explain p? It is tempting to define a self-explanatory proposition negatively as

---

10   Cf. note 6 of Chapter 2.

a true proposition such that as soon as one grasps its truth, one grasps that seeking an explanation for it is mistaken. But that is not quite right. Suppose the PSR is false and there is some contingent proposition p that happens to have no explanation. Then, let p^* be the proposition

(68) p has no explanation and p.

As soon as one grasps p^* one grasps that it cannot have an explanation – that one would be mistaken to ask for its explanation. But, plainly, p^* is not self-explanatory: if it were, then p would have an explanation, too, and hence p^* would be false.

More positively and plausibly, one might say that a self-explanatory proposition is a true and understandable proposition such that, necessarily, as soon as one understands it and believes it to be true, one has explained why it is true, or at least one has the resources to explain it. There is no more mystery. Therefore, any true and understandable proposition such that as soon as one has understood it one has to know that and why it is true will be self-explanatory. Hence self-evidently necessary claims such as that $1 = 1$ or the principle of noncontradiction will be self-explanatory. However, it is not completely obvious that these kinds of propositions exhaust the class of the self-explanatory.

Lest it be said that the claim that $1 = 1$ is a mere unexplained "brute" fact, compare the reaction one might have to the claim that $1 = 1$ and some complex mathematical claim p that I know to be true but whose proof I do not know, say, that there are no finite skew fields. I could be genuinely puzzled by p in a way in which I would not be by the claim that $1 = 1$. Suppose that God then told me that although p is true, the published proofs are invalid and in fact p is a Gödelian nonprovable proposition. I think it would be reasonable to continue to find p mysterious in a way in which the claim that $1 = 1$ is not. An appropriate way to characterize the situation would be to say that p is a brute fact. But $1 = 1$ is not a brute fact: there is no puzzle (not even an insoluble one) as to why it is true – once you see that $1 = 1$, what is there to be puzzled about?

6.3.2.c The Causal Objection. One might object to the notion of a self-explanatory contingent proposition as follows. All explanation of contingent propositions is causal. If a proposition is self-explanatory and contingent, then it must causally explain itself; that is, the worldly state of affairs it reports must be a *causa sui*. But the notion of a *causa sui* is clearly self-contradictory. However, this assumes that all causal explanation of a proposition is in terms of something's causing the reported state of affairs.

123

But perhaps causality is implicated in a more complicated way in the explanation of a self-explanatory contingent proposition.

Let us hold on to the idea of explanation's being causal. This suggests that when we seek an explanation of a contingent proposition, we seek an explanation of the form, C causes E. Could this be self-explanatory? That would require that that C causes E should explain why C causes E. Inter alia, it would seem to require that C causes E should explain why C existed or took place. This is absurd: the causal activity of C cannot explain C. Thus, the existence of C must not be the sort of thing that demands an explanation. If C is a being or the causal activity of a being, then that being will have to be a necessary one, because even if there are self-explanatory contingent propositions, a self-explanatory contingent *being* would be too much to swallow. Moreover, that this being causes E will itself have to be a contingent fact.

There is on the books one candidate for this kind of a self-explanatory proposition, and this is a proposition reporting a libertarian free action of a necessary being. In fact, I think it will be clear from the preceding that only something like a report of a libertarian free action will do here. On a Jamesian libertarian view, one can argue that Jones freely chose A sufficiently explains why Jones freely chose A, modulo the explanation of Jones's existence and freedom. If so, then there are contingent self-explanatory propositions when the existence and freedom are necessary. On a different libertarian view, that Jones freely chose A for R sufficiently explains why Jones freely chose A for R. Again, this would let one have contingent self-explanatory propositions. If one of these ways of looking at libertarian free will can be defended as a logical possibility, then (35) is false, and the van Inwagen argument is refuted. A defense of these ways of looking at free will is given in the next chapter.

6.3.2.d Implications for Contingent Self-Explanatory Propositions. The considerations arising from the analysis of why we do not say that Fred died because he died of being shot (Section 6.3.1.g) also help the defender of the PSR on the present horn of the dilemma, that of holding that there is a contingent self-explanatory proposition, for if there were such a proposition p, it would not have to be implausibly true that knowledge *that p* is true is sufficient to know *why p* is true. Rather, on our more generous view, for p to be self-explanatory, to know why p is true it would have to be enough to know that p is both true and self-explanatory. Now observe that while there is some plausibility that knowing that p is true is never by itself enough to know why p is true, on this view we are not claiming that.

We are, instead, claiming that to know why p is true it is enough to know that p is true and that it has the special property of self-explanatoriness. The burden of telling us why p is true is not borne by p's truth alone. To be concrete, suppose we wish to know why a necessary being freely chose A for reason R. It is perhaps not enough to know just that the necessary being freely chose A for R. Instead, we may need to add further conceptual claims about free action's being self-explanatory, and this may provide some traction. Note that, furthermore, we may be able to explain *why* free actions, or at least free actions of a necessary being, are self-explanatory (cf. Section 6.3.1.k).

7

Free Will

7.1. HOW TO EXPLAIN FREE ACTIONS?

7.1.1. The Problem

Suppose Jones freely chose A. Why did Jones choose A? The libertarian cannot allow there to be any prior causes that necessitated Jones to choose A. In fact, it seems, the libertarian cannot cite anything in the explanation of why Jones chose A. Thus, free libertarian choices appear to violate the PSR. In the preceding section, it was suggested that several accounts of free will might yield a way out of van Inwagen's fatalism objection to the PSR. If any of these accounts works, it will also give a way out of this objection. There were three accounts offered. The first said that a proposition of the form *Jones had desire D* or perhaps *Jones was aware of reason R* can explain why Jones chose A even if it does not necessitate it. The next suggested that *Jones freely chose A* can be self-explanatory. And the last suggested that *Jones freely chose A for R* can be self-explanatory.

7.1.2. A Jamesian Account

We will start by looking at the account that Jones freely chose A is self-explanatory. This account makes no mention of reasons for the choice: a free choice is self-explanatory, pure and simple.

Consider first the following claim that *does* involve reasons:

(69) A proposition of the form *Jones chose A for reason R*, if true, sufficiently explains why Jones chose A.

This is a claim deeply embedded in our ordinary practices of explanation: saying that an action in fact done for some reason was done for that

126

reason sufficiently explains why the action was done. It need not be a *complete* explanation, of course, because in general it fails to explain why Jones was free or why Jones existed at all, but it is a sufficient one. Claim (69) is something that a libertarian of any stripe can accept and that a compatibilist can also accept, though they may disagree whether that *Jones chose A for reason R* entails that the reason was such that Jones could have chosen against it or not.

But suppose now that a choice is made for *no reason at all*: it is just freely made. A libertarian like William James[1] insists that such things really happen, and it is in those cases that true freedom is found. In that case, there is no explanation of the form *Jones freely chose A for R*. In the next two sections, I shall argue that our libertarian will have to be committed to the claim that

(70) That *Jones freely chose A for no reason at all*, if true, sufficiently explains why Jones chose *A*.

Our libertarian is committed, first of all, to the negative claim that the explanatory role that reasons have in (69) for the compatibilist who thinks the reasons determine the action is *not* taken over in the case of a reason-less choice by anything other than perhaps Jones's freely choosing *A*. For imagine that the role that reasons play in (69) is taken over by some cause *C* outside Jones's freely choosing *A*. Then, this cause *C* will negatively impinge on Jones's freedom, the libertarian will insist, because if something outside Jones's choice has an explanatory role in the choice, a role of the same sort that reasons have in a reasoned choice, then we do not have a truly libertarian choice.

7.1.3. A Condition on a Libertarianism to Be Plausible

Thus, if the Jamesian libertarian is correct, then that Jones freely chose *A* for no reason at all is the closest we can come to explaining why Jones chose *A*. It still might be, however, that although this is the *closest* we can come to explaining why Jones chose *A*, it is still not a *sufficient* explanation of this. However, this also will not do. To see this, I will need a certain conceptual construction. For this construction, I will need to assume the PSR to be false. If the PSR is necessarily true, then this will have the character of a *per impossibile* counterfactual. Suppose we have some situation *S* involving, among other things, the activity of some cause *C*'s

1   The characterization of this view as Jamesian is due to Richard M. Gale.

127

bringing about an effect E. The construction I want is the *surgical excision of C from S*. This is a situation in which everything happens qualitatively just as before, except that C does not occur and E occurs causelessly with no explanation at all. I will assume it makes sense to talk of such excisions if the PSR is false. Excision is a very Humean operation. We just imagine a space-time where everything is as before, except there is no C, though the effects remain. However, if an object A is constituted by an object B, then the excision of B removes A. This should give one enough of an ostensive hold on the notion to allow one to understand it.

I now claim that any plausible form of libertarianism is committed to the following claim:

(71) If we have a situation S in which an agent counts as acting unfreely because of the freedom-canceling causal role that some cause C has in his action, that is, because of C's violating the condition that the action be ultimately self-originated as the libertarian insists, then the agent also acts unfreely in the situation formed by the surgical excision of C from S.

In other words, if some cause takes away freedom, and that cause is replaced by indeterministic randomness or some brute unexplained fact, freedom is still lacking. Indeterminism is not sufficient for freedom – this is, of course, universally acknowledged in the free will literature.[2] If your freedom were canceled by an overwhelming desire, then the random formation of that overwhelming desire would likewise cancel out your freedom. Nor will it do for a libertarian to say that the difference between randomness and a free choice is that free choices are intentional, for once one acknowledges that a choice can be free even if it is random as long as it is intentional, there does not appear to be any reason to object to the compatibilist claim that a choice can be free even if it is determined as long as it is intentional. Random phenomena are ones that one is no more responsible for than predetermined ones.

If we took an agent who was unfree because of determinism's being true, and changed nothing in the situation except that we replaced the deterministic laws of physics by completely indeterministic ones such that

---

2 This does not mean that every libertarian rejects the idea that randomness may be at the heart of libertarian freedom. Robert Kane (1996) has a powerful account in which quantum randomness is at the center of free will. However, Kane also thinks that there is more than *just* indeterminism at play here. That said, I do not know whether Kane's account does justice to (71). If not, then so much the worse for it.

by chance, with no explanation, everything happened as it would have in the deterministic case, we would not thereby have made the agent any freer. As J. J. C. Smart notes, he would not consider himself freer, indeed quite the contrary, if a random brain event made him run to the garden and eat a slug.[3]

The reason for this is that the libertarian's basic commitment is that an action must be up to the agent in a strong sense: the agent must be the true originator of the action. If this is violated by the impingement of some cause C on the agent's activity, then the agent is not free. However, to restore the agent's freedom it is not enough that C be surgically excised. Rather, to restore the agent's freedom, the agent or her free choice must be put in the place of C. An action is no more self-originated for being random. It is a standard objection to libertarianism that the libertarian is committed to actions' being random rather than causally originated by the agent. Any plausible libertarianism must deny this, and the libertarian's principles commit her to the denial of this.

7.1.4. Commitment to (70)

But now let us go back to the common ground. The libertarian and antilibertarian both accept that that Jones chose A for R explains why Jones chose A, in the case of a choice that results from reasons. The Jamesian libertarian who believes that freedom is ultimately rooted in reasonless choices holds that the role the reasons, or perhaps Jones's awareness of them or their impingement on Jones, play in this explanation is freedom canceling, or at least canceling of the highest sort of freedom. By (71), the libertarian, however, is also committed to the claim that the situation in which Jones freely reasonlessly chooses A is *not* just the situation obtained by surgically excising the impingement of reasons from the case of reason-determined choice. This means that in the reasonless free choice case, the Jamesian must claim that the explanatory role that reasons played in the reason-determined case is not lost. If it were lost, then this would be a case of surgical excision of the impingement of reasons. Rather, the Jamesian must hold that all the explanatory oomph that reasons had is transferred to Jones and Jones's free choice.

In other words, the Jamesian libertarian must hold that if (69) holds, then likewise (70) holds.

---

3   See Smart and Haldane (1996).

In fact, we can more generally argue that if libertarianism is at all plausible, then there must be no insuperable conceptual difficulty about explaining why Jones did A in cases of libertarian free choices. For consider Jones's doing A, and suppose that it is free. Suppose there is some aspect of this that is not in fact sufficiently explained by anything: every partial explanation we can cite for it, let us suppose, falls short of being a sufficient explanation. We could then imagine a different situation in which some outside cause causes this aspect to occur. In fact, we could more generally imagine a bunch of outside causes, perhaps supernatural ones, filling in all the gaps in the explanation of Jones's doing A. For instance, if part of Jones's doing A is an unexplained indeterministic firing of a neuron, we can imagine some process that deterministically fires it instead. Thus, we can modify the situation of Jones's doing A in such a way that all the gaps in explanation are filled by outside causes.

The resulting situation is one in which Jones's doing A does have a sufficient explanation. Now, either this is a situation where Jones is still free or it is not. If Jones is still free, then in fact freedom *is* compatible with sufficient explainability, though the libertarian will not choose this solution. Suppose, then, Jones is not free. Presumably, the reason he is not free is due to the freedom-canceling nature of these outside causes, their ensuring that the action is not self-originated in the right way. But we have supposed that without these outside causes' acting, the action was free. Thus, we have a situation in which surgical excision of the aggregate of these added external causes would make the action free, and this is contrary to (71) as generalized to a multiplicity of causes C, a generalization the libertarian is committed to for exactly the same reasons she is committed to (71). Hence, the libertarian is committed to its not being the case that there is something unexplained about Jones's action.

Consequently, the libertarian, whether Jamesian or other, is committed to the idea that sufficient explainability does not negate freedom. This opens up the door for a free-will theistic explanation of the BCCF, with even God's choice to actualize the BCCF being explained, though the details will need to be looked at more carefully. In fact, it appears that if libertarianism violates the PSR because of an unexplainability in free choices, then libertarianism is untenable. While a libertarian need not be committed to the truth of the PSR, she cannot be committed to free will actions' necessarily being violations of the PSR. And, obviously, compatibilists are likely to think that freely willed actions are *not* violations of the

PSR given that they tend to hold that free actions are explainable in terms of reasons and desires.

Thus, the free will objection to the PSR fails, whether one is a compatibilist or not. However, it is only someone who thinks libertarianism is a coherent doctrine who can use the libertarian counterexamples to van Inwagen's premises. Van Inwagen is a libertarian himself, of course, but that is only an ad hominem argument. The argument that libertarianism commits one to upholding the PSR as applied to our free actions will only impress a fairly committed libertarian. Indeed, because some libertarians think that the PSR is incompatible with libertarianism, these observations may lead them to conclude libertarianism to be incoherent, as being incompatible with the PSR and yet committed to compatibility with it. To prevent this outcome, we need to look more carefully at how free will fits in with the PSR and with van Inwagen's objections.

7.1.6. Why Did Jones Freely and Reasonlessly Choose As He Did?

We have seen the Jamesian libertarian to be committed to the claim that Jones's freely and reasonlessly choosing A explains why Jones chose A. But what explains why Jones freely and reasonlessly chose A? Presumably there is nothing more to explaining this than explaining why Jones freely and reasonlessly chose at all, and why, given that he freely and reasonlessly chose, he chose A. Suppose now that p is an explanation for why Jones freely and reasonlessly chose at all on this occasion. Let q be the proposition that Jones freely and reasonlessly chose A. Then, p & q explains why Jones chose A. In fact, however, p & q explains more: it explains why Jones freely and reasonlessly chose on this occasion and why, given that he chose freely and reasonlessly, he chose A. Therefore, the Jamesian should say the following:

(72) That p and that Jones freely and reasonlessly chose A explain why Jones freely and reasonlessly chose A.

Now, there might be a puzzlement here over what kind of a proposition p can be. Can a libertarian allow that there is an explanation why Jones freely and reasonlessly chose? But surely she can. Being determined to choose freely and reasonlessly would not negate the freedom of a reasonless choice. Only being determined to choose *some one particular way* would be freedom canceling. Think of existentialists who say we are "condemned to freedom" – that one is condemned to choose does not entail that one is condemned to choose A.

7.1.7. The Theistic Case

Consider now the case in which we have a necessary being, X, which is such that it necessarily chooses what kind of a world to actualize. Then, that the being exists and that it chooses (a) is self-explanatory, if one takes necessary propositions to be self-explanatory, or at least (b) it does not demand an explanation from a PSR that concerns contingent states of affairs. If we take the second alternative, we will have to formulate the PSR carefully so as to exclude having to explain necessary propositions, as discussed in Section 3.3. In any case, let r be the proposition that X exists and chooses. Let q be the proposition that X freely and reasonlessly chooses to bring it about that p, where p is the BCCF. Then, r & q explains p, and r & q also explains q by analogy with (72). If r is self-explanatory or if we stipulate that explanation does not need to explain necessary conjuncts, we then conclude that r & q explains r & q, and hence we have a self-explanatory contingent explainer. Thus the Jamesian certainly has available to her a way of responding to van Inwagen's fatalism argument.

The preceding model of the explanation of the BCCF may not be entirely adequate, of course. Depending on one's views of explanation and of the relation between X's will and that of human beings, as part of the explanation of the BCCF one might have to say something about the free choices of the human beings whose existence is explained by the necessary being's free choice to create them.

7.2. REASONED CHOICES

7.2.1. The Problem with the Jamesian Account

The main problem in the previous account is whether there can be completely reasonless choices. Such choices do not seem to merit the dignity of the term *free choice*. They seem, pace the Jamesian's insistence, not to be actions at all, but mere twitches. Is not the distinction between a twitch and an action that the latter is done for reasons? Of course we are familiar with the fact that the libertarian need not buy this argument. The libertarian can distinguish actions from twitches simply in terms of causality: x is an action providing it is caused by a person qua person or by a person insofar as she has a will or perhaps by the faculty of will of a person, or providing it comes from the right mode of causation, such as Chisholm's (1964) immanent rather than transeunt causation. A twitch, if we count it as caused by a person at all, is not caused by the person qua person but by the person qua animal. Of course, the compatibilist could respond that what makes an action be caused by a person qua person is that the action arises from *reasons* that the person has, and the libertarian has no way of drawing this distinction. However, this neglects the fact that the libertarian is likely to draw the distinction metaphysically, in terms of the metaphysics of persons, whether this metaphysics be dualistic, hylomorphic, emergentist, or other. The details of how the distinction would be drawn would depend on the details of the metaphysics. And some who believe in really distinct faculties could simply make the distinction in terms of what the faculty of will causes.

But even if the libertarian can make a distinction between actions and twitches, it is surely a undeniable fact about us that we *do* choose on the basis of reasons or desires. A reasonless choice does not seem to be a part of our experience: we are always assailed by reasons. Moreover, such a choice would be more befitting an animal than a human.

7.2.2. A Jamesian Response

However, the reasonless choice, in a Jamesian framework, need not be made in a context in which there are *no reasons*. In fact, it can be made in a context in which there are too many incommensurable reasons. Virtue is inconvenient; what is convenient is vice. We need to decide between virtue and convenience. We have reasons: *virtue* and *convenience* are themselves reasons, but they are incommensurable, so there is no third higher reason that subsumes both and decides which has the higher weight. And thus we must *choose* which of the reasons we will allow to govern our actions: with which values we will identify ourselves. This choice between the reasons cannot itself be guided by reasons because one is precisely choosing between all the relevant reasons – though one might admit that there are reasons and personal predilections that bias one and may skew the probabilities of various choices' being made. On this Jamesian view, what makes this a human choice rather than something that an animal does is not that it is done *out of prior* values. What makes it a human choice is the sort of things we are choosing between: we are choosing which incommensurable set of values to adopt as ours.

7.2.3. Concrete Choices

Thus would speak the Jamesian. However, this does not ring completely true in light of our notion that free choice does not rest solely in the realm of abstract choices of what values to identify ourselves with but instead also falls in the context of everyday practical choices, which choice

133

by choice form our character into the sort of character that is inclined to follow one set of values rather than another. When choosing between plagiarizing a paper and writing it, the student need not be thought of as always going through a two-step process: first, a choice whether to value convenience over virtue, and, second, action on the chosen value. Rather, the student chooses whether viciously to plagiarize or virtuously to apply herself. If she chooses the way of ease, we say that she chose this *because of its convenience*. If she chooses the road of sweat, she chose this *because of its virtue*. We do not usually posit an earlier stage in the explanation, a stage at which the agent steps back and decides whether to value virtue or convenience. Acquiring such and such a character, such and such a set of habitual value judgments, can well be a *consequence* of the action rather than a prerequisite for it.

Now, it is true that the compatibilist takes the preceding fact to tell against libertarianism. There is an explanation of the action, and this is in terms of *reasons*, in terms of what the agent *values*, say, convenience or virtue. However, this is more than our ordinary way of thinking about this gives us. When we say that she chose ease because of convenience or that she chose sweat because of virtue, we need not be implying that the student had the sort of character that necessitated her to go for convenience or that necessitated her to go for virtue. To explain the person's actions in terms of convenience we need not suppose that convenience is a stronger consideration for the person. Indeed, convenience is likely to become a stronger consideration for the person as a result of the action, as vicious actions breed a vicious character, but there is no reason to think it already was a stronger consideration. Given that our ordinary ways of talking about choice presuppose libertarianism as well, we come upon a view on which that Smith chose to plagiarize is explained by her valuing convenience, whereas had she chosen to work hard, this would have been explained by her valuing virtue, which facts are compatible with the claim that she in fact valued *both* convenience and virtue.

This account supports a suggestion made earlier that in this context would be tantamount to saying that that Smith values convenience would explain why she cheated were she to cheat and that Smith values virtue would explain why she did her own work were she to act honestly. Which true proposition is in fact explanatory of the action ends up depending logically on what action actually takes place.[4]

---

4 This is particularly clear in the quantum mechanical approach of Kane (1996).

7.2.4. Another Principle about Explanation

Suppose we then accept the following as embedded in our explanatory practices:

(73) That an agent takes R to be a reason for doing A and freely chooses whether to do A is always, if she in fact freely chose A for R, a sufficient explanation for why she chose A.

If we do not make the further move of requiring that the antecedent should specify that R is a reason taken to be stronger than all other available reasons, then acceptance of this plausible thesis about explanation gives a libertarian a way to accept the PSR. Note that in fact (73) follows from (69), which was, of course, deeply embedded in our explanatory practices. And to get out of van Inwagen's fatalism objection to the PSR, we need only suppose that the explanation for the BCCF, p, is that, necessarily, there is a being that takes some consideration R to be a reason for bringing it about that p and freely chooses whether to bring it about that p. This is not an explanation we know, or perhaps even can know, the details of: we do not know what the consideration R is, for instance. But the PSR does not say that for every contingent proposition there is an explanation that we can *know*.

The main problem with this way out was already discussed in Section 6.3, and it is that both the explanans sufficient to explain doing A and the explanans sufficient to explain doing non-A, namely, the agent's acceptance of some reason R^* for doing non-A, are true simultaneously, and one might take this to be unsatisfactory. One is likely to ask: But what explains why the agent acted on R rather than on R^*? What explains why the agent acted for the sake of convenience rather than for the sake of virtue? On this account, the answer is that it is the agent's acceptance of R itself that does the explaining. This is rock bottom, and the libertarian who takes this way out bites the bullet and admits that the reason of virtue was just as available, but it was not the one that in fact did the explaining, though it might have done so.

However, this formulation, though showing the role of reasons, takes the agent's actual free choosing out of the explanans, where presumably the libertarian thinks it must be found. There is, however, a final option that combines the previous two, and this is to take it that propositions of the form x freely does A for R are almost self-explanatory: they explain everything that calls out for an explanation in the proposition that x freely does A for R other than the existence and freedom of x and x's taking R to be a reason. If x were a necessary being, necessarily freely choosing whether to do A, and necessarily taking R to be a reason (as well as taking an incommensurable R^* that weighs against A as a reason), then that x freely chose A for R would be self-explanatory or at least self-explanatory modulo necessary truths.

The advantage of this account is that both reasons and the agent's free choice are found in the explanans. As in the reasonless choice case, we can respond to van Inwagen by citing a contingent self-explanatory action: that a necessary being freely brought it about that p for the sake of R.

In saying that that x freely chose A for R is self-explanatory (modulo existence, freedom, and appreciation of R, in the case of a contingent being),[5] one is saying that the consideration R does play an explanatory role, though not a role sufficient on its own to explain the action, and x's free choice also plays a role, albeit a role conditioned by R. Ordinarily, our search for explanation ends when we have found a person who freely chose something and when we have explained the reasons because of which she *in fact* chose it. We may not always know quite what to do about the availability to her of reasons against choosing the thing, but the natural thing to say in that case is that it was because of the attractiveness of the reason that she in fact acted on that she freely chose to act on that reason, and it is at least in part because of this attractiveness that she chose not to act on another reason – even if that other reason was just as attractive to her. Had she chosen to act on the other reason, then her action would be explained by her freely choosing to act in accordance with that other reason. It is tempting then to say, even in the context of ordinary life, "That she chose to act as she did shows that she must have taken R to be more attractive than R^*." But the words *must have* betray the fact that this is a theoretical claim. Nor is it obvious that we cannot say that what makes true the proposition that she took R to be more attractive than R^* is just the fact she freely chose to act on R.

To defend this account in full would require a complete account of libertarian free will, which would be beyond the scope of this book. Suffice it to say that it is by no means obvious that this account, or one of the previous ones, is incoherent, and this one, at least, does justice

---

5   An explanation of p modulo q is not a complete explanation of p. One might think that therefore something cannot be self-explanatory modulo something else, since if something is self-explanatory, it explains itself completely. However, a proposition might explain only an aspect of itself, in which case it is self-explanatory *modulo* another proposition. For instance, if p is any self-explanatory proposition, say that $1 = 1$, and q is any non-self-explanatory proposition, then we can say that p & q is self-explanatory modulo q.

to many of our ordinary ways of speaking. And I have argued, further, that the libertarian cannot hold libertarian-free choices to be violations of the PSR, for that would be succumbing to the randomness objection to libertarianism.

7.2.5. Counterfactuals

A point in favor of reason-based libertarian explanations is that arguably, as one would expect of many kinds of explanation, they have some robustness: they ground some counterfactuals about what would have happened under somewhat different conditions. To use an example of Plantinga's (see Adams, 1977), had Curley accepted a smaller bribe, surely he would have accepted a larger one (barring special circumstances, such as those in which acceptance of the larger one would have put him in danger of a longer jail sentence).

For a general class of examples, suppose that actually x chose A for R. Then, roughly, under the same historical circumstances at the same time, it seems that had x been even more impressed with R than actually, and no less impressed than actually with any of the other reasons in favor of A, and no more impressed than actually with any of the reasons against A, x would still have chosen A for R. Moreover, had the circumstances at that time been different in a way that did not affect x's mental state up to and including the time of the choice, x would have acted in the same way and for the same reason. Thus, someone who shot a gun into the bushes because it was fun to do so would still have shot a gun into the bushes, and for the same reason, had someone been hiding in the bushes. The previous formulations are rough and more work would need to be done to determine what exactly needs to be preserved in the antecedents of the conditionals, but the general picture should be clear.

All of these claims are compatible with the statement that x was not determined to choose A for R, that she might have instead chosen non-A for R^*. Had she chosen non-A for R^*, then a different bevy of counterfactuals would have been true, such as that had she been more impressed by R^* and each of the other reasons in favor of non-A and no more impressed by any of the reasons against non-A, she would still have opted for non-A.

Many libertarians might reject such counterfactuals.[6] However, some might well accept them. Even some, such as Robert M. Adams (1977),

---

6 E.g., Thomas Flint has rejected them in correspondence.

who are opposed to middle knowledge and subjunctive conditionals of free will in general, may accept these counterfactuals, because what grounds the truth of the claim that Curley would have accepted the greater bribe is the this-worldly fact that he in fact accepts the lesser. And if one accepts these counterfactuals, then the plausibility of the claim that reason-based libertarian explanation is a genuine form of explanation is bolstered further.[7]

At the same time, its turning out that such counterfactuals are not in fact correct would not disprove the claim that reason-based libertarian explanation is a genuine form of explanation, for it does not seem to be a necessary condition on explanation that one be able to say that the explanandum would continue to hold had matters been different in such and such ways from what the explanans describes. After all, in some cases of genuine explanation the explanandum might well entail the explanans. The most obvious case is that of reductive explanation: Fred's being elected under the British system to Parliament may well entail that he got the largest share of the votes legally cast in the riding and is explained by this entailed fact.[8]

7.3. OBJECTIONS TO LIBERTARIANISM

The constructive part of my defense of the PSR against van Inwagen's objections involved the coherence and plausibility of libertarianism. Now there are two major types of objections to libertarianism on the books.

7.3.1. Frankfurt

The first kind of objection is in examples of the Frankfurt (1969) type. The libertarian's basic intuition is that for you to be free requires that you have been able to do otherwise. Imagine that a neurosurgeon watches over you all your life and has a detailed plan for you. When she figures out that you are about to will to do something that does not match the plan, then she moves your brain in such a way that you do will what she wants you to. Suppose that in fact she never interferes with you since

---

7 For more discussion of such counterfactuals, see Pruss (forthcoming).

8 Another possibility, one that a theory of explanation should not reject from the outset, is that it might turn out that something's arising *ex nihilo* can only be caused by God's creative activity. If so, then that a brick noncauselessly arose *ex nihilo* entails that God created the brick *ex nihilo*; but that God created the brick *ex nihilo* would explain why the brick arose noncauselessly *ex nihilo*.

as it happens you were never in a situation in which you were about to act contrary to plan. In that case, surely you were free. But you could not have done otherwise than to follow the plan.

This kind of an objection does not affect the arguments of this book, for even if one thinks that it is not the case that a free agent is able to have done otherwise, to respond to the van Inwagen argument all I need is that it be *possible* to have cases in which a free agent could have chosen otherwise, a possibility in no way affected by Frankfurt's examples. Even if the could-have-done-otherwise condition is not necessary for freedom, it is at least compossible with freedom, and hence libertarian-free actions are a possibility.

But one should not give so much credit to Frankfurt. As has been noted by a number of authors, there *are* alternate possibilities under Frankfurt-type scenarios. For instance, even granting the Frankfurt intuition that in the situation as described you can act freely, it still could have been the case that you did not act *freely*. Thus, supposing you freely helped a homeless person under the neurosurgeon's watchful eye, it was still possible that you did not freely help her, even if it was not possible that you did not help her. The alternate possibility of helping nonfreely is open to you. For it could have transpired that the surgeon had to intervene and bring it about that you help the homeless person, and were that to have happened, you would not have been acting freely – the surgeon's having intentionally brought about your action would have been freedom-canceling even by the lights of many compatibilists. Any Frankfurt-type example will lead to this conclusion, since precisely by positing the possibility of the surgeon's intervening one is positing the possibility of one's acting unfreely.

Furthermore, once one has the claim that it was possible that you not have helped the person freely, one can leverage one's way into the conclusion that your volitional state could have been different in some way. For what would have been different in the possible world where you did not help the person freely? Presumably, the neurosurgeon was able to tell that you are in a state with the counterfactual property that were he not to intervene, you would not help the homeless person. There are two ways the neurosurgeon could know this. First, he could be a deity that has middle knowledge, that is, knowledge of what an agent would freely do in nonactual circumstances. The philosophy of religion literature on middle knowledge is quite intricate. One of the serious difficulties with the notion is in the question of what it is about the cosmos that makes it be true that the person has a state of being such that she would do such and such in such and such circumstances. It cannot be any categorical feature of the person that makes this true, since then the person's actions, in those circumstances, would not be libertarian free, but determined by these categorical features. Moreover, it is quite obscure, even if there were such a state of affairs, how anyone, perhaps even God, could know it.

Without relying on middle knowledge, the neurosurgeon must rely on some actual sign in her victim. Suppose that the neurosurgeon did in fact intervene and make you help the homeless person. Then there would have been something in you, say, a state S, which was such that were the surgeon to have left you alone when in S, you would not have helped the homeless person. Now, let us look carefully into where the surgeon needs to be infallible for Frankfurt's counterexample to the could-have-done-otherwise to work. The surgeon does not have to be infallible in detecting that you have S for the scenario to work. She could in some physically possible worlds err on the side of caution and force you to help the homeless person even though you would in fact have helped without her forcing you. All that is required is that in the actual world, where in fact no interference has occurred, no such mistake was made.

However, in order to have there be no possibility of your having done otherwise, the neurosurgeon cannot ever fail to detect a state U such that you would, if left alone, not help the homeless were you to be in U. Thus, it must be that whenever you are in a state such that you would not help the homeless without interference, the surgeon detects this. Consequently, there must not be a possibility for the surgeon to be wrong when she makes her judgment that you *would* help the homeless without interference, for if she were wrong in this judgment, then she would be failing to detect that you are in fact in state U.

Therefore, the surgeon actually needs to be certain not when she judges that you are in a state such that if left alone you would not help the homeless, but rather when she judges that you are in a state such that if left alone you *would* help the homeless. Thus, in the actual world where you do in fact freely help the homeless, as per plan, the neurosurgeon must know with certainty that you are in the state V of being such that it is nomically necessary that your being in V is followed by your helping the homeless. But now it is clear that there is something you could have done otherwise: you could have acted in such wise that you would not have ended up in state V, for in some of the possible worlds where you help the homeless only unfreely, forced by the surgeon, you were not in V, for the reason you were forced by the surgeon is that she did not think you were in V, and even though she need not have absolute certainty about this, it is quite possible that she is in fact right, and for the Frankfurt example to work, she must in fact sometimes be right in such judgments, since otherwise she will always be forcing you.

Now, the standard criticism of this is that the state V is not morally significant. It might just be some twitch that infallibly indicates that you will choose to help the homeless.[9] However, to suppose the existence of such is to beg the question against a typical libertarian, for the libertarian typically believes that, absent the involvement of middle knowledge in the production of V, any physical state V that has the property that a human being's being in V of nomic necessity, given the absence of external interference, is followed by her freely doing A must be a state that results from a free choice of hers. The best way to see how this works is to consider the *first* free choice made by a human being, and to note that the Frankfurt argument clearly fails there on libertarian grounds, for suppose that up to and including time t, the person has not made any free choices. At time t, on the Frankfurt scenario, she is in V and is nomically certain freely to choose to do A, absent external interference. But the libertarian will insist that if it is nomically certain given the state at t that a human being will freely do something, then some free choice must have already been made.

A different way of putting this objection to Frankfurt is from the point of view of a libertarian denial of moral luck. The denial of moral luck holds that once you have willed your deed, how it falls out is irrelevant to assessments of merit or culpability. Attempted murder and murder are equivalent as regards blame, though there are good pragmatic reasons to punish successful murder more harshly in order to give the person who unsuccessfully attempted a murder an incentive not to commit a second attempt. A libertarian who subscribes to the denial of moral luck will say that whenever you are in a position such that were you left alone it is nomically necessary that you would do A, then any culpability or merit you would have for doing A is a culpability or merit you already have, and would have regardless of whether you were prevented from doing A. Therefore, since helping the homeless person would be meritorious when done freely, then being in state V is already equally meritorious.

Thus, the Frankfurt objections to libertarianism fail on two counts. First, they fail to challenge the *possibility* of libertarian freedom, and that is all that is needed for me to answer van Inwagen. Second, they fail to

---

9   See the discussions of these sorts of arguments in Fischer (1999).

show that the libertarian must allow cases in which you did not have an alternative possibility.

7.3.2. Hume

The second kind of objection to libertarianism, going back to Hume, is that a libertarian free action, because it is not determined by the agent's character, is not something for which the agent can be held responsible. As noted earlier, the libertarian can say that whether an action is attributable to the agent as an action depends on the metaphysical relation of causation between the action and the agent or the agent's will or the exercise of the agent's will. It is worth noting now that one idea that drives the "undetermined action" objection to libertarianism is a Humean view of causation as reducible to constant conjunctions, for on that view it only makes sense to attribute an action to a person if it arises from a character whose possession is always conjoined with that kind of action. The libertarian's metaphysical answer is not compatible with a Humean account of causation. But in fact, as we have already noted in Section 2.4, Hume's account of causation is in general not compatible with the PSR – besides being implausible. It is likely that in fact *no* reductionistic account of causation along roughly Humean lines is compatible with libertarianism or the PSR, but such accounts are also likely to fall afoul of the explainability problem that Hume's account falls afoul of: that As are always followed by Bs does not *explain* why some token of A is followed by a token of B.

7.4. SUFFICIENT REASONS

7.4.1. The Objection

Of course, one might also object that the supposedly self-explanatory free-choice-reporting propositions, or else the necessary propositions that explain contingent ones, while giving causes or explanations, do not give "sufficient reasons" in the full sense of the PSR. Certainly this is true if *sufficient reason* is taken to be a "necessitating reason" as in Leibniz. However, if we simply take *sufficient reason* to be a "sufficient explanation" and let our ordinary practices of explanation be a guide to what counts as a sufficient explanation, then the PSR can stand. One can reasonably say that when an event is caused and when we have told all there is to tell about its causes, then we *have* given a sufficient explanation, even if we

142

could not have predicted the event from an account of the causes. If we accept an agent-causation model of causation, then we *can* explain a free will action by saying that it was caused by the agent and by explaining the reasons which the agent was aware of at the time of the action.

7.4.2. The Principle of Disjunctive Causation

7.4.2.a The Principle. One response that can be made is that in the case of an undetermined libertarian-free choice between A and B, the person or her will does not cause one or the other action. Rather, she causally brings it about that either she will do A or she will do B. Suppose she in fact does A. If the state of her will prior to the choice is not sufficient to determine which of the two she will do, then she or her will stands in a causal relation not to the doing of A but to the doing of A or B. What we have explained in the libertarian way is not why she did A, but why she did A or B. I have already argued that this need not follow. That it is impossible to predict from her state which she would choose does not imply that her causal relation to the action does not explain the action.

However, there is a more positive argument to be offered here. It seems plausible that any immediate cause of a disjunctive state of affairs is also the cause of at least one of the disjuncts – indeed, it is a cause of the disjunctive state *by* being a cause of a disjunct state or states. If so, then by being the immediate cause of her doing A or her doing B, the agent is the cause of at least one disjunct; it is not the doing of B, since ex hypothesi she does not do B and one does not cause that which does not happen; thus, it is the doing of A that she causes. And stating the cause of something does explain it.

The preceding Principle of Disjunctive Causation (PDC), stating that one can only count as causing a disjunctive state of affairs by causing one of the disjuncts, besides its innate plausibility, could be backed up further by a conviction that basically there are no disjunctive states or events in concrete reality, and hence they cannot stand in a primitive causal relation. Of course, we can then stipulate that when one causes it to be the case that p, one also causes it to be the case that p-or-q, though this stipulative language will sound somewhat unnatural: it implies that by causing it to be the case that p one "causes" it to be the case that p-or-$\sim p$.

The principle presupposes that it makes sense to distinguish disjunctive from nondisjunctive states. This requires some notion of the naturalness of properties, lest we decompose being massive into the faux disjunctive property of being charged and massive or noncharged and massive.

143

However, such a notion is needed in so many areas of philosophy that this is not a significant liability.

Three objections can be leveled against the PDC-based argument.

7.4.2.b First Objection: Disputing the PDC's Main Claim. One might dispute the PDC's claim that one can only be the immediate cause of a disjunctive state of affairs insofar as one is causing a nondisjunctive one. We may dismiss counterexamples in which the causal influence is not immediate. By tossing a coin, I bring it about that it lands heads up or tails up. But of course I do not *immediately* bring it about. What I *immediately* cause is that my arm should move, or that the coin should go up. This answer presupposes that there is an absolute distinction between what I cause immediately and what I cause mediately, whereas it might be thought that every instance of causation involves an infinite number of intermediate steps, much as in the paradox of Achilles and the tortoise. However, even if this is so, then the PDC can be reformulated to avoid this: Whenever x causes a disjunctive state of affairs, it causes it only by *at least as immediately* causing at least one of the disjuncts.

A better counterexample is the following. Let p be the proposition that my arm moves up. Let q be the proposition that there are aliens in the Tau Ceti system. Consider the disjunctive state of affairs of its either being the case that $(p \& q)$-or-$(p \& \sim q)$. My willing to raise my arm causes this state of affairs to be actual. However, I do not cause either disjunct, for there either are or are not aliens around Tau Ceti. If there are, then I could only have caused $p \& q$, and I certainly did not do so, since I did not cause there to be aliens around Tau Ceti. But neither have I caused there not to be aliens around Tau Ceti, so the horn of the dilemma according to which the Tau Ceti system has no aliens is no more tenable.

In response, observe that it is true that that I raise my arm entails that $(p \& q)$-or-$(p \& \sim q)$. But that my doing A entails p does not mean that I bring it about that p. That I raise my arm entails that $2 + 2 = 4$, but I do not bring it about that $2 + 2 = 4$.

7.4.2.c Second Objection: Denying Indeterministic Causation. Alternately, an objector to my argument might grant the PDC. The PDC implies that if we have a case of something that immediately causes it to be the case that A or B, even without its being determined beforehand which it will be and with the two disjuncts mutually exclusive, then the cause does in fact cause to obtain that disjunct which in fact obtains. But what if in fact there cannot be any such cases of indeterministic causation? If one believes

144

firmly enough that causation cannot be indeterministic, and one accepts the PDC, one will by *modus tollens* conclude that there cannot be a case in which something immediately causes a disjunctive state of affairs with its being undetermined which of the disjuncts it causes. But note that this conclusion is incompatible with some indeterministic interpretations of quantum mechanics, for on these interpretations, we have cases in which an experimental apparatus *causes*, say, an electron to have spin up or spin down, without its being determined ahead of time which it will be. And note that the PDC as applied to this case implies that the experimental setup does cause whichever outcome in fact eventuates.

7.4.2.d Objection Three: Equivocation. Peter Forrest has suggested that the PDC-based argument commits an equivocation. While ordinary usage does allow one to say that (a) a disjunctive state of affairs cannot be caused directly but only through causing a disjunct, and it also allows one to say that (b) where there is a cause, there is an explanation, it does not allow one to say both simultaneously. In other words, *cause* is used equivocally between the two cases. An indeterministic roulette wheel's being spun with angular velocity v causes it to land on 14, Forrest grants, but it is not the sort of cause that entails the existence of an explanation. In the indeterministic case, the wheel's being spun with angular velocity v does not explain the result, our intuitions say.

However, note first that ordinary usage really has no problem with affirming (a) and (b) simultaneously. The sense of *cause* seems exactly the same in both claims. We can think here of our ordinary intuitions about causes' being "productive" of the effects, and we will find (a) and (b) still quite plausible. What ordinary usage does tend to balk at is affirming (a) and (b) together with the explanatory claim about the roulette wheel. This suggests that if there is an equivocation, it is between the case of the roulette wheel and claims (a) and (b). But this will not do either, for in the case of the roulette wheel there is no discomfort of any sort in saying that the wheel's being spun with angular velocity v caused it to land on 00 or 0 or 1 or 2 or . . . or 36, those being all the options.

One way to analyze our attitudes to the case of the roulette wheel is to argue that it is not just the explanatory claim that we find puzzling, but the claim that the wheel's being spun with angular velocity v *caused* it to land on 14, when the result in fact was indeterministic. Thus, (b) is not needed to generate the worry. However, given the eminent plausibility of PDC, this should rather be a worry about how it could both be true that the wheel's being spun with angular velocity v caused the disjunctive result *and* that there was indeterminism as to the exact result. It is well known that intelligent people find indeterminism *itself* surprising and at times paradoxical. People find the adage that insanity is repeatedly doing the same thing while expecting a different result quite plausible. It would not be surprising if residual disbelief of indeterminism were to spill over into disbelief of some of the consequences of indeterminism.

But we can do better than this. Take a case in which the PDC forces us to say that the cause C of A-or-B is also the cause of A. We ought not say that what makes it be the case that C is the cause of A is that A is the actual disjunct of the disjunctive event A-or-B and that this disjunctive event is caused by C. That would get the order of things backward and would be unfaithful to the insight that led to the PDC. The only way C could be the cause of A-or-B is if it were the cause of A, or the cause of B, in a more basic sense. The causal connection with the disjunct is the more primitive one in what Aristotle would call "the order of nature." Thus, just as the PSR is a substantive principle that tells us that where there is a contingent fact there is an explanation, so too the PDC should be seen as a substantive principle that tells us that where there is an indisputable instance of causation of a disjunctive event, there must be a more basic instance of the causation of a disjunct. Since we have confidence that the roulette wheel was caused to land on 00 or 0 or . . . or 36, we therefore can infer that there is a particular number that it was caused to land on, in a more primitive sense of causation.

From this point of view, it is a separate question whether this more primitive sense of causation has to be deterministic or not. If it turns out that our intuitions require it to be deterministic, because we balk at saying that spinning with velocity v indeterministically caused the ball to land on 14, then the PDC provides a substantive argument for determinism in those cases in which we are willing to admit that the disjunctive event does have a cause. However, our discussion of libertarian freedom suggests that genuine instances of causation need not be deterministic. It seems genuinely correct to say that x's choosing on account of R caused action A. The discomfort present in the case of the roulette wheel seems much lesser here, perhaps because a reason R is cited, even if it is a nondetermining reason. If the citing of a reason for action turns out to be essential to the acceptability of indeterministic causal and explanatory claims, then given the PDC or the PSR the only place for indeterminism would seem to be in the actions of persons, and not in basic physics.

But one need not accept that it is essential that a reason for action be cited. If we accept a Jamesian reasonless-choice account of freedom, this is clear. But even if not, there could be some analogy between the case of actions indeterministically chosen by persons and events indeterministically caused by physical phenomena. Causation may, for instance, be a primitive relation as some singularists suppose, and it might well be that the existence of this relation is always explanatory. Or a different analysis of causation might turn out to be right, one on which there still is such explanatoriness. In these cases, our balking at the claim that the spinning of the wheel with velocity v caused it to land at 14 could just be due to our failure to understand that sort of causation in the intimate way we, pace Hume, understand our own causing of actions and the less intimate way we understand deterministic event-causation.

7.5. AN INCREDULOUS STARE

Despite all this, it may just seem a little strange to say that some contingent proposition, of whatever sort, is self-explanatory. But recall from Chapter 1 the way of looking at explanation in terms of the removal of mystery. For instance, learning that x freely chose A for R leaves no mystery about why x freely chose A for R, though there might be a further question of why x took R to be a reason or why x took R to be a reason for doing A. But suppose that we have a case in which there is no puzzlement about why R is taken as a reason for A – maybe we have a case in which the agent is of such a sort as to *essentially* be responsive to R, in the way that Aristotelian theories say a human being is responsive to eudaimonistic reasons or that theism claims God is responsive to the good, and where it is clear why R tells in favor of A.[10] Once we know that x freely chose A for R, there is no room for puzzlement about why this fact is so, modulo questions about why x existed, was free, and had the reasons she had. We can read off the explanation right from the fact.

Note that if we look at explanation in this way, then we can subsume under the standard view of the explanans as being a proposition the idea of agents as explaining freely willed actions, for the libertarian agent-causation theorist will agree that if one knows that x freely chose A for R, then there is no further mystery there to be dispelled. Reference to the agent has already been made: we are told *the agent* made an exercise of free

---

10 Cases in which we are puzzled about a particularly evil action a person did are, I take it, often instances in which we are puzzled by what sort of a reason she may have acted on, or in which we do not know why she took a consideration to be a reason, or in which it is opaque to us how this consideration tells in favor of the action.

will in favor of A under the nonnecessitating influence of R. The crucial issue is that the libertarian of whatever stripe, whether an agent-causal theorist or not, needs to say that once one knows who did A and because of what reason, there is no further mystery about why A was done for that reason. If there were, then the action's roots would in part be a brute mystery and not the agent's choice.

7.6. CONTRASTIVE EXPLANATIONS?

A common objection to the preceding attempts at explanation is that while they may explain why the agent did A, they do not explain why she did A rather than the incompatible action A^* for which she had reason R^*.

7.6.1. "Rather Than" Sentences

First I will show how the defender of the PSR can concede this. Yes, there is such a thing as contrastive explanation: "Why is it that p rather than p^*?" But there is also *propositional* explanation, explanation of p. Take a standard case. "Why did Fred eat the banana?" Without a contrast class, the request for explanation is ambiguous between, say, "Why did Fred eat the banana rather than the apple?" and "Why did Fred eat the banana rather than sit on it?" To the first, one might answer that Fred preferred the banana to the apple, and to the latter, that he was hungry and eating rather than sitting satisfies hunger.

It is commonly alleged that there is something more to explaining why p *rather than* q holds, something that goes beyond explaining why p holds and why $\sim q$ holds. Moreover, it is alleged, that Fred freely was impressed with R may explain why Fred did A, but not why he chose to do A rather than A^*, where there is some other reason, R^*, that Fred in fact was impressed by and that militated in favor of A^*. I could bite the bullet. That Fred was impressed by R explains why he did A rather than A^*. If he had instead freely chosen to do A^*, then although it would have been no less true that he was impressed by R, his doing A^* rather than A would have been explained by his being impressed by R^*.

However, I can reject the explanatory demand by saying that it does not arise out of a demand for explanation of a *proposition*. I never claimed that every "Why is it that p rather than p^*?" question about contingent matters has an answer. Rather, every "Why is it the case that p?" question about contingent matters has an answer. Every contingent proposition has an explanation, but "that p rather than p^*" is not a proposition or else does not express a different proposition from p & $\sim p^*$. But if p^* is incompatible with p, then there does not seem to be anything more to explain in the proposition that p & $\sim p^*$ than just to explain p and show the incompatibility of p and p^*. The "rather than" has the pragmatic force of showing what kind of an explanation we are looking for instead of affirming a different kind of state of affairs.

I now need to argue for the claim that what makes for the difference between "p rather than q holds" and "p & $\sim q$" is not that they express different propositions, but either that the first does not express a proposition at all, or that it expresses the same proposition as the second but also has a force that goes beyond the expression of a proposition.

Let us look at the distinctive force of "p rather than q." What are the truth conditions? It is clearly necessary for the truth of "p rather than q" that p be true and q be false. Can we say anything more? The following sounds very strange:

(74) It is the case that the dinosaurs are extinct rather than that the Moon is made of blue cheese.

But is this false? First, observe that in some circumstances, and not ones that differ in respect of dinosaurs and the Moon, (74) is assertible. For instance, suppose I tell you that exactly one of the following propositions is true:

(75) that the dinosaurs are extinct
(76) that the Moon is made of blue cheese.

I then ask you which one and you might well respond with (74).

At the same time, under ordinary circumstances, (74) does not appear to be assertible. But I will argue that it does not appear correct to say that under ordinary circumstances, (74) is false. For if it were, then we would have to say that under the circumstances in which you have been told that exactly one of (75) and (76) holds, it is no longer false. And were it false even under these circumstances, it would not be assertible then except by someone ignorant of some relevant fact, and yet under these circumstances no ignorance of a relevant fact is needed for assertibility. Hence, if ordinarily (74) is false, then (74) makes a nontrivial claim about the circumstances that goes over and beyond the truth of (75) and falsity of (76). Presumably this is some claim that implies that either subjectively or objectively there is some kind of a choice to be made between (75) and (76) – that somehow they are *alternatives*.

In other words, it seems that if one takes (74) to be ordinarily false, then a partial analysis of "p rather than q" is that it entails something like the proposition that

(77) p & $\sim q$ and the propositions p and q are "alternatives."

But now consider the strangeness of saying, under ordinary circumstances,

(78) It is not the case that (75) rather than (76) holds. But were you to have told me that exactly one of these two claims holds, then it would have been the case that the dinosaurs are extinct rather than that the Moon is made of blue cheese.

Yet on the interpretation we are now trying out, (78) is actually true under ordinary circumstances. Consider now my special circumstances in which (74) is appropriate. The following strange claim would then be true:

(79) Although it is the case that the dinosaurs are extinct rather than that the Moon is made of blue cheese, this would not have been the case had we not spoken with one another.

This is so because for had we not spoken with one another, (75) and (76) would not have been "alternatives."

Moreover, on this interpretation and under these special circumstances, to explain why (75) rather than (76) holds would require that I explain why it is that (75) and (76) are "alternatives." Thus, an explanation of why (75) rather than (76) holds would be something like the following:

(80) The dinosaurs became extinct because of a massive asteroid impact, the Moon is not made of blue cheese because it came into existence out of rocklike material and blue cheese is not made out of this kind of material, and you had told me that either the dinosaurs are extinct or the Moon is made of blue cheese, but not both.

Surely the phrase "and you had told me . . . but not both" is an interloper here. Note, too, that if we took (77) to be a *complete* analysis of "p rather than q," then interestingly, there would be no great difficulty in offering an explanation of why Frank did A rather than A^*: we would just have to explain why he did A and why it is that A and A^* were "alternatives."

Thus it does not appear that distinction between the cases in which (74) is or is not appropriate is marked by a difference in truth value. Moreover, we have seen that under ordinary circumstances (74) is not false. If it expresses a proposition and is not false, then given classical logic, it is true. Let us suppose, for now, that (74) does express a proposition. Then, it is true. Generalizing, since nothing in the argument depended on the special structure of the example, it follows that the truth conditions for "p rather than q" are the same as those for "p & $\sim q$." In particular, the proposition that p & $\sim q$ entails the proposition that p *rather than q*.

We can now make the following move. Suppose that r entails s, and we have a proposition u that gives a complete explanation of why r holds and why r entails s. Then it is highly plausible that u explains why s holds. This is not the case for incomplete explanations, ones that explain only one part of r. I cannot leverage an explanation of why Jane killed Bob and why it is that the claim that Jane killed Bob entails the claim that Bob existed into an explanation of why Bob existed. But that is because, typically, my explanation of why Jane killed Bob does not explain a certain aspect of the situation reported by the proposition that Jane killed Bob, namely, why Bob exists. A complete explanation of why Jane killed Bob would explain how every aspect of the reported situation came about, and hence would explain why Jane and Bob existed.

If this is correct, then a PSR for noncontrastive propositions entails a PSR for contrastive propositions, and indeed we can construct explanations of contrastive propositions for free out of complete explanations of noncontrastive propositions combined with some facts about language that explain why p & $\sim q$ entails that p *rather than q*. An obvious objection, however, is that the whole point of introducing the contrastive propositions was to highlight the fact that in the cases of interest, complete explanations have not been offered.

I can grant this objection, however, and offer another principle. Given an explanation of why it is that necessarily r holds if and only if s holds, and an explanation (even an incomplete one) of why it is that r holds, I can produce out of them an explanation of why it is that s holds. Since on the hypothesis currently under examination, "p & $\sim q$" has the same truth conditions as "p rather than q," this principle would also be enough to get us contrastive explanations for free out of noncontrastive ones. Again, however, there seem to be counterexamples to the principle. For instance, that Jane thought Bob was trying to kill her explains why Jane killed Bob, but we cannot leverage ourselves from this to an explanation of why *Jane killed Bob and Bob existed*, even though we know why exactly the truth conditions for the latter are the same as for "Jane killed Bob." Here, however, it does not appear so painful to bite the bullet. For instance, we can say, "That Jane thought Bob was trying to kill her and that Bob existed explains why Jane killed Bob and Bob existed." Of course, we

151

have not explained everything there is to be explained – that is why this is an incomplete explanation – but we have done enough to get out of the apparent counterexample.

Thus, the hypothesis that "p & $\sim q$" and "p rather than q" have the same truth conditions does give a way out of the difficulty for the defender of the PSR. Since the hypothesis follows from the claim that *that p rather than q* is a proposition, and since the difficulty does not arise if the claim does not hold, this is quite satisfactory. But let us suppose that the reader does not accept either my entailment or my "if and only if" principle. Is there any way out for the defender of the PSR?

Well, consider that one natural way of making sense of what we have arrived at on the assumption that rather-than claims express propositions would be to say that "p & $\sim q$" and "p rather than q" express the same proposition but differ in implicature. Thus, it is not appropriate to say "p rather than q" when p and q do not count as "alternatives," but the proposition *that p rather than q* does not say that they are alternatives. I would now like to argue that this natural solution is actually correct. For suppose it is not. Then, the claim *that p rather than q* tells us something about reality, something else than the mere claim p & $\sim q$. It is intuitively clear that if this is so, then in fact the claim that *p rather than q* is *richer* rather than poorer. It adds something of a propositional nature. Intuitively, what it adds is a certain kind of emphasis on p's occurring despite the real alternative that q offered. But any attempt to state something like this would make the proposition *that p rather than q* entail that p and q are "alternatives," and we have already seen that there is no such entailment.

Since the claim (74) needs to be taken to be true even under ordinary circumstances, assuming that *that p rather than q* is a proposition, our explanation of what it is that the claim *that p rather than q* adds to the claim p & $\sim q$ cannot rely on the assumption of some kind of a contrast between p and q. Of course, we can try conditionalizing on this assumption and saying that "p rather than q" means

(81) p & $\sim q$ and if p and q are some sorts of "alternatives," then p occurred despite the "opposition" (epistemic or objective) of q.

This would mean that while (74) is true both under the ordinary and the contrived circumstances, it is true on account of different situations' obtaining in the two cases. In the ordinary case, it is true on account of the facts that the dinosaurs are extinct while the Moon is not made of blue cheese. In the contrived case, it is true on account of these facts together with the fact that of the two alternative propositions you offered me, the first one was the correct one.

This account is needlessly complex. It seems much simpler just to deny that there is a difference in propositions expressed between "p & $\sim q$" and "p rather than q" and to find the difference in something pragmatic. Moreover, not only is the account needlessly complex, but it is implausible, for it is implausible to say under ordinary circumstances

(82) It is the case that the dinosaurs are extinct rather than that the Moon is made of blue cheese. This would still have been so even if you had written down the two claims (75) and (76), but it would have been true on account of something further then.

It does seem, thus, that we should not mark the distinctive force of "p rather than q" in terms of a propositional difference from p & $\sim q$. This is compatible with the claim, congenial to the defender of the PSR, that the two express the same proposition, and it is compatible with the equally congenial claim that "p rather than q" does not express a proposition.

7.6.2. Isn't All Explanation Contrastive?

But this response misses the point, it will be contended. *All* explanation is contrastive. Thus, it makes no sense to explain merely p. One needs to specify which aspect of p is to be explained. However, in defense of the existence of nonconstrastive explanation one can say that as long as one explains *any one* aspect of the proposition and transfers the other aspects to the explanans, one can count as having given an explanation of the proposition. The explanation will not be ultimate or even complete in this case. But it will be an explanation. For instance, one can explain why Fred ate the banana by saying that Fred chose to eat the banana because he was hungry. This is neither an ultimate nor a complete explanation, since it leaves unexplained why it was the banana that he chose to eat. But this point gets transferred to the explanans: "Fred chose to eat the banana because he was hungry." The PSR restricted to propositions then applies once again to this explanans. And it may be that when explaining this explanans one will have to mention Fred's preference for bananas over apples.

In other words, one can say that one has explained a proposition, though neither ultimately nor completely, as long as one has explained one aspect of the reported state of affairs and transferred the mystery about the other aspects to the explanans. But then the propositional PSR can be invoked again for the explanans. In fact, by employing chains of explanations in this way, one will end up explaining all the mysterious aspects just through propositional explanation. This suggests that the standard propositional PSR is really just as strong as a PSR calling for the explanation of all particular aspects of states of affairs and is meaningful if the latter is. (Compare a similar argument made in the Introduction.) Nonetheless, it may be that neither is quite as strong as a contrastive PSR – the defender of the propositional PSR is free to concede that without going on to defend the stronger principle.

7.6.3. No Concession

However, I need not make the concession that the version of the PSR that I am defending does not require contrastive explanations. I have already claimed that in the kind of case at issue, the proposition that the agent was impressed with R could be reasonably taken to explain why she acted on R *rather than* on R^*. It is true that had she acted on R^*, then that she was impressed with R^* would have explained why she acted on R^* rather than on R, and it is further true that she was impressed with *both* R and R^*. This way of talking seems quite consistent with ordinary language and is a part of ordinary language that a libertarian should retain despite compatibilist critique: she did this because of R and if she acted otherwise it would have been because of R^*. At the same time, once one is dealing with contrastive explanation, one should not say that that she was impressed with R and R^* explains why she acted on R. In the case of a contrastive explanation, the explanans must make for some contrast between the alternatives. But it need not be true, appearances to the contrary, that the explanans must be such that it would have been false had the relevant possibility alternate to the explanandum been true.

This was on the account that it is the reasons that do the explaining. On the self-explanatory account, we can also handle contrastive cases. Take first the Jamesian case. Why did Fred do A rather than A^*? Well, Fred did A rather than A^* because he freely chose A rather than choosing A^*. Why did Fred freely choose A rather than A^*? This is self-explanatory, modulo the question of why Fred existed and was free: once you know that he freely chose A rather than A^*, you know why this happened. Our libertarian cannot admit that there is something unexplained here because to do that would be to succumb to the randomness objection. And the same can be said about the non-Jamesian case in which it is self-explanatory, modulo existence, freedom, and antecedent value judgments, that Fred freely chose A for R.

Note that the "modulo" here is something that may require further clarification that we are now in a position to supply. An explanation of p modulo q is a nonfull explanation of p: it fails to explain one aspect of the state of affairs that p reports, the aspect being the state of affairs that q reports. To get a full explanation of p, one needs to take the explanation of p modulo q and add in a full explanation of q.

7.7. THE MODESTY OF THIS ACCOUNT AND SOME ALTERNATIVES

7.7.1. The Modesty Objection

This account of explanation appears to be rather weak. One might naturally say that the strength of an explanation, q, of p is measured by the conditional probability $P(p \mid q)$. But, as Peter Forrest has noted, my account of explanation allows for this probability to be quite small, and the "explanation" afforded is thus quite modest. For instance, suppose God chooses to create some one world from a set B of worlds of cardinality κ but has no reason to prefer one to another. This seems to be a coherent possibility, and it appears that on my account of explanation, God's making a free choice about what world from B to actualize will explain why w_0 is actual. If κ is infinite, then the probability that w_0 would be actualized is going to be infinitesimal, however, and so the explanation is very modest.

However, whether this would indeed count as an explanation on my account depends on whether one takes the reasonless model of free choice or not. The Forrest objection applies only on the reasonless model, since on the reasoned model to explain why w_0 is actual, one would have to state what reason favored w_0 over the other worlds, and so the reasoned model of free choice explanation rejects the possibility of a situation as described by Forrest. One might think that this is so much the worse for my account, since the situation Forrest describes is plainly possible. But that possibility is not completely obvious: one might think that, objectively, each possible world would have some distinctive considerations in its favor and some distinctive ones against it, and God could choose to actualize w_0 on the basis of the reasons in favor of it. We will discuss related issues in Chapter 9, but here it is worth noting that the reasons could be analogous to artistic ones.

An artist could choose between two potential works of art she could create not on the grounds of one work's being overall better than another, but simply on account of one work of art's exhibiting such and such a valuable feature (in a wide sense of *valuable*) that the other does not exhibit, even if the other work exhibits other features, equally or more valuable. Thus an artist producing an abstract painting may choose to exemplify rectangularity in some position because of the unique value that the rectangularity serves, a value incommensurable with the value that circularity would have served there. Had this artist chosen to exemplify circularity, the unique value that circularity served would have been the reason. And the explanation in terms of this value is a genuine explanation even if there are infinitely many other values that could have been served. Why this feature and not another? Because of the value of *this* feature.

7.7.2. Could We Require High Probabilities?

On either model of free choice I need to bite the bullet and insist that the sufficiency of an explanation has little to do with the probabilities induced. I am defending the necessity of the PSR. Suppose Jones chooses to do A on account of reason R and we have a very strong explanation, so that the probability that given the antecedent conditions he would choose to do A is very high. Still, on libertarian grounds we need to say that in the same circumstances he still could have chosen not to do A. The probability of that choice would, then, have been very low. But a PSR that has necessity would require that it be given an explanation, and since the action was free, the explanation would have to involve Jones's improbable free choice. It does not seem, thus, that a libertarian can coherently accept a PSR that involves a high degree of probabilistic connection between the antecedent conditions and the eventual action.

One might try an account that is careful about choosing on what the probabilities are conditional. Thus, suppose that when Jones chooses to do A it is on account of R, while not doing A would have been on account of R^*. The choice is made in circumstances C in which Jones is impressed by both R and R^*. Then, we can insist that the explanation involves *just* Jones's being impressed by R and does not at all include C. Thus, what is high is $P(\text{Jones does } A \mid \text{Jones is impressed by } R)$. But while it would be incoherent to say that both $P(\text{Jones does } A \mid C)$ and $P(\text{Jones does not do } A \mid C)$ are high, there is no incoherence in saying that $P(\text{Jones does } A \mid \text{Jones is impressed by } R)$ and $P(\text{Jones does not do } A \mid \text{Jones is impressed by } R^*)$ are both high. Thus, perhaps, the condition of high probability *can* be coherently required. However, this only pushes the problem further back. To counter the fatalism argument, we are interested in the case in

156

which Jones is actually God and the choice is the first free choice ever made. Now, the only way that P(God does A | God is impressed by R) and P(God does not do A | God is impressed by R^*) can both be relatively high is if P(God is impressed by R^* and God is impressed by R) is relatively low.[11] But what, then, explains the conjunction of God's being impressed by both R and R^*? Since the probability is low, the conjunction is a contingent claim. Since the choice whether to do A or not is the first choice in the explanatory order, we cannot explain this contingent claim in terms of an earlier choice. Nor can we simply say, "It is explained by its being probable," since it is *not* probable.

Thus, the defender of the PSR must insist that what gives sufficiency to explanations is that mystery is taken away, for example, through the citing of relevant reasons, not that probability is increased. Observe that mere high probability does not take away mystery. For there is nothing innately more *mysterious* about a low-probability event than a high-probability event. It is no more mysterious that Smith wins the lottery than that he loses it.

7.7.3. Morris's PSR

Consider the following version of the PSR, inspired by ideas of Forrest that he in turn attributes to Thomas V. Morris. Say that q is a "maximal explanation" of degree 1 of p provided that q is a strong explanation, that is, one in which the probability of the explanandum given the explanans is at least $1 - \varepsilon$, where ε is an infinitesimal. Then say that q is a "maximal explanation" of degree n provided that q explains p at least modestly, and there is a maximal explanation of degree $n - 1$ for why there is no stronger explanation, if $n > 1$. We say that q is a maximal explanation if it is a maximal explanation of degree n for some finite n. Again, the strength of explanation is measured probabilistically. *Modest explanation* here is the term for the kind of explanation I defend in the context of the PSR, though I do not endorse this description. The Maximal PSR

---

11 Let B be the event that God does A and let D and D^* be, respectively, the events that God is impressed by R and by R^*. Then $P(B \mid D) = P(B \mid D \ \& \sim D^*)P(D \ \& \sim D^*) + P(B \mid D \ \& \ D^*)P(D \ \& \ D^*)$ and $P(\sim B \mid D^*) = P(\sim B \mid \sim D \ \& \ D^*)P(\sim D \ \& \ D^*) + P(\sim B \mid D \ \& \ D^*)P(D \ \& \ D^*)$. Without loss of generality, suppose $P(B \mid D \ \& \ D^*) \leq 1/2$. (The argument in the opposite case is essentially the same, but with starred and unstarred events interchanged and with B and $\sim B$ interchanged.) Let $p = P(D \ \& \ D^*)$. Then, $P(B \mid D) \leq (1 - p) + p/2 = 1 - p/2$. Thus if $P(B \mid D)$ is high, say, 0.9, then p must be low, in this case no more than 0.2.

then states that there has to be a maximal explanation of each contingently true proposition.

However, the notion of a maximal explanation does not seem to fit well with intuitive notions of informative explanation. Suppose that we are in a possible world of musicians and painters where each couple when conceiving a child decides indeterministically, through direct biological control over genetic material, whether the child would have a strong love for music or a strong love for painting. Surprisingly, parents' choices have no correlation with their own artistic preferences: both kinds of children have probability 50 percent. The children then make a career choice at age eighteen, and 90 percent of the time choose in accordance with their love for the particular kind of art, whether music or painting. Now Bob and Jane's son chooses music despite having a love for painting. He does so on account of his appreciation of the objective value of music, an appreciation that is weaker than his appreciation for painting. What I have just given is surely the most informative explanation that can be given. But it is not the strongest in the probabilistic sense, since it is a 10 percent probability explanation, while if we take the situation back to just before the child's conception, we can give a 50 percent probability explanation, since at that time the probability that the child would become a musician was 50 percent. The latter explanation is "stronger," but it is surely less informative. It does not enlighten us as much. This is yet another aspect of the fact that explanation is not prediction.

7.8. CONCLUSIONS

Seemingly, I gave three accounts of how to reconcile libertarian free will with the PSR. But only two of them are substantially distinct. On the one hand, we have the Jamesian reasonless-choice account. On the other hand, we have a perhaps more satisfying reasoned-choice account. This account has two versions: Either we say that *that x freely chose A for R* is self-explanatory modulo the explanation of why *x* existed, was free on the occasion, and was impressed by *R*, or else we say that *that x freely chose A* is explained by some claim such as *that x was impressed by R* or *that x chose freely while impressed by R*. The two versions amount to the same thing: they both say that once we have said that *x* freely chose *A* for *R*, then the only thing left that is unexplained is why *x* existed and was both free and attracted by *R*. The difference between the two versions seems to come down to a preference for the way one phrases explanations. But there is a substantial difference between a reasoned-choice model and a reasonless-choice model. And while one can defend the compatibility of both with the PSR, the reasoned-choice model appears more satisfying explanatorily.

Note, however, that if the defender of the PSR insists that we must opt for the reasoned-choice account, not just because – as seems very likely – it is a better account of free will, but because only it is compatible with the PSR, then it seems she will have to dismiss the possibility of indeterministic effects where there are no agents involved and would also ultimately have to acknowledge that the PSR plus the denial of fatalism entails the existence of God. If one wished both to acknowledge the fact that *x freely chose A* is unsatisfactory as a self-explanation *and* leave open the door for indeterminism in cases in which there is no agency, one could, however, say that the reason *x freely chose A* is unsatisfactory as a self-explanation is that we know that the sort of causation involved in "freely doing" requires reasons, and this knowledge makes us request a reason, whereas in nonagential cases we would not need to.

Now, even if all of what I said about free will is disputed, if it is insisted that in fact we do not give a sufficient reason in the full sense by giving an indeterministic cause even in reasoned-choice models, one can give one final response: We can rename the PSR as the Principle of Good Explanation. In any case, even with these provisos on the understanding of *explanation*, provisos ensuring that libertarian free will explanations are recognized as explanations, the PSR remains a nontrivial principle: indeed, it would arguably be a principle strong enough to imply the necessary existence of a Creator along the lines described in Chapter 4.

Thus, we can escape the apparent incompatibility between the PSR and libertarian free will either by renaming the PSR or by accepting one of the concrete proposals for the way libertarian-free actions can be explained. Alternately, instead of accepting a concrete proposal, we might accept that the libertarian account of free will is true and also accept the argument that a libertarianism incompatible with the PSR would be deeply implausible as it would succumb to the randomness objection.

8

Quantum Mechanics

Since all experiments are subjected to the laws of quantum mechanics, the invalidity of the law of causality is definitively proved by quantum mechanics.

(Heisenberg, 1927, p. 197, trans. in Stern, 1969, p. 132)[1]

8.1. THE PROBLEM OF INDETERMINISM

If quantum mechanics is correct, on whatever interpretation, there are experimental setups such that no amount of observational knowledge of the initial system could possibly predict the outcome. An electron goes through a magnetic field in the Stern-Gerlach experiment in a superposed spin state |UP> + |DOWN>. It will take an upward or downward path through the magnetic field, and if quantum mechanics is correct, no observation of its physical configuration prior to the performance of this kind of experiment can possibly reveal which it will be.

The standard indeterministic interpretation of quantum mechanics has it that not only can no observation of the prior physical properties of the system, including of the electron, allow us to predict the outcome of the

---

1 It is interesting that the argument Heisenberg has in mind for this conclusion may in fact be quite fallacious. Heisenberg writes: "In the sharp formulation of the law of causality: 'when we know the present with precision we can calculate the future,' not the conclusion is wrong, but the premise. On principle we *cannot* know the present in all its determining factors" (Heisenberg, 1927, p. 197, trans. in Stern, 1969, p. 132). But a conditional is not falsified by the falsity of its antecedent. Of course, to be charitable, on positivistic grounds one might well think that the impossibility of knowing a fact of the matter sufficient to determine the future entails the nonexistence of such a fact of the matter, and Heisenberg does write: "[O]ne might be led to the conjecture that behind the perceived, statistical world, a 'real' world is hidden, which is governed by the law of causality. But such speculations seem to us sterile and meaningless – and we wish to emphasize this opinion. Physics is only supposed to describe the connection of perceptions in a formal way" (ibid.).

experiment, but that the system lacks any physical properties, observable or not, such that were they known ahead of time, we would know what the outcome is. In other words, on this interpretation, two quantum mechanical systems that start with exactly the same intrinsic properties can behave in different ways. This is indeterminism. It is seen as challenging the PSR for exactly the reason libertarian free will is, but more deeply because the defender of libertarian free will can allow for indeterministic explanations involving the reasons for one action rather than another.

The problem, then, is that it seems we cannot explain why the electron goes one way rather than another. There is an additional problem, however, in that as we shall soon see, quantum mechanics involves correlations that do not appear to have a causal explanation.[2]

8.2. REJECTING INDETERMINISM

One response is to reject the indeterministic interpretation of quantum mechanics. An interpretation of quantum mechanics is an account of the reality described, perhaps only partially, by the physical theory, consistent with all the observational predictions that the theory makes. A different interpretation of quantum mechanics will be just as compatible with the observational predictions, and hence there will be no observational reason to prefer one to the other.

The simplest way to reject the indeterministic interpretation of quantum mechanics is to argue that this interpretation is logically untenable. If an electron will take the upward path in the experiment, then the electron has the property of being such that it will go upward. While this is correct, it misses the point of the interpretation and is useless as a defense of the PSR. For the proposition that the electron has this property says nothing other than *that the electron exists now and will go up*, a proposition that can only explain why the electron will go up if it is self-explanatory, at least given the electron's existence, that it will go up. But this proposition is not self-explanatory, and hence the PSR is not saved by this argument. Moreover, this objection against the indeterministic interpretation fails because it neglects the fact that that interpretation said there was no *intrinsic* property of the system in virtue of which the outcome could, in principle, be predicted.

---

2   I am grateful to Peter Forrest for pointing out to me that this is a separate challenge to the PSR.

8.2.1. Dispositions

One might, however, offer a different alternative to the indeterministic interpretation. The electron, let us suppose, will in fact go up. Then, it has the *dispositional* property of being such that *were the experiment done, it would go up*. This dispositional property, if the proposition that the electron has it is not taken to be a mere restatement of the proposition that the electron will go up, certainly seems to be the sort of property the having of which can figure in the explanation of why the electron will go up. Or, instead of positing a bare property of being such that were the experiment done it would go up, a property that might be thought to have too much of a resemblance for scientific respectability to the *virtus dormitiva* explaining why opium makes one drowsy, one might come up with a more elaborate theory of the internal unobservable properties of the electron in virtue of which the electron is such that were the experiment done it would go up. David Bohm's interpretation of quantum mechanics claims to provide such a theory.

8.2.2. The EPR Problem

It would seem that none of this should be a problem. At the very least, we could cheaply posit the bare dispositional property, the tendency for upward movement through the Stern–Gerlach experiment. One might have some verificationist objections, but a verificationism that does not allow for dispositional properties has little chance of being right anyway. The real problem is that if we are not careful, positing such dispositional properties will in fact lead to different experimental predictions than standard quantum mechanics, predictions that in fact have been experimentally falsified. Einstein, Podolsky, and Rosen (EPR) proposed a certain scenario, in an attempt to prove quantum mechanics on the standard interpretation incomplete. Considerations based on this scenario have been used in conjunction with Bell's inequality to oppose the dispositional property solution.

Following Mermin (1981, 1985), a simple setup for EPR correlations can be described as follows, as consisting of three disconnected and widely separated pieces. In the middle, there is an emitter, from which emerge two particles, one on each side. The two particles go to two detectors set up some distance to the left and right, respectively, of the emitter. Each detector has an adjustable dial with three settings, A, B, and C, and two lights, red (R) and green (G). Each time the particle from the

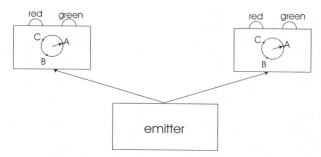

Figure 1. The experimental setup for EPR correlations

emitter enters a detector, one of its two lights will flash. The dials are set independently and randomly with all possible combinations of dial settings being equally likely (see Figure 1).

Moreover, the flashes have the following properties:

(83) When the two dials have the same setting, the same color of light will flash on both detectors. There is no way of predicting whether the common color will be red or green; both colors occur equally often statistically, and indeed on different runs on which the two dials have equal settings the color is seen to be statistically random.[3]

(84) Overall (without conditioning on dial settings), the pairs of flashes RR, RG, GR, and GG are all equally likely, unpredictable, and independent on successive runs: each has probability 1/4.

It just is a fact about quantum mechanics that we can come up with a setup having this essential structure.

Consider any one run on the dispositional-property interpretation. Then, the left particle has three dispositional properties, U_A, U_B, and U_C, which specify which color of flash would result were the left dial turned to A, B, or C, respectively. The right particle likewise has three dispositional properties, V_A, V_B, and V_C, which specify which color would result were the right dial turned to A, B, or C, respectively. Because of (83), it seems we have to suppose that for $i = $ A, B, C, the property U_i codes for green if and only if V_i codes for green, and likewise in the case of red the two properties code for the same color.

3   More precisely, if C_n is the common color on run n and $D_n(S)$ is the event that the dials have the same specific state S on run n, then $P(C_n = R \mid D_n(S)) = P(C_n = G \mid D_n(S)) = 1/2$.

163

Thus, when the two particles leave the central transmitter, the properties U_A, U_B, and U_C of the first match up, respectively, with the properties V_A, V_B, and V_C of the second. Unfortunately, a special case of a result known as Bell's inequality shows that this contradicts the conjunction of (83) and (84). For we can now think of the central system as producing codings for triples of colors, say, the triple GRG, when the particles are such that U_A and V_A both code for green, U_B and V_B both code for red, and U_C and V_C both code for green.

Within our experimental setup, let E now be the event that both flashes are of the same color. (Recall that the dials are set randomly.) Observe that the probability of E given the central emitter's producing a system dispositionally coded for the triple GRG can be computed as follows. The dials are set randomly and independently. Thus, there are nine equally likely pairs of dial settings, AA, AB, AC, BA, BB, BC, CA, CB, and CC. With the coding GRG from the transmitter, only five of them, namely, AA, AC, BB, CA, and CC, will yield E, that is, the same color. For instance, the pair AC will yield it because with the coding GRG, we will have U_A code for green, and V_C also code for green. Thus, E given the coding GRG is achieved at exactly five of the nine settings, and hence the probability of E given GRG is 5/9. The same is true for any other coding in which the three colors in the coding are not the same. On the other hand, the probability of E given the coding GGG or the coding RRR is 1. Therefore, the probability of E given any one specific coding will be 1 if the coding has all colors same and will be 5/9 on any other coding. Hence,

(85) $P(E) \geq 5/9$.

Thus, the lights will flash the same color in at least 5/9 of the experiments.[4] But by (84) they will do so in half of the experiments. Therefore, $1/2 \geq 5/9$, and that is absurd.

This means that there are correlations between the measurements at the two receivers that cannot be explained in terms of a common cause. This both challenges the idea that one might explain away the indeterminism of quantum mechanics by positing hidden dispositional properties and produces another challenge to the PSR: What explains the correlations between the results observed at the two receivers?

---

4 This proof is due to Mermin (1985, pp. 43–44).

8.2.3. Locality

It seems to follow that there cannot be any dispositional properties of the particles that explain why the results are as they are. There is, however, one part of the preceding argument that can be challenged. I wrote that it seemed that because of (83), the dispositional properties of the two particles had to be correlated in such a way that, say, when U_A was such that were the left dial turned to A, green would result, then likewise V_A would be such that were the right dial turned to A, green would result, and likewise for all other dial numbers and colors. The argument for this claim can be spelled out as follows. Suppose, for a reductio, that in some run of the experiment U_A was such that green would result were the left dial turned to A, while V_A was such that red would result were the right dial turned to A. Now it might seem at first sight that this contradicts (83), which claims that same colors result from same dial settings. However, there is no straightforward contradiction here, for it might be that in this run of the experiment, in fact, even though the particles have properties as described, the two dials will not in fact be both turned to A.

If we added the further assumption that what dispositional properties the particles have does not depend on whether the dials are set to measure these properties, then we would indeed get a contradiction to (83), for then the assumed setup in which U_A coded for green while V_A coded for red could indeed have physically occurred were both dials set to A, and a contradiction to (83) would ensue. This further assumption can be broken up into two subassumptions. The first states that what dispositional properties one particle has in no way depends on how the dial will be set. This is a straightforward consequence of the fact that we are dealing with dispositional properties about what the particle *would* do were the dial set a certain way – those dispositional properties cannot depend on whether the dial is in fact set that way. The second is *locality*: what dispositional properties one particle has cannot depend on how the other, widely separated dial is set. If there could be such dependence, then we could always say that once the left dial were set to, say, B, then the opposite particle would "learn" that it should have a dispositional property to produce the same color, were the right dial set to B, as the first particle is going to produce.

Locality is not a metaphysically necessary condition. Newton's theory of gravity was nonlocal: what one particle in one corner of the universe did affected what happened to another particle in another corner of the

165

universe instantaneously. This is more problematic given relativity theory. First of all, relativity theory says that no signal can travel faster than light. However, the setup described cannot in fact be used for actual *signaling*, as it turns out – one cannot use the dials on one end to transmit information to the other end. It is true that at the other end the same color will result *if* the dials are set the same way, but a person at the other end cannot know whether the dials are set the same way. And if one just decrees ahead of time that the dials are to be set in the same way, then no information can be transmitted from one receiver to the other: the two receivers will flash the same color, but there is no control that anyone at either receiver has over what color that will be, and such control would be needed for signaling.

More seriously, however, instantaneous action at a distance given relativity theory is closely akin to backward causation, for if A and B are simultaneous spatially separated events in one reference frame and A causes B, then we can find another reference frame in which in fact B is earlier than A. Hence, there will be backward causation in some reference frames if there is simultaneous causation in any one reference frame, unless one is willing to say that which event causes which depends on the reference frame. But the latter conclusion would be unsatisfactory vis-à-vis a concept of causation that is objectively explanatory. Of course one might simply suppose an absolute reference frame, say, one identified with naturally defined "surfaces of homogeneity" (Smith, 2002).

However, one might be willing to tolerate a modicum of backward causation – for instance, backward causation of B by A when A is later than B in some but not all reference frames (i.e., when A and B are "spacelike" separated) – if this backward causation is unable to give rise to paradoxes, and the fact that one cannot instantaneously *send* signals from one receiver to another suggests that paradoxes will not result. Or, alternately, one might simply posit that there *is* an absolute reference frame, and the fact that A is later than B in some reference frames is unproblematic if A is not later than B in the specially distinguished absolute reference frame. And while this would indeed be contrary to the spirit of relativity theory, it would be compatible with all the observational consequences of relativity theory – for we could not observationally *tell* which reference frame was in fact the absolute one.

All of these solutions would seem to allow for the possibility that one might have some kind of a deterministic quantum mechanics and to explain the EPR correlations.

8.2.4. The Conceptual Possibility of Deterministic Quantum Mechanics

Accounts of quantum mechanics that make it deterministic by positing certain dispositional properties or lower-level unobservable properties that ground these dispositional properties are known as *hidden variable* theories. Currently, the most serious such theories are the Bohmian ones, though there is currently no fully relativistic Bohmian theory, and there are problems facing extension of Bohmian theories to quantum field theory.

The technical problem lies in formulating a precise scientific theory that gives correct observational results in line with quantum theory and that is not ad hoc. If all we want is to see that it is *conceptually* possible to have a deterministic theory that gives the same observational results as quantum mechanics, it is easy to see that this can be done. For instance, take a neo–Leibnizian theory that says that every point of space is a monad, and this monad has encoded within it a list of all the events that will happen throughout time at that point, and through an internal causal process it goes deterministically through these events as time passes. Moreover, we have Leibnizian preestablished harmony so that the occurrent events in the universe as a whole fit the statistics predicted by the correct physical theory.

It is, of course, a little difficult to fit *us* into this theory, for on Leibniz's own theory we were monads, while here we are not. However, even this is not insurmountable. Trying ecumenically to show how the doctrine of transubstantiation fits into his system, in his correspondence with Des Bosses,[5] Leibniz supposed that monads could be united into a "substantial bond," and thereby made into an extended substance, whose monadic constituency might shift over time. We can use this to fit us into the picture: we are, one might suppose, shifting agglomerations of space-time-point monads, and what we perceive is a function of those monads that fall into the substantial bond. If we want to allow for nondeterministic free will, we can suppose miracles, too, whereby we, who are not monads, affect the monads.

This whole theory is crazy. However, it *is* a deterministic story and shows that it is possible to produce a theory with a deterministic metaphysics that is compatible with the observational results. And, of course, there is always occasionalism, as a way out of the difficulty here: a supernatural entity, or some physical entity at an initial time t_0, could just

---

5   Ariew and Garber (1989, pp. 197–206).

directly cause all events at all times, in accordance with certain statistical laws. The point is not that these accounts are true – they surely are not – but that their availability shows that there is a definite possibility of avoiding indeterminism, even if Bohmian approaches fail.

8.3. INDETERMINISM AND PSR

However, probably, the defender of the PSR should not be very afraid of indeterminism. After all, if we insisted that all explanations be of a deterministic sort, then the PSR would indeed become incompatible with contingency by the van Inwagen argument as well as with libertarian free will. One way to explain contingent events nondeterministically is provided by the reasonless-choice models of free will. We could understand the phrase *randomly caused* to be analogous to *freely chose* and say that the system's initial state and its randomly causing A explains why A occurred. Here, we can invoke the principle that when we have given the causes of an event, we have explained why the event occurred. We might also opt for a more Aristotelian solution, abandoning the requirement that explainers are propositions and saying that what explains why A occurred is the substance or substancelike cause of A, acting through substance-causation.[6] This cause could be either the experimental system, or if one accepts that indeterminism only happens through observation, the cause of the indeterministic result could be a human observer.

In response to the objection that in an indeterministic case, the cause only causes A or B to occur, and not A itself, we can return to the Principle of Disjunctive Causation. Disjunctive states only enter into causal relations through their disjuncts' doing so. Thus, the cause indeed causes A. This is made even more plausible in this case in that physical causal relations presumably are between physical systems and/or their physical states. But quantum mechanics on the standard interpretation does not provide us with disjunctive states. This might seem surprising given what one may have heard about Schrödinger's cat, that unfortunate creature that, as a result of an indeterministic lethal-gas-releasing process, is in a state that is a mix of being alive and being dead (assuming cats do not count as observers, because if they did, that would mess things up). However, the cat is in a *superposed* state, $|\text{DEAD}> + |\text{ALIVE}>$, and neither in the DEAD state nor in the ALIVE state. Were it in a disjunctive state, either it would

---

6 This view is due to Haldane in Smart and Haldane (1996).

be in the DEAD state or it would be in the ALIVE state. The superposed state is not a disjunctive state since if x is in the disjunctive state A-or-B, where A and B are pure states, then it is either in the pure state A or in the pure state B (or in both), while something that is in the superposed state logically cannot be in either of the two pure ones. It is upon observation that the cat exits the superposed state and enters either the DEAD state or the ALIVE state, with previous conditions being insufficient to determine which. Then it is either dead or alive, precisely by virtue of being dead or by virtue of being alive. But its being dead-or-alive is not technically a quantum mechanical state then: it just is in the DEAD state or is in the ALIVE state, and hence it is plausible that it is the DEAD state that enters into causal relations and likewise the ALIVE state enters into causal relations, while any disjunctive state of affairs – not a quantum mechanical state in the technical sense – supervenes on the nondisjunctive states and causal relations apply to the disjunctive state of affairs only stipulatively.

However, this would only answer one of the two challenges of quantum mechanics. The other challenge was that of the explanation of EPR correlations. This, too, can be met without making matters deterministic, for instance, by allowing some backward causation or supposing an appropriate absolute reference frame. Or, if one is willing to accept purely nomic explanations that do not cite causes, one might just be satisfied that there is a law of nature that such correlations take place. Whether this would be satisfactory and what it would come down to in the end depend on the nature of laws (cf. Section 16.3).

8.4. PARTICLES COMING INTO EXISTENCE *EX NIHILO*

A variant of the quantum mechanics objection is that according to quantum field theories particles go into and out of the quantum vacuum at random.[7] However, the quantum vacuum is not *nothing* (cf. Davies, 2001, p. 241). Moreover, all this happens nomically, and unless one is a Humean about laws of nature, one should admit that there is a reality that underlies the laws (laws of nature will be discussed further in Section 16.3). Thus, the only part of this objection that should be any worry is the "at random." But now what was said before is once again applicable. We can say that the system, in this case the quantum vacuum, indeterministically causes these events. Or we can opt for some hidden variable theory. To

---

7 I am grateful to J. Brian Pitts for this version of the quantum mechanical objection.

see that some such theory is logically possible and compatible with any evidence we might get, just imagine that there is an absolute reference frame, albeit one that cannot be empirically detected, and that each point in space is a real entity, a monad, say, that contains a complete record of all the particles that will come to be or cease to be at that location at some point in time, and that this monad is what is causally responsible for these transitions.

9

Turning Leibniz against the PSR

Recall Leibniz's argument that the PSR entails that space and time cannot be absolute, since otherwise it makes sense to ask, but by the nature of the matter it is impossible to answer, why the universe is situated in space and time where it is, rather than all moved over spatiotemporally. This can be turned around into a reductio ad absurdum of the PSR: space and time are absolute; hence the PSR is false.

The general structure of the argument is this.

(86) There is a possible world w^* just like the actual world in all qualitative features but nonetheless differing from the actual world in terms of the numerical identity of some entity (an object, a place, a time, etc.).

(87) If two worlds w and w^* have the same qualitative features, then no explanation can be given for why one rather than the other is actual.

(88) Therefore, the PSR can be false; that is, there can be a contingent proposition p with no explanation.

It is plain that the argument is valid: just let p be the proposition that w rather than w^* is actual. The only question, again, is as to soundness.

9.1. IN FAVOR OF (86)

Premise (86) asserts the existence of a world qualitatively identical to the actual one yet somehow different. There are several ways of substantiating (86). One way is via a spatiotemporal translation as in Leibniz: just imagine all the contents of space-time having been moved over. Another is through considerations of counterfactuals. Would it not have been possible for you to have occupied precisely the role I occupy and for me to have occupied

171

precisely the role you occupy? If this were to have happened, then a world qualitatively identical to ours would have been actual.

The intuition about personal identity swapping is, of course, very controversial. One might say that we are constituted by some qualitatively describable aspects of our roles. But an argument can be given, if not for the actual truth of (86), then for a weaker claim that can easily be seen to suffice for the above anti-PSR argument:

(89) There are possible worlds w and w^* just like one another in all qualitative features but nonetheless differing from the actual world in terms of the numerical identity of some entity (an object, a place, a time, etc.).

For this argument, I will need the notion of a *property expressible in general terms*, or *general property* for short. This is a property that could be expressed in a language lacking proper nouns of particulars, demonstratives pointing out particulars, or operators that rigidify terms referring to particulars. The definition leaves open the Kripkean possibility that some general properties are defined in terms of demonstratives or rigidifying operators pointing out universals: for example, "*this* kind of liquid" or "*the* (understood as a rigidifying operator) property of electrons responsible for their mutual repulsion." A *temporalized general property* is defined in the same way as a *general property* except that proper nouns rigidly referring to moments of time, demonstratives pointing out moments of time, and operators that rigidify times are permitted. Thus, every general property is a temporalized general property, but the converse only holds if time is relational.

I will also need the notion of a *t-bounded general property*, for a given time t. This is a temporalized general property F such that the proposition that x has F does not make any contingent claim about what happens after time t. Characterizing this notion precisely is a nontrivial task. For logically simple properties F, a start of a characterization might be to require that the proposition that x has F is compatible with time's coming to an end after t.[1]

By *interchange haecceitism* I will mean the doctrine that there are two distinct possible worlds whose descriptions in terms of the temporalized general properties of their contents are the same. Such two worlds must differ solely in the numerical identities of entities in them as there is no

---

1 Cf. Gale (2002a).

other way for them to differ. Interchange haecceitism is just equivalent to (86)'s being true at some possible world.

Now consider the Principle of Identity of Indiscernibles (PII). This holds that there could not be two entities that are indiscernible, that is, that have the same general properties. Many take the PII to be implausible. Could there not be a world with two qualitatively identical black spheres? Could the world not be perfectly symmetrical, and so I would have a twin symmetrical with me? Could there not be two qualitatively identical angels? The PII has a stronger cousin: The Temporalized PII (TPII) states that, necessarily, for any objects x and y, if t is a time such that at least one of x and y existed prior to t and for every t-bounded general property F it is the case that x has F if and only if y has F, then x is identical with y. I will be only interested in the restriction of the TPII to physical, enduring objects. Observe that the notion of a temporalized general property enters similarly into both the definition of haecceitism and that of the TPII.

It is prima facie quite plausible that the PII is false. The falsity of the TPII is even more plausible, since it asserts that there cannot be two entities that, even though perhaps now discernible, had been indiscernible up to some time. I will now show that if the TPII is false, then interchange haecceitism is true.

If the TPII is false, then it is possible for there to exist two beings x and y and a time t prior to which at least one of the beings existed and such that for every t-bounded general property F, x has F if and only if y has F. Since I have restricted the TPII to physical enduring objects, x and y can be taken to be physical and enduring. Consider now a possible world w_0 containing two such beings x and y. Note that in fact *both* x and y existed prior to t: otherwise, they differ with respect to the possession of the t-bounded general property's *being existent prior to t.*[2]

I am going to need a technical assumption concerning the rearrangement of items in worlds. The technical assumption in its initial form is as follows:

(90) For any possible world w and physical objects x and y that exist at t in w with y also existing at some time after t, there is a possible world

---

2 If one thinks that even temporalized existence is not a property, then one has to modify this argument slightly. One way to do this is to note that if one of x and y exists prior to t, it has some shape, say, S at some time prior to t. Then, consider the property F of *having shape S at a time prior to t*. This is a temporalized t-bounded general property had by one of x and y, and hence had by both. But anything that has F exists prior to t.

$w_{t,x}$ at which it is the case that x exists at no time after t but y exists at some time after t.

This assumption follows from an intuition about the rearrangeability of items within a world – for instance, it is entailed by David Lewis's rearrangement principle (Lewis, 1986, Section 1.8).

One might object to the assumption on Kripkean grounds. Perhaps there is a physical object x that has the essential property of continuing to exist after t, and if so, then the assumption will not be verified. Alternately, one might have a theological objection. If God necessarily exists, then it might be logically impossible for a contingent being that had a certain life history to cease to exist: for instance, if someone lived a just life up to time t but suffered terribly up to t, then divine justice would make it impossible for God to allow this person to cease to exist prior to receiving the reward of this just life. But even those impressed with this argument may well grant the weaker claim:

(91) For any possible world w and physical objects x and y that exist at t, there is a possible world w_x at which x exists but does not have all temporalized general properties in common with y.

Observe that (91) follows from (90), for x and y differ in terms of general properties at $w_{t,x}$: for instance, x ceases to exist at t but y does not. Observe that (91) will be satisfied if there is some world at which x exists but y does not.

Given this technical assumption, the argument becomes quite simple. If the TPII is false, then there is a possible world w containing physical objects x and y that share all the same t-bounded general properties. Let w_x be as in (91).

I now claim that there is a world w_y that has the same description as w_x in terms of temporalized general properties, but in which the roles of y and x are interchanged in the sense that there is a temporalized general property F such that x has it at w_x but y does not, whereas y but not x has F at w_y. I will prove this as follows. Let A be a complete description of w_x in temporalized general terms: say, a conjunction of all propositions (or atomic propositions) true at w_x and expressible in general terms. Let F be any temporalized general property that x but not y has at w_x. Consider then the property S that an object u has if and only if

(92) There is a possible world w^* such that w^* satisfies A and u has F at w^*.

Observe that S is a t-bounded general property of an object, even if F is not t-bounded, for the claim that for some w^* satisfying A the object u has F at w^* is a claim about u's logical possibilities in the space of possible worlds, rather than about u's future in the actual world. Observe further that x has S at w. Therefore, since x and y have all t-bounded general properties in common at w, it follows that y has S at w.

It follows that there is indeed a world w_y satisfying A, and hence matching w_x with respect to the truth values of all propositions involving only temporalized general properties, and at which y has F. Since y does not have F at w_x, it follows by Leibniz's Law that w_x and w_y are distinct worlds. But since they agree on the truth values of all propositions involving only temporalized general properties, it follows that interchange haecceitism is true.

Thus, if the TPII is false, then interchange haecceitism is true, and (86) is possibly true. But then if additionally (87) is true, we conclude that the PSR is possibly false.

If not only the TPII but the PII is also false for physical objects, then there is a quick intuitive road to interchange haecceitism. For consider two indiscernible objects x and y in some world w. Imagine a possible world w_x where x stops existing at some time t but y continues existing. Then there will be a possible world w_y where in turn y stops existing at t but x continues existing, and we may further construct w_x and w_y such that they are indiscernible if x and y were.

Note also that the preceding argument gets around a certain difficulty. The swapping argument is most plausible when the items are most similar. It is quite dubious whether you and I could have had reversed roles. For Kripkean reasons, one might argue that had I started from different genetic material than I did, then I would have been a different person, and so I could not have played your role. On the other hand, if you and I were completely indiscernible, then swapping our roles would not make for any change of role, because ex hypothesi we would have the same roles. What the preceding arguments do is suggest that if items start out in the same roles but do not continue in the same roles, then they can be swapped meaningfully: the swap makes a difference and yet the Kripkean reasons do not seem to come into play because our roles started out indiscernibly.

9.2. A DEFENSE OF THE TPII

But is acceptance of the TPII so absurd? Ian Hacking (1975) has noted that any apparent counterexample to the PII can be reconceived as a case

Figure 2. A symmetric universe

with a more complicated relational space-time structure.[3] Consider, for instance, a situation in which we have an infinite sequence of events of the form $ABABABAB\ldots$, where all the tokens of A are indiscernible and all the tokens of B are indiscernible but with A's being discernible from B's, and where this sequence is all there is in the universe. That situation can be reconceived as a system with a circular time structure and just two events, A and B. Or consider a symmetric spatial arrangement, say, a two-dimensional universe rotationally symmetric around a central point as in Figure 2. We could just reconceive of this situation as a situation without indiscernibles but a more impoverished universe, identifying together the objects and points previously conceived of as indiscernible. In Figure 2 we would identify together the contents of all of the slices and then identify together the bounding lines. The resulting spatial structure would be a cone (see Figure 3).

The Hacking solution, however, is less satisfactory in the case of the TPII. Consider a violation of the TPII that is not a violation of the PII. For instance, the universe in Figure 2 might exist in the state as pictured for a long time, and then some of the items might gradually and asymmetrically change position, so that we would no longer have indiscernibility (see Figure 4). If we are to apply the Hacking reconception method to deny the TPII, then we must suppose that the instant the letters start moving out of place, however continuous the movement, the space

3 See also the discussion in Belot (2001).

176

Figure 3. A Hacking-type reconception of the symmetric universe

Figure 4. Loss of symmetry

jumps discontinuously from a cone to a circle, and each of the objects in the original space then fissions into four objects instantaneously. If this is too much to swallow, and if we think we *can* imagine a system in which there is a symmetric structure for a while, then we will have to deny the TPII. If further we think that given a system satisfying the TPII it was possible for the universe to have come to an end before the indiscernibles diverged, then we will also have to deny the PII, since had the universe thus come to an end, we would have had a violation of the PII.

9.3. AGAINST (86)

It is natural for a defender of the PSR to try to deny (86) and (89). (Indeed, Leibniz would employ the argument with (87) and the negation of (88) as premises and the negation of (86) as the conclusion.) After all, if the two worlds are qualitatively identical, how can they differ?

One way to put the worry would be in a verificationist mode. One might hold that a proposition that could not be verified by *any* conceivable observer is false or nonsense. But no conceivable observer could verify the difference between two qualitatively identical but numerically different possible worlds. Were things as they are in w^*, nobody could know the difference. However, while traditional verificationism must indeed reject the possibility of such a difference, it is not clear that every case of such differences must be rejected by every form of verificationism. Consider the worlds obtained by swapping who occupies your and my roles. Were things thus swapped, there would be a difference in what I perceive: I would be reading this book instead of writing it. So a verificationist way of putting the worry about (86) is not quite satisfactory.

But while the verificationist way of putting the worry is unsatisfactory, there is something right about worrying what the difference is between the possible worlds that differ only in numerical identities of objects. If we are to be realists about possible worlds and think them real entities, whether abstract entities such as collections of propositions or giant states of affairs as in Robert M. Adams (1974) or Alvin Plantinga (1974a), or concrete entities such as physical universes as in David Lewis's (1986) extreme modal realism, there is a worry about individuating them. While perhaps ordinary indiscernibles could be individuated by their spatiotemporal relations, abstract possible worlds do not stand in any spatiotemporal relations. Nor do Lewis's physical universes, because each has its own space-time structure. However, this objection supposes a realism about possible worlds. A sophisticated fictionalism such as Sider's (2002) pluriverse approach avoids the problem, because the possible worlds become mere characters in a story about the space of possibilities.

9.4. AGAINST (87)

9.4.1. Reasonless-Choice Libertarianism

The PSR defender's other option is to dispute proposition (87). If the reasonless-choice libertarian view is coherent, then that Smith reasonlessly and freely chose A is self-explanatory, except insofar as we need to explain why Smith existed and was choosing. On this libertarian view, one could thus give the Samuel Clarke answer against the Leibnizian arguments. A necessarily existent God reasonlessly and freely chooses which of w and w^* to actualize, even if the two universes are indiscernible. It might seem unbefitting of a God's dignity to make reasonless choices,

Leibniz would respond. But in the case in which the choices are between indiscernibles, this is not so obvious. It might be unbefitting of a God's dignity to make reasonless choices where there are reasons for preferring one option over another. But this is precisely a case in which there are no such reasons, and hence a God aware of this fact would not be doing anything unbecoming were he to choose without reason. If, further, one thinks that indeterministic *nonintentional* causation is possible, as in one of the possible ways out of the quantum objection to the PSR, then the absence of reasons for a God to choose on the basis of will not worry one — instead, the reason for one rather than another of the possibilities' eventuating could be some random indeterministic physical process started by God.

If one rejects random indeterministic processes as producing explanations and rejects the Jamesian reasonless-choice form of libertarianism, then the problem is more difficult. One might attempt to use a nonreasonless libertarianism here. But the problem is this: What kind of a reason could there be for a person to bring it about that w is actual instead of w^*? If the two worlds are indiscernible, there are no considerations that can tell in favor of one over the other, it seems.

Because we are dealing with a libertarianism, it will not do just to object that there are no considerations *overall* in favor of one over the other. The libertarian, of whatever stripe, holds that sometimes one can choose an option even though *overall* the weight of reasons is on the other side. But the nonreasonless libertarians may still require that there be *some* reason for choosing as one did even if the reason is weaker than (or at least incommensurable with) some reason for some incompatible action and may insist that one chose that side in part on account of that very reason, despite one's knowing it to be weaker (or knowing that there are incommensurable reasons pointing in a different direction). But in the indiscernibility cases it does not even seem possible for there to be such a reason.

Here it will be useful to recall the two forms that the argument for the existence of indiscernible worlds took. The first form was Leibniz's own and used the possibility of the universe as a whole's being shifted in time or space. This form of the argument can be disputed without undue cost by the defender of the PSR. All she needs to do is to embrace Leibniz's conclusion that space and time are relationally constituted.

The more worrisome form of the argument, however, is that based on the denial of the TPII. First off, the defender of the PSR could simply restrict the scope of the PSR to explaining purely qualitative states of affairs. The numerical identities of things need not be explained then. However, unless one thinks that numerical identities are reducible to purely qualitative features, this restriction may not be satisfactory, since it would undercut basic intuitions behind the PSR, such as the intuition that there has to be an explanation why I exist. For if one restricts the PSR to purely qualitative states of affairs, then it might be explainable why someone like me exists, but not why *I* exist.

However, if the defender of the PSR has managed to argue, as I have attempted to do in preceding chapters, and as must be done in order to refute the van Inwagen fatalism objection, that indeterministic causal explanation is a genuine form of explanation in at least some cases, then she will now be in a position to respond to this objection. There could always be some indeterministic process that causes one rather than the other situation to eventuate. It may be indeterministic as to which of two qualitatively identical twins will die earlier, but the cause of the death of the one that dies earlier, even if it is indeterministic, explains why she died earlier.

There is, however, a further difficulty that the cases resulting from the denial of the TPII present, in that one might have a way out of the van Inwagen, freewill, and quantum mechanical arguments without having a way out of this one. Suppose one admits that, indeed, libertarian free will based explanations are genuine explanations, but only when they make reference to reasons. Thus, the reasonless–choice model of free will fails – if it is taken to succeed, then we can just take Samuel Clarke's solution to the whole problem, namely, posit a God who freely and reasonlessly chooses between the indiscernible worlds. I am imagining here a libertarian who admits that once one has cited the reasons and the fact that a free choice was made, one has explained the event. The reasons need not be such as to necessitate one to act, of course, but they must be there, and they must be sufficient to distinguish between the options.

This kind of libertarianism will escape the indiscernibility objection to the PSR, but it is difficult to see how it would escape the present difficulty, for in the case of indiscernible states of affairs, no person can have a reason to actualize one state rather than another. Any reason in favor of one state is itself also a reason in favor of the other state. Thus if one thinks reasons must play a role in a free choice, and a free choice is the only example of indeterministic causal explanation, even if one thinks that one can freely choose between equally balanced or incommensurable reasons, one will have a difficulty here.

9.4.2. Haecceities and Reasons

There is, however, a possible response. If one accepts the view I dubbed interchange haecceitism, one might feel compelled to accept the existence of *haecceities*, which are thisnesses, the property of being a particular individual being. The haeccties make clear what ways the indiscernible worlds differ. There are, however, difficulties in the notion of haecceities, which thereby make the interchange haecceitism based arguments less plausible. For instance, Adams (1981) observes that there is a problem about the relation of me to my thisness, namely, the property of being me. It is not just that I have my thisness essentially. Rather, I have my thisness essentially and my thisness essentially has the property of not being had by anyone other than me. Thus my thisness has a property that cannot be specified without specifying me *de re*. It will not do to specify me *de dicto* here, for example, by saying that my thisness essentially has the property of being had only by beings that have the property of being me, since that would be just making the trivial claim that my thisness essentially has the property of being had only by beings that have my thisness. But that would not distinguish my thisness from *having green-dyed hair* since *having green-dyed hair* essentially has the property of being had only by beings that have green–dyed hair. But if my thisness has a property that cannot be specified without specifying me *de re*, then it cannot exist if I do not exist. Alternately, my thisness is essentially related to *me* and hence can only exist if I exist since nothing can be related to what is not (Adams, 1981). Therefore, my thisness cannot be a haecceity, since a given haecceity exists in all possible worlds. But my haecceity, were it to exist, would indeed be my thisness, and hence I have no haecceity.

The haecceitist might try to bite the bullet and say that if *H* is my haecceity, then I simply am *that entity that has H*. And there is no need to specify further that *H* can only be had by me, because that would be tautologous. This would also allow a reduction of *de re* modality to *de dicto* modality: the claim that I could not be a horse could become the claim that, necessarily, anything that has *H* is not a horse. Furthermore, the haecceitist may object that it begs the question against haecceitism to say that I can be specified *de re* only if I exist. Plantinga (1983), on the other hand, has questioned Adams's seemingly plausible assumption that it is an essential property of my haecceity that it is the haecceity of me, while granting that it could not be a haecceity of me were I not to have existed, just as no one could be my brother were I not to have existed. And there are additional reasons to reject an Adams-like bifurcation between qualitative properties that exist necessarily and haecceities that only exist if exemplified (see, e.g., Rosenkrantz, 1993, Section 3.III).

Or, alternately, an objector to the PSR might accept interchange haecceitism, the idea that there are possible worlds differing in the numerical identities of objects, without reifying haecceities as expressive of these identities.

Supposing on the other hand that indeed talk of haecceities can make sense, then at least sometimes reasons *can* be given in favor of acting in a way that produces one indiscernible state of affairs rather than another. Consider a question, perhaps facing God, of which of two qualitatively identical twins to give $100 to, or perhaps more radically which one to create. If there are haecceities (note that in the less radical case we only need haecceities of existing objects, which are much less controversial), then I might make reference to the fact that the value of doing good to a person is a reason that makes *de re* reference to the numerical identity of that person. When I love someone, at least in some cases I do not love someone simply as falling under such and such a qualitative description.[4] Rather, I love someone in her individuality. And likewise the value of doing good *for x* makes irreducible reference to the numerical identity of x. Therefore, even if x and y are hitherto indiscernible, the value of doing good *for x* provides a different reason from the value of doing good *for y*. It is true that given indiscernibility, and assuming further that I stand in the same relation to both (which only follows from indiscernibility if I do not have a qualitatively identical twin), neither reason is stronger than the other. The two reasons are either balanced or incommensurable. But they are, nonetheless, distinct reasons, and hence a libertarian who allows that one can freely choose on the basis of balanced or incommensurable

---

4 This can be true even if the description is historical, for I could find I was wrong in thinking that someone fell under the historical description and still *continue* to love the person, with the continuation being phenomenologically different from a case in which one stops loving one person and starts loving another. And even if I, in fact, do not continue to love the person, I might have been *committed* to this continuation and failed to live out that commitment. One might think, for instance, that this is true in cases of unconditional love, in which the love is neither conditioned on assumptions about the future nor on assumptions about the past. Of course, this raises all kinds of issues that go far beyond the scope of this book. This view of unconditional love fits well with Kierkegaard's view that genuine love does not love for reasons but does not logically require that view: It is one thing for the justification of the initial *entry into love* to be dependent on the beloved's apparently falling under a description and another for the love's continuation to depend on the beloved's actually falling under a description.

reasons will allow that in this case there are different morally relevant reasons for the two possible indiscernible courses of action.

This, then, would lead to an explanation of which of two worlds is actualized, in cases deriving from some failures of the TPII, in terms of some free person's, say God's, choosing between incommensurable or balanced reasons. But this only applies in cases in which one is doing something that in some morally significant way impacts a person or other item of moral significance. But what about a choice as to which of two indiscernible stones should exist, or which one should exist for a longer time? Could God have a reason there? One might first respond that it is the cases of persons that are most relevant vis-à-vis the preceding argument against the PSR. For one might insist that identity for nonpersons is such that role swapping is simply impossible for them, and hence the argument for interchange haecceitism in the case of nonpersons fails. But it is less plausible to suppose this impossibility in the case of persons: we have some idea of what it would be like to play a different role from the one we do.

Alternately, one might accept Augustine's claim that existence is in and of itself a good, and hence everything that exists is valuable. The choice of which stone should exist longer is, then, a very low-grade choice as to which stone should be gifted with a certain good, a choice that might well be seen as significant by a person who loves all of his creatures, including stones. Or even if one does not accept Augustine's claim, one might think that *some* moral significance can be found in any case.

10

What Survives the Criticisms of the PSR?

We saw four distinct kinds of objections to the PSR. First, we had Humean objections to the PSR understood as a necessary truth, based on the idea that in constructing possible worlds we are free to rearrange the items in the universe in any way, and in particular in a way that excises causes. We saw that this idea itself has not been sufficiently supported in any of its forms. We are also going to see in Chapter 19 that on the best available account of possibility, such rearrangement is not possible, because in fact the best available account of possibility entails the PSR.

The second kind of objection to the PSR was bound up with indeterminisms of various sorts. The fatalism objection argued that the contingency of the world was incompatible with the PSR. The free will and quantum mechanics objections argued that theories that we have good reason to believe are correct are incompatible with the PSR. Third, the Leibnizian arguments showed that without some form of indeterministic causation we cannot causally account for the possibilities of indiscernible worlds.

We saw that the libertarian cannot, on pain of succumbing to the "brute randomness" objection to libertarianism, deny that free-will causal explanations are genuine explanations, even if they are indeterministic, and I defended free-will causal explanations using several models. In defense of both free-will causal explanations and quantum mechanical indeterministic causal interpretations, further, I argued on the basis of two principles. The first simply states that by giving the cause of an event, one has always sufficiently explained it. The second, in response to the objection that in the indeterministic cases it is a disjunction that is caused, is the principle that disjunctive states of affairs do not stand in causal relations, except through their disjuncts' doing so. Note that we need not say which of the models of explanation in the case of free will works. I am inclined to prefer the reasoned to the reasonless version. The reasoned version is of two varieties. In one case, the reason the agent chose A is that she freely chose A for R, where her freely choosing A for R is self-explanatory (modulo her freedom, her being impressed with R, and her existence), and in the other she chose A for R because she was impressed with R and chose freely. Both varieties when added to the explanandum give the listener the same amount of information, though the first puts more of the information in the explanans while the second leaves some information for the explanandum. Which one is "the explanation" may simply be a verbal question.

A version of the PSR compatible with the preceding considerations is one that states that every contingent proposition has an explanation, but without its being required that the explanation always be distinct from the explained proposition or that the explanans should entail the explanandum. Moreover, *sufficient reason* needs to be understood not as "necessitating reason" but as "sufficient explanation," where we understand that a causal account is always sufficiently explanatory, even when indeterministic. It is this version of the principle that will be the primary target of the positive arguments in Part III of this book.

And, if one denies that citing the cause always gives a sufficient explanation, then one might just have to rename the PSR that will be defended "the Principle of Good Explanation." In any case, the principle that will be argued for will certainly be a nontrivial principle. As applied to the Big Conjunctive Contingent Fact, namely, the conjunction of all contingent true propositions with redundancies removed, the principle shows the existence of a necessarily existing being that is a first cause. This consequence constitutes a fourth anti-PSR argument that was discussed earlier. I argued that there should be no difficulty here, especially if we understand that necessity and analyticity need not go together.

Part Three

Justifications of the PSR

11

Self-Evidence

The premier reason why people believe the PSR and weaker versions such as the CP is that they take these principles to be self-evident, obvious, intuitively clear, in no need of argumentative support. For instance, when presented with the Parmenidean PSR-based time-shift argument against change, even when the PSR premise is made explicit, most students do not wish to make it be their critical target – sometimes, in fact, it takes quite a while before someone objects to the PSR. The public at large is likely to see the purpose of this book as silly: Why argue for the obvious? Of course once it is shown that the PSR has the implication that there is a necessary being that created the universe, one is more likely to question the PSR. But even then, undergraduate atheists seem to have a certain preference for denying the contingency of the universe rather than questioning the PSR, though of course that might simply depend on the details of presentation to them.

At the same time, the premier reason why the claim that the PSR is self-evident is rejected by philosophers is that to many of them not only does the PSR not seem obvious, but it seems to be actually false, for instance because it is seen as implying the existence of God or the falsity of quantum mechanics. We have seen that the PSR does not imply the falsity of quantum mechanics. It may imply the existence of a creator, but that is no reason to reject the PSR, since there are no good arguments against the mere necessary existence of a creator. But no matter whether the arguments against the PSR work, the very fact that some intelligent people disbelieve it seems to show that the PSR is not self-evident.

There are a number of ways of understanding the notion of a self-evident proposition. About the strongest is the following definition:

(93) A proposition *p* is self-evident if, necessarily, anyone who understands it correctly understands it to be true, and it is possible for someone to understand it.

The possibility clause is needed to rule out the counterexample of a false proposition that it is impossible for anyone to understand, if there should be such utterly incomprehensible propositions.

This notion of self-evidence has a certain similarity to analyticity. An analytic proposition is one whose truth follows from the meanings of its terms. But not every analytic proposition is self-evident in the sense of (93). The proposition that the Pythagorean theorem follows from the axioms of Euclidean geometry is analytic but not self-evident: one can understand these axioms and the statement of the theorem without understanding the theorem to follow from the axioms. Nor is it obvious that every self-evident proposition is analytic. For instance, a case could be made that the proposition that there are thinkers is self-evident in the sense of (93), whereas it is by no means obvious that it is analytic, though a theist who thinks that God's existence is analytic might say so. For I cannot understand (93) without thinking, and on Kantian or Cartesian grounds one might argue that I must be aware of myself as thinking while thinking, and thus aware of there being thinkers. It is not obvious that this is so, but neither is it obvious that it is not. In any case, the difference between self-evidence and analyticity is that the latter speaks of propositions in themselves while self-evidence concerns propositions in relation to knowers.

11.2. THE OBJECTION FROM SMART PEOPLE WHO DISAGREE

Could the PSR turn out to be self-evident in this sense? The answer seems plainly negative: Adolf Grünbaum, J. J. C. Smart, and David Hume are all intelligent people who rejected the PSR. Surely the claim that they did not understand the PSR that they were rejecting is incredible.

There is, however, a *tu quoque* response. A number of also intelligent people, such as Leibniz and Aquinas, accepted the PSR (or versions of it) and saw it as something which is such that it cannot be understood without being understood to be true: not only did they see it as self-evident, but perhaps they saw it as self-evident *that* it is self-evident. If they were wrong about this, they were wrong about the meaning of the PSR, and hence *they* failed to understand the PSR that they accepted. This response, however, is questionable. The second-order judgment that a self-evident proposition is self-evident is one that depends on further concepts, such as the concept of self-evidence, and so there is more room for error, more room for thinking one has understood a proposition when in fact one has not.

The very notion of failing to understand a proposition may seem incoherent. If Hume has failed to understand the PSR, then how can we say that he has failed to understand *the* PSR rather than some other proposition? After all, if he has failed to understand *the* PSR, then he had in mind a proposition, the PSR, which he failed to understand. And to have a proposition in mind is precisely to grasp that proposition. But this attempt to strengthen the argument against the self-evidence of the PSR fails, because there may be pragmatic features of Hume's activity that show that it was the PSR that he wanted to grasp. Obviously, he did not have the proposition before wanting to grasp it. Rather, he had a description of the proposition, such as "the proposition that Leibniz believed and called 'The Principle of Sufficient Reason,'" and he wished to grasp that proposition which fell under this description. The defender of the PSR's self-evidence, then, claims that Hume failed at this task, despite all his intelligence.

11.3. BUT ISN'T THE PSR EASY TO UNDERSTAND?

Can the task be so hard? The PSR in the form we are interested in is a relatively simple proposition that states that every contingent proposition has an explanation. Which part do the PSR skeptics fail to grasp? Would it not be philosophical incompetence, of a sort incompatible with their intelligence, to fail to grasp the notions of explanation, contingency, and proposition, or to fail to understand universal quantification?

But this question answers itself. Intelligent philosophers *do* disagree on what *explanation*, *contingency*, and *propositions* are. Obviously, therefore, some of them either fail to grasp these concepts or grasp *other* concepts than those that other philosophers include under these labels. In the latter case, they are not denying the PSR but some other proposition. For instance, it follows from the considerations in Section 2.4 that if we understand *cause* in a Humean way, then it is very likely false that every contingent event has a "cause." But since this concept of a *cause* is not Aquinas's, for instance, this in no way reflects on the CP as found in, say, Aquinas.

This, however, is only an opening gambit in the defense of the PSR's self-evidence. Competent philosophers obviously are themselves quite aware of the differences in meaning of terms such as *cause*. Hume not only meant to deny that contingent events need to have "Humean constantly conjunctive causes" but also meant to deny that they need to have "causes" as understood by Aquinas or Leibniz. But it may well be that Hume failed to understand the philosophies of Aquinas or Leibniz, of course, and hence failed to understand what he wanted to deny.

However, Hume did not simply deny the causal principle. Hume held that anything contingent that existed could have existed by itself, with its existence being a brute fact. Given this, it is not necessary for Hume to understand the details of Aquinas's or Leibniz's notions of explanation or causation to deny that the CP as understood by Aquinas or Leibniz is true. He need only understand that the CP as understood by them entails the negation of Hume's independence of existent beings thesis. Analogously, if I believed that the only enmattered intelligent beings are humans and had a crazy neighbor who believed in the existence of "superplasma"-based sapient aliens, I would not need to understand the concept of "super-plasma" to believe my neighbor's claim to be false – it would suffice that I would know that whatever my neighbor meant by it, it was a form of matter.

But observe that in fact this observation supports a defense of the PSR's self-evidence because it shows that Hume could well have denied the PSR without grasping all the concepts in the PSR. He could have denied it under the description "Leibniz's favorite principle." If his arguments for his own account of causality were cogent, then in fact he could have been at least subjectively warranted in denying the PSR without grasping it. This gives one a charitable way of understanding how an intelligent philosopher could have at least subjective warrant in denying a self-evident proposition. Of course, there are also uncharitable ways of understanding this, and we cannot a priori rule them out. The PSR is widely held to entail theism – one might deny it ad hoc for precisely that reason.

Recall, however, the objection against a Humean claim that it is intuitively clear that a brick could come into existence *ex nihilo*. One response to this claim was that we should not have undue confidence in this possibility claim as it uses a notion of possibility far removed from ordinary life. It appears that the PSR as restricted to contingent propositions is subject to exactly the same criticism,[1] while an unrestricted PSR or a

---

1 I am very grateful to an anonymous reader for this point.

PSR restricted in some way closer to everyday concepts, say, restricted to spatiotemporal affairs, would be "easy to understand" and hence it would be harder to see why intelligent people denied it if it was in fact self-evident.

Two responses could be made here. The first is that there is an asymmetry between the Humean claim and the PSR, for the ordinary concept of contingency is one of causal contingency, and this supports the PSR as we shall see in Chapter 19, while it tells against the Humean claim. Hence the Humean claim requires a departure from ordinary intuitions while the PSR does not. The second is that this does not show that the claim that the PSR is self-evident is false, but merely that to someone who does not see matters as I do, the self-evidence to me of the PSR should not have much weight, and that I, too, should be cautious in my claim.

11.4. TWO WAYS NOT TO UNDERSTAND

11.4.1. Conceptual Color Blindness

There are two models on which we could see a philosopher as failing to understand a self-evident principle. The first is a kind of conceptual color blindness. Imagine a person who does not have a grasp of moral concepts, understood in an objectivistic way. Having moral concepts could be, as Aristotle and John McDowell think it is, second nature to us. Moral deliberation practices could well be practices we need to be initiated into, just as we need to be initiated into mathematical practices, with both kinds of practices being doxastically alethic, seeking objective truths. Or perhaps the moral intuitionists are right and we have a faculty of moral intuition. Whichever view we take, we could perhaps imagine an intelligent person who lacks the faculty or initiation that gives us moral concepts. This is not obvious, of course. It might be that the structure of thought is such that without moral concepts there can be no thoughts at all,[2]

---

2 One might think that one cannot have any concepts without having normative knowledge, such as that one *ought not* contradict oneself, or that one *ought to* base one's beliefs on evidence at least ceteris paribus, or that if one thinks something is a *C* (where *C* is one of the concepts one has), then one *ought not* think it a *D* (where *D* is another one of the concepts one has). If, furthermore, rational normativity cannot be understood without understanding moral normativity (e.g., because there is no distinction between rational and moral normativity, or because moral normativity is the paradigm of normativity, or because rational obligations are a subspecies of moral obligation and derive their "oughtness" from the moral), then one cannot have any concepts without having moral concepts.

and if so, then this example will have to be taken as grounded in a *per impossibile* counterfactual.

Now, once one gains moral concepts, there might be self-evident moral truths, such as that, ceteris paribus, pain is to be relieved. These might be such that once one understands them, one knows them to be true. Consider, however, an intelligent person lacking moral concepts. Such a person will fail to grasp these moral truths and will hence fail to see them as self-evident. She might, however, hold an error theory of them, even if she fails to grasp them. For she might be, as Mackie (1977) is, a reductive materialist, and argue that it is clear – even without actual grasp of the concepts – that the concepts intended by those initiated into the moral deliberation practice or by those apparently having a faculty of moral intuition are concepts of immaterial realities, and hence positive propositions concerning these concepts are all false. Or, she might more cautiously say that the moral claims either are nonsense *or* are false, if she is not sure whether in fact the apparent concepts such as *oughtness* are genuine concepts.

We might get some sympathy for this way of looking at things if we look at a religious concept we do not share, such as the apparent concept of the *taboo*. We may not in fact be able to map *tabooness* onto our own concepts. This might make us suppose that in fact the people who talk of things as taboo are speaking nonsense. But we need not take that radical view; we could remain agnostic about whether they speak nonsense. We could instead simply think that what they are saying might be false, without actually grasping *tabooness* ourselves. We know that those who talk of things as *taboo* intend this to be an objective normative property. Should someone say it is always taboo to talk in the rain during a full Moon, we would know that her claim entails that some objective norm is always violated by talking in the rain during a full Moon. Since we do not have a grasp of tabooness, we do not know what kind of an objective norm this is supposed to be, beyond vague indications that it is neither a norm of morality nor one of rationality. But if we justifiedly believe that there are *no objective norms of any sort* against talking in the rain during a full Moon, we can know that her claim, if it makes sense at all, is false.

11.4.2. *Talking Ourselves Out of Understanding*

A second model for failing to grasp a proposition while yet denying it is a case in which one has talked oneself out of comprehending something or talked oneself out of grasping some concept. Suppose moral objectivism is true. Now imagine someone who has fallen under the sway of social constructivists or evolutionary psychologists. She has seen myriad analyses of how our engagement in practices of moral talk and deliberation can be explained sociologically or Darwinistically. After a while, she forgets that there is a distinction between explaining and justifying and thinks that once one has given a causal explanation of our practice of moral talk and deliberation, one has said all there is to be said about it: One does not need to posit moral truths to which our practice is answerable. And so she loses sight of the moral concepts with which she grew up. She no longer has normative concepts of the *dishonest*, the *just*, and the *cowardly*. She only has sociological concepts of those people or actions that have the labels *dishonest, just, and cowardly* attached to them, or she has concepts of certain functional features of human beings that are more or less adaptive.

We all know people like that. Indeed, some of us are people like that, if not in regard to moral concepts, then in regard to other concepts. We may imagine, further, that the person has at least subjective warrant in believing that the sociological or Darwinian accounts are complete accounts of the moral sphere of human praxis. But a moral objectivist who believes that once one has the concepts of *pain* and *ought*, then it is self-evident that, ceteris paribus, pain ought to be relieved need not find her belief challenged by the mere existence of the sociologically or evolutionarily minded critic. Of course, the critic's arguments may well be threatening. But the critic's existence should not be. One *can* talk oneself out of having certain concepts. If the reader finds the case of moral truths to be too dubious because she accepts the sociological or Darwinian reduction, she might simply try to imagine what the moral case will look like from the point of view of the moral objectivist. Or she may look at some other area, such as religion or mathematical realism.

The existence of intelligent critics who deny the PSR does not, therefore, disprove the claim that the PSR is self-evident in the strong sense of being such that anyone who understands it must understand it to be true.

One response may be, "This may be all fine and good for cases of moral propositions, but the case of the PSR is different. I grant that it is possible that some proposition p employing a special set S of concepts is self-evident to someone possessing S, but denied by an intelligent critic, because she fails to possess S. However, this is only true in cases in which the proposition p carries no controversial implications that the critic disputes and that can be expressed in concepts available to the critic. The PSR, however, does carry such controversial implications. For instance, it implies that there is either something outside time or something prior to the Big Bang, since it is only by reference to something outside time or prior to the Big Bang that the Big Bang, which is evidently contingent, can be explained – whatever 'explanation' might turn out to be."

However, this response misses the details of the preceding analysis. We started with the observation that it is only because the critic may understand some implications of the PSR that she can be justified in rejecting it. Likewise, the critic of moral discourse may well understand that moral discourse is such that if it is true, then reductive materialism is false. And she may understand this without grasping moral propositions, even if there are moral propositions. But (93) does not say that one can see the proposition to be true when one has understood some of its implications: one can understand some of the implications of a proposition without understanding the proposition itself.

Alternately, the critic might say, "Even were I to understand non-Humean causation, nonetheless I just would not see the PSR as self-evident." This response, however, is unsatisfactory. One's insight into what judgments one would make were one possessed of concepts that one is bereft of is obviously limited.

11.5. MORE DETAIL

But there is a more powerful response along these lines that the critic of the PSR might make: "Which part of the PSR is it that I fail to understand and that is such that were I to understand it, I would therefore end up seeing the PSR as true?" This requires more detail from the defender of self-evidence. Earlier, I used the illustration of the concept of a cause. It is implausible to suppose that every critic of the PSR, or more precisely of the CP, is a Humean about causation. It is by no means obvious what it is about the concept of causation that is such that it is self-evident that any contingent event has a cause.

I would suggest that the critic of the PSR might be blind to the nature of contingency (cf. Reichenbach, 1972, p. 61). Every contingent proposition has an explanation, the PSR avers. Intuitively, contingency is closely bound up with causal concepts: we talk of an event as contingent *on* something when the latter contributes to the event's explanation and without it the given event would not occur. Our everyday concepts of modality are, in fact, arguably causal in nature (Place, 1997; Mackie, 1998). It may be that were one to understand contingency appropriately, one *would* see the PSR as self-evident. In Chapter 19 we will in fact see that a certain causal concept of contingency, or more precisely of possibility, is such that it entails the PSR, and I will argue further that this concept is superior to alternative ones. An intuitive grasp of this might be behind the self-evidence of the PSR.

It is essential for this line of thought that the concept of contingency here not be a stipulative one, but the very same concept we employ normally, and the same concept that we find ourselves using in other plausibly self-evident claims such as that physical events in time are all contingent. On this line of thought, the critic of the PSR has either never grasped or, more plausibly, has talked herself out of the natural concept of contingency. Instead, she has a different concept. The critiques of non-Aristotelian concepts of possibility in Chapter 19 will add weight to this suggestion. At the same time, it is necessary to make sure that the correct concept of contingency not be such that by predicating contingency of the occurrences of the sort that we wish to apply the PSR to we beg the question against the PSR's opponent. For instance, it certainly would not do baldly to define an event as contingent provided it has a cause. The PSR we wish to defend would then become vacuous. Rather, the concept of contingency behind the PSR must be sufficiently closely related to our ordinary usage that it be clear that, say, the existence of horses is contingent.

This kind of an account does not impugn the philosophical competence, at least narrowly construed, of the critic. It is not philosophical incompetence to lack the correct concept, say, of contingency. Different great philosophers have different concepts under the same label. Some may be wrong – some may in fact be failing to grasp a concept that they grew up holding but have talked themselves out of since. They are philosophically wrong, but it does not follow that they are incompetent, unless one construes philosophical competence sufficiently thickly to include such faculties of right judgment that one cannot go wrong about these matters. And if one does construe competence thus thickly, then there is nothing problematic about one philosopher's calling another philosopher, even a great one, incompetent. No doubt Spinoza failed in his judgment whether to take the proposition that everything is necessary as a conclusion or a *reductio*. And if it is *this* kind of failure that we label "philosophical incompetence," then it is an incompetence compatible with greatness, and hence it is no failure in philosophical charity to ascribe such incompetence to another philosopher.

11.6. SMART PEOPLE WHO ACCEPT THE PSR
BUT NOT AS SELF-EVIDENT

A different sort of challenge is this. Some people who actually *accept* the PSR, such as Thomas Sullivan (1994), hold that it is not self-evident in the sense previously indicated. Presumably since they *accept* the PSR, they grasp it and should by grasping it see it as self-evident.

However, there are at least two possible responses here. First we may start with an observation inspired by Spinoza (cf. *Treatise on the Emendation of the Intellect*, Section 35) that it need not be that it is self-evident that a proposition *p* is self-evident for *p* to be self-evident. Spinoza may later soften this by arguing that through knowing *p* by the mode of self-evidence we also know *p* to *be* self-evident (cf. Proposition 43 of Part II of the *Ethics* and the following *Scholium*), but we need not follow him there.

Timothy Williamson has criticized the idea that we can be in a condition *C* that is luminous in the sense that if we are in *C*, then we are always in a position to know that *C* obtains (Williamson, 2000, p. 95). The problem is that there is a continuum in all mental acts and that we cannot discern tiny differences, while we can move by tiny differences from *C* to not-*C*. If we take the condition *C* to be *knowing something through self-evidence*, then this can be taken as a critique of self-evidence. While it is not obvious that there is in fact such a continuum in the qualities of all mental acts, the argument does suggest that the defender of self-evidence would be safer staying away from claiming that luminosity of self-evident knowledge if it can be avoided.

To back up this Spinozistic response further we might note that the principle of noncontradiction is very plausibly self-evident. However, a person may well grasp the principle of noncontradiction without having the concept of self-evidence. Thus, self-evidence is what justifies the principle of noncontradiction to her, but this is a justification she cannot give. And, similarly, it need not be self-evident *that* the principle of noncontradiction is self-evident.

Alternately, the defender of the PSR might say that the timid believer in the PSR who does not wish to claim self-evidence, as does the critic, fails to grasp fully the concepts in the PSR. Indeed, perhaps by listening to critics, the timid defender has talked herself out of grasping these concepts. And just as the critics deny that the PSR is true without fully understanding it, but nonetheless perhaps subjectively justifiedly because they have a description of the PSR and may be subjectively warranted in thinking that no proposition falling under that description is true, so too the timid defender might have a description of the PSR and believe subjectively justifiedly that some or every proposition falling under that description is true.

The phenomenon of holding a proposition *p* to be true without understanding it is an interesting one in general. It might, for instance, explain ordinary linguistic practice when an educated layperson makes a statement couched in scientific language that she does not fully understand, but from which she nonetheless can draw implications that she can understand. The same analysis might be brought to bear on the case of religious mysteries. For instance, a religious person need not claim actually to possess the concept *Trinity* to claim to believe that the doctrine of the Trinity is true. She might, for instance, believe that there exists a proposition very aptly expressible by the words of the Creed and that this proposition is true, without herself having a grasp of that proposition (Merricks, 2004).

11.7. THE IMPASSE

However, there is a much more trenchant response to the claims of self-evidence. Suppose the PSR is indeed self-evident and I grasp it as such. So what? There plainly are people who think it is not self-evident. My saying that it is self-evident will not convince them. Ex hypothesi, they lack the concepts involved in the PSR, and hence do not see it as self-evident. My banging my fists on the table will in no way help them gain the requisite grasp of the PSR. Thus, while my seeing the PSR as self-evident may possibly ensure that I do not have a responsibility to back it up argumentatively *for my own sake*, if I want others to share my conviction, I cannot rest with a mere claim of self-evidence. I can try to refute the unsound arguments by which a critic may have talked herself into a failure to grasp the principle. I can try to clarify the concepts so that she might have more hope of grasping them. I can discuss applications of the PSR to show that she herself may be committed to the PSR without knowing it.

And I can give positive arguments for the PSR from other propositions. For even if a proposition is self-evident, there may still be arguments that can be given for it, based on other premises that one's interlocutor is willing to accept, perhaps other self-evident premises, or other premises that in an ideal world would be conclusions drawn from the PSR but in this dialectical situation are accepted in the absence of the PSR. Of course if the PSR is evident, then there is something strange about giving an argument for it. For as soon as the interlocutor grasps the proposition expressed by the words I use to give utterance to the PSR, she will grasp it to be true. And if she does not grasp the proposition, how can she grasp an argument for it? But again this can be answered by adverting to the preceding model of how someone might believe that the PSR is true without having a grasp of it. For one might have a vague grasp of the PSR, that is, a grasp of the PSR as a proposition falling under a certain description. And then one might accept an argument for the claim that some or all propositions falling under that description are true. For instance, one might not oneself grasp the concept of a *cause*, but one might accept arguments involving the concept because one may know that they hold for any of a family of concepts that include the desired one.

11.8. MATHEMATICAL ANALOGIES

It might be helpful at this point to recall two mathematical examples. The Law of Excluded Middle (LEM) says that for every proposition p we have p or $\sim p$. It is quite plausible that this is self-evident. After all, were it not self-evident, we would be at a loss for how we could possibly get to know it. Would we prove it from other, more evident propositions? It is hard to find a proposition more evident than LEM, unless it should be the Principle of Noncontradiction (PNC), which states that for every p we have $\sim(p \,\&\, \sim p)$, but as it happens, one cannot prove the LEM from the PNC, without somewhere along the way invoking some variant of the LEM, say, in the form of De Morgan's Law and the Principle of Double Negation that if $\sim\sim p$ then p.[3] This is so because it can be proved that there are consistent quantified logics, indeed even consistent quantified logics supporting set theories, in which the LEM is false but the PNC is true.[4]

Nor do we know the LEM inductively. We could generate a proposition and then find out that it is true or find out that it is false. Unfortunately, there is many a proposition for which we have neither found that it

---

3 De Morgan's Law states that $\sim(p \,\&\, q)$ is equivalent to $(\sim p$ or $\sim q)$. Thus, if we have $\sim(p \,\&\, \sim p)$ by the PNC, then given De Morgan we have $(\sim p$ or $\sim\sim p)$. By the Principle of Double Negation we have $\sim p$ or p.
4 In a topos-theoretic framework, cf. Bell (1988).

is true nor found out that it is false. For instance, we do not know whether it is true or false that there exist aliens or that Goldbach's Conjecture (that every even number greater than 2 is the sum of two primes) holds. Now, admittedly for every proposition for which we know the truth value, we either know it to be true or know it to be false. But this is a tautology: to know the truth value is nothing other than to know which of the two alternatives holds. Nor will it do to pride ourselves on the sheer number of propositions for which we have found out the truth value and to claim that this number is likely to increase without bound, for surely we will never find out whether or not Caesar had an even number of hairs on his body the moment he died, and indeed as the past slips away from us, there will always be such propositions that we will not know.

And even some of those cases of the LEM that one can check might not be so unequivocal. How do I check that the LEM holds for Oswald's assassinating Kennedy? I may reason as follows. If Oswald did not assassinate Kennedy, there was an enormous conspiracy in the United States. There was no such enormous conspiracy. Therefore, by *modus tollens*, it is false that Oswald did not assassinate Kennedy. But to infer from this that it is true that Oswald assassinated Kennedy is to infer p from $\sim\sim p$, and the validity of this inference is, under appropriate background assumptions, equivalent to the LEM. This is not just a usual case of the need for employment of auxiliary hypotheses in experimental testing. Here, it is the very hypothesis tested that must be applied as an auxiliary hypothesis.

So we do not know the LEM empirically, even though surely we know it with certitude. But if we do not know it empirically, and do not know it by proof from more basic propositions, then it seems we must know it in some self-evidencing way. This need not take exactly the form (93), of course, but some account on which some propositions are a priori self-evidencing is needed.

As in the case of the PSR, there are people who wish to deny the LEM, namely, the mathematicians known as intuitionists. The intuitionist insists on giving mathematical proofs that do not rely on the LEM. Thus, she will reject the following proof of the theorem that there exist irrational numbers x and y such that x^y is not irrational:

(94) The number $\sqrt{2}$ is irrational, as shown in Euclid's *Elements*. Consider the number $\sqrt{2}^{\sqrt{2}}$. By the LEM, it is either rational or not rational. If it is rational, then just let $x = y = \sqrt{2}$ so that x^y is rational.

If it is irrational, then let $x = \sqrt{2}^{\sqrt{2}}$ and let $y = \sqrt{2}$. Then, $x^y = \sqrt{2}^{\sqrt{2} \cdot \sqrt{2}} = \sqrt{2}^2 = 2$ is rational. Thus, in either case, there is an irrational number raised to an irrational power that is rational. Q.E.D.[5]

Now proof (94) is, admittedly, not very informative, because it does not tell us which irrational numbers x and y are such that x^y is rational, since that depends on which disjunct in the disjunction

$$\sqrt{2}^{\sqrt{2}} \text{ is rational or } \sqrt{2}^{\sqrt{2}} \text{ is not rational}$$

is in fact true. But the intuitionist does not merely claim that the proof is not informative. Rather, she claims that this is not a proof at all. There is pragmatic value, of course, in having intuitionists around because they are likely to search for more informative proofs and encourage others to do so. But nonetheless, I take it, the intuitionist is wrong in taking the LEM to be false or doubtful, even though there is no denying that the intuitionist can be a highly intelligent person – indeed, great cleverness is needed to do mathematics in the absence of the LEM.

Note that just as in the case of the PSR, so too one can challenge the skeptic about the LEM with a pragmatic inconsistency – both use the principles in daily life. They may, however, both claim that there is a significant disanalogy between the daily life cases and the special cases in which the PSR or the LEM does not apply. In Chapter 16 we will examine the issue of the everyday applicability of the PSR and what evidence it lends to the PSR as a whole.

One might think that there is a significant disanalogy between the PSR and the LEM, in that the LEM is a much lower-level principle that is employed much more often in daily life, while the PSR is a much higher-level principle. However, the PSR, too, is used often in daily life. Alternately, one might note that the LEM just is so much simpler than the PSR, or that it does not lead to conclusions as controversial as those to which the PSR leads. It is not clear, however, why this difference in degree should bar the PSR from the very possibility of being self-evident.

Or one might insist that the LEM is a principle so basic to human conversational praxis that it is simply impossible to be a talker, a participant in the human society, while denying the LEM, whereas people like Adolf Grünbaum and David Hume certainly are talkers and participants in human society. But then so are intuitionists like Brouwer!

5   This elegant proof is a part of mathematical folklore. I remember first seeing it as a kid in the pages of *Discover* magazine.

All these objections based on the simplicity or basicness of the LEM suggest that perhaps a different analogy might be helpful. Consider the Axiom of Choice (AC) from set theory, to which we have already alluded. Recall that the AC, in its primary official formulation, states that if a set A is a collection of disjoint nonempty sets, then there is a set S that contains exactly one member from each of the disjoint sets. Finite cases are obvious and do not need a special axiom. If $A = \{\{1, 2\}, \{3, 4\}, \{5, 6, 7, 8\}\}$, we can just let $S = \{1, 3, 8\}$.

The AC is a principle of plenitude for sets. In a different equivalent form, it says that the Cartesian product of any number (finite or infinite) of nonempty sets is itself nonempty, where the Cartesian product of, say, three sets A, B, and C is the set of triples (a, b, c), where a is a member of A, b is a member of B, and c is a member of C. For a finite number of sets, the number of members in the Cartesian product is equal to the product of the numbers of the members of the respective sets. Intuitively, then, if we have an infinite number of nonempty sets of which we are taking a Cartesian product, the cardinality of the product should be larger. And so we are likely to accept the AC, which simply says that the cardinality of the product is nonzero.

But for all of its initial plausibility, the AC leads to at least one counter-intuitive conclusion. For instance, as mentioned in Section 3.1, it implies that we can decompose a solid ball into a finite number of disjoint subsets that can then be reassembled, by rotation and translation, into two solid balls of the very same diameter as the original ball – this is the Banach-Tarski paradox. Lest one run and buy a sphere of gold in the hope of enriching oneself through endless multiplication of gold, I should hasten to add that just as proof (94) did not give a procedure for finding the irrational number that when raised to an irrational power yielded a rational number, so too the AC-based proof here gives no algorithm for cutting up the sphere. And even if it did, it would not be an algorithm we could follow, because the pieces would not be solid, but would have something in common with, say, the aggregate of all the points with rational coordinates – except they would be weirder, in that at least some of them would lack a well-defined volume. Because of this weirdness of the piece, I think one would not be wrong in putting this counterintuitive conclusion down to the weirdness of the mathematical continuum – the sphere's being a continuous entity.

The philosophical root of the controversy behind the AC is that it posits the existence of a set S containing one member from each of the disjoint member sets in A, even though in general there need not be any effective procedure for *constructing S*. In this, the AC is like the LEM. The LEM claims that p or $\sim p$, but there need not be any effective procedure for determining which of the two is the case.[6] If one is not bothered by mathematical objects or truths in the absence of effective procedures for constructing or verifying them, then one may well not be bothered by the AC, just as one will not be bothered by the LEM. It may be worth noting that there is some, perhaps superficial, similarity to the PSR in this respect: the PSR does not itself give us a procedure for *finding* or *stating* the explanation – indeed, if we had such a procedure, then we could apply Inference to the Best Explanation in the place of the PSR.[7]

Of course the theoretical utility of the AC, its mathematical fruitfulness, might well count pragmatically in favor of it. But it is not clear how this fruitfulness should constitute *evidence* for the AC. All this might lead one to think that the AC is simply self-evident. Just as we cannot prove the LEM without basing ourselves on things equally "controversial" (to the intuitionist), so too we know we cannot prove the AC without basing ourselves on things just as controversial, since it turns out that at least Zermelo-Fraenkel set theory conjoined with the AC is consistent if and only if Zermelo-Fraenkel set theory conjoined with the denial of the AC is consistent.

There is, however, a disanalogy between the PSR and the cases of the AC and the LEM. While it may well be that we cannot find an argument for the PSR based on premises with greater innate intuitive plausibility than the PSR, we will find arguments for the PSR based on premises that *in fact* should appeal to a class of philosophers who do not themselves accept the PSR. However, there is no reason to think the possibility of giving dialectical arguments for the PSR is in fact a reason to deny its

---

6 One might wonder whether there are any logical connections between the LEM and the AC. It turns out that in an appropriate setting, the AC entails the LEM but the LEM does not entail the AC (cf. Bell, 1988, Theorem 4.31).

7 In light of footnote 6, one might wonder whether there is any logical connection between the PSR and the AC. One can give a somewhat tongue-in-cheek sketch of an argument for the equivalence of the PSR and the AC, given a causal principle applicable to chains of contingent events. As we saw in Section 3.1, given the AC *and* this CP, it follows that there is a first cause for every event. This we might take to entail the PSR. On the other hand, given the PSR, it can be argued that there is a God (see Chapter 4). If it could be argued that God has to be all-powerful in an appropriate sense, and in fact Jerome Gellman (2000) has argued that such a God as the PSR yields would have to be, then, as Robert Meyer (1987) quips, given a set A of disjoint nonempty subsets surely *God* could choose a subset containing one element from each one! Alas, this tongue-in-cheek argument probably fails since an omnipotent God can only do what is logically possible, and if the AC is false, then it is probably necessarily false and hence God cannot make such a choice.

self-evidence. After all, Aristotle gave dialectical arguments for the Principle of Noncontradiction.

11.9. WHAT SELF-EVIDENCE COULD BE

Now that perhaps the reader's confidence that the PSR *might* turn out to be self-evident has been fortified, let us turn back to the question of what that would mean. We started with a strong notion of self-evidence on which a true proposition is self-evident if it is understandable and cannot be understood without understanding that it is true. It is plausible that if the PSR is self-evident in this sense, then indeed those who understand it *know* it. It is not obvious, however, that they know that they know it.

One might, however, accept that the PSR is self-evident in this sense and still argue that those who accept the PSR because of its self-evidence lack knowledge, because there are *defeaters* available – namely, the arguments against the PSR. After all, understanding a proposition to be true is not the same as knowing it to be true. We have seen that the main arguments against the PSR fail or depend on dubious premises such as the impossibility of libertarian-free actions, but there could well be people to whom the PSR is self-evident, who are aware of the counterarguments and who are not aware that the counterarguments have been answered or who disagree with the answers. It is not clear whether *these* people should count as *knowing* the PSR, even granted that it is self-evident. However, the mathematical cases might convince one that there are basic propositions that it is right to hold on to even in the presence of apparent counterarguments. One might think that part of claiming the LEM to be self-evident is a claim that all evidence against it is thereby trumped. This might lead one to the following even stronger version of self-evidence:

(95) A proposition p is self-evident if, necessarily, anyone who understands it correctly understands it to be true, and it is possible for someone to understand it, and understanding p makes the agent have indefeasible knowledge of p for as long as she understands p.

But it is highly implausible that at least the AC should be self-evident in *this* sense. Suppose a very competent and honest mathematician came up to me and told me that the proof that the AC is consistent with Zermelo-Fraenkel set theory if and only if the set theory is consistent on its own has been found to be wrong, and that in fact it has been shown that the AC is false. It would be irrational for me to conclude that because the AC is in fact true, the speaker is either mistaken or lying. Of course, the defender of the AC's self-evidence in this strongest sense could simply claim that no one of us *in fact* understands the AC. But if so, then the self-evidence of the AC is, even if true, useless to us in every way.

It is not obvious, however, whether someone who holds the LEM to be self-evident would be irrational in rejecting the LEM in an analogous case. And if she were not to be irrational, then it might well be that likewise the defender of the PSR would not be irrational – if it is *in fact* the case that the PSR is self-evident.

No doubt the very strong formulations of self-evidence in (93) and (95) will strike many readers as highly implausible, at least as applied to the PSR. Be that as it may, I think the preceding considerations show that even these very strong formulations can be defended. If the PSR is true, then there is at least no evident absurdity in thinking it to be self-evident in these ways. A fortiori, there is nothing absurd about the PSR's being self-evident in some weaker way, such as in virtue of some fallible faculty of metaphysical insight by which we discern the truths of metaphysical propositions, or in the sense that all *normal* or *unbiased* agents who understand the PSR understand it to be true. We know the difficulties in spelling out such views. And all of these views have one thing in common: They are unhelpful when trying to convince a skeptic of the PSR.

Finally, we should make a cautionary distinction. There is a difference between claiming that instances of the PSR are self-evident and claiming that the PSR itself is self-evident. For instance, one might argue that we all find ourselves with a truth-directed faculty that when presented with a contingent state of affairs produces in us a belief that that state of affairs has an explanation. Such a faculty is going to be reliable, since most states of affairs we are presented with under normal circumstances do in fact have explanations, and hence this faculty will provide us with *knowledge*, on both the reliabilist epistemology and on Plantinga's Reformed epistemology, in normal circumstances. At the same time, its being so will be largely useless to those who, because of the presence of defeaters or of a malfunctioning explanation-assuming faculty, do not have this knowledge.

Suppose that it is further in fact the case that the PSR is *always* true, not just true in central cases, and that the faculty mentioned gives us the assumption of an explanation in all cases of a state of affairs taken to be contingent. Could one who has this faculty functioning properly with no defeaters claim in fact to know the PSR to be true in all cases? On the reliabilist or Reformed epistemologies it is the actual functioning of a reliable and/or truth-directed faculty that bestows knowledge. Knowledge that the faculty *would* in circumstances C bestow warrant on the belief that p does not itself bestow warrant on the claim that p would be true in C. Nonetheless, the fact that the faculty *would* bestow warrant on p in C might yield some evidence for p's being true in C, since one might think that, ceteris paribus, it is more likely that such a faculty is right in any random set of circumstances than that it is wrong.

This suggests that we need to distinguish between *cases* of the PSR's being self-evident and the PSR *itself's* being self-evident. For many applications this will make no difference, even for global Cosmological Argument types of cases in which we ask why there are any contingent entities at all, since in these applications we will be applying the PSR to particular cases. However, if it is only cases of the PSR that are self-evident, then other PSR-based arguments may be questionable. For instance, repeated applications of the PSR might be problematic, as in "If p has an explanation q, and q is contingent, then q must have an explanation," for we are not actually given q. The faculty by which we assume the existence of an explanation does not apply to propositions that are not given to the faculty.

On the other hand, one might compare the case of logic. It may be that our inferential faculties only deliver judgments of the form "*this* instance of *modus ponens* (or LEM) is valid," but not of the form "*all* instances of *modus ponens* are valid." Nonetheless, by reflecting on these faculties, we might well become convinced – and perhaps warrantedly – that their deliverances would be true in other cases. How this reflection would work is not clear. Perhaps it would require an insight that *modus ponens* as such is self-evidently valid. So perhaps the defender of the PSR as on the whole self-evident cannot confine herself to defending merely the weaker claim that cases of it are self-evident.

A confession: The PSR is self-evident to me. But since this will carry little weight with skeptical readers, we shall move on to arguments for the PSR.

11.10. PARADOXES

A final objection to the notion of self-evidence is that it seems that any decent paradox has self-evident premises, but these premises are not all true. Thus, there are false self-evident claims, and it is difficult to see how self-evidence can be conclusive evidence.

A quick answer is that such claims will not be self-evident according to (93) or (95), since these claims expressly say that the proposition is *correctly* understood to be true. But this does little to assuage the worry, for now the question comes down to whether the person to whom, say, the PSR is self-evident has *correctly* understood it to be true. The defenses of the possibility that the PSR is self-evident have shown that one can think one understands when one does not understand. Likewise one can think one correctly understands something to be the case when one does not.

Nonetheless, in the favorable cases the understanding may indeed provide conclusive evidence. Consider, for instance, the fact that in normal cases, my seeing myself as thinking that p provides conclusive evidence that I am thinking that p. Nonetheless, if Spinoza, Kierkegaard, and Wittgenstein are right, there are times when people think that they are thinking that p when they either are not thinking at all or are thinking about something else altogether.[8]

---

8 Formulating the second part of this thesis precisely is difficult because the cases of interest are ones in which, because of a deep confusion, the person is unable to entertain p. But then if she cannot entertain p, how can she think that she is entertaining p? However, as discussed, she may think that she is entertaining a proposition falling under s, where s is some description under which p falls. Thus, Kierkegaard seems to think that many people of Denmark are wrong that they are even thinking the (irreducibly *de se*) thought *that I am a Christian*. One way to make coherent sense of this is to say that such a Dane thinks that he thinks a thought with the logical form *I am a . . .* and further thinks that the blank in the thought is filled in with the same concept that the apostles expressed by the word "Christian." (It is a little bit more complicated than that, actually, because Kierkegaard also throws into question the "I" part of the thought.)

12

Three Thomistic Arguments

Recall St. Thomas's distinction between existence, *esse*, and essence, *essentia* or *quidditas*. Thomas took it as obvious that every thing needed something by virtue of which it had being, and took this needed "something" to be a causal relation in the case of contingent things. Is there an argument on Thomistic principles for this intuition of his? I will argue that there is. Indeed, I will discuss three arguments, of which at least the second works, and there is something to be said for the third. While the first argument is, I believe, unsound, together the first two arguments can be seen as handling two horns of a dilemma, depending on which way the *esse-essentia* distinction is taken.

12.1. FIRST THOMISTIC ARGUMENT: THE REGRESS OF EXISTENCES

12.1.1. The Regress of Existences

Consider a puzzle about a given existing thing, say Socrates, on Thomistic principles. Socrates has an essence and an act of existing. When we say that Socrates exists, we are talking about his act, A_1, of existing – this act of existing is the truthmaker for the claim that Socrates exists. At the same time, the act of existing is itself something that exists – if it did not, it could not ground Socrates' existing. Socrates' act of existing is not a necessary being, since then Socrates would be a necessary being. Thus, A_1 itself contingently exists. What is it in virtue of which A_1 itself exists? Well, it does not exist in virtue of A_1's essence, since it is not a necessary being. Thus, it exists in virtue of its own act, A_2, of existing. And so on ad infinitum. Socrates exists in virtue of A_1, A_1 in virtue of A_2, A_2 in virtue of A_3, and so on. And unless we posit a first cause, which the opponent to the CP will not want to do, there is no B in virtue of which all the A_k exist.

A crucial assumption here is that Socrates does not exist in virtue of *himself*. This follows from the fact that he is not identical with his existence, and, surely, on a Thomistic view that in virtue of which it is true that he exists just is his existence. If Socrates were identical with the existence of Socrates, the regress would be stopped at the first step. That Socrates is not identical with his existence, however, follows from the following considerations, for were Socrates identical with his existence, then on an Aristotelian metaphysics that sees the essence as a component in that which has the essence, it would likewise be true that Socrates' essence would be identical with his existence or a part thereof. The latter option can be disposed of easily: to talk of "parts of existence" is to commit a category mistake. Moreover, the existence, on Thomas's account of something that does not exist in virtue of its essence the way a necessary being would, is that which must be added to the essence to make the entity exist, and if so, then the essence is not a part of the existence. Thus, Socrates' essence would have to be identical with his existence, and hence with Socrates, or at least Socrates would exist in virtue of his essence. But this implies that, necessarily, if Socrates' essence exists, so does Socrates. But Socrates' essence does exist, at least in the mind of those who think of Socrates, and hence it follows that Socrates exists. But Socrates is in fact dead. Of course, there may well be life after death, but then just run this argument in a world in which it is true that Socrates ceases to exist with death.

Thus, the Thomistic account of existence appears to give rise to a regress. There are two points to be argued for now. First, that the regress would indeed be vicious. Second, that the generation of the regress can be curtailed – but only by rejecting the possibility of a thing whose *esse* arises neither from its essence nor from outside the thing.

12.1.2. *The Viciousness of the Regress*

Not all regresses are vicious. If p is a true proposition, then it is true that p, true that it is true that p, true that it is true that it is true that p, and so on. There is no difficulty in this regress because it is not a regress of grounders. It is not the case that p is true *because* it is true that it is true that p. But consider a different case. Suppose we thought that our knowledge that p depended on our knowing that we know that p, and suppose further that we thought these were distinct exercises of knowledge. Then we would indeed generate a *vicious* regress. Likewise, as Aristotle takes for granted in the first book of the *Nicomachean Ethics*, the regress of pursuing F_1 for the sake of F_2, F_2 for the sake of F_3, and so on, would indeed be vicious.

One suggestion for when a regress is vicious is the case in which it is a *grounding-type* regress, such as a causal, explanatory, or justificatory regress. In those cases the chain of groundings as a whole is without grounding, and it is as if we explained why the Earth does not fall down by positing an infinite series of tortoises beneath it to hold it up – the infinite series is of no more use than one tortoise, and one tortoise is indeed of no more use than the Earth itself. Nor will it do in a grounding-type regress to say that there is no cause, explanation, or justification to the chain as a whole, because these regresses occur precisely in contexts in which a cause, explanation, or justification is *required*. Thus, if the infinite chain of purposes generated by the argument of the first book of the *Ethics* is all there is, then in fact ultimately we act for no purpose at all – and it is a basic tenet of Aristotelianism that this is not so.

This point has been questioned heavily in the case of causal or explanatory regresses. Hume claimed that in those cases a sufficient explanation of a chain of causes or explanations is in the internal explanatory relations between the members of the chain. I argued in detail in Section 3.1 that this is false, but at the moment let me even concede the causal case. Nonetheless, other cases remain in which it is plain that a regress would be vicious. The ethical case, for instance, comes to mind. If after giving an infinite chain of purposes (speaking faster and faster as we go on, to make sure we say it in a finite amount of time) a friend asked us, "And what is *all that* for?" we would realize that even having given the infinite chain we have returned to the problem that started it all. The very problem of purposeless action because of which we embarked on the regress has reappeared.

The case of the regress of existences is equally vicious. We have here a basic ontological dependence in Thomistic metaphysics: each existent item depends on its act of existence in the most intimate way in which it can depend, namely, for its existence. But if the act of existence itself exists, as it must if it is to be something real, then its existence further depends on another act of existence, and we have a regress. But exactly the same problem reappears at the level of the infinite chain of existences.

211

The chain is something, and its existence must also depend on its act of existence. And hence the problem that started the regress is present at the level of the regress as a whole.

We have a basic metaphysical dependency: each thing depends on its existence, without which it could not possibly be, and there is no avoiding the conclusion that an infinite chain of such existences would be like the chain of tortoises apparently keeping up the Earth but in fact not helping to do any grounding at all. In fact, the dependency here is a truthmaker dependency: the truthmaker of the claim that the given object exists is its *esse*; the truthmaker of the claim that its *esse* exists is the *esse* of that *esse*; and so on. If this chain regresses with no overarching *esse* by virtue of which all the others exist, then there ultimately is nothing by virtue of which it is true that the given object exists, and hence the given object does not exist.

Of course this depends on the basic Thomistic ontology. If one thinks that the *esse* of a thing is not itself something real that the thing depends on, then one will not see this regress as any more vicious than the regress started from the observation that if *p* is true, then it is true that *p* is true.

12.1.3. How to Stop the Regress

One way to stop the regress is to insist that at some point in the chain, say, at A_n, we have an *esse* whose existence is identical with itself: $A_{n+1} = A_n$. On Thomistic principles, such an *esse* would then be a necessary being – since the item itself as a whole would be identical with its *esse*, in particular its essence would be identical with its *esse*. But hence whatever it is that exists in virtue of it would also be a necessary being, and hence A_{n-1} would be a necessary being, and going back along the chain we would find that the initial object is a necessary being.

But it is always better to stop a regress before it even starts. The *esse* of the initial object is perhaps not *to be simpliciter* but *to be caused*. Thus instead of leading us to a further *esse* in virtue of which the first *esse* can be truly said to exist, we are led to an efficient cause. The strategy here at first sight seems to be the same as in Aristotle's *Metaphysics* H.6, which is the culmination of the ontological investigation of substance. There, Aristotle struggles with the question of what it is by virtue of which the form and the matter are united into one entity. We can see that the problem is similar. Positing a further *entity* by virtue of which the form and matter are united would generate a vicious regress – for we would need a yet

212

further entity to unite this entity to the form and matter. Aristotle notes, however, that

> the proximate matter and the form are one and the same; the one potentially and the other actually, so that to search for a cause or ground of the oneness [of matter and form] is like looking for the cause or ground of being one [in general]. For a particular thing is one, and what is potentially and what is actually are in a way one, so that there is no cause or ground [*aition*] unless [*plēn ei*] it is something that moves it from potentiality to actuality. (*Metaphysics* H.6, 1045b18–22, my trans.)

What Aristotle seems to be doing is conceptually recasting the initial situation. It is a mistake to look for that in virtue of which the matter and form are one when by *in virtue of* we mean some sort of indwelling ground of unity. The only thing to be looked for is the efficient cause that moved the item from potentiality to actuality, that is, which caused the union of the matter with the form.

Thus, we can stop our regress of existences by replacing a grounding relation, whereby the existence of an *esse* is grounded by a yet further *esse*, with a causal relation. Unfortunately, there are two interrelated serious objections to this approach to arguing for the CP on Thomistic grounds.

12.1.4. Why Do We Need a Cause at All?

The first objection is that once we see that there is no need for the *esse* of Socrates to have another *esse* that makes it true to say that the first *esse* exists, because all we need is a cause, then it is not clear why we need a cause at all. There is a difference between ontological grounding relations and efficient causal relations. When we sought that in virtue of which the *esse* of Socrates exists, we were looking for an ontological ground, a ground required by an ontology on which there is a distinction between *esse* and *essentia*, for if we take that ontology seriously, then it seems the *esse* must itself have an *essentia*, namely, *being the esse of Socrates*, and an *esse*. But the causal relations seem to answer an explanatory question, not an ontological question about the nature of Socrates' existence. And so the initial reasons for generating the regress do not require us to posit a *cause*. Once we have seen that we do not need a regress of existences, we do not thereby see that we need a regress of causes.

In the passage from *Metaphysics* H.6, the efficient cause that makes for the transition from the proximate matter – the matter from which the object can be generated in a single transformation – to the final object does not actually do any work in explaining the unity of matter and form. Aristotle says that there just is no ground or cause *unless* it is an efficient cause, but this does not constitute an assertion *that* there is an efficient cause, much less an argument for such a cause. Aristotle is telling us that it is ridiculous to look for the cause why matter and form are one, because that is like looking for a cause for why some object, say, a horse, is one. And the latter is plainly absurd. There is no *aition* of its being one, except at most an *aition* in a different sense, namely, whatever caused the horse to exist in the first place. The point is that the search for the principle of the unity of matter and form is a mistaken search. Invoking Aristotle as a parallel to the preceding Thomistic argument thus undermines the argument, for one can likewise say that what the problem of the regress of existences shows is that we need to see *esse* and *essentia* differently, and then the problem will disappear. We do not need to suppose an efficient cause – Aristotle discusses the efficient cause only to clarify what kind of cause can *at most* be said to be present.

The preceding criticism does appear both to be plausible exegesis of Aristotle and compatible with Aquinas's commentary on *Metaphysics* H.6. However, it is not a sufficient answer to the puzzle of the regress of existences. The problem of the regress of existences might be seen to be closely parallel to the problem of the unity of form and matter. Why is essence united to existence? Surely this is a silly question: the existence simply actualizes the essence, just as an Aristotelian form simply actualizes the matter. But the question is not silly at all in either context. For when we talk about the form's actualizing the matter, it is as if we thought of the form as existing independently of the matter. Once we think of the form as not existing independently of the matter, the language of actualizing becomes more puzzling. That is why one might well think that even if Aristotle does not make this point in H.6, although his admission of the possibility of cause of the transition from potentiality to actuality at 1045b22 makes room for it, an Aristotelian system *will* need to suppose the form's priority to the matter. But this is accomplished precisely through having the form preexist in the efficient cause, either as the form of that cause, as when one animal generates another, or intentionally in the mind of an agent acting as cause.

In the Thomistic context, the problem is at least as serious. The essence has no being apart from the concrete instantiators of it and apart from the minds that know it. In talking of its "actualizing" the essence, we say that the *esse* brings the essence into ontologically mind-independent existence. But this requires that the *esse* indeed be an independent factor, an independent *principle*, that enters into the matter. But then it is right and proper, and for exactly the same reason, to ask about what makes this real thing, which must be prior to the essence considered as mind independent if it is to actualize it, be.

12.1.5. The Esse of Socrates Is Socrates' Being Caused

However, once we realize that the *esse* of Socrates is *Socrates' being caused*, then the whole puzzle disappears. For *Socrates' being caused* is a radically different sort of thing from a substance. Something like the *esse-essentia* distinction should still apply to it, though in a different way. The essence of *Socrates' being caused* is actualized by nothing other than the causal activity of Socrates' cause, whatever that cause might be. To put it awkwardly, what this account posits is that Socrates' cause, or maybe its *engagement in causal activity*, is the *esse* of Socrates' being caused.

There is a problem here, though. Imagine Michelangelo's deciding whether to make a statue of David or of Saul, and suppose we take this to be a libertarian-free choice. Suppose, further, for simplicity that Michelangelo has a will so powerful that simply deciding which statue to make makes that statue come into existence. Then, the *esse* of the David is *the David's being caused*. Now, the *esse* of the David's being caused is Michelangelo's will or perhaps Michelangelo's will's causal exercise. But Michelangelo's will and his will's causal exercise can exist even without *the David's being caused* existing. For he could have chosen to make a statue of Saul instead. So in what sense can Michelangelo's will be said to be the *esse* of the David? This leads us to the conclusion that, given libertarian free will, one and the same thing could have been the *esse* of more than one possible object. But if this is so, then it is not enough to know that the *esse* of *the David's being caused* exists to know that the David is caused, that is, that the David exists as caused.

This reasoning applies more generally as an argument against Thomas's *esse-essentia* system. Suppose that it is always the case that that the *esse* of A exists entails that A exists. As before, generate a regress of existences. Thomas will reject the possibility of this regress's being infinite, and let us follow him in this. Then the regress must terminate in something whose *esse* and *essentia* are identical, and hence that is a necessary being. By knowing that this item exists, we can know that everything else in the chain exists, then, at least link by link. Thus, the given contingent object ends up being such that its existence is entailed by the existence of a necessary being. And that is absurd – the given object would not be contingent then.

This argument shows that Thomas, were he to accept the regress of existences argument, could not consistently hold that the *esse* of a contingent being is such that its existence entails the existence of the being. Thus, he would be committed to the principle that there is no entailment from the existence of the *esse* of a contingent being to the existence of that being. But surely he *is* committed to there being such an entailment by his whole *esse-essentia* analysis. The very reason for positing the man's or phoenix's *esse* was that we observed that in knowing their essences we did not know them to exist. By implication, knowing the *esse* of Socrates lets us know that Socrates exists. But there is a *de re / de dicto* ambiguity here. Knowing the *esse* of Socrates *as the esse of Socrates* lets us know that Socrates exists. Thus, that the *esse of Socrates*, read *de dicto*, exists does entail that Socrates exists. But let "*X*" be a proper name for the *esse of Socrates*. Then that *X* exists need not entail that Socrates exists: *X* could be the *esse* of something else, if the preceding arguments hold. Thus, we can clarify Thomas's argument in a way that does not make it result in a contradiction upon being faced with the issue of libertarian free will. And it is a clarification Thomas is committed to, since he is committed at least to God's having libertarian free will, even if the debate continues whether on his view creatures have libertarian free will.

Of course, much still needs to be worked out in detail in such an account. Is the *esse* of Socrates just *Socrates' being caused*, or is it just *being caused*? The latter would mean we all have the same *esse*. This is not what Thomas intends, but it is not obvious that the system rules it out. Thomas does insist that God is not our *esse*. But on the preceding account if God directly creates *x*, *y*, and *z*, then while God is perhaps not the *esse* of *x*, *y*, and *z*, God is the *esse* of the *esse* of *x*, and of that of *y*, and of that of *z*. Another point to be noted is that the cause of Socrates not only causes the *esse* of Socrates to *be*, but also causes it to be the *esse* of *Socrates*.

Next, note that if Socrates' *esse* were *Socrates' being causelessly existent*, then we would indeed have a serious problem. For on Thomas's ontology, that *esse* would need another *esse*, something in virtue of which it can be said to exist. Now, to block fatalism, the general conclusion that we must have cases in which one and the same item is the *esse* of more than one potential item must remain in play. However, in this case, the relation

216

of the *esse* of *x* to *x* in the chain of existences starting with Socrates is never going to be causal, since Socrates is causeless, ex hypothesi, and anything that causes the existence of the existence of . . . of the existence of Socrates causes Socrates to exist. Therefore, the relation of the *esse* of *x* for *x* will have to be some stronger form of grounding, perhaps some sort of truthmaker-style grounding, or some logical-entailment style of grounding. But this is presumably not going to allow for indeterministic grounding: if item *A* grounds item *B* in this strong sense, then the existence of *A* had better entail the existence of *B*. Only a causal grounding relation is loose enough to deny this entailment (compare the discussion of free will and quantum mechanics in Part II).

12.2. SECOND THOMISTIC ARGUMENT: THE INTERDEPENDENCE OF EXISTENCE AND ESSENCE

12.2.1. *The Nonuniversality of the* Esse-Essentia *Distinction*

There is a different approach to the CP also based on the *esse-essentia* distinction, but with that distinction interpreted differently. While the first argument supposed the universality of the distinction, we start this time by denying that the distinction is universal enough to allow us to start the regress of existences. Socrates needs an existence and essence, but the *esse* of Socrates does not need this – an *esse* is a different kind of item.

In fact, even if we take the first account, we still must allow *some* types of items not to have a distinction between *esse* and *essentia*, for as we saw, there will have to be cases in which the same item X, which is in fact the *esse* of A, could have been the *esse* of something else, say, B. Thus, it is an accident of X that X is in fact the *esse* of A. Accidents are items in the Thomistic ontology. Denote this accident of X, namely, the accident of X's being the *esse* of A, by Y. Now, if every kind of item has the distinction, then consider the *esse* and *essentia* of Y. This generates an infinite regress, the first steps of which are

(96) A

(97) The *esse*, X, of A

(98) The accident, Y, of X that X is the *esse* of A

(99) The *esse*, X_1, of Y

(100) The accident, Y_1, of X_1 that X_1 is the *esse* of Y

(101) The *esse*, X_2, of Y_1

(102) The accident, Y_2, of X_2 that X_2 is the *esse* of Y_1

To arrest this regress we have to deny at some point that the *esse-essentia* distinction is conceptually applicable or claim that the *esse* of one of the accidents is identical with its *essentia*. Suppose we take the latter option. For definiteness, let us suppose that the *esse* and *essentia* of Y_2 are identical. Then, Y_2 is a necessary being on Thomistic principles. But since an accident would not exist if that which it is the accident of did not exist, a necessary being can only be an accident of a necessary being. Hence, X_2 is a necessary being. Moreover, since Y_2 is the accident of X_2's being the *esse* of Y_1, it follows that it is a necessary truth that X_2 is the *esse* of Y_1 (this does not commit a *de re / de dicto* mistake if accidents are identified in such a way that if H is the accident of B's having property F, then necessarily if H exists, then B has F). Hence Y_1 exists necessarily. Therefore so does X_1, since Y_1 is an accident of X_1. And so on. We finally conclude that A is a necessary being. Thus, this option is unavailable.

This leaves only one option. We must at some point deny the applicability of the *esse-essentia* analysis. On the account of Section 12.1, we will presumably do so at the level of the accident Y of X that X is the *esse* of A – and, indeed, Aquinas explicitly denies that accidents ordinarily[1] have an *esse-essentia* composition (*Summa Theologica* III, 77, 1, objection 4 and reply 4). We will say that all we have is the fact of X's being the *esse* of A. We have predication, but we do not need to reify it into the kind of entity that needs an *esse-essentia* distinction. There is some justification for thinking that an *esse-essentia* analysis applies to the *esse* of A, because this *esse* in some sense "does" something, namely, actualizes the essence of A, and hence is to be thought of as an active principle, as something sufficiently substantial that it should need a distinction between *esse* and *essentia*. But perhaps we need not say the same about an accident, which is but a modification of a more substantial entity and receives all its reality from that entity, at least in the ordinary course of events.[2]

But we may reasonably disagree. We can take the preceding problems as a sign that we should not push the *esse-essentia* distinction too far. Thus,

---

1 The exception is that of them after transubstantiation. Cf. note 2.
2 Thomas allows, in his account of transubstantiation, for an accident (say, whiteness) to remain in existence after the substance it is the accident of ceases to exist (*Summa Theologica* III, 77, 1). Nonetheless, it is does not seem possible that an accident should exist without that of which it is an accident's *having existed* at some point, and that is all that is needed for the previous discussion of the second regress (Thomas himself admits that the individuation of the accidents after transubstantiation supervenes on their individuation prior to transubstantiation, and the latter individuation is through that of the subject they had inhered in, that is, the bread and the wine: *Summa Theologica* III, 77, 1, reply 3).

perhaps indeed the distinction should not apply to the *esse* of Socrates itself. Once we say this, our initial regress of existences is arrested at the first step. We have the *esse* of Socrates, but no *esse* of the *esse* of Socrates. Moreover, if we take this view, we no longer have any need to take the controversial view that the same item could serve as the *esse* of more than one possible item. In fact, there is good independent reason not to take this view, which in turn is good reason to reject the claim that the *esse-essentia* distinction applies to an *esse*, for if the same X could serve as the *esse* of more than one possible item, then X has a certain independence. If the *esse* of Socrates can *only* be the *esse* of Socrates, then a statement that the *esse* of Socrates exists can be taken to be a longwinded way of saying that *Socrates* exists, just as the statement that the accident of Socrates' wisdom exists can be taken to be a longwinded way of saying that Socrates is wise. But if the *esse* of Socrates could have been the *esse* of Clinias, instead, then no such paraphrase is possible, and hence the *esse-essentia* distinction should kick in for the *esse* of Socrates, leading us back to the first version of the argument.

Thus let us then explore the view on which each act of existing can only be the act of existing of one item. Socrates' *esse* can only be the *esse* of Socrates. This shows that there may be an interdependence between the *esse* and *essentia* that is not visible if we simply characterize Aquinas's view in terms of "the priority of existence over essence." Our first view did, indeed, allow for a completely unambiguous such priority, and to the extent that one thinks either Thomas's view or the truth of the matter exhibits such a priority, one will opt for that view. But this one does not. The essence of Socrates is needed to specify what the act of existing of Socrates is: it is the act of existing of *Socrates*.

12.2.2. The Interdependence of Essence and Existence

But at the same time, essence really does depend on existence. This is the Aristotelian moment in Thomas's thought. If there were no minds, there would be no essences of nonexistent things. As it is, there might be such essences, because the essence of a house could have existed in the mind of an architect even if no houses had ever been made. Indeed, it might have to be admitted that in God's mind there are in some sense all kinds of essences of nonexistent things that God could make. But once we admit the existence of God, then we have the CP for free: if there is a first cause, then everything indeed has a cause. For the moment let us restrict ourselves to essences *as existing mind-independently*. Thomas does hold that it is different for an essence to exist in mind than for it to exist in a thing, and of course he must be right. Otherwise, when we think of a house, there is a house in our mind, and we do not need to build a house – we just need to find a way of getting ourselves into this house!

The mind-independent existence of the essence of Socrates *does* depend on Socrates' existence, given an Aristotelian ontology. But as we saw, likewise Socrates' existence depends on Socrates' essence in some way. The essence can be characterized independently of the existence: "I can know what a man or a phoenix is and still be ignorant whether it exists in reality" (Aquinas, 1949, chap. 4). We thus have a puzzle.

In the case of Socrates, we get out of the difficulty as follows. The nature or essence of the human being, as found in Socrates' parents, precedes Socrates temporally. Through a causal activity in which their nature or essence itself plays a causal role – we must not think of a nature or essence as something causally inefficacious in an Aristotelian setting – Socrates is generated. Socrates' existence is something new on the scene. Socrates' essence is new only qua the essence *of Socrates*. It is already on the scene in his parents. Thus, in one sense essence precedes existence. The essence as found in the cause is prior in the order of explanation to the existence of the effect. At the same time, the existence of the cause – the *esse* of the mother and the *esse* of the father of Socrates – precedes that essence.

12.2.3. Individual Essences

This leads to a natural question. Is the essence as found in Socrates numerically the same as the essence as found in his parents? In the case of Aristotle, substituting *form* for *essence*, this is a disputed exegetical point. Aquinas says:

> If someone should ask, then, whether the nature [of the human being] so considered [i.e., in itself] can be called *one* or *many*, neither should be granted, because both are outside the concept of humanity and both can be added to it. If plurality were included in the concept of humanity, it could never be one, although it is one inasmuch as it is present in Socrates. Similarly, if unity were contained in its concept, then Socrates' and Plato's nature would be one and the same, and it could not be multiplied in many individuals.
>
> Nature or essence is considered in a second way with reference to the act of existing [*esse*] it has in this or that individual. (Aquinas, 1949, chap. 3)

The last sentence of the first quoted paragraph clearly says that at least in some sense, the nature or essence is many. Yet the next sentence suggests that we can talk of a single nature as found in many individuals.

220

The question is an important one here, for if numerically one and the same essence were found in Socrates and his parents, then the preceding solution to the puzzle of bidirectional priority between *esse* and *existence* might be quite satisfactory: Socrates' essence is prior to his existence, because his essence preexisted in his parents. But if Socrates' essence is different from that of his parents, then it is not the case that the essence of Socrates is prior to the existence of Socrates in any sense. If we were dealing with Aristotle, we might try to solve this by shoehorning him into a commitment to diverse individuals' sharing numerically one essence, though the resulting view would be rather implausible once one identifies an Aristotelian essence with a form, and hence with a soul. But Thomas does want to maintain a difference between the essence of Socrates and the essence of his parents.

However, we can consider the essence of Socrates in two ways: first, as instantiated by an individual existing in a particular place in space and time (Thomas talks of individuation through "matter considered under determined dimensions"),[3] and, second, as not designated in this way. The essence of Socrates, while not numerically identical with the essence of his parents, is nonetheless *generically* identical to it, Aquinas will insist. And this is good enough to solve the puzzle about the mutual priorities between *esse* and *essentia*. What needs to condition the *esse* of Socrates, what needs to delimit it, is not so much that it is the act of existing of *Socrates* but that it is that of a *human being*. The humanity of the existent object is indeed prior to the existence, in the sense that to specify what sort of an existence we have in view, we need to specify that it is a human existence, an existence of a human being. And the generic essence of a human being as such is to be found in Socrates' parents – not, indeed, a second essence of them, but their own individual essences considered generically.

12.2.4. *Further Differentiation of Existences*

This, however, is not quite enough. It does guarantee that the *esse* of Socrates and the *esse* of Alexander's warhorse Bucephalus are numerically distinct. One is a human and the other an equine *esse*. But we started this discussion by offering it as an alternative to the first Thomistic argument for the CP, premising our alternative on the idea that the *esse* is not an independent principle that can actualize more than one essence, and

---

3 Aquinas (1949, chap. 2).

hence it is not the sort of thing for which we should in turn seek another *esse-essentia* distinction. Thus we also need to differentiate the *esse* of Socrates from the *esse* of Clinias. But this we can do through the matter of Socrates, the matter considered as initially occupying such and such a spatiotemporal location, which initial location defines Socrates' identity. Or at least a traditional Thomist account would say something like this, given Thomas Aquinas's (1949, chap. 2) talk of matter as designated in three dimensions. If we depart from Thomas further, we might consider the identity of chunks of matter as primitive, though doing so may create other problems.[4]

Thus, in the case of objects that have a cause, there is a solution to the problem connected with the mutual interdependence of essence and existence. The existence is determined or conditioned by the essence considered generically, in a way in which it does indeed precede the existent object, and, in the case of a material object, the matter. At the same time, the essence considered individually depends on the existence, as Gilson famously insisted. Note, too, that this solution involves something stronger than the CP for substances. It involves a claim that an object having an essence must arise from another object that has generically the same essence – or else, to return to an option that we had set aside but now can restore, from a minded object that had this generic essence existing in its mind.

12.2.5. Alternatives and Objections

This is an argument for the CP from Thomistic principles to the extent that this or some other solution involving the CP is required for solving the difficulty. To complete the argument, thus, we need to examine

---

4 The most notorious of these problems is the problem of constitution. Thinking of the identity of a chunk of matter as definitory of the identity of a substance may require that the chunk be identifiable independently of that substance, for instance, through preexisting. Thus we have to have a chunk of matter with a primitive identity survive across substantial change. This, however, raises problems of constitution, because it allows us to speak of a chunk of matter, and its identity, and a substance, and its identity, so that we can ask ontological questions about what it is that unites the matter with the form, and how the matter is related to the substance. And we cannot then take the solution that, as a reading of *Metaphysics* H.6 would say, there is in a sense no difference between the matter and the substance. But if we accepted only the spatial dimensions of matter as definitory of the identity of the substance, then we could allow that in substantial change the matter itself changes numerically, while remaining the same spatially. The matter would no longer be identifiable apart from the substance, and the problem of unity, that is, of constitution, dissolves as Aristotle shows in H.6.

alternatives. One alternative solution would be to reject entirely any precedence of essence over existence. Of course the problem of what it is in virtue of which the *esse* of Socrates is different from the *esse* of Bucephalus remains. But we can solve this without talking of any prior essence at all. Rather, what makes the *esse* of Socrates different from that of Bucephalus is just that the two have different matter.

This is problematic, however, especially if we accept the Aristotelian intuition that when a horse dies, the substance in question ceases to exist. But when Bucephalus dies, his matter keeps on existing. Since we are now working on the view that the same *esse* cannot be the *esse* of two different entities, say, Bucephalus and Bucephalus's carcass, it follows that the *esse* of Bucephalus cannot depend for its identity *solely* on the identity of the matter.

However, one might argue instead that the identity of an enmattered object supervenes on the identity *and properties* of matter, that is, whether *A* is identical with *B* can only depend on the relation between the identity of the chunks of matter in *A* and *B* and on the properties of this matter, such as electric charge and momentum. Thomas can, however, accommodate such a supervenience claim in his ontology. Thomas holds that it is the form of an enmattered object that is responsible for the properties of the matter, including the matter's dimensional properties, to the extent that these properties are not imposed upon the object from without. And it is the properties caused from within that are responsible for an object's identity. What makes a colt the same entity as the adult horse is the development of the properties of the colt into those of the adult horse, directed by the colt's own system. What makes a brazen sphere the same sphere at two different times is the causal interconnections between the positions and properties of the particles at the first stage and those at intermediate times. If external influence disturbs these interconnections too much, for instance, by replacing all of the brass at once, we are dealing with a different object. Thomas will then say that the essence *is* involved in the causal properties of the matter of the object, and hence making identity depend solely on these does not get one away from the essence.

A more serious problem for my argument is this. Let us grant that the *esse* of Socrates does depend in some way on the essence of the human being and the essence of the human being depends on an existence either of a human being or of a mind thinking about human beings. But why cannot the *esse* of Socrates and his essence come into existence simultaneously and causelessly?

There is no problem with the *esse* of Socrates and his essence's coming into existence simultaneously. That certainly happened when Socrates was formed in Phaenarete's womb (assuming this was his mother's name, and not just a literary conceit of Plato's). However, if this is the whole story, if there is no essence of the human being preceding Socrates in existence, then we have a vicious circularity in the order of dependence. The *esse* of Socrates depends on the essence of Socrates then, while the essence of Socrates depends, for Aristotelian reasons, on Socrates himself and hence on his existence. Their coming into existence simultaneously is no help at all – for the *esse* of Socrates needs to come *before* the essence of Socrates in the order of dependence, and yet the latter on this proposed solution to the puzzle needs to come before. Our proposed solution to the difficulty only worked because the essence that the esse of Socrates depended on was not the essence of *Socrates*, but the generic essence of a human being, which we can find in any man or woman, or in a mind thinking of human beings as such.

Granted, the essence of the human being must come into existence before the existence of Socrates, at least in the order of dependence. But this still leaves two loose ends.

12.2.6. *Essences* ex Nihilo

One may object to the argument for the CP by asking whether the essence of the human being does not itself come into existence *ex nihilo*, thereby violating the CP?

However, the essence of the human being, on Aristotelian grounds, cannot exist apart from an actual human being or a mind thinking of human beings as such. Now, we have just seen that we could not have the essence of the human being's coming into existence simultaneously with an actual human being's coming into existence, with no previous existence of such an essence. So the remaining possibility here is that the essence of the human being came into existence *ex nihilo* in a mind.

But, first, this possibility does not challenge a CP for substances, if this mind is what creates human beings. The individual human being still satisfies the CP, even if the essence of the human being does not. However, this concession need not be made. This essence's being-in-mind is itself going to be a mental act, something real and with causal power. Thus, it may well be that we can apply the *esse-essentia* distinction to this mental

224

act, and, if so, then we will have to be able to find a cause of this mental act's existence in terms of something else in which we can find the same essence as the essence of this mental act.

12.2.7. Noncausal Dependence

The second, and more potent objection is to ask why the dependence between the existence of Socrates and the essence of the human being must be causal. This objection envisions one of two scenarios. On one scenario, there is a mind that thinks about human beings, but there are no human beings, and then Socrates pops into existence with no cause, and in particular with no causal connection between Socrates and the essence of the human being as existing in the preexistent mind. On the other scenario, there are other human beings before Socrates, and hence the essence of the human being exists, but Socrates comes into existence causelessly, and with no causal connection between him and the essence of the human being as it is found in the other human beings. If one has Kripkean objections that Socrates could not have been conceived of parents different from Phaenarete and Sophroniscus, then let us not talk of Socrates here, but of Socrates*, a human being who pops into existence *ex nihilo* but is very much like Socrates.

Both of the scenarios do ensure that the essence of the human being is already there on the scene when Socrates* pops into existence. Thus we do not have the absurdity of an *esse*'s popping up *ex nihilo* without that essence on which the *esse* depends already present. Nor does this view commit us to the essence's existing abstractly in a Platonic heaven. However, the view is unfaithful to Aristotelian principles. The basic reason the Aristotelian rejects the idea of essences' dwelling abstractly in a Platonic heaven is that the Platonic heaven is causally separated from concrete things, and hence the Forms are not available to play any causal or explanatory role. The two scenarios under consideration will both be seen to suffer from a similar defect: the essence of the human being is not available to play the role for which it is needed.

One way to see it is this. Thomas is in fact committed to individual essences. If we accept this, then the *generic essence* is an abstraction: it is not something really there. Now, the *esse* of the real Socrates of our world, as we saw, must depend on the essence of the human being. But this essence only exists concretely as the essence of Phaenarete or of Sophroniscus or of Herodotus or the essence of the human being as

225

thought of by Protagoras or by God or by a modern genetic engineer. Each of these essences, considered generically, is an essence of the human being. However, these essences are different. If Socrates was conceived of Phaenarete and Sophroniscus, then it is *their* essences – Aquinas and Aristotle thought only Sophroniscus's but their biology was deficient – that are plainly the ones Socrates' act of existing involves, and neither the essence of Herodotus nor the essence of the human being as thought of by Protagoras or a modern genetic engineer enters in. The case of God depends on whether we follow Aquinas in thinking that the soul of each human being is directly created by God. In any case, this shows that the existence of Socrates does not depend on any essence of the human being other than that essence *as found in his causes*, whether as found formally in them, to use the phrase that is familiar to us from Descartes, as in the case of Phaenarete and Sophroniscus, or as found eminently in a mind, as in the case of God, assuming Socrates' soul was directly created by God.

Therefore, presumably, if Socrates* were to have just popped into existence *ex nihilo*, his existence would not be dependent on *any* human essence. Certainly if our real Socrates' *esse* did not depend on the essence of the human being as thought of by Protagoras, neither would the *esse* of Socrates* have depended on that essence as thought of by Protagoras were Socrates* to have popped into existence causelessly. And it would not have depended on Herodotus's essence. But neither would it have depended on the essence as found formally in Phaenarete and Sophroniscus had Socrates* not been their son, any more than it would have depended on Herodotus's essence. Nor would there be any need for the act of existing of Socrates* to depend on any essence found in the mind of God, if God were not a cause of Socrates*. Therefore, the act of existing of Socrates* would not depend on *any* essence of the human being, which we have already seen to be impossible. Thus, on Thomistic grounds, it is impossible that Socrates* should pop into existence *ex nihilo* with no cause.

Two objections can be leveled against this argument. First of all, it uses the assumption that there are individual essences, that there must be specific essences of human beings on which the act of existence of Socrates* depends, but which one cannot single out in any nonarbitrary way. Thomas does accept individual essences, but an Aristotelian critic might not. In response, one might note that even without individual essences, the act of existence of Socrates does not depend on the essence as considered in its grand overarching spread through all human beings and all minds thinking of them, but in this essence as it is found in Sophroniscus and Phaenarate and perhaps God. And the argument goes through: the act of existing of Socrates* has no x such that the essence of x or the essence as found in the mind of x is that on which this act of existing depends, contrary to what we have argued.

The second objection is much more serious, and indeed it rises to the level of a new objection against the whole Thomistic account. What if in fact the act of existence of Socrates* were to depend on *all* the essences of the human being, not just those found in Sophroniscus, Phaenarete, and the mind of God? But as it would be strange to suppose that Herodotus's essence becomes involved just as soon as we move from Socrates to Socrates*, since there is no more reason why it should be related to Socrates* than to Socrates, we will extend this to a more general account. Every human being's act of existence depends on the essence of every other human being and on the essence of the human being as found in the mind of anybody in whose mind it is found. Thus, we can handle Socrates and Socrates* uniformly.

This objection presumably rejects the Aristotelian account of how the form of the parent is involved in the production of the child in the case of a child's coming into existence in the usual way. Rather, insofar as conditioning the *esse* of Socrates goes, the essences of Sophroniscus and Phaenarete are no more involved than that of Herodotus, though they may of course be causally involved in different ways.

The puzzle now before us is how something, namely, the *esse* of Socrates*, can come into existence causelessly *ex nihilo* but always already dependent on something else. Its coming into existence causelessly *ex nihilo* suggests it is an independent thing. So how can it be dependent on something, as it must be on the essence?

And why is it that the *esse* of Socrates* cannot come into existence when there are no human beings in existence or in thought already? What is there about a thoroughly humanless reality that precludes the causeless event of Socrates' *esse* popping into existence from happening? One could perhaps imagine a positive reality's preventing something from happening causelessly. Maybe the presence of a rock in a place in space can prevent Socrates from materializing there causelessly. But how can a causeless event *need* anything to make possible its occurrence?

And besides this, the very idea that the essence of the human being should condition the *esse* of Socrates* without a causal connection between this essence and the *esse* is very un-Aristotelian. As noted before, such a notion damages the Aristotelian critique of Platonic Forms.

12.2.8. Conclusions of Argument

What we have seen, thus, is that there are two different Thomistic ontologies that can be given, depending on whether one thinks that the *esse* of an object itself is subject to *esse-essentia* analysis or not. Each ontology requires the CP to overcome difficulties. Thus, indeed, the CP is at the heart of Thomistic metaphysics. Whether the PSR is at the heart of it, too, depends on the connections between the CP and the PSR, which were discussed in Chapter 3. How good an argument for the CP this is would depend on a more thorough analysis of Thomistic metaphysics and especially of the *esse-essentia* distinction.

The CP argued for on the second Thomistic ontology is one that combines a principle that says that contingent objects – that is, ones that have an *esse-essentia* distinction – have causes, and that the essence of the effect is found in the cause, either formally, as when the cause is of the same sort as the effect, or eminently, as when the essence is in the mind of the cause. This has theological implications, of course. Assuming that the essence of the human being is generically different from the essence of any other animal, and given that human beings have not always been around, then it follows that at some point a mind that had thought the essence of the human being created a human being, though of course not necessarily *ex nihilo* – perhaps, for instance, using the matter of a nonhuman animal. One might avoid this conclusion by supposing, implausibly, that the essence of every animal, say, is generically the same, and the difference between Socrates and Bucephalus is only quantitatively greater than that between Socrates and Napoleon. But then we require a mind to have created the first animal or at least the first living thing.

This approach to the CP thus leads not just to Cosmological Arguments but to teleological ones as well. John Haldane (Smart and Haldane, 1997, pp. 98–106) has recently resurrected teleological arguments of this form. Of course, some will take these theological conclusions to discredit the metaphysics on which all this is based. But since there is no strong evidence against the mere conclusion that there is a mind that designed every species and endowed members of the species with essences, this would be irrational. Note that evidence for evolution is beside the point here: such a mind might well have employed evolution as its means of production.

And evolution taken by itself fails to explain why animals have the essences they do, the Thomist will insist.[5]

12.3. THIRD THOMISTIC ARGUMENT: SUBSTANCE-ACCIDENT ONTOLOGY

Bruce Reichenbach (1972) and more recently Mark Nowacki (1998) have given an argument for the CP based on a substance-accident ontology. On this ontology, if something is not dependent on anything, then it is a substance. Now, consider a contingent object, say, Bucephalus. Bucephalus has an existence. This existence is either dependent on something or not. If it is not dependent on anything, then Bucephalus's existence is a substance. But that is an absurd conclusion. If Bucephalus's existence is a substance, then it makes sense to think of it on its own, without Bucephalus. But that is plainly absurd. Note that this argument fails as applied to a being such as God who, according to Thomas, is identical with his existence.

There is a very serious direct objection to this argument. If the existence of y is to be an accident of some other substance x, then we are using *accident* in a sense too far removed from focal uses such as when we say that snubnosedness is an accident of Socrates or that greenness is an accident of the chair. Furthermore, there is something uncomfortable for a Thomist in adopting the preceding argument. Presumably, in the case of an object y immediately caused by God, the substance that y's existence depends on is God. Since the dependence here is supposed to be accident-substance dependence, it follows that y's existence is an accident of God. But Thomas thinks, on the basis of arguments that to a Thomist are very plausible (*Summa Theologica* I, 3, 6), that God has no accidents. If one responds by saying that the notion of *accident* is used here in an extended sense, then one endangers the whole argument.

A different response to the argument would be a Platonic-Fregean one. The existence of Bucephalus is really an accident of the essence of Bucephalus, namely, the accident of its being instantiated. The essence of Bucephalus is then a substance. However, we should not insist on the claim that a substance *causes* its accidents, our Fregean will tell us, and in particular the essence does not cause its being instantiated. So the fact

---

5 The argument in this section has a significant similarity to one given by Barry Miller (1983). However, Miller's argument starts with the controversial assumption that one could not refer to a nonexistent individual.

that the existence of Bucephalus is an accident of something, such as the essence of Bucephalus, should not thereby force us to admit that it is *caused* by something. The latter criticism can be detached from the Platonic-Fregean ontology, in fact. Granted, the existence of Bucephalus depends on something in the way that an accident depends on that of which it is the accident. But why should we think this dependence to be causal? After all, will not even the defender of the CP admit that some accidents are *passive*, such as Bucephalus's being shod, with the substance of which they are accidents having little or no causal input?

Since the relationship between a substance and its accidents need not be causal, the Reichenbach-Nowacki argument seems only to yield a dependence principle: every contingent being is dependent on something else.

But there may still be something more to the argument as an argument for the CP. For suppose *y*'s existence has no cause but does depend on some substance *x*. One may worry how a *dependent* being, an accident, can come into existence causelessly. After all, if something comes into existence causelessly, is it not thereby an *independent* being? Are we equivocating on two senses of dependence, accident-substance dependence and causal dependence, or do these two senses have something in common that would help make this into a valid argument?

13

Modal Arguments

13.1. THE STRATEGY

One strategy for substantiating a principle is to start with a weaker and thus dialectically more acceptable principle, and then show that the weaker principle implies the stronger one or that the kind of intuitions that lead to the weaker one also lead to the stronger one. Nowhere has this strategy been as prominent as in ontological arguments for the existence of God. Instead of asking the atheist to accept that God exists, the ontological arguer asks the atheist to accept a prima facie weaker and more plausible claim, such as that possibly God exists or that we have a coherent concept of God. However, the theist has either previously defined God to be a being whose existence is necessary or in some way from which necessary existence provably follows. Therefore, the theist's interlocutor becomes committed to the claim that possibly necessarily God exists. But by the axiom S5 of modal logic, if possibly necessarily p (i.e., MLp), then necessarily p (i.e., Lp). Hence, necessarily God exists.

When formulated so baldly, the argument simply begs the question. Consider it written out:

(103) ML(God exists).
(104) Therefore, by S5, L(God exists).

It is a difficult problem to make precise the notion of "begging the question." This example argument does not beg the question merely because it has only one nonlogical premise. After all, any valid argument with multiple premises can be replaced by one with a single conjunctive premise. The reason this ontological argument begs the question is subtler. Ordinary language does not deal in nested modal operators.

231

Arguably, part of the *meaning* of modal operators in nested contexts is encapsulated in the axioms they satisfy. Therefore, one does not count as understanding what (103) says unless one understands that the "M" and "L" are governed by S5, that is, unless one understands that "ML" can be replaced with "L." To accept (103), one must understand it. But to understand it, one must understand that it is equivalent to (104). Although a full analysis of "begging the question" is not available, it is clear that any argument in which a premise cannot be understood without being understood to be equivalent to the conclusion does beg the question. This analysis of the argument is due to Richard Gale.

This is not to say that all ontological arguments beg the question. The argument may be less bald. Rather than assuming S5, it might include a substantial argument for S5.[1] Or, alternately, rather than baldly defining God as a certain kind of necessary being, it might start by defining God in some other way, say, as that than which nothing greater could be conceived, and then showing that anything that satisfies this definition must also be a necessary being. However, even so, the ontological arguer must be careful lest her premises be such that they cannot be understood without one thereby understanding that they imply that ML(God exists).

13.2. SULLIVAN'S ARGUMENT FOR THE CP

A strategy similar to that of the modal ontological argument has been tried by Thomas Sullivan (1994) in an argument for the CP. A very similar argument can also be found in Leftow (1988). Sullivan first assumes that every event possibly has a cause:

(105) $\forall E(M\exists C(C \text{ causes } E))$.

The person skeptical of the CP no doubt has Humean intuitions that there are lots of possibilities. Any given event might come to exist without a cause, and hence the CP could well be false, but likewise it might come to exist with a cause. It thus appears reasonable for Sullivan to ask his interlocutor to accept (105).

Now, we do not have a full analysis of causation. However, Sullivan offers as a partial analysis that if C causes E, then C is a necessary condition for E. Let me make a friendly amendment here, because as it is

---

1 For instance, Plantinga (1974b), pp. 108–112.

formulated we are not going to reach the conclusion.[2] Sullivan's intuition requires not only that C is a necessary condition for E, but that C's causing E is a necessary condition for E. Thus, on this partial analysis of causation:

(106) L $\forall C\forall E$ (C causes $E \supset$ L(E occurs $\supset$ (C causes E))).

Now suppose E actually occurs. By (105), let w be a possible world at which C causes E. Then, it is true at w that L(E occurs $\supset$ (C causes E)) by (106) for some C and E. Therefore, it is actually true that ML(E occurs $\supset$ (C causes E)). By S5, it follows that L(E occurs $\supset$ (C causes E)). Hence, since E actually occurs, it follows that

(107) C causes E.

The argument from (105) and (106) to (107) is clearly valid given S5. Is this a good argument for the CP? This depends. One might argue that if (106) is partly constitutive of the meaning of *causes*, then one cannot understand (105) without understanding the nested modalities as collapsing via S5 as in the preceding argument. This, however, is less plausible than in the case of the modal ontological argument, because the deduction of (107) from (105) and (106) is harder to see at a glance than that of (104) from (103). What counts as question begging is relative to the logical powers and dialectical position of one's interlocutor. Thus, to a sufficiently smart logician, both arguments would be question begging: the smart logician would not assent to (105), if (106) is partly constitutive of the meaning of *causes*, unless she already accepted the CP.

On the other hand, rather than having (106) be partly constitutive of the meaning of *causes*, one might take it to be a substantial metaphysical thesis about causation. Unfortunately, the argument on that interpretation becomes unsound. For while Sullivan is free to *stipulate* that *causes* behaves as (106) suggests – though note that if he uses the word in a nonordinary sense, then one's intuitions behind (105) may be deceptive – (106) is false on the ordinary interpretation of *causes*, since (106) entails that if an event E is caused by C, then it is an essential property of E to be caused by C. But certainly if E is something like *there being a great fire in Rome in the first century*, an event which no doubt actually had some cause, quite a number of different events *could* have caused E: Nero's soldiers could

2 The problem is that Sullivan assumes only that if C is a cause of E, then C is a necessary condition for E. He shows that if it is possible that E has a cause C, and E is actual, then C is actual as well. But it does not follow from this that C is actually a cause of E.

have set Rome afire, the Goths could have sneaked in much before their heyday and lit Rome, a particularly unfortunate series of lightning strikes could have occurred, and so on, with each of these events' being capable of being solely responsible for E. Therefore, it is false that it is an essential property of E to be caused by C.

There is more plausibility here if one thinks of E as a rigid designator of an event rather than a definite description. As Quentin Smith (1994b) suggests, one might argue on Kripkean grounds that the causal history of an event is essential to it. If so, then if E is a rigid designator of an event, and E is in fact caused by C, then E could not have been not caused by C. However, the Kripkean considerations are quite controversial. And the argument threatens to become closer to being question begging. For if the Kripkean considerations are correct, then essentiality of cause might be part of the concept of a rigidly designated event. If so, then to understand (105) is to understand it as saying that possibly E is *essentially* caused by some event. But perhaps, as in the case of the modal ontological argument, one cannot understand the nested modal operators (in this case *possibly* and *essentially*) without understanding that the "possibly" can be collapsed out, and then the argument becomes question begging.

13.3. THE WEAK PSR

13.3.1. The Argument

Sullivan's argument is not the only attempt to derive a version of the PSR from a weaker version that claims that the stronger possibly holds. A different approach is to be found in the context of a new Cosmological Argument for the existence of God by Richard M. Gale and me. Consider the Weak PSR, which says that every contingent proposition possibly has a complete explanation:

(W-PSR) $\forall p$ (p is contingently true $\supset$ M $\exists q$ (q completely explains p)).

Here, the word *explains* is used in such a way that the proposition that q explains p is guaranteed to entail both p and q. A proposition can only explain if it is true and a proposition can only be explained if it is true. The W-PSR is weaker than the PSR despite the PSR's concerning *explanation* and not *complete explanation*, because the PSR entails that there is not just an explanation for every proposition, but a complete one (see Section 1.4), that is, one that explains every contingent aspect of the explanandum.

Now, as it turns out, the W–PSR entails the PSR for contingent propositions, for suppose p is a contingent true proposition. For a *reductio*, assume p has no explanation. Let p^* be the proposition

(108) that p and there is no explanation for p.

Observe that p^* is contingent and true since p is. Therefore, by the W–PSR there is a possible world w at which p^* has a complete explanation. Suppose that q completely explains p^* at w. Now, if a conjunction of two propositions has been completely explained, then so has each conjunct. Hence, the first conjunct, p, of p^* is also explained by q at w. Hence, it is true at w that p has an explanation. But q explains p^* at w, and hence p^* is true at w, and hence there is no explanation for p at w. Hence, p does and does not have an explanation at w, and that is absurd. Therefore, the assumption that p has no explanation leads to absurdity. Thus, p has an explanation, and so the W–PSR entails the PSR for contingent propositions.

13.3.2. Does This Beg the Question?

Although a version of this argument has been criticized by Graham Oppy (2000) as being question begging, it is in general not, unless the reader be too much of a logician. Certainly it is possible to understand the W–PSR without understanding that it entails the PSR, for it is only when we apply the W–PSR to p^* that we can conclude that p has an explanation. It is certainly not necessary for understanding a universally quantified claim such as the W–PSR that one should understand the implications of every instance of it – if it were, then the categorical syllogism *All men are mortal; Socrates is a man; therefore, Socrates is mortal* would be question begging. All one needs to understand is what the W–PSR asserts of each proposition, and this one can do without seeing that the full PSR follows.

13.3.3. An Alternate, Incompatible Principle

But from the fact that this argument for the PSR does not beg the question, it does not follow that it is sound. The argument is indeed valid, and the only controversial premise is the W–PSR. One way to object to the W–PSR is to produce an alternate plausible principle that is incompatible with the W–PSR. For instance, the Humean who agreed with the W–PSR on the grounds of the plenitude of the space of possibilities might say that she not only thought the W–PSR to be necessarily true, but on

235

exactly the same grounds of plenitude thought that, necessarily, every contingent proposition is possibly unexplained:

(109) $\forall p$ (p is contingent $\supset$ M (p and $\sim\exists q$ (q explains p))).

However, the necessary truth (109) is incompatible with the necessary truth of the PSR, and the latter is entailed by the necessary truth of the W–PSR. The Humean may then claim that there is an epistemic tie between (109) and the W-PSR as competitors for the title of a necessary truth – both are equally plausible, but they cannot both be necessary truths.

This particular form of the objection is easily countered: (109) is just false. The proposition that there exists a beautiful work of human art is a contingent proposition that cannot lack an explanation, for, by definition, any work of human art is produced by an artist, and the artist's production will explain the existence of the work. There is, thus, no such thing as an unexplained work of human art. Similarly, that there is a caused rock is just explained by the activity or occurrence of the cause of a rock.

But the objector is not done. Consider the following more worrisome claim incompatible with the W-PSR:

(110) M $\exists p$ (p is contingently true and p is unexplained).

Grounds of modal plenitude support this alternative. Moreover, (110) might seem to be preferable to the W-PSR on the grounds that the W-PSR is universally quantified while (110) is merely existentially quantified.

However, there is more than one reason to prefer the W-PSR to (110). The idea of a contingent proposition's lacking an explanation is prima facie less comprehensible than that of its having an explanation. The ordinary person is puzzled enough by the idea that something might not have an explanation, and how much more puzzling is the idea of something that could not have an explanation.

Moreover, an intuition about something's possibly lacking an explanation requires the existence of a world about which a negative fact holds, whereas an intuition about something's possibly having an explanation requires only the existence of a world in which a certain positive fact holds. One claim to be made now could be that negative facts are more ontologically mysterious. One might, for instance, argue that ultimately there are only positive states of affairs, and any negative state of affairs must be constructed out of positive ones. Thus, the state of affairs of there not being any unicorns might be constructed out of the presence of objects logically incompatible with unicornicity in every part of space. But it is not at all clear how one might similarly handle the state of affairs of a proposition's not having an explanation. After all, prima facie, an explanation need not involve anything material, so simply filling all of space with objects whose existence is incompatible with the existence there of a causal factor explaining the explanandum will not do. This is not to say that the problem cannot be solved, but just that it is a strike against confidence in (110).

And there is a related reason not to trust the intuition about (110). In ordinary modal talk, we rarely imagine whole cosmoi. Rather, we imagine parts of cosmoi. When thinking about what would happen were Hitler never to have been born, our imaginative survey is fairly limited: it reaches only to Earth, and perhaps other parts of the solar system, between the late nineteenth century and maybe the twenty-first century. Our modal intuitions about this hypothetical possibility do not include statements about what would happen, say, in the Andromeda galaxy as a result. Our thinking is *local*. Now, given an event E caused by C, it may well be easy to imagine E in the absence of C. To do this, we only need to imagine a cosmos where there is something incompatible with the presence of C where C was. But to imagine the event E as not caused *by anything at all* would require a quite detailed exercise of modal imagination. We would have to imagine a *whole* cosmos, not just a part of one, because no state of a *part* of the cosmos is sufficient to guarantee that E lacks a cause, for, after all, it is always logically possible that there be a cause outside the part we have imagined. Thus, imagining something's lacking a cause or explanation is a case in which we should not trust our modal intuitions very much. Therefore, (110) is something we should be cautious about endorsing.

13.3.4. Range of Application of the W-PSR

A final objection to the W-PSR is, however, more serious. To show that the PSR follows from the W-PSR we applied the W-PSR to a rather extraordinary second-order proposition, one involving a quantification over all propositions, namely,

(111) p and $\sim\exists q(q$ explains $p)$.

But it is quite possible that when we assented to the W-PSR we were only thinking of its application to simple first-order propositions.

One solution to this is to use a more complicated proof of the implication from the W-PSR to the PSR, one that only uses first-order propositions, though with the final PSR and initial W-PSR being restricted to explanations of contingent first-order propositions:

(112) $\forall p$ (p is first order and contingent $\supset$ M $\exists q$ (q is first order and q completely explains p)).

The proof needs the assumption that any two distinct worlds differ in the truth value of a contingent first-order proposition. Let the Big Conjunctive Contingent First-Order Fact (BCCFOF) of a world be the conjunction of all contingent first-order propositions in that world, with any logical redundancies omitted in order to root out set-theoretic paradoxes. This itself is a contingent first-order proposition. Our assumption implies that two distinct worlds have different BCCFOFs. More strongly, if two worlds are distinct, then the BCCFOF of each world is false in the other. To see this, suppose w_1 and w_2 are distinct. Then there is some contingent first-order proposition r that is true at one and false at the other world. Then the BCCFOF of the world at which r holds will contain r while the BCCFOF of the other world, the world at which $\sim r$ holds, will contain $\sim r$. It follows that the BCCFOF of each world will be false in the other world.

Now, let p be the BCCFOF of the actual world. Then, by the W-PSR there are a world w and a proposition q such that q completely explains p at w. (Note that no assumption is made about whether q itself is first order.) Then, p is true at w, since only true propositions have explanations. But p is the BCCFOF of the actual world, and by the remarks of the previous paragraph, it follows that w must be the actual world. Hence, q actually explains p. Now any true first-order contingent proposition is contained in p. Hence, if p has an explanation, so does any true first-order contingent proposition, since in completely explaining a conjunction we have explained the conjuncts.[3]

Unfortunately, this approach, too, requires that we apply the W-PSR to a fairly contrived proposition, the BCCFOF of the actual world, and it can be argued that our modal intuitions – and we know modal intuitions are in general fallible by seeing how puzzled we get about various philosophers' cases – about such contrived propositions are not as reliable as our intuitions about more restricted propositions. Whether

---

3 This version of the argument is close to the argument in "A New Cosmological Argument" (Gale and Pruss, 1999), where (in a slightly modified context) it is further shown that q is a proposition reporting an intelligent and powerful necessary being's freely bringing it about that p.

this criticism is completely fair is not clear, but it does weaken the argument.

13.4. CAUSALITY AND COUNTERFACTUALS

13.4.1. *The Effect Would Not Have Occurred without the Cause*

The W-PSR-based argument and Sullivan's argument give us two desiderata for a modal argument for a version of the PSR. The argument should not require that we apply the weaker modalized version of the PSR to some particularly contrived proposition or event. Nor should the argument require a contrived and counterintuitive notion of causation that almost immediately leads from possibly having a cause to necessarily having a cause.

Sullivan claimed that a cause was a necessary condition for the effect. While this requirement is too strong, surely at least something like the following fact is true: that C causes E entails that were C not to have existed or taken place, E would not have taken place. This is not a complete analysis. Moreover, it requires that in cases of causal overdetermination we describe C carefully, for instance, as a disjunctive event. But this counterfactual claim is certainly a part of the notion of causation. David Lewis thought that this was a complete analysis of causal connection, but this further controversial claim will not be needed.[4]

Suppose that an airplane crashes as a result of metal fatigue in the ailerons. Then the following nested counterfactual is true: Were the plane hit by a surface-to-air missile, then the plane would have crashed and it would have been the case that were the plane not hit by a surface-to-air missile, the plane would, or at least might, still have crashed. The plane would or might still have crashed because of the metal fatigue in

---

4 One might argue as follows against Lewis's more general claim. The recently shown failure of Lewis's own semantics for counterfactuals properly to exclude absurd cases of backtracking counterfactuals in which the consequent is in the antecedent's past (Elga, 2001; Pruss, 2004b) strongly suggests that a semantics for counterfactuals will have to presuppose an asymmetry between the past and the future. One might further argue that there are no scientific asymmetries sufficient to ground an asymmetry of such philosophical significance, and this might lead one to the Kantian view that the asymmetry in time supervenes on the asymmetry of causation: the past is just that region of time where (at least most of) the causes of present events are situated and the future is just that region of time where (at least most of) the effects of present events are situated. But if the asymmetry of time is presupposed in a semantics for counterfactuals, and the asymmetry between cause and effect is presupposed in the asymmetry of time, then at the pain of circularity one cannot analyze causation in terms of counterfactuals.

the ailerons. Analogously, one might say this. Suppose that an airplane crashes for no reason at all. Then the following nested counterfactual is true: Were the plane hit by a surface-to-air missile, then the plane would have crashed and it would have been the case that were the plane not hit by a surface-to-air missile, the plane would, or at least might, still have crashed. The plane would or might still have crashed for no reason at all. But this results in the absurdity that in the counterfactual world w where the plane is hit by a surface-to-air missile, and where no other crash-inducing causes are available (since the counterfactual that moved us from the no-cause world to w presupposed only one added cause – the surface-to-air missile), it is the case that were the missile not to have hit, the plane would or might still have crashed, contradicting the fact that the missile is the cause in w of the plane's crashing.

As it stands, the argument may be thought to rest on improperly assimilating the case in which the plane crashes for no reason at all to the case in which the plane crashes for some specific reason. In the latter case, when we move to a counterfactual world by positing a new cause we generate a case of overdetermination, and hence a case in which the effect would still happen even without the new overdetermining cause. But in the case in which the plane crashes for no reason at all, the counterfactual world in which a cause is posited is a world where there is only one cause, and hence the counterfactual that were the cause not to have occurred, the effect would not have taken place is intact.

13.4.2. A Precise Argument

We will see, however, that we can make a variant of the preceding argument into a valid and plausible argument for the CP. We will need a certain precise version of the observation that were the cause not to take place, the effect also would not. The version says that if E is in fact caused by C, then E would not have occurred were no cause of E to exist:

(113) $(C \text{ causes } E) \Rightarrow (\sim\exists D\ (D \text{ causes } E) \to E \text{ did not occur})$

where $p \to q$ stands for "were p to hold, q would hold," and where $\Rightarrow$ marks entailment. We also need a *might* operator: $p \diamond\!\!\to q$ will stand for "were p to hold, q might hold." The two operators are related as follows: $(p \to q) \Leftrightarrow \sim(p \diamond\!\!\to \sim q)$.

Premise (113) takes into account the possibility of overdetermination, in which more than one event occurs, each of which is sufficient to cause E. It also takes into account the possibility that perhaps, were C not to have occurred, some other event D would have caused E. For instance, if members of some group are asked to volunteer to execute a traitor, then it might well be that Jones's shooting the traitor causes the death of the traitor, although were Jones not to have shot the traitor, someone else would have and hence the traitor would still have died.

Since we are dealing with events, what will be argued for will be a CP. Our first weak version of the CP is that every event possibly has a cause, and this is our second premise:

(114) $\forall E$ (E occurs $\supset$ M $\exists C$ (C causes E)).

The third premise is from the preceding discussion of counterfactuals. Were the cause not to have occurred, the effect would not have occurred.

David Lewis proposed the following analysis of counterfactuals for a possible proposition p: $p \rightarrow q$ holds providing there is a (p & q)-satisfying world that is more similar to the actual world than any (p & $\sim q$)-satisfying world is (Lewis, 1986, sec. 1.3). While this analysis is doubtless not correct in all its details,[5] the intuitive idea of a connection between counterfactuals and possible worlds remains. When we try to see whether $p \rightarrow q$ is true, we mentally move to a world relevantly similar to our world, but in which p holds, and see whether q holds in every such world. Which features we must carry over from the actual world to the counterfactual world for it to count as "relevantly similar" is a difficult question. One might well say that, to the extent that p allows, one needs to carry over laws of nature and the past of p, while Lewis insist that "relevant similarity" has to do with being as similar as possible to the actual world. If, on the other hand, we think that there is some world relevantly similar to our world in which p holds but q does not, then we say that were p to hold, q might not hold.

In modal logic, the Brouwer Axiom, which is entailed by S5, says that if a proposition p is actually true, then necessarily that proposition is possible. In terms of accessibility, this says that if we were to move to a world accessible from the actual world, the actual world would be accessible from that world: the accessibility relation is symmetric. But perhaps the best way to think about the Brouwer Axiom is to think of it as encapsulating the observation that in any counterfactual situation we might consider, the events of the actual world would remain as alternate possibilities.

---

5   See, for instance, Edgington (1995), Elga (2001), and Pruss (2004b).

There is an analogue of this observation in the case of counterfactuals:

(115) $(q \ \& \ p \ \& \ \mathrm{M}{\sim}p) \supset ({\sim}p \rightarrow (p \ \Diamond\!\!\rightarrow q))$.

If we actually have both p and q holding, and then move to a relevantly similar world w in which p does not hold, so as to evaluate a counterfactual with antecedent ${\sim}p$, the events of the actual world are going to be relevant for the evaluation of counterfactuals in w. Hence, if we ask in w what would happen were p to hold, we need to say that q might happen since q in fact happens in the actual world.

Consider how (115) plays out in a paradigmatic case. Suppose p claims that Jones freely chose to set fire to a barn and q claims that Jones was arrested. Then, were Jones not to have set fire to the barn, it would have been true that were he to have set fire to the barn, he at least *might* have been arrested. In the case in which p reports the occurrence or nonoccurrence of some punctual event in time, we can think of the space of possibilities as a branching structure. Were p not to have occurred, we would have gone on a different branch from the one we in fact went on. But were we to have gone on that branch, it would have been true that were p to have occurred, events *might* have gone just as they have *actually* gone. The fact that events *have* gone a certain way witnesses to the relevance in the counterfactual world of the possibility of their going this way. In this sense, (115) is an analogue to the Brouwer Axiom.

We also need two further obvious axioms dealing with counter-factuals:

(116) $(p \Rightarrow q) \Rightarrow (p \rightarrow q)$.
(117) $((p \rightarrow q) \ \& \ (p \rightarrow {\sim}q)) \Rightarrow {\sim}\mathrm{M}p$.

Entailment relations are stronger than counterfactual conditionals, and it cannot be that both q would hold were p to hold and ${\sim}q$ would happen were p to hold, unless p is itself impossible.

But now (113)–(117) imply the CP. Let q be the true proposition that event E occurs. For a reductio, let p be the true proposition that there is nothing that causes E, that is, ${\sim}\exists D$ (D causes E). By the weak CP of (114), $\mathrm{M}{\sim}p$. Thus, by the Brouwer analogue (115), we have

(118) ${\sim}p \rightarrow (p \ \Diamond\!\!\rightarrow q)$.

Let w be any possible world at which ${\sim}p$ holds. Then, w is a world at which E has a cause. Since nonexistent and nonoccurrent things can neither cause nor be caused, E occurs at w as does a cause, call it C. Applying (113), we see that it is true at w that were no cause of E to have existed, E would not have occurred; that is, it is true at w that $p \to \sim q$. Since this is true at every world at which E has a cause, that is, at every world at which $\sim p$ holds, it follows that

(119) $\sim p \Rightarrow (p \to \sim q)$.

But $p \to \sim q$ is equivalent to $\sim (p \diamond\!\!\to q)$. Thus, by (116)

(120) $\sim p \to \sim (p \diamond\!\!\to q)$.

By (117) and (118) it follows that $\sim Mp$. But p was assumed to be true, and true propositions are possible and hence absurdly $\sim Mp$ and Mp.

Thus, the assumption for the reductio is false, and so p is false. Hence, there is a cause of E, and the CP follows. Note that the CP follows here not just for individual events, but for chains of events, provided one assumes that for any ungrounded chain it is possible that the chain should have a cause. As argued in Chapter 3, once one accepts the CP, one should also accept the PSR.

13.4.3. The Possibility Premise

The most controversial two premises in this argument are the possibility premise (114) and the Brouwer analogue (115). As for (114), we get it for free in some cases. For instance, when it is claimed by a Humean that there is nothing absurd about a brick's coming into existence without a cause, it is plain that it is possible for a brick to come into existence with a cause – since that is how they generally do it. The objector to the PSR is not very likely to object to (114). It would be a strange kind of contingent event that was just incapable of being caused. One might scruple at the possibility of any given *chain's* being caused, on the other hand, if one wished to extend (114) as described in the previous paragraph. One might particularly worry how a chain that extends infinitely far back into the past could be caused. One answer is that it is possible for there to be a being outside time that causes the chain. Another might be that it is possible that there be an eternal being simultaneous with the chain that causes every link in it, thereby leading to causal overdetermination, because the link at one time would be caused by both the eternal being and the preceding link.

13.4.4. The Brouwer Analogue

13.4.4.a Lewis's Semantics. The real difficulties are with (115). The first difficulty is that (115) cannot be a conceptual truth on Lewis's semantics for counterfactuals. According to David Lewis, $p \to q$ is true if and only if either p is necessarily false, or there is a p & q-world closer to the actual world than any p & $\sim q$-world, where by an r-world I mean simply a world where r holds.

Write Aw for a proposition true at w and only at w. We might take Aw to be the BCCF of w, or we might take Aw to be the proposition that w is actual. Let $q = Aw_0$, where w_0 is the actual world. Let w_1 be any other world, and let $p = \sim Aw_1$. Then, q & p & $M\sim p$ holds. Consider the antecedent of (115). This says that there is a $\sim p$-world w at which $p \diamond\!\!\to q$ and that is closer than any $\sim p$-world at which $\sim(p \diamond\!\!\to q)$. In fact, there is only one $\sim p$ world, namely, w_1. Thus, the antecedent of (115) says simply that $p \diamond\!\!\to q$ holds at w_1. Now, $p \diamond\!\!\to q$ is equivalent to $\sim(p \to \sim q)$. The proposition $p \to \sim q$ holds at w_1 if and only if there is a p & $\sim q$-world that is closer to w_1 than any p & q-world is. Now, there is only one p & q world, namely, w_0, and a p & $\sim q$-world is just a world different from w_0 and w_1. Thus, $p \to \sim q$ holds at w_1 if and only if there is a world different from w_0 and w_1 that is closer to w_1 than w_0 is. Thus, $\sim(p \to \sim q)$ holds if and only if no world is closer to w_1 than w_0 other than w_1 itself.

Thus, if (115) holds, then no world, other than w_1, is closer to w_1 than the actual world, w_0. It is already deeply implausible that this should be true for every w_1, namely that the actual world should be the closest neighbor to every other world. But if (115) is a conceptual truth, then this will have to hold not just when w_0 is the actual world, but for any other world w in its place. Thus, for every pair of distinct worlds w_1 and w, there is no world closer to w_1 than w is, other than w_1 itself. This shows that given *any* world w_1, there are no worlds w_2 and w_3 distinct from w such that w_2 is closer to w_1 than w_3 is. All worlds are equidistant from w_1. By Lewis's semantics it follows that no nontrivial counterfactuals hold, where a counterfactual is nontrivial providing its antecedent is false and does not entail the consequent. Thus, one cannot accept both (115) and Lewis's semantics as conceptual truths.

However, all *we* need (115) for is the special case in which q reports an event and p reports the nonexistence of an event under a certain description (namely, under the description of being a cause of the event reported by q), and it might well be that in those cases (115) could still hold on Lewis's semantics. The previous counterexample was generated using very special propositions – the proposition q was taken to be true at exactly one world and the proposition p was taken to be false at exactly one world. Ordinary language counterfactuals do not deal with such special propositions, and hence it might be that the intuitions supporting (115) do not

244

require us to make (115) hold for these propositions, and hence these intuitions are not refuted in the relevant case by the counterexample.

This, however, is shaky ice. One might perhaps more reasonably take (115) to entail a refutation of Lewis's semantics. In any case, Lewis's semantics are known to be flawed, especially when applied to propositions like the ones in the preceding counterexample. To see one flaw in them, suppose that w_0 is the actual world, and we have an infinite sequence of worlds $w_1, w_2, w_3, \ldots$ such that w_{n+1} is always closer to the actual world than w_n is. For instance, these worlds could be just like the actual world except in the level of the background radiation in the universe, with this level's approaching closer and closer to the actual level as n goes to infinity. Let p be the infinite disjunction of the Aw_n for $n > 0$. Fix any $n > 0$. On Lewis's semantics we then have

(121) $p \rightarrow \sim Aw_n$

as w_{n+1} is a p & $\sim Aw_n$-world that is closer than any p & Aw_n-world, since there is only one p & Aw_n-world, namely, w_n, and w_{n+1} is closer than it. This implies that it is true for *every* disjunct of p that were p true, that disjunct would be false! But surely there has to be some disjunct of p such that were p true, that disjunct at least *might* be true.

As does the counterexample to (115), this counterexample deals with propositions specified as true at a small (in the case of p here, infinite, but still only countably infinite and hence much "smaller" than the collection of possible worlds, which is not only not countably infinite but not even a set)[6] set of worlds. This shows that there is something wrong with Lewis's semantics, either in general or in the handling of such propositions.

To see even more clearly, though making use of a slightly stronger assumption about closeness series, that there is a commonality between a problem with Lewis's semantics and the Lewisian counterexample to (115), suppose the following principle of density: For any nonactual world w, there is a nonactual world w^* closer to the actual world than w is. This should at least be an epistemic possibility: our semantics for counterfactuals should not rule it out. Let w_0 be the actual world and put $p = \sim Aw_0$. Then, by the principle of density, on Lewis's semantics, there is no possible world w such that were p true, w might be actual, that is, such that $p \diamond\rightarrow Aw$. For suppose that we are given a w. First, note that it is hopeless to start with the case in which w is w_0 since p and Aw_0 are logically incompatible. Next, observe that we in fact have $p \rightarrow \sim Aw$. For let w^* be any world

6 Pruss (2001).

245

closer than w. Then, w^* is a p & $\sim Aw$-world that is closer than any p & Aw-world, there being only one of the latter, namely, w. Thus, we do not have $p \diamond\!\!\rightarrow Aw$.

But surely if p is possible, then there is *some* world that is such that it might be actual were p to hold. Lewis's semantics fails because of its incompatibility with this claim, on the previous not implausible principle of density which should not be ruled out of court by a semantics of possible worlds. Note further that the failure here is precisely a failure in the case of a might-conditional $p \diamond\!\!\rightarrow q$ with p of the form $\sim Aw_1$ and q of the form Aw_2, which is precisely the kind of might-conditional that appeared in the analysis of the previous counterexample. Lewis's semantics makes too few might-conditionals of this sort true, and it is precisely through failing to make a might-conditional of this sort true that it gave a counterexample to (115).

Thus, rather than having run my argument within Lewisian possible worlds semantics, I have run it on an intuitive understanding of counterfactuals, which intuitions do support (115). It would be nice to have a complete satisfactory semantics for counterfactuals. Lewisian semantics are sometimes indeed helpful: they are an appropriate model in many cases. But as we have seen, they do not always work. Other forms of semantics meet with other difficulties. We may, at least for now, be stuck with a more intuitive approach.

If we want more precision here, we might speak as follows. To evaluate $p \rightarrow q$ and $p \diamond\!\!\rightarrow q$ at a world w, we need to look at some set $R(w, p, q)$ of "q-relevant p-worlds relative to w" and check whether q holds at none, some, or all of these. If q holds at all of them, then $p \rightarrow q$ and $p \diamond\!\!\rightarrow q$. If it holds at none of them, then neither conditional is true. If it holds at some but not all of them, then $\sim(p \rightarrow q)$ and $p \diamond\!\!\rightarrow q$. The difficulty is with specifying the q-relevant p-worlds. Proposition (115) then follows from the claim that the actual world is a q-relevant p-world relative to every world w which is an r-relevant $\sim p$-world relative to the actual world for any possible r and q. This is plausible, and somewhat analogous to the Brouwer Axiom. However, this does not let us embed the discussion in a precise semantics because we do not have an account of what $R(w, p, q)$ is.

13.4.4.b An Apparent Counterexample. David Manley (2002) has come up with the following apparent counterexample to (115), which I modify slightly. Suppose our soccer team wins twenty to zero. Then, it is true that the team won overwhelmingly in the actual world w_0. What would have happened had our team not won? Presumably the score would have been

246

rather different, say, twenty to twenty, or zero to five, or something like that. Suppose the score is one of these – that we are in a possible world w_1 where our team has lost. Then, it is *not* true that were our team to have won, it would have won overwhelmingly. If our team in fact failed to win, as at w_1, then worlds where the team wins *overwhelmingly* are much more distant from our world than worlds where it wins by a bit. Thus, it is true at w_1 to say that were our team to have won, it would have won by a tiny amount. Putting this together, we conclude that were our team not to have won, then were it to have won, it would have won by a tiny amount. But this is incompatible with (115), which claims that were our team not to have won, then were it to have won, it *might* have won by a large amount.

Unfortunately, this account also relies on David Lewis's semantics and again does so in a context in which Lewis's semantics fail. For, by the previous reasoning, if we are in a world where our team has not won, then we should say that were it to have won, it would have won by exactly one point. But this need not be true. Perhaps were it to have got ahead by a point at some point in the game, then the other team would have become disheartened and lost by more. We can even more clearly see the problem in the Lewisian reasoning if we substitute a game very much like soccer except that its scores can take on any real value: perhaps instead of a flat one point for a goal, one gets a real-valued additive score depending on how close to the middle of a goal one hits. Then, by the preceding reasoning, were our team not to have won, it would be true that were it to have won, it would have won by no more than one-tenth of a point. Worlds where one wins by no more than one-tenth of a point are closer than worlds where one wins by more than that. But this reasoning is perfectly general, and the one-tenth can be replaced by any positive number, no matter how tiny. But this is absurd. It is absurd to suppose that were our team not to have won, it would be true that were it to have won, it would have won by no more than 10^{-1000} points.[7]

13.4.4.c A Modal Counterargument. Just as the W-PSR-based argument was objected to with a counterargument based on (110), so too one might try to balance the modal-counterfactual argument with the intuitive plausibility of the claim that possibly there is an uncaused event. However, the premises of the modal-counterfactual argument have the dialectical

---

7 This is similar to the coat thief example cited in Edgington (1995).

advantage that they prima facie do not take a stance on the necessary truth of the CP and do not beg the question against the opponent. They are somewhat lower-level principles about causation and counterfactuals, while the Humean claim is simply a denial of the necessary truth of the CP.

13.5. CONCLUSIONS

The modal–counterfactual argument is a valid argument for the CP. The premises of the modal argument are all quite reasonable. We thus have reason to believe the CP, reason beyond the self-evidence considerations, even if we do not accept deep Thomistic ontological theses. Moreover, as one can run the same argument in the case of chains rather than individual events, then the methods of Section 3.1 can leverage our results into a more global form of the CP, as long as we can argue for the possibility of each contingent chain's having a cause. This more global form differs little from the PSR.

14

Is the Universe Reasonable?

Often the following argument is attributed to the defender of the PSR: The PSR says that reality is rational. It is irrational to suppose reality to be irrational. Hence, it is irrational to deny the PSR. Typically, this argument is given only a straw man, quickly refuted, and the defender of the PSR is associated with an evidently unsound argument.

The argument as given is plainly valid, at least:

(122) The PSR says reality is rational.
(123) It is irrational to suppose reality to be irrational.
(124) Thus, it is irrational to deny the PSR.

Of course, one might be a skeptic about the PSR, neither denying nor affirming it, and escape the argument thus. Now while the argument is valid, acceptance of (123) may rest on a confusion between irrationality within a belief operator and outside it. To hold that reality is irrational need not prima facie be an irrational belief, just as for me to hold that Jones is irrational need not be irrational.

But there could be a little more to the argument than this. The PSR is one of our basic assumptions about how the world works; our belief in it increases our confidence and resolution in our search for truth and explanation. Prima facie, a stepmotherly nature might not support our scientific research. However, once we suppose nature to be thus stepmotherly vis-à-vis the PSR, recalcitrant in the face of our drive to seek explanations, then one might reasonably worry that our other intuitive expectations about the world, such as that it conform to our senses, might be frustrated. A world where the PSR fails is a world unfriendly to us, and if it is unfriendly in that way, who is to know how far its unfriendliness extends. Thus, denial of the PSR means that the world is irrational in the

249

sense of not conforming to our ways of thinking in one way, but if in one way, why not in more? And so the specter of skepticism looms ahead. Since skepticism *is* an irrational stance, this might be taken as support for (123).

However, the support is meager, since the universe plainly does disappoint some of our epistemic expectations. For instance, quantum mechanics shows that either there is an indeterminism of a sort that disappoints us in our scientific endeavors *or* there are hidden variables beyond empirical reach (or both).

But there is an argument not a far step from this one that has not been sufficiently explored. We have a *desire* to seek explanations. This makes it plausible that in fact there *are* explanations, since as a species we do not have desires for things that do not exist at all. Of course, it does not follow that there are explanations for *everything*.

However, one way of looking at our desires to seek explanations of various particular things is as merely symptomatic of a single human drive to understand it all, a basic human desire to explain everything there is, holistically but perhaps only sketchily. On this view, our piecemeal curiosities do not give rise to search for cosmic explanation, but it is the latter that gives rise to our piecemeal searches for explanation. Of course, even without the search for cosmic explanation we might have practically motivated and evolutionarily explicable desires for explanation. We might want to know why the lion runs the way it does, so that we might be better able to kill it. We might want to know why plants grow in one setting rather than another in order to be better agriculturists. However, these practically minded interests are not the disinterested desire to know for the sake of knowing that Aristotle evokes at the beginning of his *Metaphysics*, a desire born of wonder rather than of pragmatic exigencies.

It is quite compatible with our pragmatically motivated interests that we also have an overarching striving for an understanding and explanation "of it all," and our piecemeal interests derive from this. If so, if this is indeed one of our basic human desires, and if our basic human desires are all satisfiable, then it *is* possible to "explain it all," though no doubt we could only know the global explanation sketchily. Thus, the BCCF has an explanation, and hence so does everything else. Or at least, it is metaphysically possible that the BCCF has an explanation – but as we saw in Section 13.3, this implies that the BCCF in fact *does* have an explanation.

This argument obviously will not impress an existentialist sort of philosopher who is quite willing to admit that we are thrown into a cold and indifferent world, with desires that do not match it. But such a story is its own counterargument, for why should we have a basic human desire that is so much out of step with reality? It is true that our disinterested wonder about "the reason for it all" has produced modern physics and has thus been an evolutionary benefit to us, but the wonder at the world as a whole is older than modern physics and in the past had much less in the way of practical application.

This is not the strongest of the arguments for the PSR, but it does provide some evidence, for that we desire something is indeed evidence, albeit defeasible, for its possibility.[1]

---

1 Note, too, the resemblance between this argument and Thomas Aquinas's argument for the claim that knowledge of God is our ultimate end: we will not be happy until we know the causes of things, and thus we will not be happy until we know God, who is the first cause (*Summa Theologiae* I–II, 3, 8).

15

Explanation of Negative States of Affairs

15.1. THE ARGUMENT

Here is a pattern of explanation we all accept, which was already met with in Section 3.4: "Why did the yogurt fail to ferment? It failed to ferment because none of the usual explanations of fermentation, namely, the presence of bacteria, were there to explain it, and there was no unusual cause. Why did the dog not bark? It did not bark because no stranger approached it and none of the other possible causes of barking caused it to bark." These are perfectly fine explanations, and they are not elliptical for longer explanations, though of course they are not *ultimate* explanations since one may ask why no stranger approached the dog.

In these explanations, we explain a negative state of affairs by noting that the positive state of affairs that it is the denial of lacked an explanation. But now observe that this form of explanation presupposes a PSR, at least for positive states of affair, for if such a PSR does not hold, then one has failed to explain the negative state of affairs. If it is possible that a dog should bark without cause, then in saying that there was no cause for the dog to bark we have not explained why the dog did not bark. We may have explained why a nonbrute barking did not occur, but we have not explained why a *brute*, or unexplained, barking did not occur.

Our acceptance of the preceding explanations as nonelliptical is thus a sign of our tacit acceptance of the PSR.

15.2. THE DEFECTIVENESS OBJECTION

"The explanation is in fact defective. We have not explained why there is no brute barking. But in ordinary life we are satisfied with such a defective explanation."

This objection creates a mystery where there is none. Once we know that none of the causes of the dog's barking have occurred, we know why the dog did not bark. There is no longer a mystery about why the dog did not bark. The only scope for mystery is why none of the causes of the dog's barking have occurred. Of course our ordinary pattern of explanation could be mistaken, and the objector could take a revisionary view of our ordinary ways of thought. However, note what the objector has become committed to: No longer merely objecting to the claim that all propositions have an explanation, she has pointed to a class of propositions that everybody thinks *are* explained and has said that these in fact are not fully explained, and indeed necessarily are not fully explained if the explanation offered is the only possible one.

15.3. THE NOMIC NECESSITY OBJECTION

"It might just be nomically necessary that the PSR holds, or that it holds for the sorts of cases, say, physical events, in which we ordinarily use this pattern of explanation."

Note that this objection does not say that the PSR *necessarily* holds of these sorts of cases but not of others. That would be an unjustified ad hoc restriction, since there is no metaphysical reason why one should think the PSR as a necessary truth to hold only for them, unless one accepts the PSR on dubious Kantian grounds. However, if the PSR holds only of nomic necessity, then the restriction to these states of affairs is quite plausible. We shall see in Section 16.4, however, that the PSR should not be thought of as holding merely of nomic necessity. Thus the reply to this objection will have to wait.

16

The Puzzle of the Everyday
Applicability of the PSR

16.1. THE ARGUMENT

No one wants to deny the PSR wholesale. We all assume that airplane crashes have causes and consider it much more likely that an inspection team overlooked a cause that was there than that there was no cause. Generally, the person denying the PSR will still accept a restricted version, such as that, at least as a contingent matter of fact, every physical event in time has a prior cause, or perhaps that most macroscopic physical events have prior causes.

No one thinks that bricks pop into existence *ex nihilo* from time to time. The disagreement between the upholder of a robust form of the PSR and the PSR skeptic is over the status of this proposition. Is it simply a generalization contingently true, or true with high probability, or is it the result of a basic metaphysical *ex nihilo nihil fit* type of PSR? It is a common dialectical move that when the defender of the PSR appeals to homely cases, the opponent insists that the homely cases only support a contingent, and perhaps only true "for the most part" (to use an Aristotelian phrase), version of the PSR. But it is a mistake for the PSR's opponent to think that victory has been achieved in this way.

Let it be granted that the PSR is not metaphysically necessary and may not even hold for all events. It is still a mystery as to why it holds to the great extent that it does. After all, if the PSR is not metaphysically necessary, then there presumably are possible worlds where bricks pop into existence out of nothing for no reason at all. Why is our world not like that? Philosophy starts in wonder and the great extent to which the PSR at least contingently holds is surely worthy of wonder. Call this the "puzzle of the PSR's everyday applicability."

Of course the opponent of the PSR, precisely because she is such, can refuse to answer the question. She can just insist that the everyday applicability of the PSR is simply a brute fact lacking any explanation. This is a perfectly consistent move. On a Humean metaphysics on which any kind of a rearrangement of objects is logically possible, it is indeed true that there are possible worlds in which the PSR has everyday applicability, and it could thus just be a brute fact that our world happens to be one of those.

But claiming something to be a brute fact should be a last resort. It would undercut the practice of science were things claimed to be brute facts where not implausible putative explanations, propositions that would be explanations were they true, can be formulated. And in this case there is available to us a putative explanation, namely, that it is a basic metaphysical principle that the PSR holds of metaphysical necessity. We can conclude the metaphysical necessity of a fuller PSR by inference to best explanation from the everyday applicability of the PSR.

16.2. AN ABUNDANCE OF OBJECTIONS

16.2.1. *This Is Not Explanatory*

Saying that the PSR is metaphysically necessary simply transfers a mystery from a puzzle about everyday events to a mystery about why the PSR is metaphysically true. It is replacing a mystery about the physical world with a mysterious metaphysical "principle."

A coherent ontological system in which the PSR falls out of lower-level assumptions, say, about the nature of being, such as in our Thomistic arguments, would be a response to this. If such an approach works, we will have subsumed the metaphysical principle into a wider ontological system and thereby made it less mysterious. And indeed the possibility of doing so is itself evidence for any system that allows this to be done: the explanatory value of a metaphysical system is evidence for the system.

Moreover, we generally consider the subsumption of events under general physical laws of nature to be a paradigmatically good form of explanation. For exactly the same reason, subsumption under a metaphysical principle should be a good form of explanation.

16.2.2. *The PSR Is Irrefutable*

In a good use of inference to best explanation, the laws or principles inferred are refutable: one can conceive of a situation in which they could be observationally falsified. But the PSR is irrefutable, since for any observable event for which we have not found a cause, we can always suppose an *unobservable* cause beyond our ken.

In response, one might well admit that the PSR is, strictly construed, irrefutable. The cause predicted by the PSR could always be unobservable. But not being strictly refutable is something the PSR has in common with most scientific inferences. A scientist can always give up some auxiliary hypothesis to defend a proposition. We know the difficulties facing the person wishing to defend Darwinian evolution from irrefutability.[1] One can imagine pieces of evidence that would make evolution highly unlikely, but one could always suppose a more convoluted evolutionary story to get around the difficulty. Likewise, there are pieces of evidence that would make the PSR, insofar as it is inferred from experience and not on the basis of some metaphysical argument, epistemically untenable: say, if bricks haphazardly started popping into existence.

The objection that causes entirely beyond our ken could always be posited to save the PSR from empirical refutation should in fact not worry one. First of all, any ceteris paribus law could be saved from empirical refutation by positing causes beyond our ken. However, the evidence that inference to best explanation bestows on a proposition is defeated in cases in which the proposition can only be saved from refutation by positing causes entirely beyond our ken, that is, causes that can only be justifiably characterized as "entities sufficient to cause *this*," such as the *virtus dormitiva*. Second, consider the parallel of neo-Darwinian evolution. Any conceivable fossil finding could be made to fit with evolution if we allowed for causes beyond our ken. It is not a part of the theory of evolution, as such, that there are no supernatural unknowable beings redistributing fossils in strata and perhaps doctoring them. Any fossil that appeared to refute evolution could be supposed to be produced by such a supernatural cause, just as any event that appeared to have no cause could be thought to have some supernatural cause. This in no way harms the theory of evolution, and likewise it does not harm this inference to the PSR.

One response that the critic can make here is that in fact there *are* cases in which the defender of the PSR will have to advert to causes beyond our ken. For instance, quantum mechanics presents us with indeterministic events whose causes we could not know. Likewise, there was a Big Bang.

---

1 For a simple discussion, see Kitcher (1998, chap. 3).

There is very good reason to think the Big Bang could not have had a physical cause, because any physical cause would have been in time and prior to the Big Bang, whereas time starts with the Big Bang.

The quantum mechanical case was already considered in Chapter 8 and can be responded to by either the Bohmian approach or the insistence that explanations need not be deterministic.

The case of the Big Bang is more interesting. Let us suppose that the physicists who think that there can be a physical theory explaining why the Big Bang occurred are wrong – for if they are right, then the Big Bang is no objection here. If so, then any explanation of the Big Bang will involve something nonphysical. But it does not follow from this that the explanation will be beyond our ken. There might well, for instance, be some independent evidence for the existence of a deity of a certain nature, such as evidence found in fine-tuning anthropic arguments, and if so then the intentional action of this deity might be supposed to be an explanation of the Big Bang. But then because there would be independent evidence for this deity's existence, the deity would not be beyond our ken, since the independent evidence would provide for some characterization of the deity, for example, as a deity that desires organic life-forms to exist. Moreover, it might be that the supernatural being would have to be a person (see Chapter 5) and we *do* know some things about all persons: they are beings that, say, have a capability for intelligence, intentionality, and responsiveness to reasons.

16.2.3. This Inference Is Not Predictive

One way to distinguish a genuine use of inference to best explanation from a misuse of it is that good explanations are *predictive*, in the sense that they make use of laws or principles that yield further observable predictions beyond the explanandum itself. But the PSR does not yield any further observable predictions because the PSR does not say that the explanation of a proposition will always be one that can be observed.

Observe, however, that although evolutionary theory provides us with a general account of how organisms evolved, it does not *by itself* lead to further observable predictions. After all, while the theory insists that generally organisms evolved in a way that adapts to environmental conditions that harm or promote the genetic transmission of an organism exhibiting such and such a phenotype, that the environmental conditions are always observable is not part of the theory as such. Rather, that the sources of adaptive pressures appealed to are supposed to be physical and hence ideally at least indirectly observable is something that is superadded to evolutionary theory by the general edifice of scientific practice. Likewise, that the causes the PSR bids us to search for are *physical*, unless the context demands otherwise (e.g., because we have a conceptual argument that a physical cause cannot be found, as in the case of the cause of the physical universe as a whole), is an additional hypothesis.

Another example of a nonpredictive explanation would be the following. Suppose that all over the world the sky started glowing in a mysterious and beautiful way, all amputees noticed that their limbs instantly regrew, and simultaneously everyone's computer screen flashed up the message, in the person's native language: "Know that I am God and I do exist. Live your life virtuously." And then the messages disappear, the sky goes back to its normal color, but the regrown limbs stay. The simplest explanation is surely that God did all that in order to testify to his existence. But there do not seem to be any predictions that can be made on the basis of this. One cannot, for instance, make any justified predictions about whether this will happen again or not, since given that this sort of universal phenomenon does not appear to have happened earlier in history, we cannot infer that God habitually does these things.

Finally, perhaps some probabilistic predictions could be made when the PSR is applied in arguments for an intelligent first cause of the universe (see Chapter 5), since it seems we can say *something* about what an intelligent person is likely to do: an intelligent person has a nonnegligible likelihood of acting on objective reasons, and thus it is perhaps made more likely than on a naturalistic hypothesis that there should be things in the universe that such a being would have reason to make, such as orderly or beautiful or complex beings.

16.2.4. The PSR Is Metaphysically Necessary, Whereas Inference to Best Explanation Involves Only Nomic Necessities

Laws of nature are metaphysically contingent and hence are genuine subjects of inference on the basis of empirical facts. It is unacceptable to use empirical data to infer a *metaphysically* necessary truth. Hence, the argument to the PSR, it seems, fails.

However, people use empirical data to infer metaphysical necessities all the time these days. Whenever we use a calculator, we infer a metaphysically necessary truth from empirical facts. We can infer that $5 + 7 = 12$, from the empirical fact that pressing the buttons $\boxed{5}$, $\boxed{+}$, $\boxed{7}$, and $\boxed{=}$ causes the display to show 12. It might be thought that this is different from the earlier case, however, in that when we use a calculator, we do not use inference to best explanation. Perhaps, we use inductive reasoning ("calculators have usually shown correct answers") or base ourselves on manufacturer's testimony, which in turn is based on inductive reasoning about semiconductor physics. So the example of a calculator, while showing that we can derive metaphysically necessary truths from empirical data, does not show that we can do so by means of inference to best explanation. Nor does the example show that we can derive the metaphysical necessity of a true claim from empirical data. In the case of a calculator, the immediate inference might be argued to be just that $5 + 7 = 12$. The further inference that this is metaphysically necessary follows not from empirical observation but from the general metaphysical principle that all arithmetical truths are necessary.

There is thus a significant disanalogy between scientific employment of inference to best explanation and our inference of the PSR. However, this disanalogy need not be fatal, because inference to best explanation is also used outside science. Philosophers often argue that some claim is probably true from the fact that its truth would neatly solve some philosophical puzzle. Positing the existence of propositions, for instance, would help explain how beliefs are individuated. Positing possible worlds, Lewis thinks, helps solve a number of different puzzles.

However, in those cases more than one phenomenon is explained. The PSR only explains the everyday applicability of the PSR, it seems. But this is not obvious. The metaphysical truth of the PSR might also enter into an explanation of why, say, mere epiphenomenalistic property dualism is an unacceptable theory — for it fails to give the reason why physical properties are correlated with mental properties. And what further applications of the PSR could be given depends only on the ingenuity of philosophers: a number of issues were, however, already mentioned in the Introduction.

16.2.5. The PSR Inferred Is Too Broad

The empirical data at hand support only the claim that the PSR has everyday applicability, not that the PSR is true in general. Therefore, we should infer that there is a metaphysical principle that, necessarily, the PSR has everyday applicability, not that the PSR is true.

First, as a matter of general principle, in an inference to best explanation one seeks a principle that is not gerrymandered to fit the data, but has simplicity and generality. Otherwise, one could count as having explained everything by positing that, as a matter of metaphysical or nomic necessity,

259

everything is exactly as it is. Inferring only that the PSR has everyday applicability would be like inferring from the fact that every hitherto observed raven is black that, as a matter of law, every observed raven is black when observed. But the latter law does not sufficiently simply generalize from the observed data. There is a simpler and hence preferable, though stronger, law here: every raven is black all the time. The hypothesis that the PSR is just metaphysically necessary in full, rather than that the everyday applicability of the PSR is metaphysically necessary, is simpler and hence preferable.

The proposed restriction of the PSR was ad hoc. The same could be said about a restriction to physical phenomena. There is no reason to think the PSR to be *metaphysically* necessary for physical phenomena without being metaphysically necessary for all contingent phenomena. Why should contingent physical phenomena be intrinsically different from nonphysical ones with respect to explainability? Of course it may be a necessary truth that all physical phenomena are themselves contingent.

Second, a metaphysically necessary proposition that something is *probable* or holds for *macroscopic* objects is an unprecedented kind of principle, in the absence of deeper metaphysical facts. While the PSR *simpliciter* is something that could not unreasonably be thought to be a basic metaphysical principle, the claim that every *macroscopic* object has a cause or that *most* physical events have causes seems much less likely to be a metaphysical principle. This is not to say that it could not be derived from propositions that look more like metaphysical principles. For instance, one might derive it from a claim about God's necessarily existing and from a claim about what kinds of things, namely, orderly universes, a God is most likely to create. But the onus would be on the opponent of the PSR to produce such a derivation and thus show the preferability of the narrower thesis as an explanation. Note that the theistic explanation will not do, for that God necessarily exists entails the PSR, since God's creative action grounds the explanation, not necessarily deterministic, of every contingent fact, except perhaps those explained by the free will of creatures.

16.2.6. The PSR Inferred Should Have Merely Nomic Necessity

Inference to best explanation gives us laws of nature, not laws of metaphysics. Thus, we should infer from the everyday applicability of the PSR that the PSR, at least as restricted to physical events, is physically necessary.

To respond, neither the PSR nor the CP looks quite like a law of nature. For instance, although the CP is a causal claim, basic causal laws of nature tend to be of the form *every C causes a C** rather than of the form *every C* is caused by a C*, which is what the CP looks most like. The latter form is what evolutionary theory looks like – every animal evolved through such and such a general process – but evolutionary theory is not a basic law of nature.

Therefore, the form that this objection should take is not that the PSR or the CP is a basic law of nature, but rather that it can be derived from some basic law or laws of nature. One promising prospect here is the law of conservation of mass-energy, which already implies a very weak form of the *ex nihil nihilo* principle: a state of the universe with positive mass-energy is preceded in time by another state of positive, and in fact equal, mass-energy.

By itself, conservation of mass-energy will not yield a CP, since conservation of mass-energy is consistent with a piece of matter of mass-energy's being annihilated in one place for no reason at all and a piece of matter of the same mass-energy's simultaneously popping into existence elsewhere also for no reason at all. However, a localized mass-energy conservation principle, that says that the amount of mass-energy entering any region of space from an adjoining region during an interval of time is equal to the amount of mass-energy leaving it to an adjoining region, may do better.

However, no conservation-type law will yield a *causal* principle, for conservation-type laws say nothing about causation, as conservation laws are compatible with the hypothesis that there are no causal interconnections between events on different time slices, or that there is a time slice at, say, t_0 across which all dynamical quantities are conserved but no causal influences reach.

But conservation laws together with enough causal laws of the form *every C causes a C** could quite conceivably ground a causal principle about mass-energy configurations. For instance, if we had enough deterministic causal laws of the form *every C causes a C**, then given a mass-energy configuration at time t_0, we could predict the mass-energy configuration at a later time t_1, and the conservation laws might imply that no new mass-energy subconfiguration at t_1 came into existence beyond those that were predicted by the causal laws, and hence no subconfiguration at t_1 is without cause.

Thus, the objector to the PSR might be able to use laws of nature to give a coherent account of the everyday applicability of the PSR. In doing so, she will be taking it that an appropriate version of the CP is nomically necessary but not metaphysically necessary. However, we will soon see that this response does not work on all views of laws of nature.

It fails, for instance, on a plausible Aristotelian understanding of laws of nature as grounded in the powers and capacities of objects. We will in fact see that, on the Aristotelian view of laws, not only is this objection to the argument for the PSR refuted, but a fuller argument for the PSR is made available.

But first we need a general digression about laws of nature.

16.3. LAWS OF NATURE

16.3.1. Humeanism

The most basic dichotomy between views of laws of nature is that between Humean views, on which the laws of nature are merely descriptions of actual states of affairs that obtain, and anti-Humean views, according to which the laws of nature have modal import and describe something over and beyond correlations between actual states of affairs. The best argument against the Humean approach may well be the very one that Aristotle levies against Platonic Forms: Humean laws of nature do not have any causal power and fail to explain anything. That all ravens are black is only explanatorily relevant to the claim that my raven Smitty is black if its force goes beyond the mere description of the color of the ravens in existence. If it is a mere coincidence that all ravens are black, then this accidental generalization fails to explain Smitty's blackness. Indeed, explaining the blackness of Smitty by the blackness of all ravens, when the latter is a mere coincidence, is explaining the obscure by the more obscure – the coincidence of all ravens' being black is more surprising and calls out for explanation more than Smitty's happening to be black.

Admittedly, there are more complex versions of Hume's approach. Thus, David Lewis proposed that laws of nature are the propositions that figure in an account of nature that has the optimal balance of simplicity and informativeness (i.e., deductive strength). A detailed discussion is beyond the scope of this section. However, a quick objection is not out of place. It seems to be a conceptual truth that it is *physically* impossible that the basic laws of nature could have been other than they in fact are, though this may of course be logically possible. Consider now a simple, conceptually possible case. Suppose there is a basic physical law that states that a particular kind of interaction indeterministically has a 50 percent chance of producing an electron with spin up and a 50 percent chance of producing an electron with spin down. It is then *physically* possible that, by coincidence, this interaction should have *always* produced an electron with spin up: let the event of this coincidence be E. But were that to have occurred, then the assertion that the interaction always produces an electron with spin up would be no more complex than the preceding indeterministic law but would clearly be more informative. Consequently, this assertion would have been a law. But it cannot be that there are *both* a physical law that says that an interaction produces a result with 50 percent probability *and* another physical law that says it always produces that result. Hence, had E occurred, the laws of physics would have been different from what they are. But E is physically possible assuming that the law governing these interactions is indeterministic. This violates the principle that the laws of nature could not physically have been otherwise.

16.3.2. Anti-Humeanism

Let us then part company with Hume on the laws of nature. There is more to something's being a law of nature than its being true of the actual universe. We must, of course, be careful here. Suppose it is indeed a law of nature that all ravens are black. It is reasonable to say then that the law of nature is a proposition, namely, the proposition that all ravens are black. But then, it seems, we are no further ahead than the Humean, because qua proposition, it asserts nothing more than that all ravens happen to be black. However, while the proposition B that all ravens are black merely predicates blackness of the actually existent ravens, the *further* proposition that B is a law of nature says something more than just that B is true.

We can thus partially characterize dissent from the Humean position by saying that there is more to a proposition p's being a law of nature than p's being true and p's having certain *formal* features (such as being universally quantified and involving concepts that are not gerrymandered in some "grue"-some way). There are propositions p that are laws of nature in some possible worlds and yet that are not laws of nature in all possible worlds in which they are true.[2] For instance, in our world that objects fall when dropped is a law of nature, but there is a world where the laws

---

2   This need not be true of *all* laws of nature. For instance, some laws of nature might be necessary truths, if they predicate essential properties of their objects. Also, arguably, the proposition that p is a law of nature is itself a law of nature if and only if p is a law of nature, so that the proposition that affirms nomicity of the proposition that all ravens are black is a proposition that is a law of nature in every possible world in which it is true.

of nature do not constrain the movement of falling objects but where the objects *happen* to move just as they do in our world.

Now, recall the truthmaker theory. Every true proposition is true in virtue of its accurately reflecting some aspect of reality, and that aspect of reality is the proposition's "truthmaker." Now, if p is a purely categorical proposition that is a law of nature, then we can ask not just what the truthmaker of p is, but also what the truthmaker of the proposition *that p is a law of nature* is. This truthmaker must be some aspect of reality. It must thus exist, since the nonexistent cannot be a truthmaker by Parmenides' principle that one cannot talk of what is not.

We need a name for the truthmaker of a true proposition of the form *that p is a law of nature*. The name should not be an abstract noun, because this truthmaker is not an abstract entity or concept, but an actual aspect of our existent universe, whose existence has explanatory prowess. I shall call such a truthmaker a *lawmaker* of p, that which makes the true proposition p into a law. Of course, just as the "truthmaker" of a proposition need not be a person that makes the proposition true (except in special cases: the truthmaker of "Socrates exists" is a person, namely, Socrates), so too one should not read personhood into the term lawmaker.[3]

The preceding assumes the truthmaker theory, the Parmenidean claim that every truth is true in virtue of what is. However, the argument also works if we assume the Aristotelian or Lewisian theory that true propositions can be made true either by the presence of a positive reality or by the absence of one. For it is implausible to suppose that what makes the proposition *that p is a law* be true is its lacking a falsemaker, or its being logically composed of propositions some of which lack a falsemaker, since the claim that p is a law seems clearly positive. Thus, still, I maintain that there will have to be some positive reality.

It is generally accepted that laws of nature are not causes, because laws are mere propositions and propositions have no causal efficacy. However, there are contexts in which one wants to use causal language about laws of nature. One may want to say, "The law of gravitation made this apple fall." Since the law of gravitation is a mere proposition, it cannot make anything

---

3   On certain views of laws of nature, some or all lawmakers will turn out to be persons or aspects of persons. For instance, a Richard Swinburne (1968) might allow that a proposition's being a law of nature is constituted by God's directly willing it to be such, so that the lawmaker of the proposition is the will of God. Or if one thinks that ultimately all natural lawfulness supervenes on dispositional properties of substances, and if persons are substances, then the dispositional properties of persons will be lawmakers, though there will also be lawmakers that are the dispositional properties of nonpersons.

fall. But what *does* make apples fall, given appropriate initial conditions, is the lawmaker of the proposition that the law of gravitation holds. For, the explanatory relation among the proposition that $F = Gm_1m_2/r^2$ (the formula, of course, abbreviates a more complicated statement that gives the definitions of all the symbols), the proposition reporting the initial conditions, and the proposition reporting the fall of an apple mirrors a logically contingent, objective, ternary relation in nature among the lawmaker of the proposition that $F = Gm_1m_2/r^2$, the dropping of the apple, and the falling of the apple. Otherwise the law will not be objectively explanatory.

If the explanatory relation among a law-reporting proposition, an initial fact-reporting proposition, and a final fact-reporting proposition failed to mirror some kind of extramental relation in nature between the lawmaker and truthmakers, respectively, of the respective propositions, then explanatory relations would lack objectivity. But the search for explanations is a search for objective truths. Given that generally speaking we are willing to say that a relation of *causality* between events A and B is parallel to a relation of *explanation* among the propositions reporting that A and that B happened, the relation between the lawmaker of the law of gravitation, the initial conditions, and the fall of the apple is one that we can also call "causal" in an extended sense. Thus, nomological explanatory relations can be said to parallel causal relations between lawmakers and truthmakers.

So the laws of nature are not causes, but their lawmakers can be meaningfully said to have causal efficacy or causal relevance. And there must *be* lawmakers if the laws of nature are not to be Humean and if every true proposition must have a truthmaker or if Lewis's more general truthmaker/falsemaker theory holds. What I have said so far is, however, neutral between various concrete anti-Humean accounts of laws of nature. Indeed, these accounts can be seen as being nothing else than different substantive accounts of what the lawmakers are. If one thinks that the laws of nature can be reduced ontologically to the dispositional properties of substances, as an Aristotelian does, then the lawmakers will ultimately be nothing but the possession of these dispositional properties. If one thinks that a theory of physics is true on which ultimately it is space-time that moves particles around, then space-time or its properties will be the lawmaker or lawmakers. If one thinks that the idea of a law of nature is primitive, then there will be no reductive account of a lawmaker beyond saying that it is "the truthmaker of a proposition reporting that some other proposition is a law of nature."

16.3.3. Natural Necessity

Admittedly, this is not the only way of looking at the matter. One might instead make the concept of *natural necessity*[4] be primitive. If one accepts the truthmaker (or truthmaker/falsemaker) theory, then the natural necessity will have to be grounded in something, a lawmaker. However, one might be hesitant in saying that this lawmaker *causes* things to obey the natural necessities. But if the lawmaker does not cause things to obey the natural necessities, then it is not clear *why* things obey them. This may seem to be a question-begging objection in the middle of an argument for the PSR, but it is not. The main reason for positing laws of nature is to explain why things behave as they do. If it is completely obscure why things obey the laws of nature, if we have not been able to say anything about the connection between the lawmakers and the lawful events, then by stating the laws of nature we have not explained the events. It would be as if we said Jones's death is explained by Smith's pressing the trigger without anything's being said about any causal or other connection between the pressing of the trigger and Jones's death.

The defender of the natural necessity approach can say that natural necessity should be understood as analogous to metaphysical necessity. It is a category mistake to think there is some entity that causes it to be the case that $2 + 2 = 4$, and likewise it is a category mistake to think there is some entity that causes stones to fall toward the massive Earth when dropped. Both happen because of a necessity, a different necessity in the two cases, and yet their happening does not require any explanation of causal type.

However, the analogy here is mistaken. We know that the falling of a stone indeed can be explained scientifically. Were this not so, then inference to best explanation could never get off the ground since the case of invoking gravity to explain the falling of stones is as clear a case of explanation as anything in science, and one might very plausibly think that inference to best explanation is at least a *part* of the epistemology of science. Moreover, the primary nonpractical motivator for science is precisely the search for explanation. On the other hand, the notion of the explanation of metaphysically necessary truths is one that we do not have a good handle on. Is the proposition that $2 + 2 = 4$ to be explained by showing via associativity that $(1 + 1) + (1 + 1) = (1 + 1) + 1) + 1$, with 2 being defined as $1 + 1$ and 4 as $((1 + 1) + 1) + 1$? Or is it

---

4 E.g., Leckey and Bigelow (1995).

266

perhaps a self-evident arithmetical claim? Or should we choose some other set of foundations for arithmetic? In general, are all mathematical proofs explanatory? Are only some, and if so, which ones? These are all questions to which we do not have answers, but they suggest that explanation in the sphere of the metaphysically necessary might be a very different thing from explanation in the sphere of the physically necessary, and hence provide a disanalogy between the two cases. One might even say that in the case of the physically necessary we seek *explanations* while in the case of the metaphysically necessary we seek *elucidations* and *understanding*.

It is a criterion of adequacy on a theory of laws of nature that it should make comprehensible why subsumption of a physically necessary connection of events, say, a stone's being dropped and its falling, under a law *explains* that connection. Unless one were willing to erase the distinction between the metaphysically and nomically necessary – and doing so would undercut the current objection to the metaphysical necessity of the PSR – and unless one is willing to be a Humean, it seems that some causal connection needs to be posited between lawmakers and events. Otherwise, it is quite unclear how the nomicity of the laws, that is, the existence of lawmakers, is supposed to be explanatory of the events.

16.4. LAWS OF NATURE AND THE CP

16.4.1. Why Are There No Everyday Violations?

Let us return to the question of why everyday violations of the PSR or CP do not happen. Suppose we grant that the CP is not metaphysically necessary. Then why do violations of the CP not happen? Presumably, since ex hypothesi they metaphysically could happen, the answer has to have something to do either with its being objectively unlikely that they should happen or with the contingent laws of nature or perhaps boundary conditions operative in our world. The objective unlikelihood, unless it is grounded in the laws of nature the way quantum probabilities are, is most obscure. For any one decently behaved possible world at which laws of nature just like those of our world hold and the CP holds in everyday contexts, there are infinitely many possible worlds where the CP does not hold. A universe is a maximal aggregate of physical entities. Call a universe that obeys our laws of physics and has the CP holding in everyday contexts a *regular universe*.

In fact, there are infinitely many more irregular universes. To see this, let S be the set of regular universes. The set S is infinite. But it is nonetheless a *set* of some fixed cardinality. This point is not trivial, since the collection of all possible universes is not a set.[5] However, S *is* a set, because the rules or laws in accordance with which the good physical behavior of the world is defined specify the *set* of all possible continuants for any given world at any given time, for these rules specify what kinds of possible entities can come to be present in the world and how many of them can come in and when. The possibility of such specification is, I take it, analytically contained in the notion of a *regular universe*.

To make this point clearer, suppose that the kind of regularity that the world has is that which some kind of quantum field theory posits. Then, the field theory posits that the basic entities in a regular continuant will be several kinds of fields governed by certain equations. Now, a field can be represented as a function from some fixed set A to some fixed set B (e.g., a scalar field on a four-dimensional Euclidean space-time can be represented as a function from $\mathbf{R}^4$ to $\mathbf{R}$, where $\mathbf{R}$ is the set of all real numbers). The collection of *all* functions from A to B is a set denoted by B^A whose cardinality can be computed if the cardinalities of A and B are known (in the case of scalar fields on a four-dimensional Euclidean space-time, the cardinality of the set of functions from $\mathbf{R}^4$ to $\mathbf{R}$ is a cardinality known as f that is bigger than the cardinality c of the continuum). Or suppose that the kind of regularity that the universe enjoys is such as to imply, among other things, that the universe is composed of up to n (a finite or infinite number) particles, which arise from k (a finite or infinite number) different kinds, each of which kinds of particles has at most p (a finite or infinite number) different properties that can each be described by real numbers (the properties might be, e.g., charge or coordinate components of the position). Then, the set of regular universes will have cardinality at most $c^{n \times k \times p}$, where c is as before the cardinality of the continuum. And even if a universe is only regular *in some aspect* or *in some region*, we will still be able to run the argument I am about to give, but this time concerning not universes as wholes, but those aspects or regions of universes in which there is regularity. Instead of kinds of *universes*, we will then be talking of kinds of *aspects or regions of universes* and counting these. Working out the details in this extension of the argument is left as an exercise to the reader.

Now, assume the Axiom of Choice. Let a denote the cardinality of S. Let n be any infinite cardinality greater than a, for example, 2^a (the

---

5 This is shown in Pruss (2001) for possible worlds, but the same argument applies to possible universes.

cardinality of the set of all subsets of S, which Cantor's diagonal argument has shown to be greater than the cardinality of S). We will let U be a set of possible universes in which tomorrow the Earth and Sun disappear counternomically for a day and are replaced, for no cause at all, by a big cloud of photons all dancing the polka, with the number of these photons having some value between $\aleph_0$ (the cardinality of the set of integers), inclusive, and the $(n + 1)$st infinite cardinal number[6] $\aleph_n$, exclusive, which photons then disappear, the Earth and Sun return, and everything returns to normal nomic order the day after. The number of different cardinalities m satisfying $\aleph_0 \leq m < \aleph_n$ is equal to n, and so we can choose the worlds in U so that U will have cardinality at least n and hence greater than a. Moreover, since n is an *infinite* cardinality, it must be that n is *infinitely many times greater* than a.

Thus, indeed, there are a lot more of the everyday-CP-violating universes that otherwise obey the laws of physics than there are everyday-CP-obeying universes, if the violation of the CP is metaphysically possible.[7] Thus, we are unlikely to be able to say that everyday obedience to the CP is objectively probable, unless this probability can in some way be grounded in the laws.

So we are back to where we were. If the everyday violation of the CP is metaphysically possible, then it must be the laws that explain why it is not in fact violated. Should it be countered that this lack of violation is just a brute fact, one that is not itself explained, and that it is question begging to assume otherwise in an argument for the PSR, the following response can be made. The preceding argument shows that there is a presumption that the high degree of everyday obedience to the CP we observe is a very unlikely state of affairs. Even if one were willing to tolerate brute facts, a theory's positing of a very unlikely brute fact that can be specified a priori in a concise way ("the CP is satisfied") is a strong consideration against

---

6 The existence of such a cardinal follows from the Axiom of Choice. For the technically minded reader, we prove this in the nomenclature of Kuratowski and Mostowski (1976): The number n is the cardinality of a set S. Then as S is well-orderable by the Axiom of Choice (p. 254, Theorem 1), we can find an initial ordinal ω_n (often also denoted $\aleph_n$) with index equal to the cardinality n of W (p. 273, Theorem 5). By definition of the index, it follows that there are precisely n infinite initial ordinals less than ω_n (p. 273, Definition 1); that is, there are precisely n cardinalities between $\aleph_0$ (inclusive) and ω_n (exclusive). We can then let $n^* = \omega_n$. (*Note:* Throughout their p. 273, Kuratowski and Mostowki talk of "initial ordinals," where, to be strictly precise, they mean "infinite initial ordinals.")

7 For arguments of this sort in the related context of Lewis's extreme modal realism, see Forrest and Armstrong (1984), Lewis (1986, Section 2.5), Pruss (2001), and Section 19.3.2.

that theory.[8] We should in fact say that on the theory that it is just a brute fact whether the CP holds in everyday contexts, the observed high degree to which the CP holds of macroscopic events is a most surprising fact, whereas on the theory that the CP is metaphysically necessary, this fact is much less surprising (though we might reasonably still be surprised that the causes are so often observable). Thus, we have very strong evidence against the brute-fact theory of the CP's holding in everyday contexts, and should opt for the alternative.

The brute-fact and unlikely-but-random accounts dismissed, we now need to consider whether the CP, even in a restricted form, could in fact be grounded in the contingent laws of nature. As we shall see, on the preceding lawmaker account of laws the answer is negative.

16.4.2. Ceteris Paribus Laws and the CP

On a lawmaker account, as long as there is more than one lawmaker influencing, say, motion, it is very natural to think of the laws of nature as all holding ceteris paribus. Perhaps one lawmaker brings it about, ceteris paribus, that items dropped fall, while another brings it about that items magnetically repelled from the ground, ceteris paribus, move upward. Now, if we follow the Humean denial of the metaphysical necessity of the CP, then we will have to admit that whatever a lawmaker can do can also happen in a brute manner, without any cause. A rock can fall under

8 The notion of a fact that can be specified a priori in a concise way is an intuitive notion. For instance, we will use this notion when we say, upon hearing of a run of a thousand heads in a coin-tossing experiment, that surely there was something fishy. Even though the run of a thousand heads has exactly the same probability as any other sequence of a thousand outcomes, namely, probability 2^{-1000}, the run of a thousand heads could be concisely specified ahead of time, unlike most of the alternatives. There is no successful way of making this notion precise right now, though Dembski (1998, 2002) has made valiant attempts. A basic difficulty, for instance, is that the notion of a specification is language relative, and we need to avoid languages that are gerrymandered to specify precisely the description we are after. Thus, supposing that a given seemingly random run of a thousand tosses of a coin has occurred, a language might in fact be gerrymandered to include the adjective *jabberwockian*, which describes precisely *that* sequence of coin toss results, so that the run could be specified briefly: "A jabberwockian run has occurred." One needs to rule out such gerrymandering. This is most difficult in the case in which the phenomena to be specified (Dembski [2002] is concerned with things like life) are ones that were observed prior to and during the development of our language. Unfortunately, the CP is also this kind of a phenomenon, and this means that the argument must be run on an intuitive level only, at least right now. (Note, however, that we would just as much think fishy a run of a thousand heads that occurred when the English language was being formed: we *can* perhaps proceed intuitively in these matters with the help of such counterfactuals.)

270

the influence of gravity *or* it can just move this way or that for no reason. Now, just as the gravitational impulse can be countered by an opposed magnetic impulse, it is plausible that the gravitational impulse could be countered by a brute uncaused "impulse" in a direction opposite to that of the gravitational impulse. If we say that the lawmaker of the law of gravity is by itself sufficient to bring about the downward movement, and hence when the lawmaker is present the movement cannot fail to occur, then we have contradicted the fact that the law of gravitation holds merely ceteris paribus.

Of course, we might say that when we claim that we have a ceteris paribus law, we do not mean that the law operates "in the absence of a countervailing brute impulse" but "in the absence of a countervailing cause." Moreover, one might wonder about the very conceptual possibility of a brute "impulse," since an impulse is by definition that which a force produces, and hence is caused by the force, and since furthermore one might worry that there just is no concept of an "impulse" in present-day physics.

But these objections miss the point. The point is: What is it that makes it be the case that when the lawmaker is present and no other forces or laws are relevant, the lawlike behavior must occur, on the assumption that (at least in everyday contexts) it is at least nomically necessary that the behavior occur then? If we say that the lawmaker *necessitates* this behavior to occur, then we no longer have a ceteris paribus law. The metaphysical necessity of the CP would allow, however, for this question to be answered as follows: The nonoccurrence of the behavior, in the presence of the lawmaker and the absence of other causes, would itself be a causeless event and hence a violation of the CP. If we have the CP's being metaphysically necessary, then indeed the issue is clear: Events can only occur for causes, and so the causeless event of the lawlike behavior's nonoccurrence cannot occur.

The preceding argument relies on the idea that there is more than one lawmaker influencing, say, the motion of a particle – that there is not one unified law, with a single lawmaker, that governs all the motion of our particle. Moreover, it is assumed that we cannot consider the conjunction of all the laws to be something that itself does not hold mere ceteris paribus. But even if there were a unified law or conjunction of laws, it might well be conceptually possible to think of this law as ceteris paribus. Were there other influences, other lawmakers – ex hypothesi, there are not – quite possibly this lawmaker would not suffice to produce the effects. If we accept this, the argument becomes more general.

A different way to run the argument is to focus on the version of the CP that talks of the impossibility of object's coming into existence for no cause. Consider a large vacuum container. Why is it that we will not observe a brick or a stone or some other massive object's popping into existence in this container? One might start to answer this question by saying that quantum mechanics, while allowing for objects to pop into existence, makes it a very unlikely event when the object is massive. However, this, again, misses the point of the question. The lawmakers of the laws of quantum mechanics provide causes for object's popping into existence – though not *ex nihilo*, because in the presence of those lawmakers, which are not nothing. But in what way can something cause it to be the case that something does *not* brutely pop into existence? How can an *ex nihilo* popping into existence be causally prevented? We cannot prevent it in our usual way by preventing the cause from occurring or succeeding, since there is supposed to be no cause.

16.4.3. Essence and Existence

Here is yet another form of the argument. A brick has both essence and existence. On a Fregean analysis of this, the existence is a property of the essence, in the sense that for the brick to exist is for its essence to have the property of *being instantiated*. Consider the essence of a possible brick that could exist in a vacuum container. How do the lawmakers of the laws of quantum mechanics, or any other lawmakers, prevent this essence from, for no reason at all, gaining the property of *being instantiated*? After all, presumably, these lawmakers do not act on uninstantiated essences: they act, instead, on concrete existing things, transforming some into others.

One possible answer to the question is to say that the way the popping into existence of the brick is prevented is by the law-enforced presence in that place of something incompatible with the brick's presence. Vacuum is, on this view, not the complete absence of stuff. Perhaps, at least, empty space-time is there, and the presence of empty space-time is incompatible with the brick's presence there, while the lawmakers of the laws of nature continually bring it about that the empty space-time persists as it is. This answer, however, will not work if all laws are unavoidably ceteris paribus, because then the laws will not be sufficient to bring it about that empty space-time remains as it is, and so it will be incomprehensible how they guard against brute poppings-into-existence.

And there are arguments to be made in favor of all laws' being ceteris paribus. Besides the well-known arguments of Nancy Cartwright (1999), one might add another one, at least for someone who thinks that something like theism is logically possible, for, arguably, it is logically possible that, whatever lawmakers actually exist, there might coexist with them a very powerful supernatural being capable of overriding them. If so, then the laws are ceteris paribus: they function in the absence of the influence of a logically possible supernatural being.

16.4.4. The Probability of Violations of the PSR

A useful intermediate conclusion result that I will argue for now is this:

(125) If the PSR is not metaphysically necessary, then either it is objectively highly probable that the PSR is violated in many ways, or there are no objective, nonepistemic, nonfrequentist probabilities of specific events that would be violations of the PSR.

For now I will assume all objective probabilities are nonepistemic and so drop the "nonepistemic" qualifier. An "objective" Bayesian approach will be discussed in Section 17.4.2.g.

Now, frequentism is not a viable option because after all it *is* possible for coins to have come up heads in all the finitely many tosses that have in fact occurred, even though the probability of coming up heads is not 1. By an event with a *nonexistent objective probability*, I do not mean an event that has 0 objective probability. Rather, I mean an event about whose objective likelihood it makes no sense to talk. There may well be contingent events that have no objective probabilities. For instance, if there is a God, then it might be that God's freedom is so radical that there are no objective probabilities to be, even in principle, assigned to different possible cosmoi that God could create, and if there is no God, then it might well be that no objective probability could be assigned even in principle to the Big Bang.

We might convince ourselves on the grounds of there being more possible worlds with lots of violations of the PSR than those with no violations of the PSR that violations of the PSR are objectively *probable*, if we take probability in terms of world- or universe-counting in some intuitive sense, albeit it is known that this is a sense that is very difficult to quantify. Otherwise, we have to say that there is no objective probability of any possible violation of the PSR, for the only other way there could be such an objective probability would be if these probabilities would be generated by the laws of nature and this would make specific violations of the PSR be law-governed events. But if we understand law-governed events as ones arising from the causality of substances and/or lawmakers, and if we accept the thesis at the heart of the rejection of the free-will and quantum objections to the PSR, namely, that causation always gives rise to an explanation, we have to conclude that specific events violating the PSR cannot arise from any kind of causality and hence cannot have objective probabilities assignable nomically.

We can in fact reject the first disjunct in the conclusion of (125), since we do not in fact observe lots of widespread violations of the PSR, and hence that disjunct is empirically disproved. Given the implausibility of frequentist accounts of probability, it follows that

(126) If the PSR is not metaphysically necessary, then there are no objective probabilities of specific events that would be violations of the PSR.

This undercuts *all* objective nomic probability assignments if the preceding arguments are correct about there always being possibilities of violations of laws given the negation of the metaphysical necessity of the PSR. For suppose that we have an objective probability of some event E's occurring in a law-governed way given the laws. Then

(127) $P(E$ occurs$) = P(E$ occurs in a law-governed way | laws are obeyed$)P($laws are obeyed$) + P(E$ occurs for no reason at all or for some anomic reason | laws are not obeyed$)P($laws are not obeyed$)$.

Of course, we must understand the laws that are not obeyed here as ceteris paribus ones, rather than as universally true propositions. The preceding sum then involves two terms, the first of which presumably has an objective value, while the second does not. Hence the sum also does not have an objective value.[9]

The preceding arguments become particularly clear if we understand the laws in an Aristotelian way. We have a plurality of finite substances in the universe, each with its own dispositions, capacities, powers, and characteristic forms of behavior. The substances interact in various ways, for instance, through gravitational attraction or electrical repulsion. No finite substance is sufficiently powerful to be able to overcome all actual

---

9 The sum $A = B + C$ where B has objective value and C does not cannot itself have objective value, for if it did have it, then so would C as $C = A - B$. On the other hand, it is possible to imagine a sum in which neither summand has objective value but the sum does. For instance, suppose D has no objective value. Then, neither does $-D$. But the *sum* of D and $-D$ might count as having objective value 0.

and possible opposition. Now on this view, it is indeed incomprehensible how a finite substance or set of finite substances is capable of preventing the popping into existence of something new.

Moreover, one might think that anything that can pop into existence for no cause can also causelessly pop out of existence. If substances can pop into existence causelessly, then the fact that finite substances do not in fact willy-nilly pop out of existence cannot be grounded in the powers, capacities, and characteristic behaviors of finite substances.

16.4.5. Would a "Deity" Help?

The Aristotelian can, however, posit a more powerful substance that sustains in existence all existing substances and holds sway over empty regions of space to ensure that they are empty in the absence of causes. Such a substance would be a sort of deity. It is not clear whether any substance could do this if it were not itself sufficiently similar to the God of Western monotheism. Plausibly, the only way a substance could sustain in existence other substances and prevent the causeless popping into existence of new substances is if it were such as to be itself the source of being, that by virtue of participation in which all the other substances exist and apart from which no substance can exist or pop into existence. It is plausible, further, that any such substance, since it would be the source of being, would have to exist either necessarily or at least quasi-necessarily, where a being exists *quasi-necessarily* provided it exists in every nonempty world: it would be strange if the fount of being did not have quasi-necessity, at least, since that would mean that it is a mere accident that it, rather than something else, is the fount of being. This would be sufficient to guarantee the truth of the version of the CP that says that substances cannot come into existence *ex nihilo*, for in every nonempty world, then, substances would come into existence only under the influence or sway of that deiform substance.

More generally, an Aristotelian system of ceteris paribus laws arising out of the dispositions, powers, and characteristic behaviors of finite substances can only work if the CP is assumed, for only if one could rule out the possibility of lawless brute behavior not grounded in these dispositions, powers, and characteristic behaviors could any concrete predictions be made even if one knew all of the ceteris paribus laws. The lawmakers, that is, the dispositions, powers, and characteristic behaviors of substances, are such that each is incapable on its own of logically necessitating any one result. Taken all together, they also are incapable of logically necessitating

275

a result. After all, were a new substance to pop into existence, it could override their activity. This makes it plausible that the only way behavior not arising from the activities of the substances, that is, unlawful behavior, could be ruled out would be either through the efficacy of a deiform substance or through an appropriate CP's being metaphysically necessary – or both, since one might take the CP to imply the existence of a God.

16.4.6. Causelessly Ceasing to Be

Finally, observe a simple way in which a failure of the cosmic CP might lead to scientifically unacceptable results. Suppose we accept the parity thesis that a contingent being that can causelessly come to be can also causelessly cease to be. If we think that the universe as a whole causelessly came to be, say, in the Big Bang, then we must likewise suppose it can causelessly cease to be. Now, the coming-to-be of the universe was on this view a causeless event not governed by laws of nature, for if it were governed by laws of nature, then we could say that the universe was caused by the lawmakers of the laws, even if the causal connection here were indeterministic (cf. the discussion of quantum mechanics in Chapter 8). Understanding the causelessness in the parity thesis in the same way, we will have to allow that the universe as a whole can also cease to exist, in a way that is not governed by scientific laws.

But this yields a defeater to scientific predictions of the future fate of the universe: notwithstanding whatever the scientific theories say, the universe could cease to exist, in a way not governed by law. The possibility of the universe's just popping out of existence is a possibility that needs to be taken seriously, because it is a possibility precisely parallel to something that, on the theory under consideration, has in fact happened – the universe has popped into existence. While not just any logical possibility of an outré event needs to be considered, when an event of the same sort *has* occurred and one has no justified way to attribute a low probability to the event's recurring, then the canons of reason – even of inductive reason – require one to take the possibility seriously. And indeed nothing can be said of the probability of the universe's popping out of existence, since this popping out of existence is not supposed to happen in concert with the laws of nature.

Observe that this argument can be run apart from the Aristotelian account of laws of nature or the more general lawmaker account. It can be run even from a Humean point of view. But once one uses an account of laws other than that considered earlier, then the following response becomes available: "The parity thesis is false, for the universe's popping into existence at the beginning of time is, while not governed by law, not contrary to any law of nature. But the universe's popping out of existence would in fact be contrary to the laws of nature." The point is that on the more Aristotelian view, laws are of a ceteris paribus sort. But on other views, exceptions might be impossible and there might be no ceteris paribus clauses. However, let us consider the whole of the evidence available to us before we decide what counts as a law. Part of our evidence is that, ex hypothesi, the universe has popped into existence. Let us suppose that this is an event to which no available well-confirmed scientific theory can assign objective probabilities. Nonetheless, it is something we should work into our views. If we accept an intuitive parity between popping into existence and popping out of existence, then by the same token we should leave room in our laws for the universe to cease to exist. Thus, our causal laws should be of the form, *State A at t is followed by state B at t + Δt provided that the universe still exists at t + Δt*. We have no reason to dismiss the possibility of the universe's causelessly ceasing to exist if we do not accept a CP.

16.4.7. Induction

Consider a final objection. We know *inductively* that there are causes of macroscopic phenomena, simply by virtue of having found causes in the cases of many macroscopic phenomena. There are at least three problems with this answer.

The first is the worry that many of the inductive data may be neutral with respect to the PSR or may presuppose it. For instance, yes, we have an explanation of the patterns shown on cathode-ray tubes: an explanation in terms of electrons. But we have not actually seen the electrons. We infer their existence as the best *explanation* of this and other phenomena, arguably only because we *assume* that there is an explanation – or so it shall be argued in the next chapter. Now, consider the following two hypotheses:

(128) The PSR is true of macroscopic phenomena, and
(129) There are always good *putative* explanations of macroscopic phe-
    nomena, that is, propositions compatible with the phenomena that
    would explain them well were they true.

Cases like those of electrons only support (128) by supporting (129). However, there will be cases of inductive data that *do* support the PSR.

277

Sometimes we will in fact be in a position to see that in fact there is an explanation.

But this takes us to the second objection. We do not in fact *always* find explanations for phenomena. We may never know why Sextus Empiricus died or why the San Francisco earthquake of 1906 occurred in 1906 rather than 1905, however hard we might search for the explanation – though no one wants to claim, at least in the case of Sextus Empiricus's death, that there was no cause. It might be optimistically claimed that in the case of phenomena that we collectively put our mind to and that do not slip further and further from what is epistemically accessible to us, as particular historical events do, we do eventually come up with an explanation.

But it is not clear that such confidence is in fact justified historically. For instance, we have searched for centuries for the origins of life. We do have accounts of abiogenesis, but these are mere theories, for none of which do we have independent evidence. The most that can be said for these accounts is that *if* the origin of life has an explanation and *if* the explanation is naturalistic, then likely some account like one of these is true. And we do have theistic accounts, but of course theism entails a form of the PSR, since if there is a God, his activity together with that of any free creatures explains everything, at least as long as God's existence counts as self-explanatory because it is necessary. Likewise, we have a number of theories of what triggers rain, but none of the theories is sufficiently dominant for us to say with any confidence why rain happens when it does.

Of course, one might come up with a story about why these kinds of unsolved problems are particularly hard ones, concerning the distant past or very complex phenomena. And one might in fact claim, confidently, that any cases in which our concerted efforts at finding an explanation have been thwarted will turn out not to be disconfirmatory of the PSR understood as inductively supported, but will turn out to be cases in which we can explain why our doxastic faculties are simply too limited for us to be able to handle the problem or why the problem is very complex. This confidence is highly plausible, but its justification rests on a priori considerations rather than induction.

A third but most controversial consideration against the inductive justification of the PSR is that violations of the PSR would not be law-governed phenomena. Inductive reasoning, however, presupposes that we are operating within a law-governed realm, and hence cannot itself justify this presupposition. A thought experiment: Suppose you came upon a bunch of one hundred oysters and found after opening thirty of the oysters that each contained a pearl. You might justifiably conclude that they *all* contain pearls. However, suppose you further learned that in fact whether a given oyster produces a pearl is an anomic phenomenon, one with no explanation and one to which objectively no probabilities can be assigned. I would suggest that such information would make one conclude that in fact it was just a coincidence that the thirty oysters contained pearls, and hence that one cannot justifiably claim that the others would as well.

In fact one might even hold, with Bede Rundle (1986), that induction itself depends on the PSR, and then that dependence would be an argument for the PSR.

So long as relevant conditions match those when our actions have had such results [say, as the door opening when the key is turned] previously, we anticipate them following yet again. . . .

[P]art of what is at work here is a principle of sufficient reason: a departure from an observed regularity means that conditions were different on this occasion. (Rundle, 1986, p. 120, 121)

One difficulty with this argument is that we have seen that if the PSR is not to lead to fatalism, we must accept cases in which the same conditions end up with different results – for instances, cases of libertarian free will or quantum indeterminism. However, the basic point here stands. It is quite plausible to see the pattern in simple induction as starting with a claim that there is an explanation for the inductive data. Then, we try to fill out the explanation, though perhaps only to a very vague extent, for instance, "There is something *deterministic* in virtue of which all *A*s are *B*s." And then from this explanation we conclude that the next *A* will be a *B*, unless the conditions differ in that that "something" is no longer present. This suggestion leads us into our next topic.

17

Inference to the Best or Only Explanation

RATIONAL WITHOUT THE PSR?

A number of scientific inference schemes have the structure: We have a phenomenon Φ — ideally, one that comprises a cluster of different phenomena — and a number of explanatory hypotheses $H_1, \ldots, H_n$, that is, hypotheses each of which would explain Φ were the hypothesis in question true. Of these, H_i is the best or most plausible or most probable. Hence, probably H_i holds. The question of how we tell which of the hypotheses should be chosen — what "best" or "most plausible" means — is of course the area where much controversy lies, but I will avoid this question. Schemes having this general form I will label *inference to best explanation* (IBE), though some Bayesian schemes not always contained under that label will qualify, as long as the hypotheses among which one is choosing on Bayesian grounds are *explanatory*.

I will be interested in this inference scheme to the extent that it is considered to be truth-directed in a realist sense. The nonrealist about inference to best explanation will thus not be interested in what follows. Indeed, some may find the following considerations moving them to this nonrealist stance.

IBE then holds that given a number of putative explanations, the one that is in some sense best is likely true. But what if in fact the phenomenon has no explanation at all? What if the phenomenon is just a brute fact? This possibility would not, of course, itself be an explanatory hypothesis. Thus, it would not fall within the purview of IBE at all. I want to suggest that it is a possibility for which the IBE defender needs to account. Even if one solved the difficult problem of deciding which of a set of competing explanations is best and why bestness is a sign of truth, the problem of why we should think there is an explanation at all would remain. The threat of the no-explanation hypothesis is *in addition to* the well-known threat that an unknown hypothesis might explain the phenomenon. Unlike an unknown hypothesis, the no-explanation hypothesis is a hypothesis that is worked out in as much detail as any of the particular explanatory hypotheses, but it is simpler. It just states that the phenomenon happened for no reason at all.

Obviously, this is not a worry we have in everyday doxastic practices. If we find that the airplane that crashed had a metal-fatigue failure in the ailerons that would produce a crash in, say, 5 percent of flights, and if we find no other putative explanation, then we simply conclude that probably the metal-fatigue failure caused the crash. The idea that given such a simple and clear theory about how the crash could have happened nonetheless it might be that there was no cause strikes us as even more bizarre than that there should be no cause in a case in which there is no theory about how the crash could have happened.

But if the PSR fails to be necessarily true, are we right to dismiss this possibility? Why should we not consider the hypothesis of *no explanation* in addition to the explanatory hypotheses? It seems to be simpler than the other hypotheses. The probability of this hypothesis is, moreover, inscrutable, and indeed perhaps objectively the hypothesis has no probability − neither high nor low, neither 1 nor 0 − since it posits an anomic event and one might think that objective probabilities can only be assigned in the presence of laws. In other words, the possibility that the PSR might be false seems to introduce a defeater to IBE-based inferences.

There may seem to be something circular about first having argued for the metaphysical necessity of the PSR in Chapter 16 as the best explanation of why the PSR holds in everyday situations, and then arguing in this section that IBE itself depends on the PSR. This accusation would be fair if we were trying to justify IBE. But that is not the point. It is a given that IBE is a good inferential truth-directed practice. Using this practice, we can argue for the metaphysical necessity of the PSR. Furthermore, however, we can consider the argument that IBE *itself* in part depends for its success on the PSR.

17.2. PREFERENCE FOR EXPLANATORY THEORIES

We tend to prefer explanatory theories to nonexplanatory ones. Take any scientific theory, say, neo-Darwinian evolution. We can try to consider a weaker theory that is the same theory minus the distinctive causal or explanatory claims that the theory makes. Thus, instead of saying that natural selection and random mutation explain the mammalian eye, the weaker theory will say that there was such and such a sequence of organisms, that after a cosmic ray hit a DNA molecule, it changed in such and such a way, and so forth. The weaker theory is just as useful for all practical purposes, because it produces exactly the same predictions. Moreover, we can retain any counterfactual claims, if we think we need them practically. Thus, we can say that were the glass to be dropped, it would fall, as long as we do not imply that it would fall *because* of the dropping. (An occasionalist will use counterfactual discourse in this way.) Since the weaker theory does the job and fits the data equally well, why not go for it instead?

In general, given two theories that, as far as we know, fit the observed data equally well and give the same amount of predictions, but where one theory claims to explain the data and the other neither claims to explain nor not to explain – take, for instance, the claims of Hellenistic "empiricist" physicians – IBE would tell us to opt for the explanatory theory. This is an instance of use of IBE that cannot simply be reduced to Bayesian epistemology, at least not in the absence of the PSR. Both theories make the observed data equally likely. If Bayesian epistemology is to explain the difference, the difference will have to lie in the priors. But there is no reason to suppose that the explanatory theory should have a higher prior probability than the nonexplanatory theory. In fact, in general, since the nonexplanatory theories make weaker claims than the explanatory ones, they should have higher prior probabilities.

Of course it may be that we only assign a high prior probability to a nonexplanatory theory T when there is an explanatory theory T^* that is strictly stronger than T and whose prior probability is very close to that of T. If so, then confirmation of T would be confirmation of T^*. But *why* should we assign high prior probabilities only to those nonexplanatory theories that have such an explanatory theory associated with them? What justification is there for this? If there is none, then we cannot say that there is anything irrational about those who act differently. (Cf. Section 17.4.2 for probabilistic attempts to answer this question.)

On the other hand, given the PSR, we can give an account of our preference for explanatory theories. There has to be an explanation. Theory A purports to give one and is the best candidate. We say, "Eureka! We have found what we were looking for," and we accept A. On the other hand, if we had a nonexplanatory theory, we would know that even if that theory is true, we would not be done – there would be a further theory to be given.

Here is a different approach. Suppose, now, that we have a contest between two incompatible theories, A and B, of comparable complexity, where A is explanatory and B is not. If we accept B, then given the PSR, because B is not explanatory, we know that the full story either does not include B or goes beyond B. Thus, if B is correct and a part of the full story (rather than a falsehood or a merely accidental truth), the full story of the phenomenon to be explained is more complex than B and hence than A. If, on the other hand, A is correct, it might well be the full story. Simplicity bids us to prefer A, all other considerations being equal. But it does so only given some version of the PSR.

17.3. THE SHERLOCK HOLMES PRINCIPLE

Observe, finally, how strong our commitment is to the PSR, in connection with IBE in the special case in which only one explanation is available. Recall Sherlock Holmes's famous precept "When you have eliminated the impossible, whatever remains, however improbable, must be the truth," which seems at first sight to be a claim about modal logic. But actually the application of this principle uses a version of the PSR, as we see from the continuation of the quote:

[Holmes:] "We know that he did not come through the door, the window, or the chimney. We also know that he could not have been concealed in the room, as there is no concealment possible. When, then, did he come?"
"He came through the hole in the roof!" I cried.
"Of course he did. He must have done so." (Doyle, 1927, p. 111)

Holmes thus takes the elimination of all other explanations to be tanta-mount to an elimination of all other possibilities. There is no possibility of the person's coming-to-be ex nihilo in the room.

In our ordinary reasoning, if we are certain that we have enumer-ated all the possible explanations – as Holmes admittedly had not – and that all but one did not occur, then we are certain that the remaining explanation is the correct one. We do not allow for any possibility of there being no explanation. To modify somewhat an example by David White (1979), suppose that a number of zoo animals were brutally killed

283

and dismembered. We have absolutely conclusive evidence that no animal had any access to the cages in question, and only one person did. Moreover, we know that no disease or other natural event could have caused the carnage. On the basis of our absolutely conclusive evidence, only that one person could have done it, though there is no direct evidence against him. On the contrary, there is extremely strong character and circumstantial evidence in favor of this man, who was widely reputed to be a holy man who loved animals as St. Francis did. It is highly implausible that he did it. But if it is even more unlikely that anyone or anything else did it, then we will reluctantly conclude that our St. Francis did it.

The only question is whether the evidence ruling out the other possible explanations is solid. Observe, too, that, as Holmes did, no doubt the prosecutor in court will slide between talking of having eliminated all other possible *explanations* and talking of having eliminated all other *possibilities*, and no one will consider as a possibility the option that the dismembering deaths of the animals are a brute uncaused fact. Thus, in our ordinary practice, we assign zero probability to the chance that this was a brute fact. Now, there is no reason why it should be any less likely that we have an unexplained brute fact occur in a case in which there is only one available explanation than in a case in which there is more than one available explanation. Thus, in the latter cases, if we are to be consistent, we should suppose there to be no chance of there failing to be an explanation. The *strength* of this commitment to the PSR also strengthens the claim that the PSR is not itself an inductively confirmed generalization.

Observe that Holmes's principle that if there is only one possible explanation, then this explanation is correct is arguably sufficient as a replacement for the PSR in the most controversial application of the PSR, namely, its application on a global scale to the existence of the cosmos or to the Big Conjunctive Contingent Fact, the conjunction of all contingent true propositions with truth-functional redundancies removed if needed. For as we have seen it can be argued that in those cases the only possible explanation is in terms of the free action of a necessary being. Therefore, by Holmes's principle, this *is* the explanation. This argument was made by David White (1979; see also Katz and Kremer, 1997). And, of course, if we have an explanation of the BCCF, then we have an explanation of every contingent fact, and hence the PSR is true. Thus, Holmes's principle implies the PSR.

17.4.1. Restricted PSRs

17.4.1.a Restriction to Scientific Cases. Let us now consider some alternatives to the PSR that seem to do the job for philosophy of science.

(130) If p is a true proposition that can have a scientific explanation (or, alternately, p is the sort of proposition that can have a scientific explanation), then p has an explanation.

This principle would appear to exclude the BCCF or the proposition that there is a contingent being, since it seems there cannot be a scientific explanation of these facts. Thus, it is a principle that would tell the PSR to keep to its proper place and not lead us into theological realms, grand axiarchic principles, or the like.

However, in fact, (130) does not appear to accomplish the kind of limiting of the explanatory aspirations that it promises. Let S be the set of all contingent physical beings. Suppose that, in fact, all the members of S are discernible, that Leibniz's Principle of Identity of Indiscernibles (PII) holds at least contingently, in the following sense: For each member α of S there is a general nonrelational property P_α, that is, a nonrelational property expressible in general terms without rigidly referring to individuals, places, or times, such that α and only α has P_α. This is a plausible assumption. The argument extends to a more general, and even more plausible, case in which each set of mutually indiscernible contingent beings is of finite cardinality, but I will leave that as an exercise to the reader (cf. Pruss, 2004a).

Consider now the conjunction p of all propositions of the form

(131) There exists a unique contingent being x such that P_α.

Somewhat surprisingly, p is a proposition of a sort that could have a scientific explanation. It is a finite or infinite conjunction of propositions of the form (131). But such propositions *can* have scientific explanations. For instance, if one has a conjunction of seventeen propositions of the form (131), there is no conceptual problem with giving a scientific explanation of why this conjunction is true — one just explains how one of the entities came into existence, how another came into existence, and so on, making sure that one does not involve oneself in a circularity and that one also explains any apparent coincidences. In fact, plausibly, it is logically possible for p to have a scientific explanation, for there could be a larger universe in which p is still true and where p is explained in terms of the antics of contingent physical entities not falling under any of the descriptions P_α for α in S. In that universe, S would only be a subset of all the contingent physical entities, but this does not affect the argument.

Hence, by (130), p must have an explanation. But, in fact, it seems that p does not have a scientific explanation, for an explanation of p would have to make reference to entities outside S, and no scientific explanation does that, since *in fact* the set S is the set of all contingent physical beings. Thus, p has a nonscientific explanation. Thus, while the motivation for (130) was to clip the wings of the PSR and not allow us to get to nonscientific explanations, (130) fails to accomplish this. Of course, one might deny that the version of the PII used previously is even contingently true as well as denying the more general technical assumption about the finitude of cardinality of each set of mutually indiscernible contingent entities. If so, then the preceding argument would be blocked. But it is highly implausible that it is permissible to infer an explanation of p if and only if this technical assumption holds. That would seem quite ad hoc. And given that (130) fails to give one what one wanted when one proposed it, the simpler full PSR is more plausible.

Now, one might try to block the preceding argument by saying that I misunderstood what (130) is getting at. Granted, p could have a scientific explanation. But it could not have one *in the actual world* where p is in fact a report of the existence of all contingent physical beings. Thus, perhaps, the modality we want in (130) is "possibility in the actual world." But there is no such modality. Unless this modality is going to collapse into ordinary metaphysical possibility, "the actual world" must be a rigid designator. But if w rigidly designates a world and q rigidly designates a proposition, then the proposition *that q holds at w* is either necessary or impossible. Otherwise, we end up with nonsensical claims such as "q holds at w at w_1 but it is not the case that q holds at w at w_2." Hence, if "the actual world" is a rigid designator, whatever can hold at the actual world necessarily holds at the actual world. And so (130) says that p has an explanation if p has a scientific explanation, and that is a mere tautology.

But perhaps the modality in (130) is epistemic. Given that we know p to be the conjunction of *all* propositions of the form (131) for α in S, it is not epistemically possible that p have a scientific explanation. However, epistemic possibility differs from person to person, and so this would mean that p has an explanation provided it is epistemically possible

286

for at least one person – or maybe one rational person? – that it has a scientific explanation. This is an unacceptably anthropocentric principle. Besides, since views of what can and cannot have a scientific explanation differ widely among rational persons, it would follow in practice that just about any true proposition would have an explanation, except maybe propositions such as *p is true but has no scientific explanation*.

Probably, however, what someone who would propose that the modality in (130) is epistemic really means is that

(132) If p is known to be true and it is epistemically possible that p has a scientific explanation, then it is rational to believe that p has an explanation.

Such a principle would seem to do the job in practice. It allows that if one did not know that, for instance, p is the report of the existence of *all* contingent physical beings, then it would be rational to believe that p has an explanation, but it might cease to be rational if one learned that p actually reports the existence of all contingent physical beings. Likewise, if we learned that some quantum mechanical facts do not have a scientific explanation, then the principle would no longer justify us in thinking that they have an explanation.

There are other variants of the condition in the principle. For instance, one might say (cf. Callender, 2004) that it is rational to believe that p has an explanation provided that it is reasonable to think that an explanation would be fruitful, either pragmatically (e.g., by yielding predictions) or explanatorily (in terms of supplying a theory that explains other things). All of these have in common the claim that under some conditions as to what an explanation of p would be expected to be like, it is rational to believe p has an explanation.

Now, observe that such a principle does not actually reflect the totality of instances in which we are willing to accept the existence of an explanation. Suppose that scientific study demonstrated that some basic constant in the laws of nature when expressed in binary in a physically natural system of units, upon being interpreted as a sequence of 8-bit ASCII codes, spells out a dense five-hundred-page treatise in Danish that has the same combination of being enigmatic and yet insightful as the *Concluding Unscientific Postscript* of Kierkegaard. We would not exactly know what to make of it, just as we do not really know what to make of the *Postscript*. A scientific explanation would not be possible since the constant was assumed to be basic. Since the work is so enigmatic, we could not assume that the claims made in it are straightforwardly true or even accepted by the author. Besides, the content of the work might be such as not to generate testable predictions even were the content of the work assumed to be all true. Yet, surely, the rational thing to do is to believe that there was an intelligent being that was at least partially responsible for making the constant have the value it has. This does not generate predictions. It might make somewhat plausible the claim that other constants might hide other messages, but even if this claim were not borne out, we would still be reasonable in thinking that there is an explanation in *this* case.

One might think that in this case, one does not need any specific principle for inferring explanations, but simple induction will suffice. Things that look like complex literary works are all written by intelligent agents, we see. This looks like a complex literary work. Hence, it is written by an intelligent agent. But the claim that things that look like complex literary works are written by intelligent agents is no more strongly confirmed empirically than the claim that every contingent proposition has an explanation. Note that in both cases we have cases in which we do not have direct data: there are, after all, complex literary works whose authors are not known and for which we have no independent evidence that they have an author. Furthermore, even if we found out somehow – for instance, because an indisputably divine voice told us – that the mysterious treatise was not composed by an intelligent agent, we would surely at least suspect there is still an explanation and might toss around strange possibilities such as that an intelligent agent was responsible for it in a different way than by composing it (e.g., by designing a nonintelligent machine that produces Kierkegaardian prose), or that somehow the collective unconscious of humankind produced it supernaturally, and so on.

Thus, (132) does not appear sufficient. The restriction to cases in which the epistemically possible explanation is scientific appears ad hoc. It is quite unclear why the epistemic possibility of a scientific explanation gives sufficient evidence for the claim that the proposition has an explanation in a way in which the epistemic possibility of explanation *simpliciter* does not. And of course once one removes the requirement that the explanation be scientific, then the epistemic possibility of the theistic explanation of the BCCF will be enough to secure the reasonableness of thinking that the BCCF has an explanation, and hence that every contingent true proposition has one.

17.4.1.b Detailed Explanation. On the other hand, one might modify (132) by removing the restriction to scientific explanations and inserting instead a requirement that we have a fairly specific notion of a possible explanation.

(133) If p is known to be true and it is epistemically possible that p has an explanation that we can spell out in relevant detail, then it is rational to believe that p has an explanation.

To block the application of this principle to the BCCF, and hence block the movement from (133) to the rationality of believing the PSR to be at least contingently true, we can insist that the theist does not actually give a putative explanation, but gives a sketch of an explanation. For the theist says that God brought about the BCCF for some reason R, but the theist cannot say very much at all about what R is. And *something* needs to be said about R for the explanation to count as spelled out "in relevant detail" (cf. Grünbaum, 2004).

However, note that this attempt to block the application of (133) fails as a theist *can* give some epistemically possible reasons R. She may say, with Rescher's interpretation of Leibniz, that God wanted to optimize a balance of diversity over simplicity. Or she may say, with John Hick, that God wanted to create a world where creation could participate in self-creation on the level of species through evolution and on the individual level through the moral self-improvement and growth of limited persons. Or she might say that God valued the objective good of creatures' praising him freely. There are many possibilities. The theist cannot say *which* of these possible reasons is the one on which God *actually* acted. But (133) does not require that we be antecedently able to say which one of the epistemically possible explanations is the correct one. As long as we can give some sort of a relevantly detailed sketch of *an* epistemically possible explanation, that is all we need.

If one complains that all of these sketches are too vague, consider the similar vagueness that can obtain in putative explanation of why a work of art came into existence. I once saw a number of rocks piled one on top of the other, on a rocky beach in Vancouver. The rocks clearly were purposefully arranged and had some sort of artistic vision. But I could not understand their arrangement. The sketch I could give of a putative agent-based explanation would be quite sketchy indeed: someone arranged them for some artistic purpose or other. But that should be enough for purposes of (133) since this seems a fine application of (133). In fact, to this day, my knowledge of the reasons for this arrangement remains more general than any one of the mentioned proposals in the theistic case. And, in fact, I can offer a theistic proposal that would have a very similar level of specificity:

a highly intelligent agent brought about the BCCF *for some artistic purpose or other.*

Now it is true, I suppose, that if I stared at the work of art, I might eventually come up with possible interpretations that are more specific. But it is implausible that I would need to do that to be justified in simply thinking that there is an explanation. Moreover, some (many?) people do claim to find more and more meaning in the universe as they continue to live.

17.4.2. Probabilistic PSR

17.4.2.a Bayesian Approaches. Perhaps we could simply look at matters in a Bayesian way and assign a very low prior probability to causeless events' occurring. This, too, would give us what we need in daily life and science. But it is not clear what would underwrite such a probability assignment. It is rational to set one's epistemic probabilities in accordance with those objectively assigned by the laws of nature when the laws of nature assign probabilities. But this does not apply in this case, as we have seen in Section 16.4.4. It is perhaps likewise rational to choose one's probabilities in accordance with some principle of indifference. But a principle of indifference is surely not going to tell us that it is unlikely that an object will come into existence *ex nihilo.* It is not clear that any other proposed methods for choosing prior probabilities will help, unless in an ad hoc way they simply *say* that one should assign probabilities in a way that is hostile to things' coming into existence *ex nihilo.*

One might, of course, retreat into the purely subjectivist Bayesian camp. This, however, does not appear satisfactory. It means, for instance, that we cannot say anything about the irrationality of the person who is constantly surprised not to see objects popping into existence *ex nihilo* if her consistent probability assignment included a high probability of their doing so. We *can* criticize such a person on the grounds that her probability assignment was in fact bad for her – that she could not navigate well in the world. But that is not a rationality criticism, just as it is not a rationality criticism to say that it was bad for Fred not to have played the lottery, because the number that he always uses when he plays the lottery had won. It was bad for Fred not to have played the lottery, but there was, we may suppose, nothing irrational about it.

17.4.2.b An Objective Bayesianism. There is, however, an objective Bayesian approach that might help, suggested by Peter Forrest and building on Carnap's original approach. Simply lay down a constraint on prior probabilities that simpler claims are more probable, by making claims that are expressed in longer sentences in a "natural" language be less probable, where a language is said to be *natural* in this sense if it has simple terms for the more natural universals and in general it is appropriately adapted to the nature of things. Then, unpredictable states of affairs are less likely a priori because predictable states of affairs can be described more briefly: for instance, if a state of affairs is entirely predictable from an earlier state and the laws, to describe the later state of affairs we need only give the laws and the earlier state.

One very natural way to do this is to fix the simple language. Assume the language is written in a finite alphabet of cardinality n. Otherwise one may need nonstandard analysis to handle infinities, but since I am giving this only as an example of the kind of account in question, we do not need to work out the details. Assume that one of the symbols of the alphabet is an "end of sentence" marker. Now, consider a stochastic process that generates strings of symbols, terminating the string as soon as an end of sentence marker is received. This induces a probability measure on a terminated string: the probability of a string is equal to n^{-k} where k is the length including the terminator. Now condition these probabilities on the event E that the generated sentence is grammatical. This yields a probability measure on the set of all sentences that has the property that longer claims are exponentially less likely. This is not quite enough, because if we simply define the probability of a proposition p as the sum of the probabilities of all sentences expressing p, we would probably *not* get a consistent probability measure. For instance, disjunctive claims would likely be less probable than some of their disjuncts. But it is a start. Condition further on the claim that the sentence is a complete descriptor of a world, that is, that one and only one world satisfies the sentence (this can also work in terms of universes, that is, maximal spatiotemporally connected entities, rather than worlds). Now, define the probability of a world as the sum (finite or not) of the probabilities of all the sentences that are complete descriptors of it. And then define the probability of a proposition as the sum (finite or not) of probabilities of worlds at which the proposition holds.

This measure makes simpler worlds more probable than less simple ones. This seems to mean that we have reason to accept simpler laws over more complex ones, and this is exactly what we want for scientific inference. The proposal seems to make many cases come out right. More-over, it can be argued that any proposal that makes inductive claims come out the way we think they should would assign probabilities in roughly the way described. If we prefer to model epistemic credences via convex families of probability assignments, we can now take all probability assignments of the preceding sort, ranging over all languages of the right sort, and then make the convex hull of these assignments define the a priori credence distribution.

However, it does not appear that any proposal of this sort will yield a correct epistemology of probabilistic laws, because a formal proposal such as this just does not interact well with probabilistic information. Consider two worlds, each of which contains only one basic particle. According to the laws of both worlds, the particle is of type A until time t_0, at which time it changes into a basic particle either of type B or of type C, and the probability of its changing into a particle of type B is 99 percent. In world w_1, the particle changes into a particle of type B. In world w_2, the particle changes into one of type C. The complexities of the complete descriptions of the two worlds are exactly the same. Thus, any formal proposal of this sort will have to assign exactly the same prior probabilities to these two worlds. But clearly world w_1 is the more probable a priori.

The basic difficulty here is that, plausibly, in some worlds there are stochastic laws, and it seems unlikely that in all worlds the probabilities in these should match the formal ones coming from the objective Bayesianism. We need to retain the probabilities induced by these stochastic laws, since we cannot say that it is objectively just as likely that an improbable event should happen as that a probable one should. However, the probabilities that stochastic laws give rise to tend to behave very differently than the probabilities arising from the objective Bayesianism. A sequence of coin flips each of which comes up heads is overwhelmingly more likely on the objective Bayesianism than a particular less orderly sequence, but stochastic laws are going to assign the same probability no matter whether the sequence is orderly or not. We have two very different patterns of probabilistic assignments, and it does not appear we can make them work coherently together.

And the probabilities induced by stochastic laws are hard to dispute. It is very hard to dispute that if p is the proposition that a process that with probability 99 percent produces a particle of type B has occurred, then the probability that a particle of type B exists given p is 99 percent. If we denied this and allowed the probability to be 50 percent, then we would be very hard-pressed to explain why the fact that a particle of type B is produced in most experiments is evidence for p.

On the other hand, determinism appears to produce problems for the objective Bayesian as well. Suppose that the universe is in fact bidirectionally deterministic, so that the laws and a complete description of the state of the universe at any one time entail a complete description at all other times. While theoretically determinism could be unidirectional, in practice deterministic theories have been bidirectional. Then, the boundary conditions at the time of the Big Bang (these will be conditions prevailing at the time of the singularity if the Big Bang actually occurred at a point in time and limiting conditions otherwise) determine everything that happens now, and similarly the complete state of the universe now determines those boundary conditions.

Let S_0 be a complete description of the boundary conditions and let S_1 be a complete description of the state of the universe now. There does not appear to be any reason to think that, in fact, there is going to be a way of phrasing S_0 in an appropriate language that is going to produce a shorter sentence than any description of S_1. Conceivably, the initial conditions might have been very nice in a way that allows for an elegant description – maybe the energy levels at the time of the Big Bang were integers whereas now they are irrational numbers, and so on. But there is no reason to think so apart from heady metaphysics, such as theism or optimalism. In any case, suppose that somehow or other we learn (maybe an omniscient being tells us) that the present conditions when backtracked to the time of the Big Bang would yield a state whose descriptions are not shorter than those of the present time. The entropy at that time was, of course, lower, but that refers to macrostates, while the complete description in question is that of the details of a microstate. If so, then our objective Bayesianism is going to ascribe the same prior probability to the hypotheses: "The universe started in S_0 and proceeded via laws L" and "The universe started in S_1 and proceeded via laws L." Since all empirical evidence is balanced between the two hypotheses, the objective Bayesianism will not allow us rationally to say that we know that the universe is more than five minutes old. Now, we do not in fact know the details of S_1. But it would be strange to suppose that were we to learn all the details of the present state, and were we to hear from an omniscient being that the initial state cannot be described any more briefly, then we would conclude that there is a 50 percent chance that the universe started just now.

A crucial assumption in this argument was that the probabilities were assigned to microstates. If instead our objective Bayesianism assigned probabilities to macrolevel descriptions, then the lower entropy at the time of the Big Bang would solve the preceding problem. However, it would do this at a cost. First, the line between the macro and the micro seems arbitrary and subjective. Second, the objective Bayesianism is designed to ensure that simpler hypotheses are preferable, a right and noble aim. But we have this aim just as much with respect to microstates. We do not just want to be able to confirm macrohypotheses of statistical mechanics: we also want to be able to confirm hypotheses about microstates.

Finally, consider the kind of worldview on which the objective Bayesianism is plausible. Being objective, the Bayesianism has to be responsive to the world in some way. But the probabilities that the Bayesianism is based on are obtained by a probability distribution over sentences, admittedly, sentences of a language other than one of ours, but still sentences. Why should a probability distribution that is natural for *sentences* be appropriate for the world? To put it melodramatically: Why should we think that logos rules the cosmos? Such a probability assignment would be plausible if our ontology were a Tractarian one, or if we literally thought that the universe was ruled by a rational being. But apart from such metaphysics, it appears that a more Humean assignment is more appropriate. The proposed objective Bayesian assignment assigns a disproportionately high probability to arrangements in which there is a pattern, since a pattern makes for briefer descriptions. (A sequence of fifty coin flips in which the results alternate can be described very briefly by saying what the first flip was and what the pattern was.)

Intuitively, prior probabilities should be laid down in accordance with some principle of indifference. But a standard problem with principles of indifference is that the method of partitioning the state space affects the outcomes, and hence the state space must be partitioned in a "natural" way, lest bias should enter in. Choosing the partition in a way that reflects a purely human interest in linguistic description would not be acceptable unless one had some prior reason to think that such a partitioning is indeed natural, as it would be if in some appropriate sense logos ruled the universe. Note, of course, that this criticism does not apply to those objective Bayesians who are willing to assume a priori the existence of God.

18

Inductive Skepticism

The Humean inductive skeptic claims that I do not know whether a stone dropped tomorrow will fall. It is promising to try to answer the skeptic in an externalist way. The kernel of any such answer will be that my belief that the stone dropped tomorrow will fall constitutes knowledge because I have inductive grounds for this belief and in fact throughout time stones dropped fall. I will argue, however, that given an Aristotelian conception of laws, unless the PSR is in fact metaphysically necessary, this externalist answer does not work. This will yield an argument for the PSR from the premises:

(134) An Aristotelian conception of laws is correct.
(135) I know that a stone dropped tomorrow will fall.
(136) The only way (135) could be true is in light of an externalist account such as sketched previously and elaborated below.

An externalist epistemology needs to include the notion of a defeater. For instance, some might think that even if some data-input or inference is in fact reliable and even if knowledge of its reliability is not required for it to be knowledge-conferring, nonetheless if the agent falsely believes it to be unreliable then she does not obtain knowledge through it. The belief that one is gathering information unreliably is then a defeater for the relevant knowledge claims.

Consider another defeater. Suppose I tossed a fair coin ten times and by chance it always came up heads. Suppose further that it is the case that on the eleventh throw it will, also by chance, come up heads, and that that coin has never been thrown before and will never be thrown again. One does not want to say that on externalist grounds the fact that the inductive generalization that *this* coin will come up heads is knowledge. It is mere

295

chance that the inductive generalization holds – the generalization is not *nomic*.

More generally, if some information gathering mechanism is reliable not in a nomically or modally robust sense but only in the sense that *completely by chance* it has always produced the correct results and always will, the mechanism does not confer knowledge. There is a possible world where the outcome of every battle always happens, completely by chance, to match the result obtained by augury. There are only a finite number of battles in that world, and the very unlikely event of the entrails of birds sacrificed before battle always matching the outcome of the battle according to the rules of augury always occurs, as it happens. The objective probability that this event should happen in any one case is something like $1/3$ if *loss*, *victory*, and *indecisive result* are the only three possible outcomes of battle and augury, and the probability that it should happen in every case is roughly $(1/3)^n$ where n is the number of battles. This is a very small number, but still non-zero, and it may be that the event with this small probability chances to happen. But it is not the case that, even in that world, augury is in fact knowledge-conferring. The fact that augury is right only by chance is a *defeater* for the knowledge claims based on augury. On the other hand, in a possible world where augury matches the outcomes of battle in some objectively nomic way, for example, because the fighters are so superstitious that they have no chance of victory given inauspicious augury, augury-based knowledge claims might indeed confer knowledge. And even if one does not accept the preceding judgment about mere chance success defeating augury-based knowledge claims, one should still accept that the *belief* that augury works only through chance is a defeater for such claims.

The case of accidentally successful augury suggests the following as true on any plausible externalist view:

(137) The knowledge claim obtained through an inductive prediction about the future is defeated by the predicted event's *in fact* having or being believed to have small or non-existent objective probability given the present and past state of the world.

In fact, (137) may have plausibility even apart from externalism, and if so then the argument works given a greater range of epistemological theories. Inductive predictions only give knowledge of the future if the objective probability of the future event given the present and past state of the universe is in fact medium to high. This formulation shows why (137) also mentions the possibility of a nonexistent objective probability.

For there are two ways a probability could fail to be medium to high: it could be low or it could be nonexistent – neither high, nor medium nor low, neither 0 nor 1, but there being no objectively assignable probability.

Now, on an Aristotelian, or more generally a lawmaker-based, view of laws, we saw that a failure of the PSR to be metaphysically necessary implies the objective possibility of a failure of inductive generalizations. For instance, if we accept that just as things can pop into existence causelessly assuming the *ex nihilo nihil* principle fails, they can likewise causelessly pop out of existence, and if, as is plausible, no objective probability can be assigned to a causeless event, then the probability of the Earth's popping out of existence tomorrow is nonexistent. Likewise, the probability of the Earth's continuing in existence tomorrow is nonexistent. Since the stone's falling tomorrow depends on the Earth's continued existence tomorrow, it follows that there is no probability of the stone's falling tomorrow. Hence, we have a defeater for the knowledge claim that the stone dropped tomorrow will fall.

The crucial point here is that the causeless failures of laws of nature allowed by the denial of the PSR cannot have any probabilities assigned to them objectively, for it is highly plausible that objective nonepistemic probabilities can only be assigned against a background of laws or natures that explain certain events, since only against such a background are there objective tendencies which are needed to make sense of these probabilities.

Thus, against an Aristotelian background of defeasible laws of nature, the PSR must be posited to escape from inductive skepticism.

The PSR or even the CP, too, is useful as an escape from radical skepticism about the external world. *Radical* skepticism about the external world is the view that for aught that we know, it might be that the only things that exist are my present experiences and, if this is conceptually required, an ego which has no properties other than of being a contemplator of these experiences. In other words, the radical form of skepticism envisioned supposes that solipsism of the present moment is an epistemic possibility.

However, if we take the CP to be self-evident *and* take it to be self-evident that the experiences we have are contingent, then we can escape from this skepticism, for then the experiences must have causes. Since I do not experience the causes of the experiences causing the experiences, it follows that there is something outside my experience – either the causes are outside of my experience or their relation to the effects is outside my experience or both. Suppose this something beyond my experience is just the ego. The ego is not the relation of causality – to think that would be a category mistake – and hence it would have to be the cause of the experiences. But then it has a property over and beyond the properties of being a contemplator of these experiences – namely, the property of causing them. Moreover, this is a property that I do not actually perceive. Thus, the CP lets me move outside the realm of my experiences. This is not going very far, but at least it lets me make reference to items in the external world under descriptions such as *the cause of my experience of heat*, whatever that cause might in fact turn out to be.

On the other hand, it may even be the case that the denial of the PSR leads to scepticism about all sensory data, as Robert Koons (2000, p. 110) suggests. After all, consider any given piece of sensory data. It is quite possible that this piece of data came about for no cause at all, if we do not grant the PSR. Moreover, no probability can be assigned to its coming about for no cause at all. And it is plausibly a defeater for our sensory knowledge claims that there is no objective probability that can be assigned to our senses working correctly.

19

The Nature of Possibility

19.1. ALETHIC MODALITY

We use alethic modal language all the time. For instance, we say that someone did not do something she could have done, or that the existence of unicorns is possible, or that $2 + 2 = 4$ could not have failed to be true. We make counterfactual assertions such as "Were I to drop this glass, which in fact I do not, it would fall." We think it might have been the case that Hitler had never existed. In these locutions we are speaking about situations and things that are not actual, of ways the universe might have been but was not.

Moreover, alethic modal language could not play the kind of role it does in our lives if we did not take a realist stance toward it. For instance, to decide rationally between alternatives, we often need to consider what consequences would result from each alternative. To decide questions of moral responsibility we often need to decide what else could have been done. The laws of nature by which we navigate the world have counter-factual force. If we did not take our alethic modal claims to express object-ive truths, modal language could not play the role it does in these cases.

A useful way of clarifying modal discourse is to introduce the notion of a *possible world*, or *world* for short, which is a complete way that a universe might have been. The term *possible* refers here not to physical possibility, but to a broad notion of logical or metaphysical possibility, which lets one nontrivially ask questions such as whether it would be metaphysically possible for a horse to beget an owl. Once possible worlds are introduced, one can say a proposition is possible if it is true at some world, necessary if true at all worlds, and contingent if true at some but not all worlds, so that modal operators can be replaced by quantifiers. It is possible that there is a unicorn if and only if there is a possible world at which there are unicorns.

Many ordinary language modal claims seem local. "It might have been that Hitler had never been born" sounds as if it were a claim merely about the circumstances around Hitler's birth. However, in fact, in a way it is a global claim. Usually, we do not simply mean that a world in which Hitler is not born is logically possible. What we mean is that there is a world like ours in relevant respects, for instance, sharing the same laws of nature and initial conditions, or maybe even the same historical conditions up to the late nineteenth century, but in which Hitler is not born. Specifying what these relevant respects are may well be a global task, one going beyond our parochial imagination, especially if laws of nature are global. So we need possible worlds for clarification and disambiguation.

Moreover, possible worlds can be used to clarify modal claims that one could not easily explicate in other ways. For instance, a claim that people's having virtue or vice supervenes on natural facts is a claim that there are no possible worlds that share the same natural facts but that differ in respect of someone's virtue or vice. Likewise, David Lewis (1979, 1986) has shown us how to make a start on making sense of counterfactuals in terms of possible worlds. Assuming I do not drop the glass, it is true that *were I to drop the glass, it would fall* provided that some world in which I drop the glass and it falls is more similar to our world in relevant ways, especially in nomic structure, than any world in which I drop the glass but it does not fall.

If we are to be realists about alethic modal truths, then the natural question is, What makes modal propositions *true*? What are they true *of*? Plausibly, an objectively true proposition must be true *of* some aspect of reality. Or, if we do not accept the truthmaker theory and accept Lewis's more general truthmaker/falsemaker theory, what kinds of things are they that the absence of some of which and the presence of others make modal propositions true? At present, an account of modal truths involving falsemakers is not available, though I will briefly discuss a candidate later, and so I will focus on truthmaker-based accounts.

What, then, are the existent truthmakers of alethic modal claims? This question is deeply puzzling, since many alethic modal claims prima facie concern nonexistent things such as unicorns. One proposed answer is that the truthmakers of alethic modal claims are possible worlds, and we have already seen that we have good reason to believe in possible worlds even apart from this. So this takes us to the second question, What *are* possible worlds?

There are two groups of accounts of possible worlds (Lycan, 2002, p. 307). The *actualist* accounts reject any nonactual entities, any entities not found in the actual world, and thus must provide an account of the truth of modal claims in terms of this-worldly actual entities. The *concretist* accounts, on the other hand, say that there are concrete nonactual entities, such as unicorns existing concretely in concrete physical worlds different from ours, which serve as the truthmakers of modal propositions.

I will critically evaluate the most prominent contemporary concretist account, that of David Lewis (1986), according to which possible worlds are just concrete physical universes on a par with ours, and the most promising contemporary actualist account, that of Robert M. Adams (1974) and Alvin Plantinga (1974a), which claims that possible worlds are Platonic entities constructed from abstracta such as propositions or properties.[1] I will argue that both of these kinds of accounts fail to provide an adequate theory of the truthmakers of alethic modal propositions, and I will sketch an alternate actualist account based on ideas of Aristotle. Interestingly, the actualist account I will sketch will make the truthmakers be *concrete* entities. This will provide a nonreductive account of the nature of possibility, but need not provide for possible worlds − if one wants possible worlds additionally, one may have to posit the existence of a God in whose mind they exist as ideas.

And, what is most relevant here, the account will be such that the Principle of Sufficient Reason, as applied to all contingent propositions, can be read off from it. Thus, what will be shown is that an attractive account of possibility, one that avoids the primary disadvantages of the main competitors, entails the PSR.

19.2. A FORMALIST ACCOUNT

One might simply insist that there is no problem about the grounds of possibility at all. A proposition is possible provided that it is not logically self-contradictory, that is, provided it is *logically* possible. And logical possibility is quite unproblematic. We can define it through a number of syntactic rules. Axiomatic tautologies such as that $0 = 0$ are logically necessary, and anything derivable from the tautologies by a finite number of applications of some specified set of rules is also logically necessary. Anything whose negation is not logically necessary is logically possible.

---

1 For an in-depth recent discussion of both the concretist and actualist accounts, see Divers (2002).

A narrow notion of logical possibility as sketched here is indeed useful for some applications. But it fails to do justice to the full range of phenomena that fall under the head of what Alvin Plantinga calls metaphysical or broadly logical modality. It is impossible that a horse is an insect. But this is not a narrowly logical impossibility, since one cannot derive a contradiction from $\exists x(Hx \, \& \, Ix)$, unless of course one has some axiom that basically says that. But once one allows substantial claims such as that no horse is an insect to figure as axioms, then the question of the nature of alethic modality returns. For what is it that makes some true proposition be fit for axiomhood, which of course carries with it automatic logical necessity? It is no longer some formal feature of the proposition.

One might think that that no horse is an insect is true by definition, and there is no problem about adding definitions to the axioms. A part of the definition of a horse is that it is not an insect. But that is not correct, because it is in fact an empirical discovery that no horse is an insect. Prior to our knowledge of biology, it should have been an epistemic possibility that our ordinary horses are in fact genetically defective versions of a six-legged breed of pegasuses that in fact are enormous insects.

Besides this, it is plausible that all arithmetical truths are necessary in the sense of *necessary* that interests us. But Gödel's work shows that there is no formalization of arithmetic in which we can give clear and explicit inference rules sufficient to derive all the truths of arithmetic. Therefore, there will be arithmetical truths that on a formal view will not be necessary, and that is unacceptable.

Formal accounts of necessity and possibility are relative to a set of axioms and an inferential scheme. Within that limited framework, they can be useful for analyzing some concepts. But they are not enough.

19.3. LEWIS'S THEORY

19.3.1. Lewis's Solution

David Lewis (1986) has an elegant and thoroughly worked out concretist answer to both the problem of truthmakers of modal claims and the problem of what possible worlds are. A Lewisian world is, by definition, a maximal physical spatiotemporally connected aggregate. Every way that a world could have been is a way that some existing, physical world really is. This I call Extreme Modal Realism. According to the Extreme Modal Realist, there are infinitely many existing island universes, and unicorns and witches do exist, but not in our world. What makes it true to say that something could happen is just that it does happen in one of these island universes.

Lewis has a twofold argument for positing the infinitude of physical universes that he needs. The first is a cost-benefit theoretic-utility argument. Supposing there are such universes solves the problem of what makes true modal statements true, and Lewis thinks this is useful for many other philosophical purposes, such as for saying that a proposition is nothing but the set of worlds at which it is true. Given the usefulness of the theory, Lewis concludes that it is probably true.

The second argument for the theory is that as do indexical terms such as *I*, *here*, and *now*, so too the word *actual* and its cognates depend for their reference on the context in which they are tokened. If someone says, "There actually exist horses," according to Lewis she is saying that there exist horses in the universe in which she is speaking. This makes the word *actual* and its cognates into indexical terms. But all the referents of indexical terms are ontologically on par. All referents of *I* are ontologically on par with me: there is no absolute property of I-ness that accrues to me and me alone. (This is not so obvious in the case of *now*, though it will be true given the B-theory of time.) By analogy, all the referents of *actual* are also ontologically on par. Thus, the universe that is actual is not ontologically special. It must be ontologically on par with all the other nonactual universes, and hence all possible nonactual universes must exist, Lewis concludes, and must be ontologically on par.

Note, then, that considering *actual* to be an indexical gives one a good argument for believing in Extreme Modal Realism. Conversely, if one accepts Extreme Modal Realism, there is good reason to consider *actual* to be an indexical term, or at least a term that is relevantly similar to an indexical term. To see this, Lewis argues as follows. According to Extreme Modal Realism, every way that a world could have been is a way some concretely existing world is. Now, if actuality were an absolute property of a world, then there would be exactly one world that had that property. But

[s]urely it is a contingent matter which world is actual. A contingent matter is one that varies from world to world. At one world, the contingent matter goes one way; at another, another. So at one world, one world is actual; and at another, another. How can this be *absolute* actuality? – The relativity is manifest! (Lewis, 1986, p. 94)

And one can argue that our best account of how something's actuality is relative in this way is that actuality is indexical, or at least that claims of actuality are relevantly similar to indexical claims.

All this means that Extreme Modal Realism goes hand in hand with a relative, indexical theory of actuality. But is *actual* an indexical? Richard Gale (1991, chap. 5) has noted that the indexical account of actuality fails to give correct truth values for various sentences. For example, the sentence "I might not have been I" is false, because an indexical like *I* is a *rigid designator*, that is, a term that has the same referent in counterfactual as in noncounterfactual contexts. On the other hand, Gale has argued that *the actual world* is a definite description just like *the tallest person in the world*. Just as the tallest person in the world might not have been the tallest person in the world, likewise it is true to assert, "The actual world might not have been the actual world," which is disanalogous to the indexical case and shows that *the actual world* is nonindexical. In the latter sentence, *the actual world* is used nonrigidly: its second occurrence refers to the world that would be actual in the counterfactual case.

A defender of Lewis might say that the preceding is a noncentral use of *the actual world* and point to the central use as occurring in sentences like "It could have been the case that Smith was less intelligent than she is *in the actual world*." In this sentence, *the actual world* is indeed used rigidly the way an indexical is, since it refers not to the counterfactual world where Smith is less smart, but to the world in which the sentence is tokened.[2] However, first of all, the very existence of a nonrigid use, even if noncentral, already shows a crucial disanalogy between indexicals and *actual*. Second, ordinary definite descriptions also have an analogous rigidified use. For instance, one can say, with only a little awkwardness: "It could have been the case that John was faster than *the fastest person alive*."

2 It might be argued that in fact even in this example *the actual world* is not used rigidly but simply has wide scope within the sentence in which it is tokened. To see this, consider the following dialogue. A: "It could have been the case that Smith was less intelligent than she is *in the actual world*." B: "This is true, but it might not have been true." In this dialogue, B makes the arguably true claim that it might have been the case that Smith had such a level of intelligence that she could not have had a lower (this would be true if it was possible for Smith to have had *no* intelligence at all). However, if *in the actual world* were a rigid designator and the actual world were w_0, then B would be making the claim that although it could have been the case that Smith was less intelligent than she is in w_0, it could have been the case that it could not have been the case that Smith was less intelligent than she is in w_0, a claim that is evidently false if S5 is true. If we take it that B's claim is not evidently false, then we have to grant that although *in the actual world* has wide scope relative to the rest of A's assertion, it is not rigid.

Here, *the fastest person alive* acts as rigid designator: in the counterfactual context it refers to the same person as the one who in our world is the fastest person alive, though this person is obviously not the fastest person alive in the counterfactual world.

Thus the presence of both a nonrigid and a rigid use make *the actual world* much more closely analogous to definite descriptions. This and other logicolinguistic disanalogies between *the actual world* and paradigmatic indexical terms undercut the argument for Extreme Modal Realism from the supposed indexicality of actuality. However, if one accepts Extreme Modal Realism for other reasons, such as theoretic utility, one *will* see a crucial analogy between actuality and indexical terms, namely, the systematic shift in reference between different contexts of use: what *the actual world* refers to when used by a speaker in one world is not what it refers to when used by a speaker in another. The Lewisian will then say that *the actual world* is an indexical term, albeit one that is sometimes linguistically treated differently from paradigmatic ones. A stronger argument against this claim will be that in addition to the linguistic disanalogies, we will see that there is a crucial disanalogy in the ways we treat actuality and ordinary indexicals in our inductive reasoning.

Now, if we do accept the plausibility of Lewis's account of actuality, the Extreme Modal Realist account attractively answers the two basic questions of the nature of possible worlds and modality. Possible worlds are not queer ghostly might-have-beens but are full-blooded physical beings, universes like ours. And we have an apparently reductive physicalist account of possibility: A proposition is possible if and only if there is a maximal spatiotemporally connected aggregate of which it is true.

When we say that unicorns can exist, there thus is no semantic problem of explaining what we are doing when talking of unicorns given there are no unicorns. We are simply saying that somewhere in the totality of all physical universes there are unicorns. But of course the unicorns are not actual; they are not a part of the aggregate of all physical objects spatiotemporally related to my present tokening of this sentence.

19.3.2. Inductive Paradox

Lewis's theory radically revises our notions of the range of things that exist to include the things that we thought to be merely possible. Not surprisingly, this creates a number of unacceptable paradoxes.

The first of these shows that if Lewis's theory of actuality is right, then we are never justified in making any inductive inferences about the future.

But certainly we are justified in inferring on the basis of past data that, for example, something approximately like the universal law of gravitation will continue to hold tomorrow. If tomorrow I drop a glass, it will fall – and Lewis will surely not want to deny I have reason to believe this. However, I will show that if Lewis is right that actuality is indexical, then this is an unjustified inference. Since the inference that gravity will hold tomorrow *is* a justified one, pace the skeptics, by *modus tollens* it follows that actuality is not indexical, and so this argument is a reductio of Lewis's claims about the indexicality of actuality.

To see this, suppose for a reductio that actuality is indexical. Let D be a complete description of the actual world up to the present, that is, t_0, in non-future-involving terms. Intuitively, a non-truth-functionally complex sentence about a time t is "non-future-involving" provided it does not entail the existence of any instants of time after t and is compatible with the truth of an arbitrary number of tokenings of that sentence after t.[3] Now, there are at least as many possible worlds satisfying D but at which the law of gravitation fails a day after t_0 as there are worlds satisfying D but at which gravity continues to work a day after t_0. This is just a statement about logical space, one that David Lewis certainly accepts, and one that both sides in the Humean debate on induction can accept.

Suppose then I have a possible world w about which the only thing I know is that it satisfies D. I am not justified in inferring just from *this* information that gravity will work a day after t_0 in w. Since I am only talking about possible worlds at this point, this is merely a statement about logical space, and my claim follows from the fact that there are at least as many worlds satisfying D at which gravity will fail a day after t_0 as there are ones at which it will continue to hold. This, too, is a statement that people on both sides of the Humean debate can accept and should not be controversial. The mere facts that w is possible and w satisfies D do not give one reason to think gravity will continue to hold in w.

Before continuing, we need to observe one crucial fact about theoretical reason, and specifically about inductive reason. Theoretical reason is impartial with regard to merely indexical facts. If some set of nonindexical facts did not justify an inference to some further nonindexical claim, then adding a purely indexical claim to the evidence, such as "The time described is *now*" or "This took place *here*," cannot *by itself* give justification for inferring the nonindexical claim we could not infer before. Purely indexical data are irrelevant for objective reason. If, for instance, I cannot

---

3   Cf. Gale (2002a).

infer from some nonindexical inductive data about people that Alexander Pruss will do the right thing under some circumstances, then neither can I infer it when I add the additional premise that *I* am Alexander Pruss – to do so would be to commit a fallacy of partiality.

Now suppose I find out one more piece of information about w in addition to knowing that it satisfies D: I find out that w is actual. If I take the claim that actuality is indexical seriously, then just as merely learning that t_0 is now will not give me any information relevant for inferring that gravity will continue to function a day after t_0, analogously, learning that w is actual will not give me any information relevant for inferring that the law of gravitation will be true in w a day after t_0. Therefore, if actuality is indexical, I cannot infer from the fact that w satisfies D and w is actual that gravity will hold a day after t_0. Since in fact we do not have any further relevant information about *our* world beyond D and the fact that this world is actual, neither can *we* infer that gravity will function tomorrow, assuming that actuality is indexical. But this conclusion is absurd: we certainly are justified in inferring that if we drop something tomorrow, it will fall. By *modus tollens*, it follows that actuality is not indexical.

More formally, the reductio is as follows:

(138) Let D be a complete nonindexical description of the actual world up to the present (t_0) in non-future-involving terms. (Definition)

(139) D contains the claim that gravity has always held prior to t_0 and does not overall give evidence against the continuation of gravity after t_0. (Premise)

(140) Conclusions about the actual world reached by reasoning in accordance with the canons of inductive reasoning are justified, and in particular knowing that gravity has always actually held prior to t_0 justifies one in believing it will continue to hold after t_0. (Premise)

(141) There are at least as many worlds satisfying D in which the law of gravitation fails after t_0 as there are worlds in which it continues to hold. (Premise)

(142) * Therefore, knowing that an entity w is a world satisfying D does not by itself epistemically justify inferring that w is a world at which gravity holds after t_0. (Premise, justified intuitively by (141))

(143) * Theoretical reason is impartial with respect to merely indexical facts: If knowing that x satisfies F (where F is a purely nonindexical description and x is a definite description or proper name) does not epistemically justify inferring that x satisfies G (where G is a purely nonindexical description), then neither does knowing x satisfies

F and that x is I (*now, here*, etc.: any pure indexical will do) justify inferring that x satisfies G. (Premise)

(144) * Actuality is indexical. (Premise)

(145) Therefore, knowing that an entity w is a world satisfying D and w is actual does not epistemically justify inferring that w is a world at which gravity holds after t_0. (By (142)–(144))

(146) * But knowing that the actual world satisfies D and w is actual epistemically justifies inferring that gravity holds in w after t_0. (By (139) and (140))

(147) Therefore, knowing that the actual world satisfies D and w is actual both does and does not epistemically justify inferring that gravity holds in w after t_0, which is absurd. (By (145) and (146))

The claims marked with an asterisk form an inconsistent quadruple. All of them, except (144), are highly plausible, and hence we need to reject the premise (144) that actuality is indexical. Another way to look at this argument is to see it as showing that if actuality is indexical, then inductive reasoning violates (143) and hence is guilty of the fallacy of partiality. But in fact we take inductive scientific reasoning to be a paradigm of impartial reason, and hence actuality is not indexical.

Note that a pragmatic will-to-believe argument for accepting inductive consequences such as that gravity will continue to function cannot help Lewis. Will-to-believe arguments presuppose that we have reason to think that one belief *will* be more beneficial than another, and if inductive reasoning about gravity is undercut as earlier, likewise we do not have information either way about which beliefs are more likely to be beneficial.

Observe that the previous argument is not a general skeptical argument. The premise of the indexicality of actuality plays a crucial role in the deduction of (145), and so this is, rather, a positive argument that given certain premises, we do not have more reason than not to think that objects dropped in the next minute will fall. Since we *do* have more reason, by *modus tollens*, one of the premises must be false, and the best candidate for falsity is the indexicality of actuality thesis.[4]

4 Lewis (1986, Section 2.5) criticized closely related arguments given by a number of authors (see, e.g., Forrest and Armstrong, 1984). However, Lewis's criticisms do not appear to apply to the form of the argument that I have given. Lewis's most powerful objection is the *tu quoque*: whether one is an Extreme Modal Realist or not, the multiplicity of irregular worlds should challenge induction. However, in my formulation, the indexicality of actuality is essential to the argument: this is not a general skeptical argument. Of course, a Lewisian can always challenge me to give *my* account of the justification of induction. But that is not a fair demand: I am not complaining that the Lewisian has no account of the justification of

19.3.3. Identity versus Counterpart Theory

A proposition is possible if and only if it is true at some world. Taking this at face value, it is possible that I be a biologist if and only if there is some world at which I am a biologist. Since I was never a biologist in the actual world, the true claim that it was possible for me to have been a biologist seemingly implies that at some nonactual world I am a biologist, and that in turn implies that I exist not only at the actual world but at at least one nonactual world as well. Moreover, prima facie, for grounding the truth of the claim that it is possible that I be a biologist it is irrelevant whether *other* people at this or other worlds are biologists or not.

There are now two different kinds of possible world theories. An identity theorist such as Saul Kripke insists on taking these intuitions at face value. Thus, I myself exist at a number of possible worlds, at one of which I am a biologist. David Lewis, on the other hand, is a counterpart theorist and holds that each concrete entity exists in only one world. What makes it true, however, to say that I could have been a biologist is that there is a possible world at which my *counterpart* is a biologist, where my counterpart in a given world is (roughly) that person there, if he exists, who resembles me most in the relevant respects and whose resemblance to me is sufficiently close. The identity theorist will, of course, insist that what people very similar to me do in other worlds does not *make* it true that I could do those things. Although their doings would be *evidence* for my being able to do it, these doings would not be a *truthmaker* for the proposition that I can do it.

Lewis's Extreme Modal Realism now faces a dilemma. Either counterpart theory, as Lewis himself thinks, is right, or identity theory is right. Each horn of the dilemma leads to two problems: one ethical and one metaphysical.

Suppose both identity theory and Extreme Modal Realism are true. Then the following paradox results. Whatever I choose to do, in the sum total of reality, I perform all the choices that it is logically possible for me to perform. I claim that this means that what I do overall does not matter and significant parts of ethics break down.

First of all, as has often been noted, on Lewisian grounds what I choose does not matter for the totality of reality at large, since according to

induction, but that the indexicality of actuality thesis, as understood within Extreme Modal Realism, precludes the possibility of any such account, by allowing us to make a sound argument that if actuality is indexical in the way Lewis thought it was, then there is not more reason than not to accept inductive conclusions about the future.

Extreme Modal Realism the totality of all real worlds is fixed, as this totality corresponds to the logical space of all possibilities. However, this is not itself enough to generate the breakdown of ethics, as Lewis has argued. According to a nonconsequentialist such as Lewis, what matters is not that the sum total of all reality should be positively affected by one's actions, but that one's own actions be the right ones, that one be oneself virtuous, even if there are infinitely many vicious people who undo the good effects of one's actions.

However, when one adds identity theory to Extreme Modal Realism, then the ethical paradox becomes much more formidable. For then my actions do not even affect overall what kind of a person *I* am, because I really exist in infinitely many worlds, and I cannot change which ones I exist in. In some worlds I am a mass murderer, in others I am a great philanthropist, and in yet others I am a venal liar. Whatever I do, facts such as this will not change. I know that if I choose between a virtuous and a vicious action in favor of a virtuous action, I will do the vicious one anyway, in worlds equally real as ours and in a way that is as real as the one in which I do the virtuous action. Hence, moral choice does not have significance for building one's moral character, since one's overall character as a person is fixed. This is paradoxical, and hence we cannot have both identity theory and Extreme Modal Realism.

Note that this argument does not apply under counterpart theory. It is true that if I act virtuously, then infinitely many counterparts of mine will act viciously. But they are not literally *I*, and hence a nonconsequentialist can still insist that I should do my duty, not minding them, for what they do is not my business. On the identity theory, however, what they do is literally my business, since they are I.

Besides ethical paradox, there is a serious metaphysical difficulty for Extreme Modal Realism if identity theory is adopted. We have seen that Extreme Modal Realism cannot tolerate an absolute theory of actuality. Given the identity theory, Lewis's indexical alternative, however, fails. Recall that on the indexical account of actuality, a given instance of a tokening of *the actual world*, at least in central cases, refers to that world in which it was tokened.

However, according to the identity theory, that very tokening occurs in more than one world, for suppose I token the sentence "In the actual world, a cure for cancer is found in the year 2020," and suppose that the sentence is in fact false. Nonetheless, it is logically possible that I make *this* very tokening in a world in which it expresses a true proposition. After all, according to the identity theorist, there will be a world in which this sentence-type expresses a true proposition, and in which I token the sentence at numerically the same place and time as I do, having the same history, and I perform the tokening in the same way. It is highly plausible to suppose that under these circumstances it follows that in that world I make numerically the same tokening.

But if the very same tokening of a sentence containing the phrase "the actual world" occurs in more than one world, then one cannot define the extension of the phrase "the actual world" as being *the* world in which it occurs. Nor can one allow the phrase to refer to more than one world, for then it would be the case that both a world where a cure for cancer is found in 2020 is actual and a world where such a cure is not found is actual, and this entails the self-contradictory statement that actually the cure for cancer is both found and not found in 2020. Therefore, the indexical theory of actuality is not available on the identity variant of Extreme Modal Realism, and it is difficult to see what could replace it, given the unavailability for a Lewisian of an absolutist theory of actuality.

However, the counterpart horn of the dilemma is no more congenial. First of all, we have to contend with the strong Kripkean metaphysical intuitions that what my counterparts might do in other worlds cannot be what makes it true that *I* could have been a biologist. Facts about people other than me are irrelevant interlopers with respect to questions about *my* capabilities.

Second, a variant ethical paradox can also be given, albeit one that for technical reasons has to be run in a counterfactual world and needs the plausible technical assumption that there are no indiscernible worlds, a question about which Lewis himself remains agnostic. It is indeed plausible that there are no indiscernible possible worlds. First of all, the usual tool for individuating indiscernible objects is by their spatiotemporal relations. But possible worlds do not stand in spatiotemporal relations to one another. Moreover, if there were indiscernible possible worlds, one could ask the question, How many indiscernible copies of a given possible world are there? It would seem quite incredible if there were in fact exactly 3, 17, or $\aleph_{17}$ indiscernible copies of the actual world. Whatever answer one gave, whether finite or infinite, would seem arbitrary.[5]

---

5 If a Cantorian absolute infinite made sense, one might find less arbitrary a claim that there is an absolute infinity of copies of the actual world, but this would raise another problem: It would mean that there is a precise type of physical object – namely, a universe indiscernible from this one – such that there is no set of all instances for the type. And anyway, it is not at all clear that the notion of an absolute infinity of *objects* makes sense. Such a notion would seem to presuppose a bijection between these objects and the totality of mathematical entities, and

Imagine then that I am in a possible world containing a number of persons, but only one of the persons ever makes a free choice, and suppose this choice is indeterministic and that the only indeterminism physically possible in that world is whether choice *A* or choice *B* is made – before and after this choice, determinism holds sway. Let the choice in question be whether I should stick my wet thumb into a light socket. Suppose I know this would not kill me and would have no ethically significant consequences for anybody in that world other than that it would cause severe pain for a while to me. Still, it would clearly be irrational, indeed crazy, of me to perform that action.

However, if a counterpart version of Extreme Modal Realism is true, then this would not only not be crazy, but heroic, for supposing that the world described is actual, there is a nonactual world that shares the same initial conditions and laws of nature, but in which my counterpart makes the choice opposite to mine. If I stick my thumb into the light socket, my counterpart does not. If I do not stick my thumb into the light socket, my counterpart does. Therefore, there is a real sense in which by sticking *my* thumb into the light socket, I save someone else from horrible pain. This then is a heroic act of supererogation rather than a crazy act. Therefore, the counterpart version of Extreme Modal Realism is absurd.

Thus, Lewis's Extreme Modal Realism leads to ethical paradoxes, albeit different ones, whether one adopts identity theory or counterpart theory. Both horns of the identity-versus-counterpart theory dilemma involve other difficulties for Lewis's Extreme Modal Realism. Moreover, the argument from inductive reasoning applies on either horn of the dilemma. Therefore, we have a strong cumulative case against Extreme Modal Realism on the basis of paradoxical conclusions. One paradox does not completely destroy a theory, but a number of serious ones does put it in grave doubt.

19.4. PLATONISM: THE MAIN EXTANT REALIST ALTERNATIVE TO LEWIS

The most promising contemporary realist alternative to Lewis's account of possible worlds are the abstract worlds accounts promoted by Robert M. Adams and Alvin Plantinga. On their accounts, worlds turn out to

the notion of a single bijection's encompassing the totality of mathematical entities seems deeply problematic. Absolute infinity transcends the infinity in any one mathematical object, and hence presumably it transcends the range and domain of this bijection.

be abstract Platonic entities, exactly one of which is instantiated by the universe, where *the universe* is defined to be the aggregate of all existing or occurring concrete entities, and this is the world that is absolutely actual. I will focus primarily on the Adams permutation of this account.

We thus start off by introducing *propositions* as theoretical abstract entities that are the bearers of truth-values and are needed to explain what it is that sentences express, what the objects of beliefs and propositional attitudes are, and what paraphrases preserve, somewhat as electrons are needed to explain various physical phenomena. Some or all true propositions are related to things and events in the universe, with the relation being one of the propositions *being made true by* or *representing* these things and events in the universe. If things in the universe were otherwise than they are, then different propositions would stand in these relations to things in the universe — if there were unicorns, then the proposition that there are unicorns would stand in the relation of *being made true by* to some things, namely, the unicorns in the universe.

Note that the theoretical reason for believing in these Platonic propositions is largely independent of issues of modality. Adams then constructs a possible world as a maximal consistent collection of propositions. (An argument is needed that such collections exist, but let that pass.)[6] Exactly one world is then absolutely actual: it is the one all of whose propositions are true. A proposition can be said to be true *at* a world providing it is one of the propositions that are members of the collection of propositions with which the world is identical. Note that because the worlds are Platonic entities, I had to distinguish between the concrete *universe*, which we physically inhabit, and the actual *world*, which is the collection of all true propositions.

One might object to the Platonic approaches on the grounds that they all involve queer entities. Not only are we required to believe in Platonic beings, but, as Lewis notes, we are to believe that there is a magical relation of representation holding between Platonic beings such as propositions and the concrete entities that make them true, with it being contingent which propositions enter into those relations since it is contingent which propositions are true. What is it, then, that picks out one relation in the Platonic heaven rather than another as *the* relation of representation?

The proponent of these Platonic worlds can argue, however, that she has no need to answer this question. The relation of representation is

6 In Pruss (manuscript), I argue that it is plausible that such collections can be found.

one of the primitive terms in her theory, and it is not even a primitive chosen ad hoc to explain possible worlds, but a primitive needed for other explanatory purposes, such as for making sense of our practices of claiming, believing, and paraphrasing. Nonetheless, if we had some way of pointing out this relation within the Platonic universe of all relations, we would be happier as theorists.

Second, the Platonic theories are expressly nonreductive as accounts of possibility, unlike Lewis's theory. For Adams, a possible world is a maximal consistent collection of propositions, and that is just the same as saying it is a maximal *compossible* collection of propositions. On this theory, there is a primitive abstract property of possibility or consistency that applies to individual propositions and to collections of them. One could also take necessity to be the primitive concept, but this would not change anything substantially.

That the Platonic accounts are nonreductive is only a problem if a reductive account of possibility is available. However, the most plausible account claiming to be reductive is Lewis's, which is too paradoxical to accept. But while a complete reduction is probably impossible, it would be desirable to give at least a partial reduction, on which the whole realm of alethic possibility would be seen to have its root in some more comprehensible subclass. The Platonic accounts do not succeed in performing this more limited reduction either.

Adams's theory is an *actualist* one. His possible worlds are built up out of things that are actual. These abstracta actually exist – indeed, necessarily so – and an actualist theory is one that grounds possibility in actually existent realities. On the other hand, Lewis's other worlds are not actual entities by Lewis's indexical criterion, as they are not the world in which my tokening of the word *actual* in this sentence occurred. If we think of possible worlds as possibilities for our universe, then there is a sense in which Adams and Plantinga have grounded possibilities in actuality, thereby answering to the Aristotelian maxim that actuality is prior to possibility.

However, in a deeper way, the Platonic approach is not faithful to what the Aristotelian maxim affirms. When an Aristotelian says a possibility is grounded in an actuality, she means that the actuality has some powers, capacities, or dispositions capable of producing that possibility, which, of course, once produced would no longer be a mere possibility. This is clearest in the paradigm case in which the actuality is temporally prior to the possibility. Aristotle's favorite illustration is how the actuality of one man makes possible the existence of a future man through the first man's

314

capability for begetting a descendant. If we find attractive the idea that possibilities should be grounded in actuality in the stronger Aristotelian sense, then the Platonic approach will be unsatisfactory, because Platonic entities, in virtue of their abstractness, are categorially barred from entering into causal relations, and hence cannot make possibilities possible by being capable of producing them.

Moreover, the Aristotelian can argue that in fact there *are* capabilities and dispositions sufficient to ground the truth of at least *some* possibility claims. That I could have been a biologist is very plausibly made true by my capacities and dispositions and those of various persons and things in my environment. These capacities and dispositions are concrete real-worldly things, albeit ones having modal force. Hence, in fact, we do not need a Platonic realm to make at least some possibility claims true. Indeed, the facts about the Platonic realm – about propositions' having or not having some primitive property – are interlopers here. Just as the statement that I could have been a biologist was not made true by what my Lewisian counterparts in other worlds do, so too, I shall argue, it is not made true by abstract properties of Platonic abstracta. The common intuition behind both cases is that it is something in me and my concrete environment that makes the statement true.

For on the Platonic approach, what makes it possible that I was a biologist is that the abstract proposition, an entity in the Platonic heaven, *that I was a biologist* has the abstract property of possibility. But we have just seen that there are concrete capacities and dispositions in the universe that are by themselves sufficient to make it possible that I was a biologist. We thus have two different ways of characterizing possibility: one is via concrete this-worldly Aristotelian properties of concreta that really do exist – the Platonist should not deny their existence – and the other is via some abstract Platonic primitive properties of abstracta. Moreover, anything that is possible on the Aristotelian grounds will have to be physically possible, and hence also logically possible, and hence possible on Platonist grounds (though prima facie perhaps not conversely). But now we can ask: Why is this so? Why is there this apparent coincidence that anything made possible by this-worldly powers and capacities and dispositions happens to correspond to a proposition in the Platonic realm that has a certain abstract property? The Platonist is unable to explain this coincidence between powers in our universe and abstract facts about the Platonic realm, given the lack of causal interaction between the two realms.

19.5.1. The Account and Some Advantages

If one shares the Aristotelian intuition that this-worldly capacities, powers, and dispositions can make modal statements true, one might opt for a fully Aristotelian definition of (mere) possibility: A nonactual state of affairs is possible if there actually was a substance capable of initiating a causal chain, perhaps nondeterministic, leading to the state of affairs that we claim is possible. We can then say that something is possible if it is either actual or merely possible.

An approach like this has a number of benefits. Capacities, powers, and dispositions are probably the concepts closest to ordinary language notions of possibility. They are things we arguably have direct experiential knowledge of, pace Hume, by ourselves being capable of producing effects, and we can at least point out by ostension what, say, a capacity is. Moreover, despite having modal force, they are concrete. Reducing all possibility to this subclass of modal notions would thus increase the comprehensibility of what we mean in saying something is possible – at least if one finds Aristotelian intuitions appealing. The account is not a full reduction, since powers and capacities are modal notions, but it does reduce all of modality to a more basic subclass.

Furthermore, epistemological difficulties of the Platonic and Lewisian accounts are at least to some degree alleviated. These difficulties arise from the intuition that one's knowledge of a proposition must be caused by some state of affairs closely bound up with that in virtue of which the proposition is true. But if the proposition is either about a Platonic realm of abstracta or about concrete worlds causally separated from ours, then how we can know it becomes incomprehensible. However, knowledge of Aristotelian modal properties can indeed be to some extent causal. Fire has the capacity of burning us, and we observe this capacity in action when we put our fingers in it. It is possible for Bucephalus to run, and we infer this from observing relevantly similar other horses running. This is only a sketch, to be worked out more thoroughly elsewhere, but it suggests that the epistemological problems for the Aristotelian are to some extent lesser.

19.5.2. An Account of S5

Another consideration in favor of the Aristotelian over the Platonic account is that the Aristotelian ontology of possibility shows why the

useful and intuitive axiom S5 is true. The axiom S5 states that if a proposition is possibly necessary, then it is necessary. One way to argue for S5
would be to start with two intuitions. The first is that matters could not
have been such that it would have been impossible for matters to have
been as they in fact are. However events might have gone, it still would
have been true that they might have gone the way they in fact have gone.
If matters could have gone a certain way, then had they gone that way
it would have been true that they could have gone the way they in fact
went. This is the Brouwer Axiom: $p \supset LMp$. It tells us that the accessibility
relation is symmetric.

The second intuition is that we when we talk about metaphysical
possibilities, we are talking about "ultimate" possibilities. Now, if we have
a possibility operator M such that Mp can hold without MMp's holding,
then this operator does not tell us about *ultimate* possibilities. If it could
have been that it could have been that p was true, then there is a more
ultimate sense in which p could have been true. If we then deny that
Mp, we are saying that M does not tell us of the ultimate possibilities
there are, but of possibilities relativized to some way that things have
been. Indeed, in such a case there *is* a reasonable more ultimate possibility
operator, namely, MM. Thus, if we are talking of ultimate possibilities, it
is reasonable to require that MMp should imply Mp. This is the S4 axiom;
it tells us that the accessibility relation is transitive.

But of course the Brouwer and S4 axioms, understood as necessary
truths, together with the very basic modal axiom $L(p \supset q) \supset (Lp \supset Lq)$,
imply S5. (Just apply the Brouwer Axiom to Mp to conclude that $Mp \supset$
$LMMp$; then use the necessary truth of S4 to conclude that $L(MMp \supset$
Mp), and so, by the basic axiom, $LMMp \supset LMp$.)

But while this kind of an intuitive argument can be given for the truth
of S5, on a Platonic account of possibility it is difficult to see why we
should think modal reality *is* in fact such as to satisfy S5. Why should it be
the case that every abstract proposition p that is in fact true has the abstract
property of being such that LMp, as the Brouwer Axiom alleges? This is
a special case of the epistemological objection to Platonism, of course.

On the other hand, the Aristotelian account gives a neat proof of
S5. First, observe that S4 follows quickly. Suppose it is possible that it is
possible that C occurred, but, for a reductio, assume that it is not possible
that C occurred. Then, there is a state of affairs or substance A that had
the power of initiating a causal chain leading to its being possible that C.
Were it to have initiated that causal chain, then, by assumption, C would
not have occurred (since it is not possible that C occurred), but the chain

would have led to there being an item, B, capable of initiating a causal chain leading to C. But then surely A is capable of initiating the chain leading to B, and B is capable of initiating the chain to C, and putting these two things together, A is capable of initiating a chain leading to C (though A may not be capable of *ensuring* that B initiates a chain leading to C). Hence, we have shown that it is possible that C occurred, and that is absurd given our assumption that this is impossible. Thus our proof by reductio ad absurdum is complete.

The Brouwer Axiom also easily follows from the Aristotelian view, on the plausible assumption that if A initiates one chain, C_1, of events and is capable of initiating another chain, C_2, then were it to have exercised this capability for initiating C_2, it would still *have been* capable of initiating the chain C_1. It is important that what the powers of an item (state of affairs or substance) at t are and have been, the actualization of which powers grounds various possibilities, should not itself depend on which of these powers are in fact actualized, for then the powers would not be prior to the actualization.

If one disagrees with S5, one will take the preceding to count against the Aristotelian view. However, while one might have considerations that make one agnostic about S5, it is unlikely that a good argument could be given against S5, and considerations that would make one agnostic are defeated by the fact that S5 is implied by what may be the best available account of possibility. And while conclusions about S5 make the Aristotelian theory vulnerable to *modus tollens* refutation, they also show that we are dealing with a bona fide theory, a theory that while invoked to explain one phenomenon, namely, why modal alethic propositions can be true at all, can explain other phenomena and lead to further philosophical predictions. (I am grateful to Robert Brandom for this kind of point.)

19.5.3. Global Possibilities, Worlds, and the PSR

Now, one difficulty with the Aristotelian account is that while it works for *local* possibilities, such as of my having been a biologist, it is difficult to see how one could get possible *worlds* out of it. Three solutions are available. The first is just to forget about possible worlds, except as a useful *façon de parler* to be made sense of on some fictionalist account such as Sider's (2002). The second is to supplement the Aristotelian account by a Platonist account of possible worlds, except with the understanding now that facts about the Platonic realm are not what ground claims about what propositions are possible and what propositions are necessary, but rather

318

these claims are true in virtue of the properties of concreta. This hybrid account threatens, however, to fall prey to the coincidence objection against straight Platonism: Why is it not a mere coincidence that facts about the Platonic realm match up with the realm of concreta?

A third available solution is to combine an Aristotelian account of possibility with a Leibnizian account of possible worlds. A possible world, then, is a maximal idea, a thinking, in the mind of God about a world that God could initiate the production of, with God being the first cause, the substance whose causal powers ground all other possibilities. The divine ideas are not disconnected from the Aristotelian properties that ground possibility. For it is precisely by using these ideas that God plans what to create, while they depend on God's concrete capabilities. Since they are involved in the production of the cosmos, it is not surprising that we can know something about them by observing the cosmos, in a way in which it would be hard to know something about pure abstracta.

What is relevant to the project of this book is that just as the account yields S5, it also yields the PSR. Suppose p is a contingent true proposition. For a reductio assume that there is no explanation of why p is true. That there is no explanation of why p is true entails that its being the case that p is not the result of any actual causal chain of events leading, perhaps indeterministically since we saw in Part II that we can have indeterministic causal explanations, to its being the case that p. I am assuming that "leading to its being the case that q" entails leading to all of the contingent conjuncts of q's being the case – the Aristotelian account requires this in order to take account of compossibility claims.[7] Let p^* then be the proposition that

(148) p and there is no existing causal chain of events that leads to its being the case that p.

Then, let w_1 be a possible world at which p^* is false. By the Brouwer Axiom, it is possible at w_1 that p^* is true. Thus, there is at w_1 a substance or state of affairs that could have initiated a causal chain capable of leading to p^*'s being true. But if there is a substance or state of affairs with that capability, then there is a possible world, w_2, where that substance or state of affairs in fact actualizes that capability, and hence initiates a causal chain

---

7 It would clearly not do to allow that r & q is possible simply because there is one possible chain that could lead to r and another possible chain that could lead to q, since then it would be possible for someone to be smiling and not smiling at the same time and in the same respect.

that leads to p^*'s being true. Thus, in w_2 there is a causal chain leading to its being the case that p^*. But that is absurd, since p is a conjunct of p^* and p^* states that there is no causal chain that leads to p's being true, and any causal chain leading to p^*'s being the case would lead to p's being the case. Thus, our assumption that there is no explanation of why p is true is now seen as false.[8]

An Aristotelian account of possibility, thus, entails that the PSR is true for contingent propositions. Moreover, since the Aristotelian account of possibility purports to be a partial analysis of possibility, it has the property of all full or partial analyses that if true they are necessarily true, and hence the PSR will also be necessarily true.

This is a surprising result: the Aristotelian account was not, after all, developed in order to account for the PSR. We thus see how deeply the PSR is interwoven into an Aristotelian worldview. We saw in Chapter 16 that an Aristotelian account of laws of nature presupposes the necessary truth of the PSR. We now see that an Aristotelian account of possibility entails the PSR. This suggests a general form of argumentation for an Aristotelian worldview. First, start with the basic claim that possibility is grounded in actuality: something is possible precisely to the extent that there exists something actual in virtue of whose capacities it is made possible, capacities by the exercise of which a causal chain leading to the possibility's being actualized could be initiated. Next, show that S5 and the PSR follow. Once we have the PSR on the scene, we can ground laws of nature in the dispositional and related properties of existing things, and the fact that the laws will be ceteris paribus need not disturb us, since in principle once we have specified *all* the de facto existing things, then the "ceteris paribus" clause can be dropped because of the PSR: everything will be guaranteed to be accounted for in terms of the Aristotelian properties of things, since nothing new can come into existence without a cause.

Thus, what may well be the most plausible account of possibility, namely, the Aristotelian account in terms of capabilities and dispositions, entails the PSR. This gives us a final very good reason to accept the PSR. And it gives us a good reason to reject various counterfactual counterexamples to the PSR, such as the Humean ones discussed in Chapter 4. They just are not possible according to what may be the best account of possibility.

---

8 A related argument is given in Gerson (1987).

20

Conclusions

In Part I, I argued that plausibly most of the versions of the PSR and the Causal Principle stand and fall together intuitively. Then, in Part II, I argued for the failure of the objections against a PSR that states that every contingent proposition has an explanation. These arguments require that *explanation* be understood in such a way that the explanans not be required to entail the explanandum or else in such a way that contingent self-explanatory propositions be possible. The guiding intuition here was to follow our ordinary usage of *explains*, as well as a grander notion that to explain is to remove mystery. The self-explanatory is what is not mysterious once you grasp it. This means that as long as we are willing to admit that there is no mystery left about the choice when we say that a libertarian-free agent freely chose A for R, we can coherently say that the proposition reporting this choice is self-explanatory, modulo the need to explain why the agent existed, found herself free under the circumstances, and saw R as a reason.

It may be objected that the notion of explanation is not a very strong one. It certainly is not strong enough to satisfy the entailment requirement, but then again few explanations we give in everyday life are. However, the notion of explanation and the associated PSR are sufficiently strong to allow us to require answers to global questions, such as why there is a contingent being or why the Big Conjunctive Contingent Fact is true. This means that this PSR, if true, is strong enough to ground the Cosmological Argument for the existence of a necessarily existing First Cause. Of course, it is a separate question what the nature of this First Cause is, though, as I have noted in Chapter 5, there are considerations in favor of a theistic answer.

321

The PSR is not merely tenable, however, but actually true. Besides the still unrefuted possibility that the PSR is self-evident, a number of arguments are available in favor of the PSR. Abstract Thomistic considerations involving the nature of existence lead to the PSR. Likewise an analysis of plausible versions of the principle that without the cause there would be no effect leads to much the same conclusion. The best explanation of why the PSR holds in everyday contexts is that the PSR is metaphysically necessary. Our epistemic practices become quite dubious in the absence of the PSR. Finally, the best theory of what makes alethic modal claims true has, as a surprising consequence, the truth of the PSR. Note that this is not a liability for that account: a theory is made more plausible by the fact that it has nonabsurd ramifications in many areas.

All this is only the beginning. Further analysis of the PSR in the case of necessary propositions is still to be done but will require progress in the analysis of mathematical explanation. But the PSR in the case of contingent propositions is already something. Once we have seen the PSR as epistemically respectable, we can resume the classic philosophical program of examining the implications of the PSR in various areas. As we have repeated more than once, philosophy is born in wonder, and wonder is our expression of the need for explanation.

Bibliography

Adams, Robert M. (1981). "Actualism and Thisness." *Synthese* 49, 3–42.

Adams, Robert M. (1977). "Middle Knowledge and the Problem of Evil." *American Philosophical Quarterly* 14, 109–117; reprinted in Gale and Pruss (2003).

Adams, Robert M. (1974). "Theories of Actuality." *Noûs* 8, 211–231; reprinted in Loux (1979).

Adams, Robert M. (1972). "Must God Create the Best?" *Philosophical Review* 81 (1972), 317–332; reprinted in Gale and Pruss (2003).

Anscombe, G. E. M. (1993). "Causality and Determination." In E. Sosa and M. Tooley (eds.), *Causation*. Oxford/New York: Oxford University Press, pp. 88–104.

Appel, Kenneth, and Haken, Wolfgang (1989). *Every Planar Map Is Four-Colorable*. Providence, RI: American Mathematical Society.

Aquinas, Thomas (1975). *Summa Contra Gentiles; Book One: God*. Translated by Anton C. Pegis. Notre Dame: University of Notre Dame Press.

Aquinas, Thomas (1949). *On Being and Essence*. Translated by Armand Maurer, C.S.B. Toronto: Pontifical Institute of Mediaeval Studies.

Aquinas, Thomas (1947). *Summa Theologica*. Translated by the Fathers of the English Dominican Province. New York: Benzinger Brothers.

Ariew, Roger, and Garber, Daniel, eds. and trans. (1989). *G. W. Leibniz: Philosophical Essays*. Indianapolis and Cambridge: Hackett.

Bell, J. L. (1988). *Toposes and Local Set Theories: An Introduction*. Oxford: Clarendon.

Belot, Gordon (2001). "The Principle of Sufficient Reason." *Journal of Philosophy* 98, 55–74.

Cain, James (1995). "The Hume-Edwards Principle." *Religious Studies* 31, 323–328.

Callender, Craig (2004). "Measures, Explanations and the Past: Should 'Special' Initial Conditions Be Explained?" *British Journal for the Philosophy of Science* 55, 195–217.

Campbell, Joseph K. (1996). "Hume's Refutation of the Cosmological Argument." *International Journal for Philosophy of Religion* 40, 159–173.

Cartwright, Nancy (1999). *The Dappled World: A Study of the Boundaries of Science*. Cambridge/New York: Cambridge University Press.

Chisholm, Roderick M. (1964). "Human Freedom and the Self," The Lindley Lecture, Department of Philosophy, University of Kansas, pp. 3–15; reprinted in Feinberg and Shafer-Landau (2002), pp. 492–499.

Davey, Kevin, and Clifton, Robert (2001). "Insufficient Reason in the 'New Cosmological Argument.'" *Religious Studies* 37 (2001), 485–490.

Davies, Paul (2001). "A Naturalistic Account of the Universe." In M. Peterson, et al. (eds.), *Philosophy of Religion: Selected Readings*. 2d ed. New York/Oxford: Oxford University Press, pp. 231–241.

Dembski, William A. (2002). *No Free Lunch: Why Specified Complexity Cannot Be Purchased without Intelligence*. Lanham: Rowman & Littlefield.

Dembski, William A. (1998). *The Design Inference: Eliminating Chance through Small Probabilities*. Cambridge: Cambridge University Press.

Diels, Hermann, and Kranz, Walther (1985). *Die Fragmente der Vorsokratiker*. Zurich: Weidmann.

Divers, John (2002). *Possible Worlds*. London/New York: Routledge.

Doyle, Arthur Conan (1927). *The Complete Sherlock Holmes*. Garden City, N.Y.: Doubleday.

Earman, John (1986). *A Primer on Determinism*. Dordrecht: D. Reidel.

Edgington, Dorothy (1995). "On Conditionals." *Mind* 104 (1995), 235–329.

Edwards, Paul (1959). "The Cosmological Argument." In *The Rationalist Annual for the Year 1959*, London: Pemberton; reprinted in Donald R. Burrill (ed.), *The Cosmological Argument*. New York: Doubleday, 1967.

Elga, Adam (2001). "Statistical Mechanics and the Asymmetry of Counterfactual Dependence." *Philosophy of Science* 68 (Suppl.) *PSA 2000*, S313–S324.

Ewing, A. C. (1979). *Value and Reality*. London: Allen & Unwin.

Feinberg, Joel, and Shafer-Landau, Russ (2002). *Reason and Responsibility: Readings in Some Basic Problems of Philosophy*. 11th ed. Belmont, Calif.: Wadsworth.

Findlay, J. N. (1948). "Can God's Existence Be Disproved?" *Mind* 57, 176–183.

Fischer, John Martin. (1999). "Recent Work on Moral Responsibility." *Ethics* 110, 92–139.

Forrest, Peter (1996). *God without the Supernatural: A Defense of Scientific Theism*. Ithaca, N.Y.: Cornell University Press.

Forrest, Peter (1981). "The Problem of Evil: Two Neglected Defenses." *Sophia* 20, 49–54.

Forrest, Peter, and Armstrong, D. M. (1984). "An Argument against David Lewis' Theory of Possible Worlds." *Australasian Journal of Philosophy* 62, 25–46.

Francken, Patrick, and Geirsson, Heimir (1999). "Regresses, Sufficient Reasons, and Cosmological Arguments." *Journal of Philosophical Research* 24, 285–304.

Frankfurt, Harry (1969). "Alternate Possibilities and Moral Responsibility." *Journal of Philosophy* 66, 829–839.

Gale, Richard M. (2002a). "Divine Omniscience, Human Freedom, and Backward Causation." *Faith and Philosophy* 19, 85–88.

Gale, Richard M., ed. (2002b). *Blackwell Guide to Metaphysics*. Oxford: Blackwell.

Gale, Richard M. (1999). *The Divided Self of William James*. Cambridge: Cambridge University Press.

Gale, Richard M. (1991). *On the Nature and Existence of God*. Cambridge: Cambridge University Press.

Gale, Richard M. (1976). *Negation and Non-Being. American Philosophical Quarterly* Monograph, no. 10.

Gale, Richard M., and Pruss, Alexander R., eds. (2003). *The Existence of God.* Aldershot, England: Ashgate.

Gale, Richard M., and Pruss, Alexander R. (2002). "A Response to Oppy and to Davey and Clifton," *Religious Studies* 38, 89–99.

Gale, Richard M., and Pruss, Alexander R. (1999). "A New Cosmological Argument." *Religious Studies* 35 (1999), 461–476.

Gellman, Jerome (2000). "Prospects for a Sound Stage-3 of Cosmological Arguments." *Religious Studies* 36, 195–201.

Gerhardt, C. I. (1960–61). *Die philosophischen Schriften von Gottfried Wilhelm Leibniz.* 7 vols. Berlin: Weidmann; reprinted in CD-ROM form, Charlottesville, Va.: InteLex, 2001.

Gerson, Lloyd P. (1987). "Two Criticisms of the Principle of Sufficient Reason." *International Journal for Philosophy of Religion* 21, 129–142.

Grünbaum, Adolf (2004). "The Poverty of Theistic Cosmology." *British Journal for the Philosophy of Science* 55, 561–614.

Grünbaum, Adolf (1998). "Theological Misinterpretations of Current Physical Cosmology." *Philo* 1, 15–34; reprinted in Gale and Pruss (2003).

Grünbaum, Adolf (1974). *Philosophical Problems of Space and Time.* 2nd ed. Dordrecht, Holland/Boston: D. Reidel.

Hacking, Ian (1975). "The Identity of Indiscernibles." *Journal of Philosophy* 72, 249–256.

Hare, R. M. (1964). *The Language of Morals.* New York: Oxford University Press.

Hartle, J. B., and Hawking, Stephen W. (1983). "The Wave Function of the Universe." *Physical Review D* 28, 2960–2975.

Hawking, Stephen W. (1988). *A Brief History of Time: From the Big Bang to Black Holes.* New York: Bantam.

Heidegger, Martin (1974). "The Principle of Ground," trans. Keith Hoeller. *Man and World* 7, 207–222.

Heisenberg, W. (1927). "Über den anschaulichen Inhalt der quantentheoretischen Kinematik und Mechanik." *Zeitschrift für Physik* 43.

Hill, Christopher S. (1982). "On a Revised Version of the Principle of Sufficient Reason." *Pacific Philosophical Quarterly* 63, 236–242.

Honderich, Ted, ed. (1995). *The Oxford Companion to Philosophy.* Oxford/New York: Oxford University Press.

Hume, David (1779). *Dialogues concerning Natural Religion.*

Hume, David (1739). *A Treatise of Human Nature.*

Johnstone, Henry W., Jr., and Sider, David (1986). *The Fragments of Parmenides.* Bryn Mawr, Pa.: Thomas Library, Bryn Mawr College.

Kane, Robert (1996). *The Significance of Free Will.* New York: Oxford University Press.

Kant, Immanuel (1996). *Critique of Pure Reason.* Trans. Werner S. Pluhar. Indianapolis/Cambridge: Hackett.

Katz, Bernard D., and Kremer, Elmar J. (1997). "The Cosmological Argument without the Principle of Sufficient Reason." *Faith and Philosophy* 14, 62–70.

Kirk, G. S., Raven, J. E., and Schofield, M. (1983). *The Presocratic Philosophers.* 2nd ed. Cambridge: Cambridge University Press.

Kitcher, Philip (1998). *Abusing Science: The Case against Creationism*. Cambridge, Mass./London: MIT Press.

Koons, Robert C. (2000). *Realism Regained: An Exact Theory of Causation, Teleology, and the Mind*. Oxford/New York: Oxford University Press.

Kripke, Saul (1980). *Naming and Necessity*. Cambridge, Mass.: Harvard University Press.

Kumar, Dharmendra (1973). "Necessity and the Law of Sufficient Reason – III," *Journal of the [Indian] Philosophical Association* 14, 99–107.

Kuratowski, K., and Mostowski, A. (1976). *Set Theory: With an Introduction to Descriptive Set Theory*. New York: North-Holland.

Lang, Serge (1984). *Algebra*. 2nd ed. Redwood City, Calif.: Addison-Wesley.

Leckey, Martin, and Bigelow, John (1995). "The Necessitarian Perspective: Laws as Natural Entailments." In Friedel Weinert (ed.), *Laws of Nature: Essays on the Philosophical, Scientific and Historical Dimensions*, Berlin: de Gruyter, pp. 92–119.

Leftow, Brian (1988). "A Modal Cosmological Argument." *International Journal for Philosophy of Religion* 24, 159–188.

Leslie, John (2001). *Infinite Minds: A Philosophical Cosmology*. Oxford: Clarendon.

Lewis, C. S. (1960). *Miracles: A Preliminary Study*. New York: Collier.

Lewis, David (1986). *On the Plurality of Worlds*. Oxford/New York: Basil Blackwell.

Lewis, David (1979). "Counterfactual Dependence and Time's Arrow." *Noûs* 13, 455–476.

Lewis, David (1973). *Counterfactuals*. Malden, Mass./Oxford: Blackwell.

Loux, Michael, ed. (1979). *The Possible and the Actual: Readings in the Metaphysics of Modality*. Ithaca, N.Y./London: Cornell University Press.

Łukasiewicz, Jan (1961). "O determiniźmie." In J. Słupiecki (ed.), *Z zagadnień logiki i filozofii*; trans. Z. Jordan in S. McCall (ed.), *Polish Logic*. Oxford: Clarendon, 1967.

Lycan, William (2002). "The Metaphysics of Possibilia." In Gale (2002b), pp. 303–316.

Mackie, J. L. (1977). *Ethics: Inventing Right and Wrong*. Harmondsworth, England: Penguin.

Mackie, Penelope (1998). "Identity, Time, and Necessity." *Proceedings of the Aristotelian Society* 98, 59–78.

Manley, David (2002). "Comments on Alexander R. Pruss's paper 'Ex Nihilo Nihil Fit: Arguments New and Old for the Principle of Sufficient Reason.'" Paper presented at the Society for Catholic Analytical Philosophy satellite meeting at the November 2002 meeting of the American Catholic Philosophical Association in Cincinnati.

McHarry, J. D. (1978). "A Theodicy." *Analysis* 38, 132–134.

Mermin, N. David (1985). "Is the Moon There When Nobody Looks? Reality and the Quantum Theory." *Physics Today*, April 1985, 38–47.

Mermin, N. David (1981). "Quantum Mysteries for Anyone." *Journal of Philosophy* 78, 397–408.

Merricks, Trenton (2004). "Split Brains and the Godhead." In T. Crisp, D. Vanderlaan, and M. Davidson (eds.), *Knowledge and Reality: Essays in Honor of Alvin Plantinga*. Dordrecht: Kluwer, 2004.

Meyer, Robert K. (1987). "God Exists!" *Noûs* 21, 345–361.

Miller, Barry (1983). "Why Ever Should Any Existing Individual Exist?" *Review of Metaphysics* 37, 287–326.

Misner, C. W., Thorne, K. S., and Wheeler, J. A. (1970). *Gravitation*. New York: Freeman.

Neta, Ram (1997). *The Instability of Scepticism*. Doctoral dissertation, University of Pittsburgh.

Nowacki, Mark R. (1998). "Whatever Comes to Be Has a Cause of Its Coming to Be: A Thomistic Defense of the Principle of Sufficient Reason." *The Thomist* 62, 291–302.

Oppy, Graham (2000). "On 'A New Cosmological Argument.'" *Religious Studies* 36, 345–353.

Place, Ullin T. (1997). "'*De re*' Modality without Possible Worlds." *Acta Analytica*, pp. 129–143.

Plantinga, Alvin (1983). "On Existentialism." *Philosophical Studies* 44, 1–20.

Plantinga, Alvin (1974a). *The Nature of Necessity*. Oxford/New York: Oxford University Press.

Plantinga, Alvin (1974b). *God, Freedom and Evil*. New York: Harper & Row.

Plato (1961). *The Collected Dialogues of Plato*. Ed. E. Hamilton and H. Cairns. Princeton, N.J.: Princeton University Press.

Pruss, Alexander R. (manuscript). *Worlds, Possibilities and Actualities*.

Pruss, Alexander R. (forthcoming). "Prophecy without Middle Knowledge." *Faith and Philosophy*.

Pruss, Alexander R. (2004a). "A Restricted Principle of Sufficient Reason and the Cosmological Argument." *Religious Studies* 40, 165–179.

Pruss, Alexander R. (2004b). "David Lewis's Counterfactual Arrow of Time." *Noûs* 37, 606–637.

Pruss, Alexander R. (2001). "The Cardinality Objection to David Lewis's Modal Realism." *Philosophical Studies* 104 (2001), 167–176.

Pruss, Alexander R. (1998). "The Hume-Edwards Principle and the Cosmological Argument." *International Journal for Philosophy of Religion* 43, 149–165; reprinted in Gale and Pruss (2003).

Putnam, Hilary (1980). "Models and Reality." *Journal of Symbolic Logic* 45, 464–482.

Reichenbach, Bruce R. (1972). *The Cosmological Argument: A Reassessment*. Springfield, Ill.: Charles C. Thomas.

Rescher, Nicholas (2000a). *Nature and Understanding: The Metaphysics and Method of Science*. Oxford: Clarendon.

Rescher, Nicholas (2000b). *Kant and the Reach of Reason*. Cambridge/New York: Cambridge University Press.

Rescher, Nicholas (1995). *Satisfying Reason: Studies in the Theory of Knowledge*. Dordrecht/Boston/London: Kluwer.

Rescher, Nicholas (1991). *G. W. Leibniz's Monadology: An Edition for Students*. Pittsburgh: University of Pittsburgh Press.

Rice, Hugh (2000). *God and Goodness*. Oxford/New York: Oxford University Press.

Rosenkrantz, Gary S. (1993). *Haecceity: An Ontological Essay.* Dordrech/Boston/ London: Kluwer.

Ross, James F. (1969). *Philosophical Theology.* Indianapolis: Bobbs-Merrill.

Rowe, William L. (1984). "Rationalistic Theology and Some Principles of Explanation." *Faith and Philosophy* 1, 357–369.

Rowe, William L. (1975). *The Cosmological Argument.* Princeton, N.J.: Princeton University Press.

Rowe, William L. (1970). "Two Criticisms of the Cosmological Argument." *The Monist* 54, 441–459.

Rundle, Bede (1986). "Induction and Justification." *American Philosophical Quarterly* 23, 115–123.

Rutherford, Donald P. (1992). "Leibniz's Principle of Intelligibility." *History of Philosophy Quarterly* 9, 35–49.

Shapiro, Lionel S. (2001). "'The Transition from Sensibility to Reason *In Regressu*': Indeterminism in Kant's *Reflexionen*." *Kant-Studien* 92, 3–12.

Sider, David, and Johnstone, Jr., H. R. (1986). *Parmenides: The Fragments.* Bryn Mawr: Bryn Mawr College.

Sider, Theodore (2002). "The Ersatz Pluriverse." *Journal of Philosophy* 99 (2002): 279–315.

Sklar, Lawrence (1993). *Physics and Chance: Philosophical Issues in the Foundations of Statistical Mechanics.* New York: Cambridge University Press.

Smart, J. J. C., and Haldane, J. J. (1996). *Atheism and Theism.* Oxford: Blackwell.

Smith, Quentin (2002). "The Incompatibility of STR and the Tensed Theory of Time." In L. N. Oaklander (ed.), *The Importance of Time,* Dordrecht: Kluwer.

Smith, Quentin (1995). "A Defense of a Principle of Sufficient Reason." *Metaphilosophy* 26, 97–106.

Smith, Quentin (1994a). "Stephen Hawking's Cosmology and Theism." *Analysis* 54, 236–243; reprinted in Gale and Pruss (2003).

Smith, Quentin (1994b). "Can Everything Come to Be without a Cause?" *Dialogue* 33, 313–323.

Stern, Alfred (1969). "A Philosopher Looks at Science." *Southern Journal of Philosophy* 7, 127–137.

Strawson, P. F. (1959). *Individuals: An Essay in Descriptive Metaphysics.* London: Methuen.

Sullivan, Thomas D. (1994). "On the Alleged Causeless Beginning of the Universe: A Reply to Quentin Smith." *Dialogue* 33, 325–335.

Swinburne, Richard G. (1968). "The Argument from Design." *Philosophy* 43 (1968), pp. 199–212; reprinted in Baruch A. Brody (ed.), *Readings in the Philosophy of Religion: An Analytic Approach.* 2nd ed. Englewood Cliffs, N.J.: Prentice Hall, pp. 189–201.

Taylor, Richard C. (1974). *Metaphysics.* 2nd ed. Englewood Cliffs, N.J.: Prentice Hall.

Turner, Donald Albert, Jr. (2003). "The Many-Universes Solution to the Problem of Evil." In Gale and Pruss (2003), pp. 143–159.

Turner, Donald Albert, Jr. (1994). *Cosmoi: The Best of All Possible Worlds.* Doctoral dissertation, University of Pittsburgh, 1994.

Vallicella, William F. (1997). "On an Insufficient Argument against Sufficient Reason." *Ratio (new series)* 10, 76–81.

328

van Inwagen, Peter (1983). *An Essay on Free Will*. Oxford: Oxford University Press.

White, David E. (1979). "An Argument for God's Existence." *International Journal for Philosophy of Religion* 10, 101–115.

Williamson, Timothy (2000). *Knowledge and Its Limits*. Oxford: Oxford University Press.

Index

causation
backwards, 36, 86, 166, 169
circular. *See* causal circle
Humean account of, 18–19, 36–37, 91,
191
cause, first. *See* First Cause
ceteris paribus laws. *See* laws of nature,
ceteris paribus
chains of causes, 68–69, 243, 316–320. *See
also* causal chains
ungrounded, 41–42, 68
Chisholm, Roderick M., 132
circle, causal. *See* causal circle
circle, vicious. *See* vicious circle
circular explanation. *See* explanation,
circular
Clarke, Samuel, 22, 29, 178, 180
Clifton, Robert, 99, 101
compatibilism and incompatibilism, 3, 5, 15,
23, 29, 48–49, 63, 87–89, 103, 116,
124, 126–143, 146–148, 154, 156,
158–159, 161, 168, 178–180, 182–184,
205, 215–216, 279, 321. *See also* free
will; Jamesian libertarianism
complete explanation. *See* explanation,
complete
complete individual concept, 29–31
conditionals of free will, 5, 138
conspiracy, Masonic. *See* Masonic conspiracy
constructivism, social. *See* social
constructivism
contrastive explanation. *See* explanation,
contrastive
cosmological argument, 3–4, 50–54, 82–84,
99
cosmos, 4, 6, 27, 58–62, 64, 78, 87, 94, 116,
139, 237, 284, 294, 319
counterfactuals, 15, 35, 39, 60, 127,
137–139, 171, 194, 239–248, 282,
299–300, 304–305, 311, 320

Darwinian evolution. *See* evolution
Davey, Kevin, 99, 101
Davies, Paul, 169
De Morgan's Law, 200
Dembski, William A., 270
Descartes, 6, 226
determinism and indeterminism, 4, 25,
48–49, 107, 119–120, 128–129,
145–147, 159, 170, 184–185, 250, 279,
292–293, 311–312
diagonal argument, 269
Divers, John, 301
Doyle, Arthur Conan, 283

Earman, John, 48
Edgington, Dorothy, 241, 247
Edwards, Paul, 41–42, 44, 46–47, 55, 69,
85
Einstein-Podolsky-Rosen correlations,
162–164
Elga, Adam, 39–40, 239, 241
elucidation, 267
epistemology, Bayesian. *See* Bayesian
epistemology
EPR correlations. *See* Einstein-Podolsky-
Rosen correlations
esse. See existence
esse-essentia distinction. *See* existence-essence
distinction
essence, 26–27
essentia. See essence
ethics. *See* morality
evil, 7, 14, 87–88
evolution, 7, 34, 99, 195, 228–229, 250–251,
256–258, 261, 281, 289
Ewing, A. C., 87
ex nihilo nihil principle, 20–23, 47, 58–62, 71,
75, 297
excision, surgical. *See* surgical excision
existence, 26–27
quasi-necessary, 275
existence-essence distinction, 28, 68,
209–230
explanation
axiological, 87
circular, 78, 85
complete, 17–18, 127, 136, 151–152,
234–235
contrastive, 148–155
Darwinian. *See* evolution
evolutionary. *See* evolution
full, 17–19, 44, 89, 112, 119, 153, 155
incomplete. *See* explanation, complete
inference to best. *See* inference to best
explanation
maximal, 157–158
personal, 82–83
reductive, 7, 82–84, 138
scientific, 82
subsumptive, 85
systematic, 85–86

facts, brute. *See* brute facts
fatalism, modal, 15, 88–89, 97–99, 103, 122,
126, 131–132, 135–136, 139, 141, 168,
180
Field, Hartry, 6
Findlay, J. N., 91

reductive explanation. *See* explanation, reductive
regress, vicious. *See* vicious regress
regress of existences, 209
Reichenbach, Bruce R., 196, 229, 230
Relativity Theory, 89, 94, 166
Rescher, Nicholas, 3, 21, 29–30, 85–90, 98, 289
Restricted Principle of Sufficient Reason. *See* Principle of Sufficient Reason, Restricted
Rice, Hugh, 87
Robertson-Walker hot Big Bang model, 75
Rosenkrantz, Gary S., 182
Ross, James F., 98, 101–102, 120
Rowe, William L., 44, 98, 102, 112
R-PSR. *See* Principle of Sufficient Reason, Restricted
Rundle, Bede, 279
Rutherford, Donald P., 31

S4 Axiom, 317
S5 Axiom, 103, 231–233, 241, 304, 316–320
science, Aristotelian, 10
scientific explanation. *See* explanation, scientific
self-evidence, 15–16, 31–34, 64, 95, 189–208
self-explanatory propositions. *See* propositions, self-explanatory
Shapiro, Lionel S., 48
Sider, Theodore, 178, 318
skepticism, inductive, 295, 305
Sklar, Lawrence, 39
Smart, J. J. C., 129, 190
Smith, Quentin, 103, 166, 234
social constructivism, 8
Socrates, 16
souls, 221, 226
Spinoza, Benedict de, 3, 15, 18, 98, 104, 197–198, 208
Stern-Gerlach experiment, 160, 162
substantial bond, 167
subsumptive explanation. *See* explanation, subsumptive

Sullivan, Thomas D., 11, 198, 232–234, 239
supervenience, 6–10, 30, 62, 65, 68, 95–96
surgical excision, 128–130
Swinburne, Richard G., 82, 264

taboos, 194
Taylor, Richard C., 61, 64
teleological argument, 228–229
theodicy, 87
theophobia, 15
Thomas Aquinas, Saint. *See* Aquinas, Saint Thomas
time
  anistropy of, 40
  Aristotelian theory of, 27
  B-theory of, 25–26, 303
time-reversal asymmetry. *See* time, anistropy of
torture, 7
toy models, 75–76, 79, 81
truthmakers, 23, 25–26, 31, 35, 78, 90, 209, 212, 264, 300, 302, 309
Turner, Donald Albert, Jr., 88

understanding, 63, 106, 190–199, 267
ungrounded chains of causes. *See* chains of causes, ungrounded

Vallicella, William F., 44
van Inwagen, Peter, 15, 97–125, 131–132, 135–136, 138–139, 141, 168, 180
vicious circle, 16, 42, 82, 99, 102
vicious regress, 41, 210–212

Weak Principle of Sufficient Reason. *See* Principle of Sufficient Reason, Weak
Weatherford, Roy C., 48
White, David E., 283–284
Williamson, Timothy, 198
Wittgenstein, Ludwig, 24, 208
W-PSR. *See* Principle of Sufficient Reason, Weak

Zorn's Lemma, 52

31998044R00204